LINUX MADE EASY

LINUX MADE EASY

The Official Guide to Xandros 3 for Everyday Users

by Rickford Grant

NO STARCH PRESS

San Francisco

Publisher: William Pollock
Production Manager: Susan Berge
Cover and Interior Design: Octopod Studios
Developmental Editors: William Pollock, Peter Spear
Technical Reviewers: Marc Bellefleur, Neil Derraugh, Erich Forler, Michael Gale, Kevin MacPherson,
            Brian Rolfe, Jeff Tranter
Copyeditors: Linda S. Recktenwald, Bonnie Granat
Compositor: Riley Hoffman
Proofreader: Stephanie Provines
Indexer: Ted Laux

For information on book distributors or translations, please contact No Starch Press, Inc. directly:

No Starch Press, Inc.
555 De Haro Street, Suite 250, San Francisco, CA 94107
phone: 415.863.9900; fax: 415.863.9950; info@nostarch.com; http://www.nostarch.com

Library of Congress Cataloging-in-Publication Data

```
Grant, Rickford.
  Linux made easy : the official guide to Xandros 3 for everyday users / Rickford Grant.-- 1st ed.
      p. cm.
  Includes index.
  ISBN 1-59327-057-7
1. Linux. 2. Operating systems (Computers)  I. Title.
  QA76.76.063.G7245 2005
  005.4'32--dc22
                                                            2005012979
```

To "Bonnie," my wife, soul mate, and "pre-Raphaelite ballerina," who was so patient and supportive as I wrote this book

ABOUT THE AUTHOR

Rickford Grant, author of *Linux for Non-Geeks*, has been a computer operating system maniac for more than 20 years, from his early days with an Atari XL600 to his current Linux machines. Rickford spent the past seven years as an associate professor at Toyama University of International Studies in Japan before returning to Portland, OR.

BRIEF CONTENTS

PART IV: APPLICATIONS

PART V: FOR THE MORE ADVENTUROUS

CONTENTS IN DETAIL

PART I
STARTING OUT

1
WELCOME TO THE WORLD OF LINUX . . . À LA XANDROS 3

2
METAMORPHOSIS 11

3
AN ALTERNATIVE BLUE WORLD 27

PART II
GETTING THINGS DONE

4
AN UNTANGLED WEB 45

5
THERE'S NO PLACE LIKE HOME   61

6
PORTS OF CALL   81

7
CONTROL FREAKS   95

8
THE KEYS TO THE GATES OF OZ,
OR THE GATES OF XANDROS ANYWAY   117

PART III
GADGETRY

9
MAKING LASTING IMPRESSIONS   141

10
FLATBED MEMORIES

11
BECAUSE MEMORY SOMETIMES FAILS TO SERVE

12
KEEPING TABS ON YOURSELF

PART IV
APPLICATIONS

13
SURF'S UP
211

14
EAR CANDY
245

18
TIME TO UNWIND
357

19
KIDS' STUFF
379

ACKNOWLEDGMENTS

There are, as always, a good number of people who deserve thanks for the help and support they provided either while or before this book was written, and there are still others whose help will come after the book is released. I would like to acknowledge all of them now.

First, I want to thank my wife, Sumire, to whom this book is dedicated, for helping me out and encouraging me while I was writing this book and preparing to search for new digs in Portland, Oregon. My mother, Dixie Angelina Burckel-Testa, for whom my first book was originally written, again deserves great thanks for being so supportive of my various projects, helping out with the initial proofreading of this manuscript, and being a good sport in general. Then, of course, I must also thank my auntie, Danica Lucia Zollars, because were it not for her I would never have stumbled into this world of writing in the first place. Finally, to round out my acknowledgments to members of my family, thanks are due to my cousin and friend, Stephanie Garrabrant-Sierra, who coached me mercilessly for my presentation at the LinuxWorld conference in 2004, and whose enthusiasm always serves to inspire and encourage me. Thanks as well to her sweet cat, Roxanne, who soothed my nerves at the time.

Of course, as the folks at No Starch Press were the ones who actually published this book, I would like to thank all of them for what they have done thus far, and for what I know they will be doing once the book is released. Thank you all, William Pollock, Leigh Poehler, Susan Berge, Riley Hoffman, Patricia Witkin, and Christina Samuell. And although they are no longer with No Starch Press, I would like to thank Hillel Heinstein, the editor of my first book, as it was his guidance at that time that made things so much easier this time around, and Karol Jurado, who just made sense of everything for me and seemed to be able to perform all sorts of magic.

While still in the corporate scheme of things, I would like to thank Stephen Harris at Xandros for being so helpful with my sometimes inane requests and questions, and for turning me on to Skype, thus saving me tons of money.

The folks at Xandros were also very helpful in reading through the chapters of this book as I wrote them, and pointing out anything I might have missed. For this I would especially like to thank Marc Bellefleur, and all of the others who helped out in that effort: Neil Derraugh, Erich Forler, Michael Gale, Kevin MacPherson, Brian Rolfe, and Jeff Tranter.

It wouldn't be right to mention all those who performed technical edits on *Linux Made Easy* without also mentioning the developmental editor and copyeditor for the project, Peter Spear and Linda Recktenwald. Their help, suggestions, and questions helped to make this a much more rounded volume than it was when initially submitted, and for this I extend my many thanks. *Tusen tack!*

Turning now to my friends and colleagues, let me thank Donald Hammang—cyclist, life adviser, Windows expert, and keeper of the Great Saw; Sheldon Rudolph—lifelong friend, artist, composer, and my original compu-buddy from the Atari XL600 days; and Steven Young—hiker, environmentalist, ultimate gadget-geek, and the inspiration for this book. Thank you all very much. Thanks are also due to my former colleagues Settsu Uesaka, Toshiko Takagi, James Porcaro, Tracy Nakajima, Andrezej Kozlowski, and Richard Stone for both their indirect and, at times, very direct help while I was writing this book.

Special thanks are also due to those people who provided me with support or helped direct me in ways they probably do not even realize—Dick Petrie, Dr. J. Howard Cremin, and Kimberly Jo Burk.

Finally, a special thanks to my sweet little black cat and dear feline friend, Muju, who never fails to listen to whatever I have to say and keeps me sane when I'm feeling down. Meow.

INTRODUCTION

Who Is This Book For?

If you are standing in the aisle of your local bookstore reading this right now, you may well be wondering who this book is for. If you also happen to see my previous book, *Linux for Non-Geeks,* on the same shelf (oh, lucky me), you might also be wondering what the difference between the books is. So to clear things up, I will try to answer both of those questions now. *Linux Made Easy* was written with the average computer user in mind, but not just any average user. The user for whom it was written is one who, through years of working with Windows, has become tired, weary, or broke. Such a person would like to try something different and doesn't really even care what it is as long as it will work, and work well, on his or her present machine.

In a sense, you could say that this book is for Steve, my friend since fourth grade back in Los Angeles. Not too long after my first book came out, he called me to say that he had bought a copy. Unfortunately, he said that he wasn't really going to try it out because he wasn't all that interested in getting into Linux. Not that he had anything against Linux, of course; it was just that the main thing he really cared about was getting out of Windows. He only wanted to be able to hook up his PDA, send email to his friends, use the Web, and whip up a few documents and presentations when necessary—all without having to really get all that into it. It didn't matter whether it was Linux or Dogmata Fortuita Professional OS v5 (no, that does not exist), as long as it was cheap, easy, and able. To him, Linux still seemed too much trouble at the time.

Well, to my mind, and even that of my mother (for whom I had originally prepared that first book), Linux was already easy enough, and *Linux for Non-Geeks* was written to show those interested in Linux, but still afraid to try it out, that such was the case. Of course, such people were admittedly looking for an easy way in. Steve, on the other hand, was looking for an out—a no-sweat out.

When I was later introduced to Xandros, I realized that I had found what Steve was looking for—a flavor of Linux so easy to use that Windows, and arguably even Mac OS, would seem complex in comparison. Of course, in addition to the many other folks like Steve out there in the world, there are still others who specifically want to get into Linux but have found it too cumbersome to bother with for whatever reason. Xandros is a great way for such people to get into the Linux world and really use Linux. Thus, this book was written with both of these groups of people in mind.

Because such people are more interested in getting things done than in fiddling around with their systems, and because Xandros is so very easy to use, I'll pay a good deal of attention to using software and peripheral devices such as your printer or USB flash drive. I'll discuss how to run and use those applications and devices, and I'll offer tips and projects to help you to get more out of them. You'll get hands-on experience that will help you to develop basic skills that you can then build upon and apply later on. By the time you finish this book, you will be able to do all of the things you were able to do with Windows—and more.

Version Compatibility and Updates

This book was prepared for use with Xandros Version 3 Open Circulation (which comes with this book), Standard, Surfside Linux, and Deluxe Editions. Although I do not specifically cover the more technical capabilities of the Business Edition, the book can also be used with that edition as well, with any relevant differences mentioned in the text. Some applications that I discuss, such as Thunderbird, Firefox, and Skype, were not originally included in the Standard, Business, or Deluxe Editions, but users of earlier releases of those editions can easily download those applications via Xandros Networks in order to follow along.

NOTE *The world of computers is exceedingly dynamic, and there may be changes in the software or the links to the files for projects in this book after the book is released. I'll post any such changes at www.edgy-penguins.org/LME.*

Concept and Approach

As a language teacher, I have always enjoyed programming books, mathematics books, and old-fashioned foreign-language-learning texts because of their straightforward skill-based orientation, in which each chapter builds upon the skills acquired in the previous chapter. I have tried to organize this book in that manner so that you will never be called upon to do something that you have not already learned. I also like such books because they not only teach the reader how to do something, but also provide him or her with the chance to put those morsels of knowledge into practice in the form of exercises. I have therefore included several exercises, or projects, in this book where appropriate in order to give readers opportunities to apply their knowledge. This book will serve as a reference text and will also provide a dynamic learning experience, so that you can learn by doing, as they say.

The projects throughout this book have a secondary purpose as well: by working through them, you will properly configure and round out your Xandros system so that it can do anything you want. By the time you finish with this book, your system will have all the bases covered. If that is still not enough to satisfy you, you will be happy to know that you will have access to even more—an unbelievably greater amount more—via Xandros Networks, where you will find more free applications than you will probably ever need . . . but more on that in Chapter 8.

How to Use This Book

It is possible, of course, to use this book as a mere reference text that you only consult when you have a problem to solve, but that would negate the basic concept behind its design. Instead, I recommend that you first go through the entire book chapter by chapter, doing the projects along the way. This will give you a much broader understanding of how things are done (and of how you can get things done), and it will reduce the chance for anxiety, confusion, and, worse yet, mistakes.

It is best to read this book and complete its projects when you are relaxed and have time to spare. Nothing makes things go wrong more than doing things in a rush. And keep in mind that Linux and the projects in this book are fun, not just work exercises. The whole point of the Linux world, in my opinion, is that it offers all kinds of fun. So go ahead and enjoy it.

About the Conventions Used in This Book

There are only a few minor points worth noting about the conventions I have used in the book. I have put in **bold** type the words for items within your system that you need to click or directly manipulate in any way, such as buttons, tabs, menus, files, or folders, and also any text that I ask you to input. In Chapter 20, I use monospace font for any text that appears in the Console window. Any words that I wish to call your attention to, but not actually click or directly select, I have set in *italics*, which I also use when first mentioning a window or application within the text. I have also opted to use the more graphically suggestive term *folder* instead of *directory*—no doubt the legacy of my many years as a Mac user.

About the CD in This Book

The CD that comes with this book contains a full working copy of Xandros Open Circulation Edition. This is a full working Linux system that comes with most, if not all, of the applications that an average home user will need to function comfortably. These include the Microsoft Office–compatible OpenOffice.org office suite, the popular Firefox web browser and Thunderbird email client, Real Player, and the new and easy-to-use Internet telephony application, Skype. In addition to the many other applications that come on the disc, still more—an unbelievably great number more—can be easily downloaded free of charge via the bundled Xandros Networks application.

PART I

STARTING OUT

1

WELCOME TO THE WORLD OF LINUX . . . À LA XANDROS

The first time Xandros ever came into my active consciousness was when I received an email from a compu-friend of mine who wrote, "You know what's cool? Xandros!" I was a bit surprised at first, as I found it rather difficult to fathom how any seemingly sensible person would find anything "cool" about a movie in which a giant head floats around spurting out pseudo-philosophical ramblings at a heavily sideburned and primitively clad Sean Connery. After a brief moment of reflection, however, I realized that my friend had not, as I had initially feared, totally wigged, but rather that I had been mistakenly thinking about the 1974 film *Zardoz*. Quite fortunately for all involved (including you), Xandros is something completely different— an extremely easy to install and use variation of the Linux operating system.

What Is Linux?

You already know of, and have probably used, at least one of the many operating systems that exist today. Operating systems such as Windows, DOS, and Mac OS all enable the otherwise hopeless hodgepodge of electronics that is your computer to do what you want it to do.

Linux is another such operating system; however, it is quite different from those others, both in terms of its capabilities and its heritage. Linux was not created by a corporation or by some corporate wannabes out to make money. It was instead created by a Finnish-Swedish computer enthusiast, Linus Torvalds, who wanted to create a better Unix-like system that would work on home computers, particularly his. Rather than keeping his creation to himself, Torvalds opened it up to the world, so to speak, and the system was then expanded and improved upon by compu-geeks around the globe who worked to make the system better and more powerful.

Why Should I Use Linux?

People use Linux for many different reasons. For many, it is a matter of power, stability, or even personal philosophy. However, for many others, crass as it may sound, it is a matter of money. Just think for a moment about what it costs to get started with another operating system. Go to wherever it is that you go to buy software and take a walk down the aisles. Make a list in your head of all the things you want to buy and how much each costs: an office suite, a game or two, and maybe a graphics program with which to make your digital photos look better (and perhaps yourself in the process). Now do the math.

After you pick yourself up off the floor, you will understand that we are talking big bucks here. On the other hand, for the price of this book, or a tad more if you opt for even more flexibility, you will have all of the things you wanted and more in the Linux world. Despite the worries that many people have, making the move to Linux not only means savings for you, but also more computing versatility—you will not be hamstrung at some point along the way because you don't have this or that program when you need it most—you'll have it all from the get-go!

You might counter with the fact that there are a lot of freeware applications out there for other operating systems, but c'mon, let's face it, these are often rather limited in terms of their capabilities. The programs with a little more oomph are mostly shareware, and most shareware programs these days are limited in some way, or you can only use them for a month or less, unless you are willing to pay for them. Sure, their costs are relatively low, but $25 here and $35 there eventually add up to a considerable chunk of change. In addition, at least in my experience, many of those programs are just not that great.

Is It All Just About Money?

While money is important to the average user, it is certainly not the only reason for taking the Linux plunge; there are a variety of other reasons as well. As I mentioned before, Linux is noted for its stability. Try running your present system for a month without restarting occasionally and see what happens. Linux has been known to run for over a year without a hitch or a decrease in performance.

In addition, Linux is infinitely customizable; you can get your system to look and act the way you want it to without being wizarded to death. And then there are the applications that come with or are available for most Linux distributions. In addition to there being a wide variety of them, most are well up to industry snuff, with some, such as Evolution and the GIMP, being sources of envy for those outside the Linux world.

What Is a Distribution?

An operating system consists of a lot of files that perform a lot of different functions. And because there is no Linux Corporation to package and distribute the files that make up Linux, the task of getting Linux onto your computer in working order, along with the applications that you are likely to want, has fallen to a varied group of entities—companies, universities, user groups, and even private individuals. The Linux system and application collections they create are called *distributions*, or *distros*. You could bypass such distros and try to collect everything you'd need to set up a system all on your own, but you would undoubtedly lose your mind in the process. Most people, even the geekiest, opt for the distros.

There are a large number of distros, such as Red Hat, Mandrake, SuSE, Damn Small Linux, and Debian, to provide a few well-known examples. Some are geared to specific audiences, such as businesses, educators, gamers, students, programmers, system administrators, and specific language users. What makes each distro different is the specific software that is bundled with the Linux kernel and other convenience features, such as the installer and system configuration tools. Some distros are especially appropriate for home users due to their ease of installation, and Xandros is undoubtedly a leader in this area.

So Why Choose Xandros?

With so many distros out there, you may wonder if Xandros is the one for you. As I've already mentioned, different distros are geared to the needs and likes of different users. All things considered, it is pretty fair to say that if you are looking for a Linux distro that you can essentially just get down to using without any geeking around, then Xandros is a perfect choice for you.

All that said, let me point out a few things that make Xandros an attractive alternative for anyone thinking of moving over to the world of Linux:

Ease of Installation

When installing Xandros, you won't be asked a single question that will even give you the chance for a screw-up. Now you've got to admit that's pretty close to foolproof (in the most literal sense). Xandros's four-step installation process is the unrivaled champion in the ease-of-installation department.

Hardware Compatibility

Xandros is particularly adept at handling more problematic hardware configurations. In addition, Xandros arguably provides the easiest handling of peripheral devices such as scanners and flash memory units.

Debian-Based

Xandros is based on the Debian distribution, one of the most popular Linux distributions. As a result, there are probably more applications available for Debian than any other distro. Most of these work with Xandros and can easily be found and installed via the Xandros Networks application that comes with every Xandros edition.

Xandros Networks

The Xandros Networks application makes finding and installing applications (and there are lots of them) an unbelievably simple and even enjoyable task.

Good Level of Windows Friendliness

Xandros is configured to work as comfortably as possible with the world of Windows. Not only does it allow you to easily browse Windows machines connected to whatever network you happen to be on, but it also allows you to easily make your machine a Windows-Linux dual-boot setup, thus permitting you to have both systems installed on your hard disk at the same time. To help you with the setup, it can even create and resize partitions for you, and as you will find out in the next section, you can even run numerous Windows applications and plug-ins if you upgrade to the Deluxe Edition of Xandros.

The Different Flavors of Xandros

Xandros, like many other distros, comes in both free and pay (for-sale) versions. The free version, such as the one bundled with this book, is called the Open Circulation Edition. It comes with a large number of programs, including the Microsoft Office-compatible OpenOffice.org office suite. It lacks a few of the bells and whistles found on the for-sale editions, such as unlimited CD burning speeds (Open Circulation provides only a maximum 2X burn speed) and the ability to burn DVDs (Open Circulation doesn't handle DVD burning), but it is still a fully functional and completely satisfactory operating system. And you can install applications that are comparable to most of those it lacks for free.

The for-sale editions can be classified into home and business categories; given the target audience of this book, I will cover only the home category. The Standard Edition provides you with unlimited CD burning speed and 30 days of technical support via email. The Deluxe Edition adds to the mix an additional 30 days of tech support and two additional CDs containing a wide variety of extra applications. It's an ideal choice for those with slow Internet connections who want to get everything set up fast. The Deluxe Edition also comes bundled with CodeWeavers' CrossOver Office, which allows you to run numerous, though not all, Windows applications, such as MS Office, and enables your browser to utilize Windows-based plug-ins such as QuickTime and Windows Media Player. That's an option that may be very valuable to you depending upon how important it is to you to run Windows applications. A new addition to the Xandros line is Xandros Surfside Linux, which is geared toward the hardcore web surfer. It is pretty much the same as the Home Edition, but it also comes with anti-virus software, the Internet telephony application, Skype, and a Platronics headset.

Hardware Compatibility

Well, now that I've covered all of this background business, let's get the ball rolling and prepare to install. It is pretty safe to say that Xandros will run on most computers today. Of course, this statement comes with a major caveat: you just never know if all is well until you are up and running, and because there are so many minor parts to and peripherals for your machine, it is difficult to say whether or not each part will cooperate with your installation.

If you are going to buy a new machine on which to run Linux, then it is reasonable enough to check things out first, but if you are going to install it on the machine you have, I recommend just diving in. Being the reckless character that I am, searching the Web to figure out if things will work or not seems a bit of a nuisance to me. You can spend hours poking around and still end up not being sure. You might also be misled into thinking that Xandros won't work on your machine when in fact it actually will. You can find out for sure by just trying to install it. If it works, it works; if it doesn't, it doesn't. Assuming you still have the system discs for whatever OS you were using before, you will have lost nothing but a little time.

If my damn-the-torpedos approach isn't really your style, and you would prefer search the Web to see if your hardware is supported by Linux in general, you can, of course, do this, but you need to know what model of hardware you have. To be able to find out anything of value, you should at least know what motherboard, processor (CPU), and monitor you have. Identifying your CPU and monitor should be easy enough, but the motherboard may require a bit more searching. If you have no documentation that clearly states what kind of motherboard you have, then just open up the case of your computer and look at your board, which is a giant green (sometimes brown) circuit board into which just about everything in your machine is connected. You needn't worry about damaging something because you don't need to touch anything (so don't). You may need a flashlight to find it, but the model name and number should be stamped there somewhere, either in the middle of the board or around the edges. Mine, for example, says quite clearly in the middle of the board, "AOpen MX46-533V." You should be looking for similar information.

Once you have that information, you can do a variety of things to check out your motherboard's compatibility with Xandros. First of all, you can check the Xandros hardware compatibility search page at http://support .xandros.com/hcl-search.php, though its database lists only a portion of the hardware that is actually compatible with the system. Alternatively, search the Xandros support forums at http://forums.xandros.com or post an inquiry asking if anyone knows if such-and-such hardware will work with Xandros. This works for other hardware devices too. Just write that you are a newbie and want to know if anyone has had any experience using Xandros with the board (or other hardware) in question. You will probably get quite a few responses, because Linux users are usually rather evangelical and try to draw in new users. You can also do a Yahoo or Google search, typing in your motherboard's make and model plus the word **Linux** or **Xandros**.

Hardware Requirements

All worries about compatibility aside, the following are the basic hardware requirements:

- Intel Pentium 2-4 or Celeron processor, or any AMD K6/II/III, Duron, Athlon, or Athlon XP/MP processor
- A minimum of 1.5 GB of hard disk space (Xandros recommends 3 GB), though for my money, having at least 10 GB would be best
- Sufficient memory (RAM)

Now that we're on the subject of RAM, I have a bit to say. The official specs tell you that you need a minimum of 64 megabytes (MB) of RAM to run Xandros (though 128 MB is recommended to run it comfortably). However, the way I see things is that no matter what OS you are dealing with, whether Windows or Macintosh or Linux, whatever they tell you is enough memory is sure to be too little, and when you have too little memory, no matter what system you are running, well . . . weird things just seem to keep on happening. Applications seem to take years to open, or don't open at all; menus take forever to render their little icons; and freezes and general system meltdowns just happen much more often.

My basic rule of thumb, regardless of the specific OS, is that you need the recommended (not the minimum) memory plus at least 128 MB. This gives your system (and you) a bit of elbow room, and in most cases makes your computer seem to move a tad quicker. After all, it is quite a waste to have a pretty speedy CPU and yet not be able to appreciate it because its hands are tied by a lack of memory. That's like trying to do jumping jacks in a broom closet. Not that many people do jumping jacks anymore or even have a broom closet, for that matter.

The bottom line is this: ignore what the official specs say about how much RAM you need and just put in more. You won't regret it. Fortunately, Xandros's recommended 128 MB, plus my recommended additional 128 MB, comes to 256 MB, which is well within the amount of RAM that most new systems come with these days.

And what if you don't fall into that 256 MB category? Well, memory is relatively cheap these days, so I say just go for it. Since you're saving money on applications by installing Xandros, you should have enough extra cash to buy enough RAM to make your life easier.

Where Do I Go from Here?

Now that you know more about the world of Linux in general and Xandros in particular, it's time to get down to it. Turn off that DVD of *Dawson's Creek* season 4 that you've been watching (I'll save you the suspense—Joey and Pacey do break up at the end), strap yourself down in front of that computer, clip on your spurs, and go straight to the next chapter. Of course, if you've already taken the plunge and have Xandros installed on your machine, then you should head straight over to Chapter 3 to get started.

2

METAMORPHOSIS

Installing Xandros on Your Machine

If you have already installed Xandros on your machine, you can skip right over this chapter and go on to the next one. If, however, your machine is still Xandros-free and you are ready and raring to change that state of affairs, then you had better stay right where you are and read on. In this chapter, I will review everything you need to do before I guide you through the installation steps to get Xandros up and happily running on your machine.

NOTE *If you are computerless at the moment or are contemplating buying a new machine, you might want to just forgo this whole chapter on installation and go out and buy a machine with Xandros preinstalled. Information about the availability of such machines is given on the Xandros site at http://www.xandros.com/partners/oempcs.html. As for the rest of you . . . read on!*

Single or Dual-Boot Setup?

Before getting started, you first need to decide whether to install Xandros as the only operating system on your machine or to create a dual-boot setup, which lets you easily choose to run Xandros or Windows each time you start up your machine. You see, it is possible to have both Windows and Xandros installed on the same machine and for them to happily coexist.

Creating a dual-boot setup in Xandros is incredibly easy, but you do need to have a hard disk with enough space to accommodate the two systems comfortably in their own partitions. Most computers these days come with at least a 60 gigabyte (GB) hard disk, which I would say is the bare minimum required to accommodate the 2 gigs required by Windows XP (not including space required for other applications) and the 3 gigs required by Xandros. Of course, the bigger the partitions (and, logically enough, the hard disk), the smoother things will be for you when running either system.

In my own case, I started out with just such a dual-boot setup, so I can tell you firsthand that it all works just fine. The only problem I found was that over time, I just stopped using the Windows side of things completely—I just had no need to go there. However, having so much disk space taken up by a Windows system I wasn't using anymore seemed a waste of prime real estate, so eventually I just dumped the whole thing and went for a straight Linux-only setup.

That said, unless there is some application that you really need but is not available on the Xandros side (probably some game), I'd go ahead and dump your Windows system (and all the viruses and spyware that have buried themselves in there) and go for the Xandros-only setup. Xandros has most of what you will need anyway, and because OpenOffice can read and write MS Office files, you'll be well-enough connected, if that is of concern to you.

But What If I Want My Windows Back?

You may be thinking that if you do as I suggest and dump your Windows system, you'll end up having to install it again if you don't like Xandros. That would be a considerable waste of time and energy, to be sure. However, believe it or not, there are advantages to my suggestion even if your no-go scenario turns out to be the case.

You may have noticed that your Windows system, as you've used it over time, has gotten sort of gunked up—it is no longer the quick little kitten it used to be. Menus don't pop open as quickly as they used to, things take longer to start up than they did before, and you find yourself asking "What the Sam Habberdack is that?" all the time as mysterious things happen with increasing frequency.

This is just the nature of the beast, and a very good way of getting things back to normal is to reinstall the whole thing. This will also rid your system of any spyware or viruses it might have embedded in it. So even if you do decide to come back to Windows later, you'll be doing yourself a favor, because it should run better and more safely than before. It's a little more work up front, but in the long run you'll be a happier camper.

Protecting You from Yourself

During the installation process, you will be asked to create and type in three things: an administrator password, a username, and a user password. Deciding on these now so as to get things out of the way is a good idea. If you are like most Windows home users, however, you might not be quite sure about why you need all this information, so I will fill you in now.

Xandros, like most Linux distros, tries to keep you and the actual workings of the system somewhat separated by all but forcing you to do your day-to-day work in a *user account*. When you install software or perform certain other system chores, however, you are asked to momentarily dip into the *administrator account* (also known as *root*), usually by merely typing in the administrator password when prompted to do so.

Compared to what you are probably familiar with in Windows, where every user account is an administrator account when set up, this might seem a bit cumbersome. Maybe so, but it is a great idea that provides you with much better security (both systemic and psychological), because it protects you from yourself by limiting any screwing up you do to your user account alone. In fact, even the MS boys recommend that you do this with Windows—just open your Windows Help page and do a search for "why not administrator" and see for yourself.

In addition to security, this setup can also add convenience and privacy. With your administrator-account powers, you can create additional user accounts at any time, as you would on Mac OS X or Windows XP. For example, say that your family wants to use your computer, but you don't want them messing around with your files or, worse yet, blitzing the whole system in some way. You could use one account for yourself and then add additional accounts for your daughter (Erika), your son (Jethro), and your spouse (Pat).

Under this system, when any one of them starts up your computer, they will only be able to log in to their own account. You can also set things up so that they will not be affected by the settings of any of the other users, and their settings will not affect anyone else's.

Now that you understand the root/user distinction, decide upon a root password and a user password. You will be using the user password every time you log in, so make sure it is something that you won't forget and, more importantly, won't mind typing in every day. You won't really need the root password as much, although you will be using it quite a bit while doing the projects in this book. Still, it should be something that you will remember, because it is very important.

You will also need to come up with a username for yourself. It could be as simple as your initials (my username is *rg*) or the name of your favorite tropical fish, such as *neontetra*. Whatever you choose, it will appear on your screen once you've logged in, so make sure it is a username you don't mind seeing every day. Having to see "Stinky's Home" on your computer screen day in and day out could prove a little annoying, if not embarrassing.

NOTE   *Your username can consist of any combination of numbers, underscores (_), hyphens (-) and lowercase letters. The first character, however, must be a letter. It also cannot have any spaces.*

Once you've decided upon your username and your root and user passwords, make sure that you write them down on a piece of paper or in a book (something that you can't delete). Keep them at hand until the installation process is over and you have gotten into the swing of things. After that, you can store them in some safe place—but don't forget, as I am prone to do, where that safe place is. The information is very important, and it is easy, as time rolls by, to forget such things, which you definitely do not want to do. Holding onto your root password is most important of all, because without it you won't be able to do certain things, such as install packages or add users.

Pre-installation: Can You Boot from CD?

Before you go on to the installation (Project 2B), make sure that your computer is set up to boot from your CD drive. Most machines these days are set up to do this, so you probably don't have to do anything special. If you're not sure and don't feel like tinkering around, you can find out by just going right to the installation steps in the next section. If the Xandros installation screen appears, you can just keep going. On the other hand, if you suddenly boot up in Windows, you will have to make some adjustments.

Probably the only thing you have to do is restart your machine and then press whatever key the screen tells you to press in order to enter your BIOS setup. This is usually DELETE or F1, but not all machines are the same. If the onscreen information passes by so fast that you miss it, you can check your user's manual to see what the correct key is. Once you get into the BIOS setup, change the boot sequence so that your CD drive is first. The method of doing this will differ depending on your machine, so see your user manual.

Project 2A: Creating a Boot Disk (If You Need One)

In the extremely unlikely event that your machine cannot boot from a CD at all, you will have to create a 3.5-inch boot diskette, which you can do very easily while using your (or someone else's) Windows system. To do this, you must first boot up your machine in Windows. Once you are at your Windows desktop, insert the Xandros Install CD. The Xandros Desktop Autorun Wizard (Figure 2-1) will appear. Just click the **Next** button to proceed.

1. In the new Wizard window, click the radio button next to the words *Floppy diskette*, as shown in Figure 2-2, and then click **Next**.

2. All you need to do now in order to create the boot floppy is to click the **Create Floppy** button, as seen in Figure 2-3. You will then be prompted to insert a floppy disk, so first label a 1.44 MB, 3.5-inch floppy disk as *Xandros 3.0 Boot Disk* and put it in your floppy drive. Once you've done that, click the **OK** button in the disk prompt window. The creation of your boot floppy will now begin.

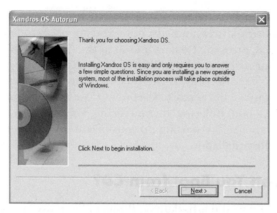

Figure 2-1: Creating boot disk with the Xandros Desktop Autorun Wizard in Windows

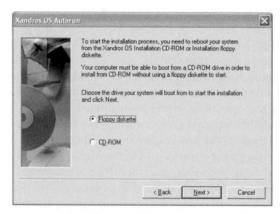

Figure 2-2: Enabling the Floppy diskette option in the Xandros Desktop Autorun Wizard

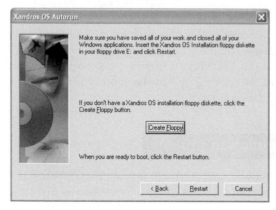

Figure 2-3: Creating a Xandros boot disk

3.   Once the floppy has been created, leave it and the Xandros Install CD in their respective drives, and, assuming you are ready to begin the installation process, press the **Restart** button in the Autorun Wizard in order to restart your machine. You will then be ready to proceed by following either the Xandros-only or the dual-boot installation instructions that follow. If you are not ready to start now, close the Autorun Wizard window and remove both disks for the time being. You can then insert the two disks later on (before starting up your machine) when you are ready to perform the installation.

Taking the Plunge—Installing Xandros

Now that we've got all the background information down, let's get on with it and install Xandros on your machine. Fortunately for you, installing Xandros is amazingly simple, and you would probably be able to do it all on your own without any coaching from me. Still, since you forked out the cash for this book, you might as well let me be your copilot here and guide you along so that you can feel a bit more confident about what you are doing. All in all, the whole process, depending on the speed of your hardware, should take less than 30 minutes, making it faster (and I think easier) than a Windows XP or Mac OS X installation. And keep in mind that with XP and OS X you are only installing the operating system itself and just a few bundled applications. In a Xandros installation, you are installing not only the operating system itself, but also most of the applications you will most likely need to use. You will thus be getting a lot done in one fell swoop.

One more thing before we start. Some people approach installing a system with a great deal of trepidation. The process makes them nervous, as if the house were going to go up in smoke during the process. Well, the house may go up in smoke, but not because of the installation process. As long as you have backed up your data, you will be OK. If you screw up the installation the first time out, so what? Just start over again. No harm done, as you have nothing to harm. Just make sure that you give yourself more time than you need for the process. Don't start installing one hour before you have to be at work, or before you have to meet your friend downtown. Rushing makes people do weird things. Make things easy on yourself by giving yourself plenty of time . . . and by backing up any data you would mourn the loss of.

That said, let's get to it!

Project 2B: The Installation Process

If you are going to set up your machine so that Xandros is your only operating system, go directly to Step 2. If, however, you are going to set up your machine to run both Xandros and Windows (dual boot), start with Step 1.

1. **Defragment Your Hard Disk (Dual-Boot Setups Only)**   If you would like to create a dual-boot setup, which allows you to start up in either Windows or Xandros, it is best for you to first defragment your Windows hard disk before proceeding. This will make the installation process faster later on when Xandros shrinks your Windows partition so as to make space to install itself.

    While still running Windows, open the My Computer window, right-click the icon for your hard disk, and select **Properties**. You can now defragment your hard disk (in Windows XP) by clicking the **Tools** tab in the Properties window and then clicking the **Defragment Now** button at the center of the window (Figure 2-4). In Windows NT, you can do this by going to the **Start** menu and selecting **Control Panel** ▸ **Administrative Tools** ▸ **Computer Management** ▸ **Disk Defragmenter**, while in Windows 98 and some other versions, you can do the same by selecting **Programs** ▸ **System Tools** ▸ **Disk Defragmentator**.

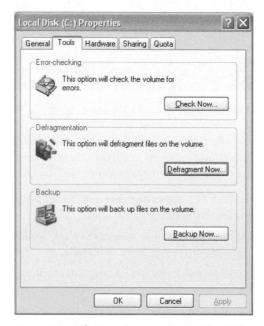

Figure 2-4: Defragmenting your hard disk in Windows

2. **Start 'er up**   Place the Xandros Install disc in your CD drive (and a boot floppy in your floppy drive, if your machine cannot boot from CD), and start or restart your machine.

3. **Welcome**   After your machine starts, you'll see its usual hardware BIOS screens, which appear regardless of the system you are using. After that, the first Xandros screen, a semi-graphical and predominately black opening screen will appear. This will be followed by the first screen of the Xandros Installation Wizard—the Welcome screen (Figure 2-5). All you need to do when it appears is click the **Next** button.

Figure 2-5: The Xandros Installation Wizard's Welcome screen

NOTE *With some hardware configurations, your installation may hang (get stuck) after the words "Initializing kernel" appear in the predominately black semi-graphical opening screen. If this happens to you, just do the following:*

a.   *Turn off your machine by pressing and then holding the power button until the machine powers down.*

b.   *Power on the machine again, and as soon as the black, semi-graphical opening screen appears, press the* SHIFT *key. A list of installation options will then appear.*

c.   *Use the down arrow key to select the second installation option, ACPI 2 Setup, and then press* ENTER.

d.   *If the installation seems to hang again, follow the same procedure over again with each of the other installation options until the installation proceeds as described. One of the options should do the trick.*

4.   **License Agreement**   Read through the license agreement in this wizard screen (Figure 2-6), click the radio button next to the words *I accept this agreement,* assuming you do (and if you don't . . . well, then we're done), and then click **Next**.

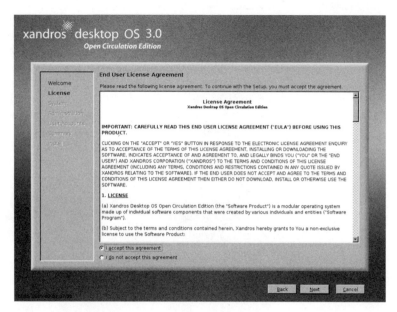

Figure 2-6: The Xandros License Agreement

5. **Installation Selection**   The following screen, which you can see in Figure 2-7, allows you to choose between an express and a custom installation. The Express installation is essentially a full one, so stick with that by clicking the radio button next to the words *Express install*, and then click the **Next** button in order to proceed.

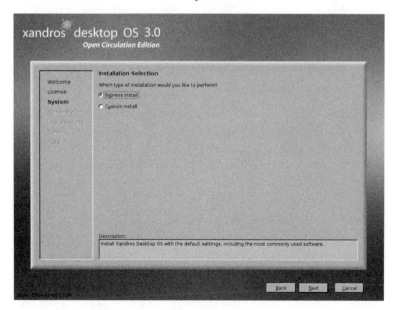

Figure 2-7: Choosing the type of installation you want to perform

6. **System Configuration**   In this screen (Figure 2-8), Xandros checks to see what you want to do with what is already on your disk. If you already have an earlier (or even the same) version of Xandros on your machine, you will be asked if you want to keep the data in your Home and root folders (but not global settings and custom installed packages, unfortunately) on your hard disk or if you want to replace the whole thing with a fresh install. If, however, you have Windows occupying your entire hard disk, as most people do, you will be asked if you want to keep that system by resizing its partition (and thus making room to install Xandros) or if you want to overwrite it with Xandros. Make the choice appropriate for what you want to do, and then click **Next**.

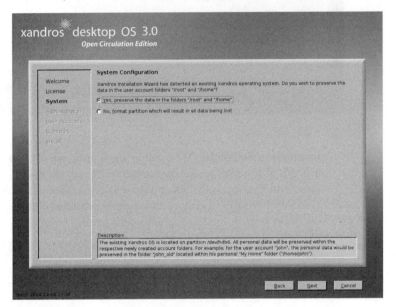

Figure 2-8: Deciding what to do with what's already on your hard disk

NOTE   *You can only resize a Windows partition if there is enough empty space within it. If your Windows-only hard disk is already almost filled to the max and if there is not enough space, the installer will not provide you with the resizing option; it will instead only allow you to replace Windows with Xandros. You can then either cancel the installation (with no harm done to your present system) and give up, or you can restart in Windows, trash as much unused stuff as you can, and then try again.*

7. **Administration Configuration**   In this screen, as seen in Figure 2-9, you will input that root (also referred to as "administrator") password that I told you to prepare earlier. Type it in each of the two boxes, and then if you want to change the default computer name, do that as well. Just be sure to use only letters, numbers, underscores, and dashes—and don't make it any longer than 15 characters. When done, click **Next**. Be sure to remember what your root password is, or you won't be able to install any applications or change certain system settings in the future.

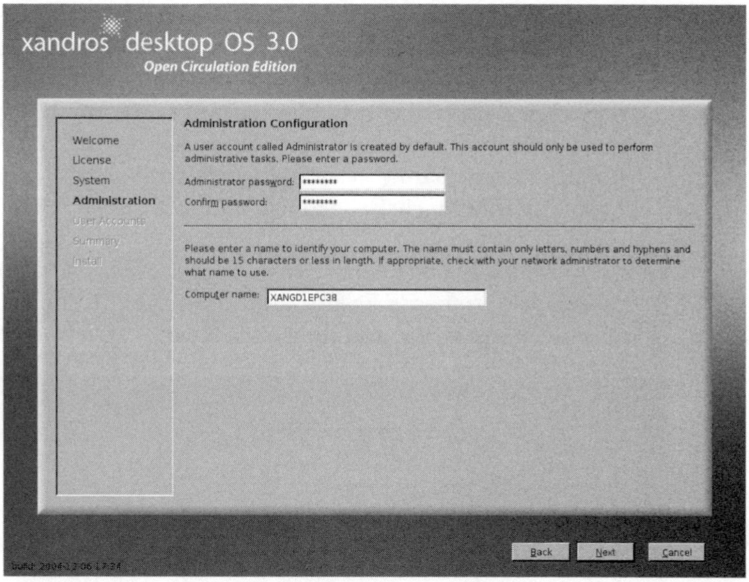

Figure 2-9: Inputting your root password

8. **User Account Configuration** In this screen (Figure 2-10), you are asked to type in your username, your real name, and a user password. You can also give your computer a unique name if you like, though this should really only matter if you are going to be using your computer on a network. Once you have filled in the boxes with the appropriate information, click **Next**.

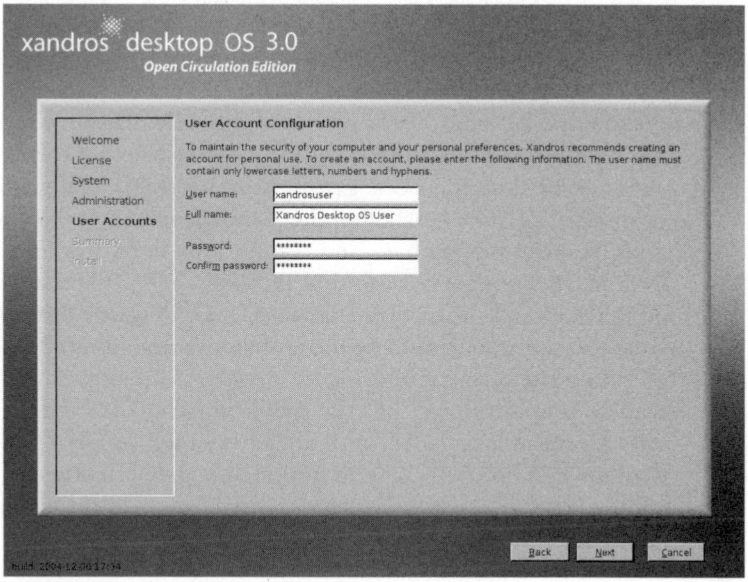

Figure 2-10: Inputting your username and password

9. **Installation Summary** In the final installation screen (Figure 2-11), the Installation Wizard shows you what it is going to install, where it is going to install it, what it is going to do with what is already on your hard disk, and a few other details. Pay special attention to the top line, *Install method*, to make sure that it matches what you are hoping for. In the case of a Windows partition resizing, it should say: *Resize Windows partition*. If everything looks as it should, click the **Finish** button.

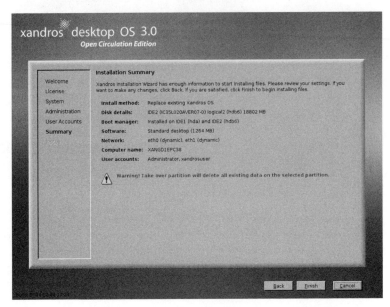

Figure 2-11: A last-minute check before beginning the actual installation

If you are creating a dual-boot setup, the Xandros installer will begin resizing your Windows partition and then create and format partitions in which to install itself. If you are creating a Xandros-only setup, the installer will skip the resizing process and begin to create and format partitions. In either case, when it is done getting your hard disk ready, the installer will begin the process of installing the Xandros system and its bundled applications. You can now sit back and rest for a spell. Rather than sitting around fretting, why not get back to that *Dawson's Creek* DVD that I told you to turn off in Chapter 1, or go downstairs and take your dog Sputnik for a short walk—30 minutes should be more than enough in most cases.

Once the installation process is complete, Xandros will tell you so in a small pop-up window. Click the **Exit** button in that window. Xandros will soon eject the install CD automatically and tell you in a full-screen message to remove the install CD (and floppy disk, if you needed one). After removing the disks, press ENTER (as also instructed to do on-screen) to restart your machine.

When your computer restarts itself, you will be greeted by the boot loader screen, where you will see a list of startup options. If you've set up a dual-boot machine, use your arrow keys to move down to the *Windows XP* (or other Windows version) entry in that list. Press ENTER, and Windows will start up just like it did before you installed Xandros. For the time being, however, and any time you want to boot up in Xandros, just accept the default startup option, **Xandros Desktop 3.0**, by pressing ENTER (or just wait a few seconds) and Xandros will start up automatically. Naturally, if you chose to set up a Xandros-only machine, the Windows option will not be available.

After a short while, the login screen will appear. In that screen, make sure your username is the one shown in the login window next to the words *User name.* If it is not, click the arrow button at the right side of the *User name* box, and select your username. Next, type your password, and then click the **Login** button. The Xandros First-Run Wizard will then soon appear to take you through the exceedingly simple post-installation process. Fortunately, there is really little to do here other than click the **Next** button a few times, but I'll walk you through things anyway. Oh, and if you are worried about making a mistake or missing out on something, don't—you can always run the wizard again later at any time. Here are the steps for the wizard:

1. **Welcome/Mouse Configuration**   Select *Right hand* or *Left hand,* and then click **Next** (Figure 2-12).

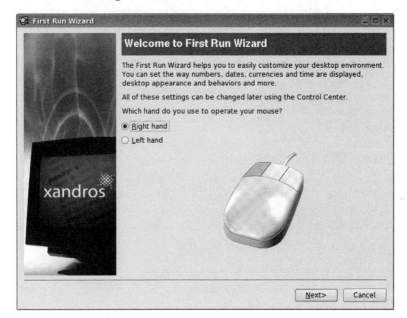

Figure 2-12: The Xandros First Run Wizard's opening screen

2. **Regional Settings**   Set the appropriate locale and keyboard layout, and then click **Next** (Figure 2-13).

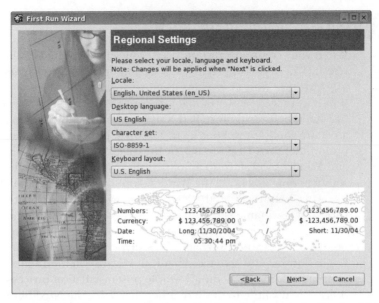

Figure 2-13: Adjusting your locale and keyboard settings in the First Run Wizard

3. **Date and Time**   The defaults in this screen of the wizard (Figure 2-14) should be correct here, so, assuming they are, click **Next**. If not, you can adjust them now.

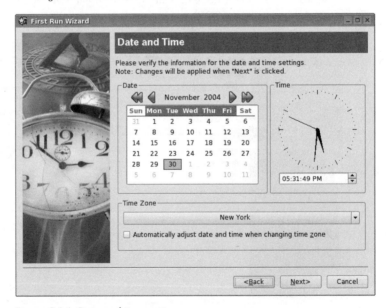

Figure 2-14: Date and time settings

4. **Connect to the Internet**   In Chapter 4, I will be covering in greater detail how to set up your Internet connection, so for now just click **Next**.

5. **Printers**   Setting up your printer will be covered in detail in Chapter 9, so for now just skip over this step by clicking **Next**.

6. **System Behavior**   In this screen (Figure 2-15), you can alter the look of your desktop; however, as I will also be covering this topic later on in Chapter 7, just skip over this step as well by clicking **Next**.

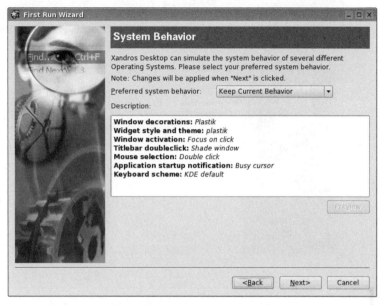

Figure 2-15: The First Run Wizard System Behavior screen

7. **Registration**   Because we have not yet set you up to connect to the Internet, select *I do not want to register my Xandros product at this time* (as shown in Figure 2-16), and then click **Next**.

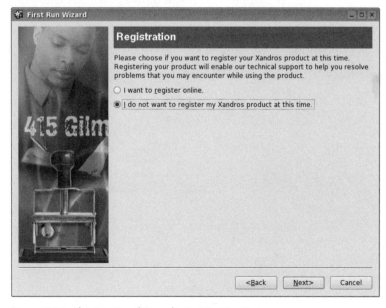

Figure 2-16: The First Run Wizard's Registration Screen

8. **Finish**   This is the final screen of the First Run Wizard (Figure 2-17), and the only thing you have to do is click the **Finish** button.

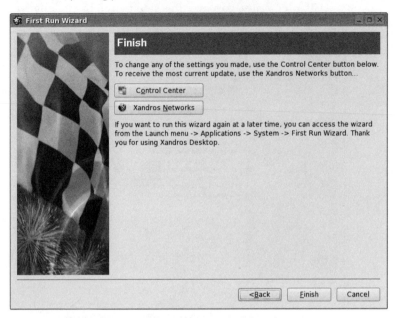

Figure 2-17: The final screen of the Xandros First Run Wizard

If you made any regional setting changes during the post-installation process, Xandros will pop up a small window telling you to restart the desktop so that the changes can take effect, so go ahead and click the **Restart** button to get that out of the way. If you didn't make any changes, the First Run Wizard will close, and you'll be ready to roll. Your new Xandros Linux system is now installed, set up, and ready to go. If you're really eager to get down to the nitty-gritty of using it, go right to the next chapter. See you there. Aloha.

3

AN ALTERNATIVE BLUE WORLD

Getting to Know the Xandros Desktop

Now that Xandros is installed, you will perform a simple, one-step process whenever you turn your computer on. This process will then deliver you to your new desktop.

Soon after powering up, you will be greeted by the Xandros boot loader screen. From this screen you can choose to boot up in Xandros by simply pressing the ENTER key or, even more simply, by just waiting a few seconds, which will have the same effect. If you created a dual-boot setup, you can use your cursor keys to scroll through the various options and select **Windows**, press ENTER, and then boot up in that operating system instead. Of course, if you are going to use this book, you won't want to choose this option now.

NOTE   *If you at some point want to boot Windows and you see more than one entry for it, choose the first entry. If you get some sort of error message and Windows does not start, reboot and try the next Windows entry.*

Assuming that you do indeed want to follow along with me here, and are thus forgoing the Windows boot option for the time being, the only thing you have to do next is wait a few somewhat lengthy seconds for the login screen to appear.

The login screen consists of a tiny window at the center of an empty blue screen. In that window, you will see the username you chose during the installation process just above an empty box in which you need to type the user password (not the root password) that you also entered during the installation process. Once you have entered your user password, click **OK** or press ENTER to proceed. If you are the only person using your computer, and thus find the login step a needless chore, don't fret. I will show you how to bypass it in Chapter 7. For now, just bear with me.

Welcome to Xandros's KDE Desktop

A relatively short while after logging in, you will finally arrive at your new desktop, which you can see in Figure 3-1. The graphical desktop that Xandros uses is called KDE, which is one of the two most popular desktop environments in the world of Linux.

Figure 3-1: The Xandros desktop

You can see that the desktop isn't all that different from what you might be used to in a Windows environment. But don't be completely fooled; despite the similarities, things are different enough to be interesting. There are three main elements that you will probably notice right off the bat: the desktop icons, the Panel at the bottom of the screen, and the Launch menu button at the far left corner of the Panel. I will focus on these elements in this chapter.

Desktop Icons

As you can see, there are five icons on the desktop: Trash, Home, Quick Start Guide, Web Browser, and Xandros Networks. To makes things simple, we'll start with the easiest and, no doubt, most familiar of these: Trash.

Trash

There is nothing mysterious about Trash . . . at least nothing mysterious about the desktop trash icon. It functions just as it does in other operating systems. Drag a file you no longer need or want to the trash icon, and the can will bloat up. If you want to empty the trash, just right-click the trash icon and, from the pop-up menu, select **Empty Trash Bin**. If you drag something into the Trash that you are not supposed to, you will be informed that you can't do that. All very simple and familiar, no matter from whence you came.

Home

As you will notice, the home icon is the image of a house (home) on a folder. This should tell you that it is your Home folder—something like a mix of My Computer, My Network, and My Documents in a Windows system. This is where all your files will be saved to, all your downloads will be downloaded to, and all your music will be ripped to. It is your territory, and even if you are on a multi-user machine, nobody except you (assuming you are the only one who knows the root password) will be able to nose around in there. It is also where you can access the other storage devices on or connected to your computer (such as floppy disks, CDs, and so on), or other computers on your network.

Quick Start Guide

This icon opens a clear, basic reference guide that deals with the essentials of using your system.

Web Browser

This icon is a launcher that you can double-click to open your Internet web browser. You'll find detailed information on your web browser and other Internet-related applications in Chapter 13.

Xandros Networks

This icon is another desktop launcher with which you can run the Xandros Networks application. Xandros Networks is an amazingly simple-to-use application that allows you to update your system, purchase upgrade versions of Xandros, and download and easily install an unbelievably vast amount of free software. Because Xandros Networks is so useful, and because it is one of the most attractive features of using a Xandros Linux system, I'll be covering it exclusively in Chapter 8.

The background of your Xandros desktop is decorated with a rather handsome image with the look of cool-blue brushed steel. If so inclined, you can replace that background image, often somewhat peculiarly referred to as a *wallpaper* with any picture of your choice. You can choose one of the other wallpapers that come with your Xandros system or a photo you've downloaded from your digital camera.

You can also download desktop wallpapers from the Internet. Both http://art.gnome.org and www.kde-look.org have lots of wallpapers available, as do many other sites. If you're interested in cars, many of the major automobile manufacturers (Ford Canada and Saturn, for example) have wallpapers of their latest models available for download. Many music and film star fan sites are flush with wallpapers too.

3A-1: Changing Wallpapers

To change the wallpaper on your desktop, start out by right-clicking any open space on the desktop and selecting **Properties** in the pop-up menu that then appears. A configuration window will appear.

To choose one of the wallpapers that comes bundled with your system, click the drop-down menu button next to the word *Picture* in the Background section of the window (the button itself will say XandrosBlue the first time around). A menu will appear that lists all of the wallpapers available for you to choose from (Figure 3-2). Select one, then click **Apply**. The wallpaper you selected should then appear on your desktop. Give this a try with a few of the other wallpapers in the list until you find one that suits your fancy. When done, press **OK**.

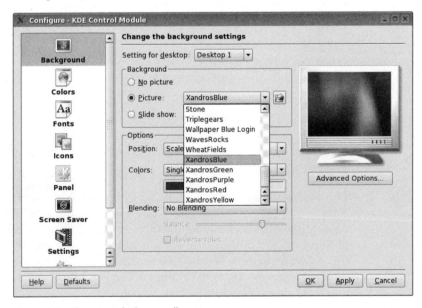

Figure 3-2: Changing desktop wallpapers

If you would like to use one of your own photos instead, as I do on my own desktop (Figure 3-3), or a wallpaper you've downloaded yourself, the process is slightly different. Rather than clicking the drop-down menu button next to the word *Picture* in the configuration window, click the little button with a picture of a half-opened folder instead. A Select Wallpaper window (Figure 3-3) will then appear.

Figure 3-3: Choosing an image of your own as your desktop wallpaper

In that window, click **Home** in the left pane of the window, and then find the image you want to use in the right pane. Once you have located it, select it by clicking it once, and then click **OK**. The Select Wallpaper window will then close, leaving you with the original configuration window (Figure 3-2). In that window, click **Apply**. The image you selected is now displayed on the desktop (Figure 3-4). If you are satisfied with the results, click **OK**; if not, try again.

Figure 3-4: Your own image (my own, in this case) displayed on the desktop.

3A-2: Setting Up a Desktop Slideshow

A very cool feature in KDE is the ability to have your desktop wallpapers automatically change every few minutes (or even seconds). This feature, like that available in Mac OS X Panther, will come in very handy once you've finished Chapter 11 and have downloaded images from your digital camera, because your desktop can then become a dynamic photo album that you can view all the time you are working at your computer—all very fun and pleasant, unless, of course, your computer is loaded with pictures of your ex. Ouch!

To set things up, open the configuration window as you did in 3A-1 (right-click the desktop and select **Properties**), and then select **Slide show** in the Background section of that window. The **Setup** button will become active, so go ahead and click it. The Setup Slide Show window (Figure 3-5) appears.

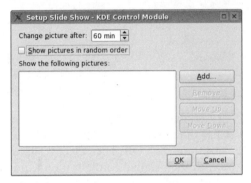

Figure 3-5: Setting up a desktop slideshow

To start setting up your desktop slideshow, you first need to decide which pictures to include. These can consist of your own images, wallpapers you have downloaded, the wallpapers that come with your Xandros system, or any combination thereof. To get started selecting, click **Add**. Once you've done this, the Select Wallpaper window (which you saw in Figure 3-3) will appear. Find an image you want to add to your slideshow, and click **OK**. The image you selected will then appear in the big box in the Setup Slide Show window. You can now go on and repeat the process for all the other images you want to add.

In the setup window, you can also decide how often you want your desktop images to change by adjusting the numbers in the box next to the words *Change picture after.* You can also set the order in which an image will appear by selecting it and then clicking the **Move Up** or **Move Down** buttons at the right side of the window. If you prefer, you can also have the images appear randomly by selecting the box next to the words *Show pictures in random order.*

The Panel

Now that we've covered all there is to cover about the main part of the desktop, let's move on to the next major desktop component, the Panel (Figure 3-6), which is located at the very bottom of your screen. You will notice that the

Panel holds a number of items. Some of these are program launchers that allow you to start up a program with a single mouse click, while others are utilities of one sort or another. To fill you in on what each of these items is for, I'll give you the blow-by-blows here, covering the items from left to right.

Figure 3-6: The Panel

Launch

Clicking this brings up the Launch menu, which is the access point for the majority of your applications and for your preferences, settings, and other configuration tools. I will discuss this a bit more near the end of the chapter.

Thunderbird

Your email application, which is Mozilla's latest answer to Outlook Express. (Looks like an envelope being held by a blue thunderbird.)

Firefox

Your web browser. Essentially, it's Netscape with a difference or two. (Looks like an orange fox wrapped around the earth.)

Xandros File Manager

This launcher is a one-click alternative to the Home icon on your desktop. Clicking it launches a Xandros File Manager window, opened to your Home folder. From that folder, you can access your files, view the contents of other drives, or mount other computers on your network. (Looks like a small file cabinet.)

Help

Provides information on using the various features and applications of your Xandros system. It is not the same thing as the First Start Guide on your desktop. (Looks like a life preserver.)

Show Desktop

Clicking this hides all open windows, thus allowing you to see the desktop itself. Very, very handy. (Looks like a pencil and sheet of paper on a blue square.)

The Taskbar

The taskbar is essentially invisible if you do not have any windows open. When you have windows open, rectangular icons for each window appear here, just as they do in Windows.

Pager/Virtual Desktops

An application that allows you to switch between virtual desktops (I discuss this in Chapter 4). (Looks like a pair of squares, one blue and one green, labelled 1 and 2.)

KLaptop

An application that appears if you're using a laptop computer. It allows you to check the status of your batteries and adjust relevant settings. (Looks like an electrical plug next to a battery.)

Sound Mixer

A control that allows you to adjust the overall volume of your system. (Looks like a small speaker.)

Xandros Update

An application that periodically checks with Xandros Networks for the availability of system updates. (Looks like a small globe, most likely with an exclamation mark in a small square.)

Lock/Logout

A pair of buttons with which you can log out (right button—looks like a power button) or lock your screen (left button—looks like a lock). Locking your screen is a handy means of keeping other people's noses out of your business while you sneak away from your desk to get a cup of coffee. When you click the **Lock Screen** button, Xandros will run a screen saver (or just blacken your screen if no screen saver is selected). To use your system again, just move the mouse or press any key and Xandros will prompt you for your user password. Once you input the password, the screen saver will disappear, and you can get back to work or whatever else it was you were doing.

Switch User (not shown)

This button, which shows two people standing, appears only on systems whose video card drivers support it. It allows you to switch between user sessions without having to quit running applications. A sort of logout without really logging out.

Clock

The obligatory and ubiquitous desktop clock and calendar.

Hide/Show Panel

Click this button to hide or show the Panel. (Looks like a small black arrow.)

Project 3B: Customizing the Panel

The Panel is not a static thing. You can add launchers (program shortcuts or aliases), utilities, and even amusements to make it do almost anything you want it to, within limits, of course. In the various stages of this project, you will customize your Panel to make things more convenient for you as you make your way through the rest of this book. You are, of course, free to change any of the customizations I ask you to make, or to just pick those that are of interest to you, but I'd suggest performing at least a few of them so that you can get a feel for things.

Each of the following subprojects is very simple. Most are point-and-click procedures that you should be able to handle without any difficulty.

3B-1: Deleting a Launcher from the Panel

Deleting items from the Panel is a very simple procedure. A good candidate to work with is the Help Center launcher, because it also appears in the Launch menu and this is an extra copy. Freeing up Panel space will make room for other items more to your liking that you may want to add.

To delete the Help Center launcher, here is all you have to do:

1. Right-click the **Help Center** launcher in the Panel.
2. In the pop-up menu, select **Remove Help Button**.

3B-2: Adding a Launcher to the Panel

Now that you have an empty space left behind from where the Help button used to be, let's fill it in with something more useful. A good candidate would be the Calculator, which everyone needs to use at one time or another.

Here's how to add the launcher:

1. Right-click the open space left behind after removing the Help button.
2. From the pop-up menu, select **Add Application Button ▶ Applications ▶ Accessories ▶ Calculator**.

3B-3: Adding a Menu to the Panel

You can add whole menus to the Panel as well as application launchers. A good choice would be the OpenOffice.org menu, because most people use these applications quite frequently.

Here's what you do to add the menu:

1. Right-click the open space to the right of the Calculator launcher you've just added.
2. From the pop-up menu, select **Add Application Button ▶ Applications ▶ OpenOffice.org ▶ Add This Menu**. Be sure to select **Add This Menu** in the very last submenu that appears, as shown in Figure 3-7.

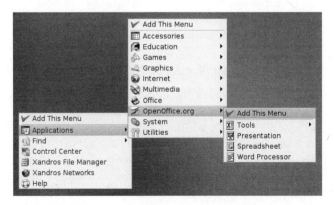

Figure 3-7: Adding the OpenOffice.org menu to the Panel

3B-4: Moving Items Within the Panel

When the OpenOffice.org menu button that you added to the Panel in subproject 3B-3 appears, it will most likely be located far from the other application launchers that are at the left side of the Panel. Having the menu over there with the others would be the most logical arrangement, so in this part of our project we are going to do some moving.

Here's what you do to move the menu button:

1.   Right-click the **OpenOffice.org** menu button (or any other Panel item you want to move that won't move by dragging alone).

2.   From the pop-up menu, select **Move OpenOffice.org** (or whatever the name of the item you're trying to move is).

3.   Your cursor will now look like an arrowhead-tipped crosshair. Without holding down either mouse button, move the mouse to the location where you would like to place the menu button—in this case, just to the right of the Calculator launcher. The menu button will follow along.

4.   When the menu button is where you want it to be, click the left mouse button, and you'll be done.

3B-5: Adding a Quick Browser for Your Home Folder to the Panel

In addition to application launchers and menus, you can also add Special Buttons to the Panel. The Launch and Show Desktop buttons are examples of these Special Buttons. A very handy Special Button you might want to consider adding is a Quick Browser. A Quick Browser allows you to view the contents of any folder you specify, in menu form, from the Panel. A logical and convenient choice for this project would be a Quick Browser for your Home folder, an example of which you can see in Figure 3-8.

Here's what you need to do to add a Quick Browser for your Home folder:

1.   Right-click any open space in the Panel.

2.   In the pop-up menu, select **Add ▶ Special Button ▶ Quick Browser**.

3.   The Quick Browser Configuration window will now appear. The default path in the text box next to the word Path will be /home/*your_username* (mine, for example, says /home/rg). Click **OK**.

3B-6: Adding a Weather Monitor to the Panel

In addition to application launchers and menus, you can also add mini-programs (called *applets*) to the Panel. Each of these applets performs a specific function, usually adding a bit of convenience to your desktop in the process. The applets at your immediate disposal include an in-panel sound-configuration tool, a dictionary lookup input box (discussed in Chapter 13), and the Clock, which is already present in the Panel by default. One the most popular applets, however, is the weather monitor, called KWeather.

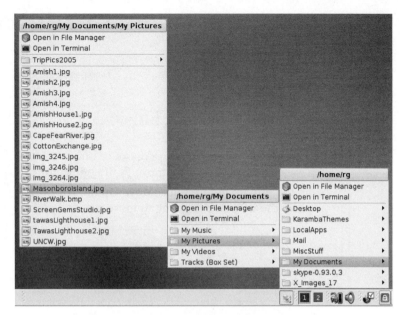

Figure 3-8: A Quick Browser button for your Home folder in action

You should note that because this applet periodically uses the Internet to check for the current conditions in the location you choose, it is best used if you have an uninterrupted Internet connection such as cable or DSL.

Here's how to add the Weather applet:

1. Right-click any empty space in the Panel.

2. From the pop-up menu, select **Add ▶ Applet ▶ Weather**. A warning message will most likely appear at the top-left corner of your screen saying, "The requested station does not exist." This is logical enough, because you have not yet selected a weather station to monitor.

3. The applet is added to the Panel. To select a weather station, right-click the **Weather** applet and select **Configure KWeather**. The KWeather Configure window (Figure 3-9) will then appear.

4. In the configure window, click the blue link that says **Lookup Your ICAO Code**. Your web browser will then open up to the National Weather Service website.

5. Scroll down to the section that says Display All Stations In a State (or Display All Stations In a Country, if you live outside of the United States). Select your state or country, and then click the button that says **Display All Stations In**.

6. The page that then appears will list all the weather stations in that state or country. Find the location you want to monitor and note its four-letter code. Detroit Wayne County Airport, for example, is KDTW.

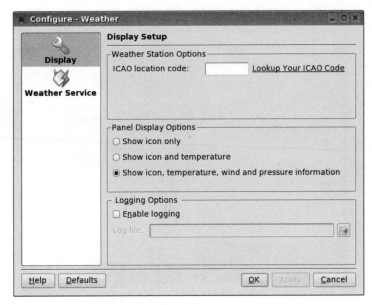

Figure 3-9: Selecting a weather station to monitor in the KWeather Configure window

7. Close your browser, and then input the four-letter code for the station you want to monitor in the *ICAO location code* box near the top of the Configure window. To save Panel space, you will probably also want to select *Show icon only* in the Panel Display Options section of that window. Once you are done, click **OK**.

8. The Weather applet in the Panel should now show in graphical form the current weather conditions for the location you've selected. To see a more detailed report, click the applet. A window like that shown in Figure 3-10 will then appear.

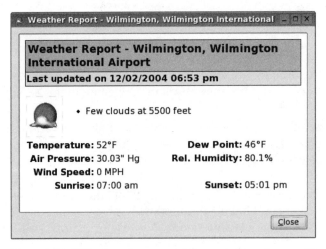

Figure 3-10: KWeather gives you a full report of weather conditions in your chosen location

More Panel Fun

In addition to the basic customization you've just done in the previous project, you can do a lot more to change the Panel's behavior. Most of these options are available by right-clicking any open space in the Panel and then selecting **Configure Panel**, to bring up the Control Center Settings window (see Figure 3-11).

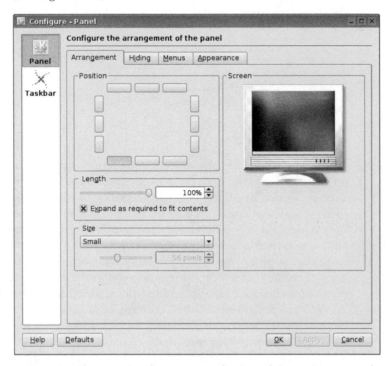

Figure 3-11: Changing Panel properties in the Control Center Settings window

From this window, you can change the position of the Panel, alter its size, change its color, or make it (but not the launchers on it) invisible, though this won't look particularly attractive. You can also set the Panel so that it will automatically disappear when you are not using it and reappear when you bring your mouse cursor into the area where the Panel normally resides. If you like the icon zooming feature in Mac OS X's Dock, don't feel left out; you can even get the icons in your Panel to do the same. (In fact, if you really want to get carried away Mac-ifying your desktop, you'll find out how you can do it in Chapter 8.) Anyway, don't be afraid to play around and give things a try—that's half the fun!

The Launch Menu

At the far left corner of your screen is the Launch button. You can access just about everything there is to access in your system from here. In a sense, the Launch menu is very much like the Start menu in a Windows system. When you click the **Main** menu icon, all of the applications and utilities available to you are exposed (Figure 3-12).

Figure 3-12: The Launch menu

As you can see, the menu is broken up into three sections, each of which is clearly labeled. The uppermost of these sections, Most Used Applications, is dynamic in that its contents change according to what programs you use most often. Because you will not have used any applications other than the First Run Wizard when you first open the Launch menu, that should be the only application listed there at that time. The items in the other two sections (All Applications and Actions) are primarily static, which means that the items listed there will remain the same unless you install a new application, in which case a launcher for that application will be added to the menu.

You will find, however, that some applications do not automatically add a launcher to the menu once installed. In such cases, you can run the launcher-less applications by selecting the Run Command item in the menu and then typing in the command for that application (as discussed in Chapter 8). Alternatively, you can use the Menu Editor application (discussed in Chapter 18) to add a launcher to the menu manually, which is useful if the application is one you use frequently. You can also use the Menu Editor to customize the menu to your liking.

What each item listed in the All Applications and the Actions sections does should either be self-evident (such as Help, Find, and Recent Documents) or will be discussed elsewhere in the book. That being the case, I will not delve any further into these things at this point.

Virtual Desktops

All of the major components of the desktop have been covered, so it is now time to discuss a rather unique and convenient feature in Linux: virtual desktops. And the best way to understand what this virtual-desktop business is all about is to just give it a try.

In your KDE Panel, click the **Weather** applet, the **Calculator** launcher, and the **Xandros File Manager** launcher. You will then have three windows open in your present desktop, or workspace. Now look at the Virtual Desktops applet on your Panel. The left half of the icon should be blue; this is your present workspace. Click the right half of the icon, the green half, and all your open windows will suddenly disappear.

Actually, nothing has really disappeared—you are just viewing a new desktop. All your other windows are still open and running in the previous desktop. In this second desktop, you can open something else: go to the **Launch** menu and select **Applications** ▸ **Games** ▸ **Cards** ▸ **Solitaire**. The Solitaire card game will soon appear.

You now have windows open in two different desktops, and you can switch back and forth between them. To do so, just go to the Virtual Desktop Applet in your Panel and click the left box, which will take you to your original desktop. Once you've done that, you can then click the right box again to go back to your game desktop.

As you can imagine, this feature has some potential benefits for you, in addition to helping you avoid clutter. Just imagine that you are at work typing up some long document in OpenOffice.org Writer. Eventually, you get a bit tired and decide to goof off a bit by playing Tetris for a while. To do this, you switch to another desktop where you open and play the game. A bit later, when you notice your boss making the rounds of the office, you simply switch back to the first desktop so that you look busy when he walks by and says, "Keeping yourself busy, Boaz?"

Phew!

Shutting Down

Well, now that you know your desktop environment so well, you may feel like calling it a day and shutting down your machine. To do so, just go to the **Launch** menu and select **Logout**. A small window will appear with three buttons to choose from: Logout (default), Shutdown, and Restart. Click **Shutdown**, and the shutdown process will begin.

When it is all done, the system will tell you on-screen that it is now safe to turn off your computer. Usually, the system will turn the computer off automatically after a few seconds. On a few machines, however, the system cannot power down your machine. You will know if this is so in your case because the message telling you that it is safe to turn off your computer will just sit there. . . forever. If you see those words on the screen and nothing else happening for 15 seconds or so, then just power down the machine manually by pressing the Power button. It is completely safe to do so at that point.

Getting Out of a Jam

At this point, you've pretty much been introduced to your desktop. Now is probably a good time to arm you with some information that will help you out of any jams you might get into as you progress through the rest of the book and get further into working with your Xandros system. You probably won't have to resort to what I am about to describe often, if at all, but it is always good to be ready just in case. After all, no matter what operating system you use, weird things are bound to happen.

Basically, there are two sure-fire remedies to employ when things go south. If one of your applications stops responding, meaning that it just sits there and does nothing, which sometimes causes other applications to appear to do almost the same, you have to kill it. That sounds a bit ominous, but it is just a temporary kill, so don't worry. If you are really lucky, and have the patience to wait for a few seconds (like 30 or so), the system may realize the problem itself, and pop up a window telling you, as you will no doubt already know, that application *X* does not seem to be responding. It will then politely ask you if you would like to kill the process. Because you certainly do want to do that, just click the **Kill** button, and the problem will be solved.

If your system doesn't show the window telling you it knows there's a problem, and thus does not volunteer to kill the application for you, you can take matters into your own hands by pressing the CTRL, ALT, and ESC keys in relative unison. Once you do that, your cursor will change in appearance from a harmless arrow into a much more frightening skull and crossbones. After that micrometamorphosis, all you have to do is click once anywhere in the offending window and the problem will, more times than not, be solved. If you suddenly change your mind before you click in the offending window, and you want to get things back to the way they were, just right-click anywhere and the skull and crossbones will be gone.

If your whole system seems to have slugged out, and you can't get anything to work, you can try to get out of the problem in the manner I have just described, by skull-and-crossboning the last application you were working with when the problem began. If that doesn't work, you will have to resort to slightly more drastic measures. The first of these is to press the CTRL, ALT, and BACKSPACE keys in unison, which will cause your system to log you out and bring you back to the login screen. Doing this will cause you to lose any data that you have not already saved, but whatever will be will be, as Doris Day used to say (or sing). That is why it is always a good idea to frequently save whatever it is you happen to be working on—you just never know when things might go wrong. Finally, in the unlikely case that the CTRL + ALT + BACKSPACE combo doesn't work either, try pressing the CTRL, ALT, and DELETE keys in unison, which should cause your entire system to shut down and then restart.

As I said, problems that will bring about the need for such keyboard maneuvers should be rare, so don't start worrying too much. If they do occur, however, be sure to calm down and try to relax. Take a breath, think about something unrelated for a moment or two, pet your cat, and then come back to your computer and try to get logical. Acting out of panic, and I guarantee this, only causes bigger problems in the long run. After all, as my friend once said, "The only thing you get by speeding to work is a traffic ticket." Stay cool and just think of problems, should they arise, as learning exercises.

PART II

GETTING THINGS DONE

4

AN UNTANGLED WEB

Setting Up Your Internet Connection

These days, average home-computer users spend more time at their computers surfing the Web and writing email messages than doing just about anything else. Even if you're not much of a surfer, there are still numerous other applications that aren't really Internet applications per se but that still make use of the Internet in some way in order to gather data. The Panel Weather applet, when accessing weather data, and Xandros File Manager, when gathering song and album information while ripping and encoding audio files, are good examples.

That said, having a computer that isn't hooked up to the Internet is like buying a new Maserati and then refusing to take it out of the garage.

Connections

To get connected to the Internet, you must have the right hardware. There are a number of possibilities in this area, including high-speed local area networks (LANs), cable modems, and ADSL connections from phone companies.

Most computers also have an internal 56 Kbps modem or can be connected to external dial-up modems for slower connections over regular phone lines. Depending on what you've got, setting things up on your system should prove a cinch in the case of LAN connections and cable modems. It might be slightly more of a challenge in the case of dial-up connections.

High-Speed Connections

If you have a high-speed Internet connection from your cable television company, or if you are connected to the Net by a *local area network (LAN)* at your office, you are really in luck, because these setups are probably the easiest to deal with. Most likely, all you have to do is connect the Ethernet cable from the wall (if you are using a LAN), or from your cable modem, to the port of the network card on your machine. After that, once you start up your machine you should be ready to go. If you have a high-speed connection from your phone company (ADSL), you will have to follow pretty much the same procedure as that for a dial-up modem, as explained later on in the chapter.

NOTE *In case you're not sure what an Ethernet cable looks like, it is a round cable, about one-eighth of an inch thick, with a plug at the end that looks like an oversized phone plug, as you can see in Figure 4-1.*

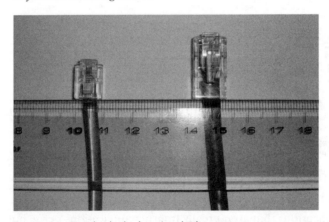

Figure 4-1: Standard telephone and Ethernet connectors compared

If you have a problem getting online, and you are trying to connect to the Net via a LAN or cable modem, the problem could very likely be that your network card is not supported by your system. This is relatively rare, but fortunately, easily remedied (by replacing it).

The problem could also be that your network or service provider does not automatically assign addresses via *DHCP (Dynamic Host Configuration Protocol)*. DHCP is a means by which your Internet provider can automatically (dynamically) provide your system with the configuration information it needs in order to connect to the Internet. If your provider does not utilize DHCP, you will have to get the necessary information about settings from the network administrator or service provider and enter them yourself.

Setting Up a Cable or Ethernet Connection for Providers Not Utilizing DHCP

To input your cable or Ethernet settings yourself, run the Control Center (**Launch ▸ Control Center**), and click **Network** in the left pane of the Control Center window when it appears. In the list of subcategories that then appears below that, click **Network Connection**. When the Network Connection module appears in the right pane of the window, click the **Administrator** button, and then type your root password when prompted to do so.

The right pane of the Control Center will soon be outlined in red, and everything within it will be active, meaning that you can alter its contents. Click the **Interfaces** tab, and then, once in the new tab, make sure that *Enable Network* is selected, click **Specify Static Address**, and input the appropriate addresses as instructed by your network administrator or Internet provider (Figure 4-2). When you are finished, click **Apply**, and then close the Control Center window.

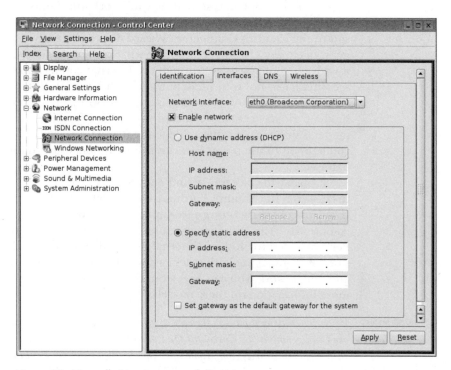

Figure 4-2: Manually inputting network IP settings

NOTE   *If you are wondering what IP and DNS are all about, you can simply think of them in this way: the DNS translates the easy-to-remember URLs that you have come to know, such as www.yahoo.com, into numerical, or IP, addresses that the Internet can understand. The address http://www.yahoo.com thus becomes http://216.109.118.68. You can type the numerical version into your browser later to see for yourself.*

Internal Dial-up Modems

Many, if not most, of you are still using dial-up Internet connections, which means that you need to have a traditional dial-up modem to reach beyond your box to the outside world. These modems, in case you've forgotten, are those wonderful machines that whistle, chime, screech, and spit whenever you dial up your Internet provider. I suppose you could think of them as noisy telephones in need of a good burp.

The biggest drawback to dealing with modems in Linux is that very few modems are supported. On the positive side of things, though, once you do find a modem that works, it is relatively easy to set up. The main reason behind this compatibility problem is that most built-in modems are software dependent, and the software they depend on is part of, or designed for, Windows. Such modems are thus called *Winmodems.*

Of course, the Linux community has been working on ways to deal with these Winmodem beasts so that they will work with Linux systems. Though support for the wide variety of Winmodem models out there is still rather spotty, the Xandros Connection Wizard does a pretty good job of trying to get yours to work. If you are not sure what kind of modem you have installed, my advice would be to go through the Internet connection setup process to see whether or not your modem works with Xandros. If it doesn't, you can replace the modem with one that is known to work, preferably a true-hardware modem. *Hardware modems,* in case you are not familiar with the term, are modems that are not software dependent and thus work with whatever system you happen to use them. You can think of them as telephones without a handset.

Probably the best way to find out which modems do work with Xandros is to check out the Xandros hardware-compatibility database (http://support .xandros.com/hclv3) or go to Xandros User Forums (http://forums .xandros.com) and ask for suggestions. The US Robotics models 56K V.92 Performance Pro Modem (internal slot) and 56 PC Card Modem (PC card slot, for laptops) are both true-hardware modems that are easily available and said to work. You can check out the US Robotics site (www.usr.com) for more information on these models.

WARNING *When purchasing a modem, beware of generic, no-name internal modems that say they are Linux-compatible. Check out the Internet first to verify such a claim. Sometimes such modems are only compatible after you do all sorts of dreadful things to your system that even a hardcore Linux geek wouldn't want to bother with. A cute little Tux icon on the box doesn't necessarily mean that the modem is Linux-friendly.*

External Dial-up Modems

If you find that the dial-up modem you have does not work with your Xandros system, the best solution is to buy an external serial modem. An external modem sits in a box outside your computer, and it connects to the serial port in the back of the computer, which is the one that looks like a hole with little prongs in it (see Figure 4-3). Because the modem doesn't use your operating system to operate, it does not tie up system resources while it's busy, which may result in a possible pick up in computer speed.

Figure 4-3: Serial port and connector

Most external serial modems should work with your system, or at least that is what most people will tell you. If you are worried and are looking for a sure thing, Zoom Telephonics (www.zoom.com) makes an external serial modem that is compatible with Linux, and they say so right on their site. The US Robotics 56K V.92 External Faxmodem is also said to work, though I haven't tried out this model myself.

If you find another model that you think will do the trick, before you commit to it by slapping down the cash, do a Yahoo or Google search with that modem's make and model number, along with the word "Linux," and see what search results you get. Of course, you can also try out one of the Linux forums and ask about the modem make and model there. There are a lot of people in the same boat as you, so you are sure to get plenty of opinions and advice.

Setting Up a Dial-up or ADSL Connection

If you are going to use an external modem (ADSL or dial-up), first power down your computer, connect the modem to the computer and the phone line, power on the modem, and then restart your computer. Once your computer is up and running again, you will have to set things up so that your modem can communicate with your Internet provider. This is pretty easy to do, and through this process you can also make sure that your modem, especially in the case of dial-up modems, actually works with your system.

To do this, you will use the Xandros Connection Wizard, which you can access by going to the Launch menu and selecting **Applications ▶ Internet ▶ Connection Wizard**. The steps of the wizard are pretty much self-explanatory, but I will point out a couple of steps that might be puzzling or at least unfamiliar to you.

The first page of the wizard (Figure 4-4) is quite simple, because it merely asks you what type of connection you are trying to configure. You can configure a connection for more than one type of device, so if, for example, you have a laptop computer that you haul back and forth between home and work, this might be of great interest to you. Just be sure to configure the connection for the type of device you are connected to at the time, and then run the wizard again later when you are connected to the other device. Once you have made your selection, click **Next**.

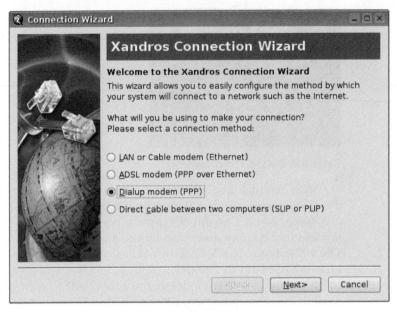

Figure 4-4: The Xandros Connection Wizard

The next page of the wizard (Figure 4-5) is another area that might be unfamiliar to you. In this page, you will be asked which users will be allowed to use the connection service you are configuring. If you are the only person using your computer, or if you want everyone who is using your computer to be able to access the Internet, accept the default All users. If you want to allow yourself, but nobody else, Internet access, select *User*. If you want to allow some users to have access and others not (such as access for you, your spouse, and oldest kids, but not the real young'ns), click *Selected group* (you can set up the details later). Once you have made your selection, click **Next**.

If you are trying to set things up using a Winmodem, the next page of the wizard warrants a special mention (if you're not working with a Winmodem, you won't even see this page). The Connection Wizard will check to see what kind of modem you have connected to your machine. It will then display the results of that search in the next page of the wizard, next to the word *Device* (Figure 4-6). You can just click **Next** unless you also see a list of drivers in the bottom pane of the wizard window (next to the word *Driver*). If you see drivers listed, select one of them (and just take a guess if you're not sure which one to use), and then click the **Load** button. In this case, the wizard will test the driver you selected. If it works, the wizard will tell you so in a pop-up window. Then you can click **OK** to close that window. If it doesn't work, go back and try one of the other drivers. Once you find a combo that works, click **Next**. If nothing works . . . well, it's time to do some shopping.

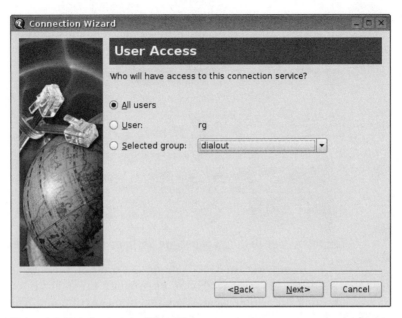

Figure 4-5: Deciding who will be able to use your Internet connection in the Connection Wizard

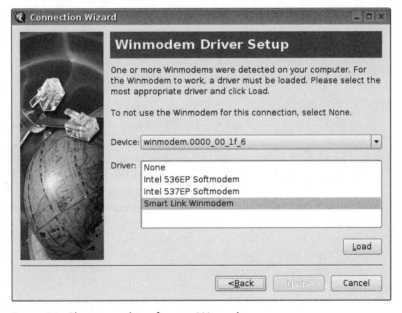

Figure 4-6: Choosing a driver for your Winmodem

The rest of the wizard will be easy enough to figure out. Just be sure to have the account information you received from your Internet provider in hand as you proceed. Once you come to the final page of the wizard and click the **Finish** button, the Connect to the Internet window (Figure 4-7) will appear. This is the same window that will appear any time you choose to connect to the Internet in the future.

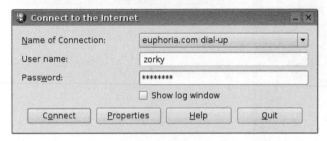

Figure 4-7: Connecting to the Internet

Changing Your Dial-up Connection Settings from Pulse to Tone Dialing

There are two ways in which telephones transmit the numbers you dial when you try to call someone. The most common these days is tone dialing, which transmits the phone number you dial by means of tones. When you frequently dial a certain number, you probably have noticed that the number seems to have a distinct tune, which in fact it does. You might even have caught a misdial at times when dialing a number because the tune for that phone number sounded wrong.

The other, increasingly less common, phone number transmission protocol is *pulse* dialing, which transmits the phone number you dial by means of pulses, one pulse for a 1, two pulses for a 2, and so on. If you have pulse dialing on your line, you will probably know it, because you can hear the pulses, or clicks, when you dial.

When you set up an Internet dial-up connection via the Connection Wizard, things are automatically set up for tone dialing. If you happen to have a line that requires pulse dialing, you will have to make a simple modification. To do this, open the Connect to the Internet window (**Launch ▸ Applications ▸ Internet ▸ Connect to the Internet**), and click the **Properties** button. When the Properties window appears, click the **Protocol and Hardware** tab, and then click the **Properties** button in that tab.

In that Properties window, click the **Commands** tab, and then click directly on the word **ATDT** (to the right of *Dial*). The area directly surrounding the word will then transform into a text-input box, as you can see in Figure 4-8. In that box, change the current entry, *ATDT*, to **ATDP** (the last letter in "ATDT" is either T for tone or P for pulse), and then click **OK** in both of the open properties windows. After that, you'll be ready to go.

Connecting and Disconnecting Dial-up Connections

To get connected to the Internet via your dial-up connection, go to the Launch menu and select **Applications ▸ Internet ▸ Connect to the Internet**. After double-checking that your modem is on (if it is an external modem), click **Connect** when the Connect to the Internet window appears. A small window, Figure 4-9, will then appear and show you what's going on while your modem goes through its dreadful routine of making spitting, hissing, and churning noises until you are finally up, running, and ready to surf. You will know that you have established an Internet connection when your Connect to the Internet window automatically minimizes. It will continue to be accessible in the Panel.

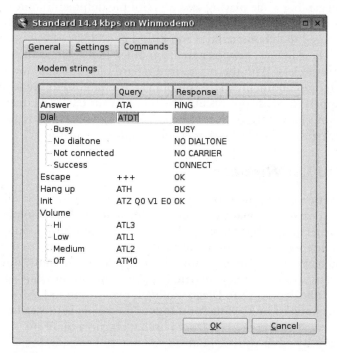

Figure 4-8: Changing your dial-up connection settings from tone to pulse dialing

Figure 4-9: The Connect to the Internet window shows what's going on as it tries to connect

Once you are done surfing around, you can disconnect from the Internet quite easily by clicking on the minimized **Connect to the Internet** window in the Panel and then, when the window bloats back up to its original size, clicking **Disconnect**. You can then click **Quit** in the Connect to Internet window to finish things off.

An Untethered Connection—Wireless

The great thing about laptop computers when they first came out was that they freed people from their desks. People could do whatever they needed or wanted to do on their computer wherever they wanted. As a cross-legged-on-the-floor kind of guy, it was really great for me, as I could plop my laptop down right there on the floor in front of the TV, and then sit there writing and gaming while playing *Wall Street* for the umpteenth time on my VCR. Yes, everything was great, but then came the Internet. Laptops suddenly became tethered to telephone lines and Ethernet cables.

Fortunately, laptops have been unleashed again as the computer world goes wireless. With the right wireless hardware, you can now use your computer just about anywhere you can catch a wave, so to speak. Whether you happen to be at your breakfast table, on your backyard deck, in the library of your university, or at your local Starbucks, you can now go online without having to physically hook up your computer to anything.

Do I Need to Go Wireless?

Whether or not you should join the fray and go wireless is still primarily a question of personal choice or individual needs. For example, if you don't have a laptop, you will have a hard time of it, as Linux support for desktop wireless hardware is not really ready for prime time. If, on the other hand, you have a laptop that you would like to plop down on the dining room table and use during dinner (married readers beware), or while sitting in the Santa Fe depot in San Diego waiting for your train to L.A., or while sitting in your hotel room looking for things to do during your vacation in Seattle, or just while sitting on your front porch taking in a bit of sun, then why not go for it? Whether you are ready to commit, still considering, or just plain curious, read on.

Wi-Fi

To get up to speed in the wireless world, you should first be aware of the three wireless protocols commonly in use today: 802.11a, 802.11b, and 802.11g, which are collectively referred to as *Wi-Fi (wireless fidelity)*. In case you are wondering, a protocol is basically a data-transmission format that has been generally agreed upon, in this case by the *IEEE (Institute of Electrical and Electronics Engineers)*. Of these three 802.11 protocols, average home users need only concern themselves with 802.11b and 802.11g, because the hardware for these protocols is considerably less expensive than that for 802.11a, which is primarily used in large office environments.

The faster of the two protocols is 802.11g, which has a transmission speed of 54 Mbps; the 802.11b's speed is 11 Mps. Linux support for 802.11g wireless cards, however, is still developmental at best, which means that you had better stick to the 802.11b protocol when selecting a wireless card. Although this may sound like an undesirable limitation, it is pretty much irrelevant in the real-world scheme of things because the speed of your Internet conection is still most likely to be slower than the capabilities of your 802.11b hardware. . . .

First of all, the 802.11b protocol is still more commonly used than the newer 802.11g. Most public wireless-access areas *(hot spots)*, such as airports, university campuses, and hotels, still use the 802.11b protocol. Even if the 802.11g protocol is used in such places, or even if someone in your family has a 802.11g-based system up and running in your house, you can still connect to the Net with your 802.11b network card, because the two protocols are compatible, which means that you can use a 802.11b with a 802.11g WAP and vice versa (not so for the 802.11a, however).

Finally, the somewhat lower speed of the 802.11b devices will most likely matter very little to you unless you are forking out an awful lot of money to your Internet provider each month for some extreme bandwidth. After all, the average transmission speed of most home cable Internet connections is still less than the 11 Mbps speed of 802.11b, so don't fret too much. Just remember that a traditional dial-up telephone modem has a maximum transmission speed of 56 Kbps, or 56 *thousand* bits per second, though such speeds are rarely achieved in reality; 11 Mbps is 11 *million* bits per second. That is plenty fast for the average mortal.

Hardware

To create your own home Wi-Fi setup, you need at least two pieces of hardware: a *wireless access point (WAP)* and a wireless *network interface card (NIC)* that goes inside your computer, both of which you can see in Figure 4-10. These two devices act like a pair of transceivers, communicating with each other via radio signals rather than over a wired connection. The WAP transmits data it receives from the Internet source device (such as your cable or ADSL modem) to the computer and receives data transmitted by the NIC that's inside the computer. The NIC, for its part, receives transmitted data from the WAP and transmits data from the computer back to the WAP.

Figure 4-10: All you need for a Wi-Fi setup—an access point and a network interface card

The basic differences between a wired and wireless Internet connection setup can be seen in Figure 4-11. In the typical wired setup, a cable from your high-speed Internet source device is directly connected to your computer by an Ethernet cable. If you are using a cable modem, for example, you would have an Ethernet cable going from your cable modem directly into the Ethernet port of your computer. It's very straightforward and simple. In a Wi-Fi setup, you are basically replacing that direct-Ethernet-cable connection with radio signals. The Ethernet cable from your Internet source device is in this case directly connected to the wireless access point, rather than to your computer.

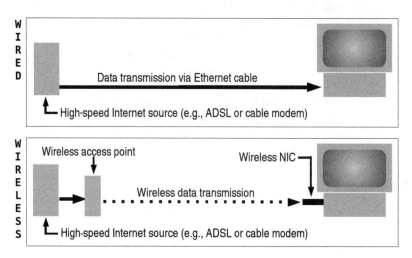

Figure 4-11: Wired and wireless Internet connections compared

What is connected to your computer is the wireless NIC. This is most frequently a PC card that you plug into one of the PCMCIA ports on your laptop (or into a special adapter on desktops). The NIC and access point then communicate with each other via radio waves rather than a hard-wire connection—a sort of virtual wire, if you like.

Wireless Access Points

If you want to set up a wireless system in your home or office, then the first thing you will need to get is a WAP. Fortunately, Linux compatibility is not really much of an issue in this department, because the access point doesn't physically interface with your computer. In addition, because the 802.11b and 802.11g protocols are compatible with each other, it doesn't really matter what type of access point you use. This is not to say that you needn't pay attention to what you are getting, because there is one type of wireless access point you will want to avoid.

While whatever wireless access point you use should work right out of the box without the need for any special settings, there are a number of settings that you might want to consider, especially for reasons of security. You can usually input or change such settings by opening a web browser and then typing in the IP address of the wireless access point, which is generally printed somewhere in the user's manual. Once you do this, a web page will appear in which you can change or input the various settings available. You do not need to be connected to the Internet when doing this, however, as these settings pages are actually embedded within WAP itself.

Unfortunately (for Linux users, anyway), there are a few WAPs that require you to use Internet Explorer to handle such browser-based settings. Because a Linux version of Internet Explorer does not exist, you will find yourself stuck unless you have a Mac or Windows machine somewhere else in the house to complete the job. Worse yet is the fact that some machines do not support browser-based settings at all. Instead, they require you to install special Windows software to do the job. When selecting hardware for your wireless setup, it is obviously best to stay clear of WAPs of this kind.

Wireless Network Interface Cards

The other piece of hardware you will need for your wireless setup is a wireless NIC, which is actually the only hardware you will need if you just want to go wireless when you are outside of your home. Because these cards plug directly into your system, you must find and use a card that is Linux-compatible. Xandros comes with several wireless drivers built in, so if you use a card that is compatible with one of those drivers, you will have smooth sailing.

Most wireless NICs are PC cards that pop into the PCMCIA slot at the side of your laptop computer (Figure 4-12). However, there are also NICs that plug into one of your machine's USB ports or one of its PCI slots. Unfortunately, Linux support is still pretty much limited to NICs of the PC card variety, though there are other Linux wireless drivers available for those other NICs.

Figure 4-12: A two-card PCMCIA slot

I don't really recommend going this non-PCMCIA NIC route, because doing so is not the simple slip-in-the-CD-and-double-click procedure that it can be in other systems. Adding a driver to Linux usually involves mucking around with the Linux kernel itself, which is a cumbersome and even daunting process, especially for a beginner. Most drivers eventually make their way into future releases of the Linux kernel, so for now I would strongly recommend sticking to hardware that is supported by the drivers that are included with your Xandros distro.

If you already have an NIC, you can just try it out to see if it works by going through the set-up steps in the following section. If you are going to go out and buy an NIC, or are thinking of doing so, and do not want to waste your hard-earned cash experimenting, you will want to check things out more thoroughly. Before getting started, you should first check out the Xandros hardware compatibility database (http://support.xandros.com/hclv3) or the Xandros User Forums (http://forums.xandros.com), where you can also ask for suggestions.

Setting Up Your Wireless Card

Setting up a Linux-compatible wireless PC card is actually relatively simple. It is probably best, though not essential, to first physically connect your WAP to your Internet source and then turn on the WAP. Once it is up and running, plug your wireless NIC into the PCMCIA slot on your computer. Any LEDs on the card might light up at this time. If not, they will do so after you finish configuring the card.

Once your card is inserted into the machine, it is time to configure the system to deal with the card, which is all very easy. First open the **Control Center** via the Launch menu, and then, once it opens, click the + symbol next to *Network*. In the subcategories that then appear, click **Network Connection**. The Network Connection module will then appear in the right pane of the window. Click the **Administrator** button in that pane, type your root password when prompted to do so, and then, when the module reloads, click the **Interfaces** tab.

Once in the Interfaces tab, make sure that **eth0 (Wireless Device)** is selected in the drop-down menu next to the words *Network Interface* (Figure 4-13). After that, click **Enable network**, and then select **Use dynamic address (DHCP)** or **Specify static address** (and input the appropriate settings), according to what your provider requires. When you are done with all that, click the **Apply** button. Your NIC should then be active and ready for action, so you can close the Control Center window now.

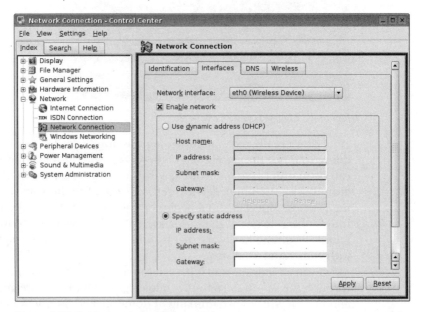

Figure 4-13: Setting up your wireless card

Releasing and Renewing Your Wireless Connection

There will be times when you want to turn your wireless card off, such as when you use your laptop on an airplane, or when you just want to flush the IP address in your Network settings *(release)* and update the settings with the IP address of a new network *(renew)*, such as when you move your desktop from one wireless hotspot to another without rebooting your computer.

This last point might seem a bit mysterious to you, so I will explain things briefly at this point. When you boot up your computer, your wireless card (NIC) performs a scan of available networks (WAPs) in order to see which one it can connect to. Once it finds a network, it gathers an IP address from that network via DHCP in order to allow you to access the Internet. Utilizing release and renew allows you to change WAPs without having to reboot your computer or when your machine, for whatever reason, just can't seem to do so on its own.

To turn off your wireless card or release the current IP address in your network settings , just follow these steps:

1. Go to the Launch menu and select **Control Center**.
2. Click the + icon next to Network, and then click **Network Connection**.
3. When the Network Connection module appears in the right side of the Control Center window, click the **Administrator** button, type your root password when prompted to do so, and then click **OK**.
4. Click the **Interfaces** tab.
5. Once in that tab, uncheck the **Enable Network** box, and then click **Apply**.
6. Click **OK** in the warning window that then appears to complete the process.

The boxes in the DHCP part of the window will now be empty, meaning that you have successfully released your settings and disabled your card. If you would like to reactivate your card later on, or if you would just like to refresh the IP address settings now, you basically do a variation on the same theme: check the **Enable network** box, click the **Apply** button, and then click **OK** in the warning window.

You can also release and renew your IP address by following steps 1–4, and then clicking the **Release** button. Once the boxes in the DHCP part of the window are empty, click the **Renew** button. When a new IP address appears in the DHCP part of the window, click the **Apply** button, and then click **OK** in the warning window that then appears.

5

THERE'S NO PLACE LIKE HOME
Working with Your Files in the Xandros File Manager

Double-click your ruby slippers and you may well end up in some dust bowl of a town in Kansas, where some nasty old lady is trying to have your dog sent to the pound—and in a wicker basket, no less! Double-click the **Home** icon on your desktop, however, and you will find yourself looking at the Xandros File Manager—a much happier place to be, all things considered. The Xandros File Manager (commonly referred to as *XFM* on Xandros user group forums) is arguably the most important part of your system. It allows you to access your files; view your digital images; browse other computers connected to your network; copy files to and from your Windows partition (if you have one); browse the contents of CDs, floppies, and other removable storage devices; burn CDs or DVDs; and even rip and encode music from audio CDs. Because the capabilities of this jack-of-all-trades are so great, I will be covering most of its features in this chapter and the next, while mentioning yet other features elsewhere throughout the book.

Navigation

When you launch the Xandros File Manager, by double-clicking the **Home** folder on your desktop or single-clicking the **XFM** launcher on the Panel, it will open up to your Home folder (Figure 5-1).

Figure 5-1: The Xandros File Manager

At this point in the game, the only two things you will find there are two icons: Desktop and My Documents. Double-clicking the **Desktop** icon will show all the files and launchers you happen to have located there, which at this point should just be the five desktop launchers we discussed in Chapter 3. Double-clicking the **My Documents** folder, on the other hand, will reveal the three folders that Xandros has already set up for you there: My Music, My Pictures, and My Videos.

Two Navigation Methods

Xandros provides you with two methods of navigating through your files: using the XFM navigation buttons and using the XFM file tree.

Navigating via the XFM Navigation Buttons

Once you've done some digging around in your various folders, you can move back and forth between them by using the three XFM navigation (arrow) buttons located below the Address bar (Figure 5-2). The left and right arrow buttons are very much like those you would use in a web browser—the left arrow takes you back to the folder or file you were just viewing, while the right arrow takes you back again to whatever you just left. The up arrow, on the other hand, brings you up one folder per click. If this doesn't seem clear to you at this point, give it a try later on when you have more files and folders with which to play around. You'll get the hang of it soon enough.

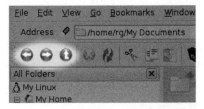

Figure 5-2: The Navigation buttons in XFM

To get double-click access to the other options available to you from the Xandros File Manager, such as your Windows partition or a CD or DVD, you can just click the up arrow button while in your My Home folder, or click once on the **My Linux** button in the left pane of the XFM window. The various devices and options will then appear in the right pane (Figure 5-3). We will be covering these items later on in this and the next chapter, so just hold off on fiddling with these for now.

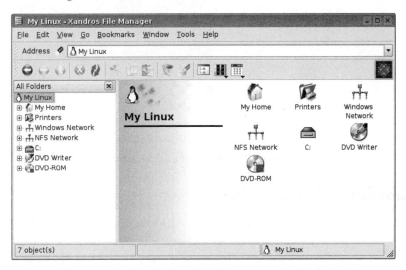

Figure 5-3: Accessing it all in the Xandros File Manager window

Navigating via the XFM File Tree

One of the most obvious things you'll notice in a Xandros File Manager window is the presence of a file tree, which appears in the left pane of the XFM window, which should be quite familiar if you're coming over from a Windows environment. You can use this file tree to navigate through your file system rather than using the double-click/arrow-button method I just described. Clicking any of the icons in the file tree will reveal the contents of that folder, network, or device in the right-hand pane. You can also view the subfolders within that tree by clicking the + symbol next to any item. Obviously, if there is nothing within that item, nothing will appear.

To have a look for yourself, click the + symbol next to My Home, and then click the + symbol next to the My Documents folder, which appears after that. Beneath the My Documents folder in the file tree you should see the three subfolders that Xandros has already set up for you: My Music, My Pictures, and My Videos. At this point, you probably don't have any files in any of these three folders, but if you do . . . say, some photos in the My Pictures folder . . . clicking that folder would reveal (in the pane on the right) the image files you have stored there, as you can see in Figure 5-4.

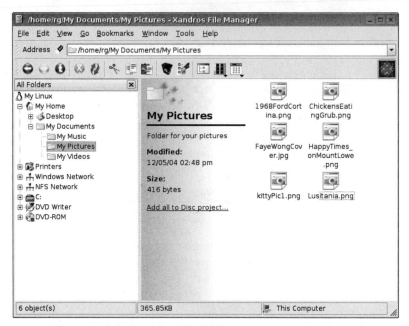

Figure 5-4: Viewing the contents of a folder via the file tree in XFM

Bookmarks Within XFM

Another very handy feature of XFM is that it lets you create bookmarks. You are no doubt familiar with creating bookmarks for web pages that you frequent, but why on earth would you want to create bookmarks within your file system? Well, imagine that you have a folder that you often need to use but that it takes an excessive number of mouse clicks to reach. To reduce your risk of repetitive stress injury (RSI) and the risk of developing carpal tunnel syndrome (CTS), you can reduce the number of clicks needed to get to the folder by navigating to that folder once, and then, in the Bookmarks menu of the XFM window, selecting **Add Bookmark**. After that, whenever you want to get back to that well-buried folder, you can just click the **Bookmarks** menu, and that folder will be right there waiting for you on the menu.

For example, let's say that you frequently need to deal with a particular group of images you've downloaded from your digital camera to your hard disk. The photos are in the *Summer in Wilmington* folder within the *My Albums* folder, which is located within your *My Pictures* folder, which is located in your

My Documents folder. That's a lot of clicking. By clicking your way to that folder once and then bookmarking it, getting to it in the future will be a mere two-click endeavor via the Bookmarks menu (Figure 5-5). You'll be saving your weary hand up to six mouse clicks every time you want to go to that folder.

Figure 5-5: Using the XFM Bookmarks menu

Creating Folders and Renaming Files in XFM and on the Desktop

Two of the most common file-related procedures in any system, creating folders and renaming files, are easily performed in the Xandros File Manager. To create a folder in XFM, right-click any open space in the right pane of the XFM window, and then select **New Folder** in the pop-up menu.

To rename a file in XFM, right-click the file and select **Rename** in the pop-up menu. The filename below the file will then be highlighted. You can then rename the file and then press ENTER to complete the process or just click any open space within the window to complete the process. Remember to retain the original file extension (.doc, .png, .jpg, and so on) when you rename a file.

To create a folder or rename a file on the desktop, the procedures are essentially the same as those for XFM. To create a folder, right-click directly on any open space on the desktop, and then select **Create New ▶ Folder** in the pop-up menu. To rename a file, right-click the file, select **Rename** in the pop-up menu, type the new name, and then press ENTER or click any open space on the desktop. You can also rename a file by clicking the file once to select it and then pressing the **F2** key.

Copying and Moving Files in XFM

Copying and moving files within the Xandros File Manager is a pretty straight-forward endeavor, although it might be slightly different from what you are used to in your previous operating system. In most other operating systems, dragging a file and dropping it in a new location moves the file to that new location. In XFM, however, that same *drag-and-drop* procedure copies the file, thus leaving you with two copies of the file, each in a different location.

Copying a File

Keeping that warning in mind, you now basically know how to copy a file: click the file, and keeping the mouse button depressed, drag the file to wherever it is you want to create the copy. You can drag it to a folder within the right pane or to a folder within the file tree in the left pane. Once the mouse cursor is over the destination folder, that folder will be highlighted. It is then safe to release the mouse button. A window will then appear (for a very short time in the case of small files) that indicates the progress of the copying process. When that window is gone, the copying is complete.

Moving a File

Moving a file is almost exactly the same process I have just described, except that you need to use the right mouse button instead of the left one. To move a file, right-click the file you want to move, and then drag it to the target folder in either pane of the XFM window. Once the target folder is highlighted, release the mouse button. A small pop-up menu will then appear (Figure 5-6).

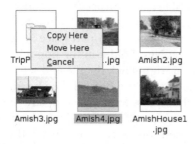

Figure 5-6: Moving files in XFM

In that menu, move your cursor (without holding down either mouse button) over **Move Here**, in order to select that option, and then click once with your *left* mouse button. A progress window will appear for a brief time until the process is complete.

Copying and Moving Files on the Desktop

You can also save files to your desktop, as you could with your previous operating system, but there's more than one way to do so:

- To copy a file from the desktop to the Xandros File Manager, while you are holding down the left mouse button, drag the file from the desktop, and then drop it in the right pane of the window by releasing the mouse button. If you would like to copy the file to a folder other than the one open in the right pane, you can drop the file directly on the target folder in either the right pane or the file tree in the left pane. If your XFM window is minimized, you can still drag the file from the desktop, then hover the cursor over the XFM entry in the taskbar and wait for the window to appear in the foreground.

- To move a file from the desktop to XFM, first copy it to XFM, and then drag the original file to the trashcan.
- To copy or move a file from XFM to the desktop or to a folder on the desktop, hold down the left mouse button and then drag the file to the desktop and release the file. A pop-up menu appears (Figure 5-7). Select **Move Here** to move the file or **Copy Here** to copy it. When you have made your choice, click the *left* mouse button.
- To move or copy a file from the desktop to a folder on the desktop, drag and drop the file using the left mouse button.

Figure 5-7: Pop-up menu when copying and moving files from XFM to the desktop

Another Way to Copy and Move Files

You can also copy or move files by cutting and pasting them in XFM or on the desktop. To do so, right-click the file that you want to copy or move, and then, in the pop-up menu, select **Copy** (to copy the file) or **Cut** (to cut the file from its present location and move it to a new location). Then left-click your selection. Now drag the file to where you want to copy or move the file, right-click the mouse, and in the pop-up menu, select **Paste**. Finally, click the left mouse button, and you're finished.

Creating a Desktop Link to a File in XFM

Rather than copying or moving a file from XFM to your desktop, you can create a link (or shortcut) to the file. To access the file, you would just double-click that link.

To create a link on your desktop to a file within XFM, drag the file to where you want to create the link using the left or right mouse button, and then release the mouse button. In the pop-up menu that appears, select **Link Here**, and then click the *left* mouse button.

Extracting and Creating Archived Files in XFM

In addition to its many other capabilities, the Xandros File Manager allows you to easily open and create archived files without installing any additional software. If you've ever dealt with a ZIP file in Windows or a StuffIt file (.sit) file in Mac OS, you have experience with archived (also referred to as *compressed*) files. Basically, when you compress a file, you are taking a single file or, more often, a group of files and shrinking them to a size that takes up less disk space. This is very useful when trying to squeeze as much as you can onto a floppy disk or a CD, or when trying to send files over the Internet. Most applications you downloaded from the Internet thus come in this fashion.

Most archived files in the Linux world are created with some variation of the *Tar* program. The archives created in that format are therefore often referred to as *tarballs* and usually end with the extension .tgz. Of course, Linux can also create and extract ZIP archives, so the compression format used for a particular archive usually reflects the system on or for which it was created.

Extracting an Archived File

There are a couple of ways to extract the contents of an archived file, but the easiest is to double-click the archived file, right-click the folder you find within, and then select **Copy** in the pop-up menu. After that, navigate to wherever it is you want to place the folder, right-click any open space in that window, and then select **Paste** in the pop-up menu.

If the files within the archive are not already in a folder of their own, you will have to create a folder for them first, using the more conventional methods you learned earlier in this chapter. Once you've done that, select all of the files within the archived file, right-click any one of them, and then select **Copy** in the pop-up menu. After that, navigate to the new folder you've just created for your new files, right-click any open space in that window, and then select **Paste** in the pop-up menu.

Creating Your Own Compressed Files

Now that you know how to extract the various types of compressed file formats out there, you probably should also know how to create your own. As a general rule of thumb, the format you choose to use should reflect the system of the person who will ultimately be opening the archive. That said, if you are creating archives for Windows users, use ZIP; for Linux or Mac users, use TGZ.

Creating a Tarball (TGZ File)

How about if you want to create your own tarball in XFM? No problem; just follow these steps:

1. If you want to place multiple files in the same archive, first create a new folder, name it appropriately, and then place all the files you want to add to the archive into that folder. (If you want to archive only a single file, you can omit this folder-creation and file-moving step.)
2. Next, right-click the folder (or the single file) from within XFM, and then select **Create TGZ Archive** in the pop-up menu.
3. The archive will automatically have the name of the folder or single file you clicked, plus the extension .tgz. In a matter of seconds (slightly longer for bigger archives), the new archive will appear next to the folder that you just moments before right-clicked, and your mission will be complete.

Creating a ZIP File

The procedure for creating a ZIP archive is essentially the same as that for creating a tarball: create a new folder, copy or move all the files you want to place in the archive in that folder, right-click the folder, and select **Add to ZIP Archive** in the pop-up menu. Once you've completed those steps, an *Add to Zip Archive* window (Figure 5-8) will appear with the name of the folder you're archiving given as the name of the soon-to-be-created ZIP file. Assuming that name will do, all you have to do is click **OK**, and the process will be complete within a few seconds—maybe less. If, however, you suddenly remember that you forgot to add a certain file to the archive, you can choose to add it at this point (before clicking **OK**).

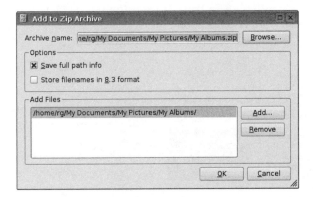

Figure 5-8: Creating a ZIP archive

To add a file to your under-construction ZIP archive, click the **Add** button in the bottom half of the Add to Zip Archive window. Another window, *Add files or folders*, will then appear, and from that window you can choose other files to add. Once you have found the file you want to add, select it and then click **Open**. The file you chose will then appear in the list at the bottom of the Add to Zip Archive window. To add yet another file, repeat this procedure again. Once you have finished adding files, click **OK**.

What if you want to add files after the ZIP archive is already created? Well, just treat the archive like a regular folder and do a copy-and-paste routine. Here's what you would do, step-by-step:

1. Select the file (or files) you want to add to an existing ZIP archive, right-click it (or them), and then select **Copy** in the pop-up menu.

2. Next, double-click the ZIP archive you will be adding to.

3. When the window for that archive opens, right-click any open space within that window, and then select **Paste** in the pop-up menu.

Xandros File Manager as an Image Viewer

Another one of the handy things about XFM is that it can act as a sort of picture viewer and previewer. If you click once on any graphics file, a thumbnail of that file will appear in the left side of the right pane of the XFM window, as you can see in Figure 5-9.

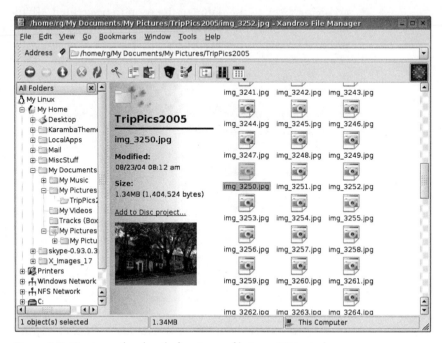

Figure 5-9: Viewing a thumbnail of an image file in an XFM window

You can also have your graphics files appear as thumbnails, rather than icons (as shown in Figure 5-10), by going to the **View** menu and selecting **Thumbnails**. This lets you see your graphics files without having to use any other special imaging software. Admittedly, this feature is no longer unique in the world of operating systems, but it is handy nonetheless. What is more unique to Xandros, as you will learn shortly, is that same functionality works for text files too.

When you double-click a thumbnail of an image in XFM, that image will appear at a larger size in the right pane of the XFM window (Figure 5-11). At the same time, a set of controls will appear with which you can browse through your images at an enlarged size, rotate them, adjust the level of magnification, or even run an in-window slideshow. This is all very cool, especially for a mere file manager.

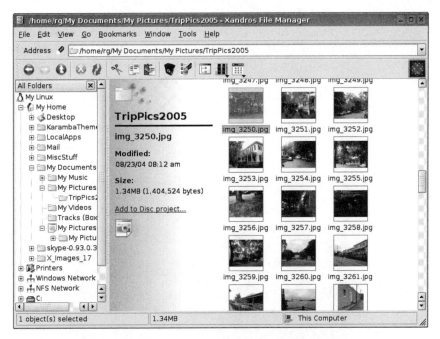

Figure 5-10: Viewing your graphics files as thumbnails rather than icons in an XFM window

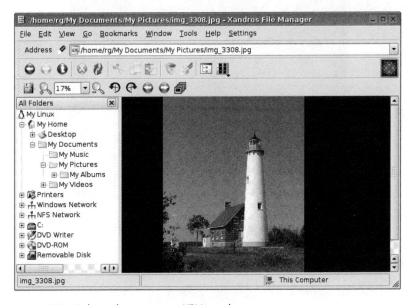

Figure 5-11: Enlarged image in an XFM window

If you would like to see an image at a size beyond the constraints of the right pane of the XFM window, you can do so by right-clicking the thumbnail of the image in question and selecting **Open With ▶ Image Viewer** in the pop-up menu. The image will then appear in its own window, as you can see in Figure 5-12. In Image Viewer (also called KView), not only do you have all the viewing options you do when viewing images in an XFM window, but you can also have your images fill the entire screen by selecting **Full Screen Mode** in the Settings menu and then selecting **Fit Image to Window** in the View menu. To get back to normal, just go to the **Settings** menu again and select **Exit Full Screen Mode**.

Figure 5-12: Viewing an image in its own window

Using XFM to View Text and PDF Files

In addition to letting you view graphics files, the Xandros File Manager allows you to read the contents of text files (those saved with a .txt file format), again without the need for any other software. If, for example, you have some notes that you jotted down and saved as a text file, you can simply double-click the file's icon in the right pane of the XFM, and the file's contents will be displayed in the XFM window. XFM can even do the same for PDF files, acting as a simple PDF viewer. Just clicking a text or PDF file will even give you a small preview of that document in the left-hand side of the XFM window, as is the case with graphics files. Of course, you can always opt to read a PDF file in a window of its own by right-clicking the PDF file you want to view and selecting **Open With ▸ Acrobat Reader** in the pop-up menu (Figure 5-13), or, if Acrobat Reader doesn't seem to do the trick, **Open With ▸ PostScript Viewer**. Text files can be read in a similar fashion by selecting **Open With ▸ Text Editor**.

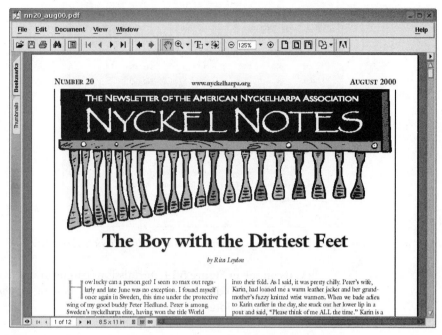

Figure 5-13: Viewing a PDF file in Acrobat Reader

Changing File and Folder Permissions Within XFM

You will find, as you make your way along in the Linux world, that occasionally you come across a file that your system will not allow you to alter. When you open up such a file in the appropriate application, the title bar will often say *Read Only*, or when you try to save the file, you will get a *Permission Denied* message. Messages of this type are telling you that the file is write-protected, meaning that you do not have permission to alter the file. In all likelihood, the only time you will encounter this situation in Xandros is when you copy files from a CD to your hard disk or when you copy files from your Windows partition to your Linux partition. This is another way that Linux tries to protect you from harming your system, though in the case of copied CD files, it may not be clear to you how it's protecting you.

If you want to alter a file or gain access to a folder that is write-protected, it is possible to do so in an XFM window as long as you are listed as the owner of that file or folder. To change file or folder permissions, just right-click the file or folder in question and then select **Properties** from the pop-up menu.

Once the Properties window opens, click the **Permissions** tab, and you will see who the owner of the file or folder is and what you are allowed or not allowed to do with it (see Figure 5-14).

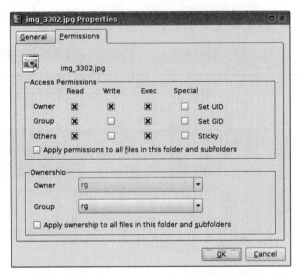

Figure 5-14: Changing permissions in an XFM Properties window

As you can see in Figure 5-14, permissions can be granted or denied to the *owner* of the file or folder (you), to a specified *group*, or to *others* (everybody else). These permissions are:

Read   Permission to view the contents of a file or folder

Write   Permission to alter the contents of a file or folder

Execute   Permission to run a program or script

In general, you needn't worry all that much about setting permissions for your own files, because you are really the only one who has access to your user account. The main exception to this is when you transfer files from a CD to your hard disk. In this case, the files likely will be write-protected, meaning that you cannot alter the files until you change their permissions.

If you are dealing with a write-protected folder or file, you can change the file's permissions to allow you to alter it by clicking the checkbox under the word *Write* in the *Owner* row. Once you have finished, click **OK** and you'll be free to do what you like with that file.

Using XFM with Your Windows Partition (for Dual-Booters Only)

If you set up a dual-boot system when you installed Xandros, you can also get read-only access to the files in your Windows partition, but not the programs, via the Xandros File Manager. To do so, follow these steps:

1. Click the **C:** icon in the file tree in the left pane of the XFM window (or whatever drive contains the files you want). The contents of your Windows C: drive should appear on the right-hand side of the right pane of the XFM window (Figure 5-15).

NOTE *You will only have read access to the partition (see the left-hand side of the XFM window, which tells you this), which means you can copy files from, but not to, the Windows partition. Although this may seem a bit inconvenient, it is probably best in the long run, because it protects the integrity of your Windows system and can help to prevent any problems from occurring the next time you decide to boot up in Gatesville.*

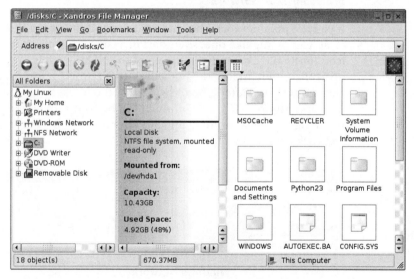

Figure 5-15: Getting read-only access to your Windows files

NOTE *Assuming your files are stored, as most people's are, in your Windows My Documents folder, you can access them by double-clicking the **Documents and Settings** folder.*

2. Once the contents of that folder appear in the right pane, look for the folder with your Windows username (mine says *rg*) and then double-click that folder.

3. Finally, double-click the **My Documents** folder that appears in the right pane, inside which you should be able to find all of your files. If you happen to have saved some files to your Windows desktop and would like to access them, double-click the **Desktop** folder instead of My Documents.

NOTE *Creating a bookmark in XFM for this Windows My Documents or Desktop folder might be a pretty convenient thing to do now that you know how.*

Dealing with Your Network in XFM

If your computer is connected to a local network, as is often the case with office computers, you can also browse the computers connected to that network, and assuming you have permission from your network administrator to do so, you can also have read and write access to the files located there.

Browsing Your Network

If you are on a network, the chances are good that it is a Windows network, or at least acting like one, so to start browsing, click the **Windows Network** icon in the file tree in the left pane of the XFM window. A window may pop up at that point asking for your Windows Network password. If it does, just click **Cancel**, and after a bit of searching, the workgroups located on the network (Figure 5-16), one of which will be your own computer, will appear in the right pane. If nothing appears after a few seconds, try clicking the **NFS Network** icon in the file tree.

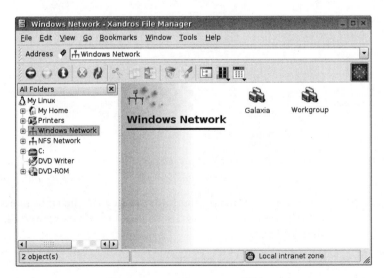

Figure 5-16: Network workgroups shown in an XFM window

Once the workgroups appear, double-click the workgroup that you belong to; the various computers belonging to that network will then appear (Figure 5-17). Search through the list until you find the host computer that you have permission to log on to (ask your network administrator if you're not sure), and then double-click the icon for that computer.

Mounting a Network Share

At this point, a small window will appear showing your username and asking for your password. Be aware that the username and password you chose for your Xandros system may be different from those for your network. My Xandros username, for example is *rg*, while my username for my office network is *grant*. My passwords are also different, but I'll keep that information to myself. At any rate, your situation may be similar to mine, so be sure to input the appropriate information. Once you have done so, click the **OK** button.

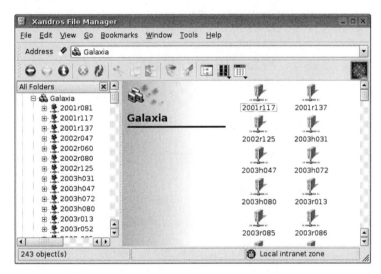

Figure 5-17: Browsing through the computers connected to your network

You should now be able to see the contents of the host computer in the right pane of the XFM window. Look for the folder with your network username (or any other folder you have permission to use), and then double-click it if you just want to see what's inside. If you want to access the folder for file-writing or copying tasks, click it once to select it, and then click the **Mount this share** link at the left side of the right pane of the XFM window.

A new window, Mount Network Share, will now appear. In this window, you will see three text boxes: *Share to mount, Mount point,* and *Connect as.* The information in the first and last of these three boxes is information regarding the network; the network needs to knows what you are trying to mount and who you happen to be. The middle box, however, contains information for your own computer. The *Mount point* box tells your system where in your file system it should display the files on your network share, or folder.

This may sound a bit confusing, but I will try to simplify things a bit. Your Xandros system, like all other Linux distributions, sees the world as a series of files and folders. In order to display the files on your network share, it needs a folder in which to do so. Again, this is no different from what happens when you insert a CD or floppy into your computer—your computer mounts the disk and then displays its contents in a folder, which, unbeknownst to you, is located on your hard disk at /mnt/cdrom0, or, in the case of a floppy, at /mnt/fd0. Of course, you needn't worry about these details.

What you do need to worry (or at least think) about, however, is where on your disk you want your system to place the folder it will use to mount your network share or shares. The default location in the Mount Network Share window is /home/Xandros_username/share_name, which is fine enough. I would personally recommend creating an intermediary folder of sorts, however, especially if you have more than one share you are going to be mounting. To do this, change the text in the *Mount point* box to read **/home/Xandros_ username/Network_Shares/share_name** (of course, substituting *your* username for the Xandros_username in that string). Your window should then look something like Figure 5-18.

Figure 5-18: Creating a folder with which to mount your network share

Whether or not you take this extra step is strictly up to you, but because whatever folder you create for this purpose will appear in your Home folder, I think you eventually will appreciate the lack of confusion that this extra folder will bring about. Either way you decide to go, once you are ready, click **OK**.

At this point, because you do not already have a network shares folder or one with your network username, another small window, somewhat frighteningly titled *Error*, will now pop up asking you if you want to create the folders in question. You do, so click **OK**.

Accessing the Files on Your Mounted Network Share

You can now access the files within your network share by going to the newly created folder within your Home folder. Remember that the files in that folder are only displayed and accessible there; they are not actually physically present on your hard disk, so if you use your computer while not connected to the network, the folders will be empty.

Anyway, assuming you have read and write permissions from your network administrator, you will not only be able to copy files from your network share but also copy files to that share. In addition, you can actually work with files directly on your share as if they were right there on your hard disk. Say, for example, that you have an OpenOffice.org document on your share. You could, if so inclined, double-click that file, make whatever changes you want to make, and save it—all without the document ever sitting on your hard disk.

Future Network Logins

Once you have things set up, you will not have to go through this rather laborious process again. Every time you start up your machine, your system will attempt to automatically mount your network share. Shortly after the Xandros desktop appears on your screen, two windows will appear—one informing you that your system is attempting to restore your network connection and another asking you for your network password (Figure 5-19). If you want to mount your network share, type your password, and then click **OK**. You can then view your network files in the folder you created in your Home folder (Network_Shares/network_username).

Figure 5-19: Typing in your password during subsequent logins

If you would rather not mount your network share at that time, you can click **Cancel** instead. This will bring up yet another window asking you if you would like to permanently remove a given share from your list of automatically connected network shares. If you need to mount your network share only occasionally, or if you are using a notebook computer that you actually move from work to home and back, it is probably a good idea to click **Yes**. If, on the other hand, you do prefer to be prompted every time you boot up, click **No**. Either way, you can still mount your network share whenever you want to, using the method I described earlier.

6

PORTS OF CALL
Working with Floppies, CDs, DVDs, and Other Removable Media

While the multi-gigabyte hard drives that almost all computers have today allow you to store what seems like an infinite number of files, there may be times when you want to back up those files or give them to others. In fact, many of the files you have on your hard disk are not files you yourself created on your computer, such as word processing files, but actually came from outside sources. After all, you probably have a good many digital photos you've received from friends or family as email attachments; word processing or spreadsheet documents that you unfortunately received from work (also most likely by email); and still other images and PDF files, fonts, and even applications that you've downloaded from the Internet.

While most file transfers these days seem to be done via the Internet, it was not too long ago that the main way to transport files from computer to computer was by floppy disk, which was also how many average users went about backing up their hard disks. Needless to say, this was a much slower and more cumbersome way of going about things. Still, despite our newfound love of digital spontaneity, hard storage media types have not gone the way of the dodo, great auk, and Carolina parakeet. In fact, not only do they continue to be used, but the range of removable storage media available to us has actually expanded to include Zip disks, DVDs, and, more recently, USB hard disks, flash drives, and memory card readers.

Given the diverse ways in which people use their computers today, being able to use these various forms of hard storage media has thus become more or less essential. Whether it be for importing photos from your digital camera, listening to music and watching movies on your computer, or just backing up all the valuable items you have stored on your hard disk, you eventually will have to deal with at least some of the various forms of hard media available in the computer world today.

Fortunately, the Xandros File Manager makes this all quite easy by acting as a port of sorts (hence the title of this chapter—a stretch, I know), from which you can easily load and unload data to and from the various media that drop anchor at your machine. Whether you insert floppy disks, CDs, or DVDs into their respective drives or connect any other storage device to one of your USB ports, you will be able to access those media via the Xandros File Manager.

Floppies

When the original Macintosh computer first came out, one of the coolest things about it was that it used 3.5-inch floppy disks (also known as *floppies*). At the time, I thought that those disks, with their hard casing and sliding metal doors protecting the media itself, were the incarnation of high-tech cool. Times change, of course, and there are fewer and fewer people using floppies these days.

The reason for this change is simple: files have just gotten too big for floppies. The audio, video, and image files most people deal with these days are gigantic. You'd be lucky, for example, to fit more than three digital photos on one floppy disk. Compared to CDs, Zip disks, memory cards, and the like, floppies are also too slow. You could practically feed the cat, make a cup of coffee, and read the first three pages of the newspaper in the time it takes to write a good number of files to a floppy. (Well, okay, that's an exaggeration, but floppies are slow when compared to the alternatives.)

Despite being small and slow, floppies are still used by a dwindling number of people who have no other way of transferring files to removable media, or who just want to hand over one or two small word processing documents to another person who can read no other type of media. You may be one of these people, or you may have to send files to or receive them from someone in this situation.

Writing to and Copying from Disk

Using floppies on your system is easy enough: just insert the floppy into its drive, open XFM, and then click the **Floppy** icon near the bottom of the file tree in the left pane of the window. The contents of the floppy will appear in the right pane. To copy, add, or remove files to or from the floppy, use the various methods I described in Chapter 5, and immediately the data will be written to (or removed from) the disk. When you have finished, eject the floppy manually.

NOTE *When you remove a floppy from the drive, the files displayed in the right pane of the XFM window will remain. This is a temporary state of affairs, however, so don't worry. Just click any other folder in the file tree until the contents of that folder are displayed in the right pane. After that, just click the Floppy icon in the file tree again, and the files previously displayed there will be gone.*

Formatting Floppies

Before you can actually write anything to a disk, that disk must be formatted. This is true of any kind of storage media—your hard disk, CDs, storage cards in your digital camera, or floppy disks—though it is sometimes done before you buy the media. By formatting a disk, your system (at your request) lays down a sort of map on the disk that specifies where data can be stored.

NOTE *Because there are, and have been, many operating systems, there are many such formats for floppy disks. Linux can read both Linux-native ext2 formatted disks and Windows/DOS FAT formatted disks. It can also create either format.*

Most floppy disks these days are sold preformatted in DOS format, so you probably don't have to worry much about this; however, if you do need to format an unformatted floppy disk, or even an already used one from which you want to erase all the data, the process is simple.

1. Insert the floppy into its drive, and then open the Xandros File Manager. Click the **Floppy** icon in the file tree of that window, and then click the words **Format Floppy** at the left side of the right pane of the window. A Floppy Disk Formatter window should appear, as shown in Figure 6-1.

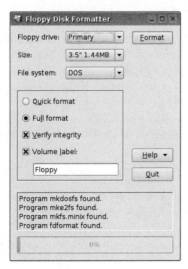

Figure 6-1: Formatting a floppy disk

2. In this window, you can specify the *density*, or capacity, of the floppy (1.44 MB or 720 KB), the file system type (ext2 or FAT), and the name for the disk. Once you have done so, begin formatting the floppy by clicking the **Format** button.

3. A small window will appear asking if you are sure you want to proceed. Click **Continue** and the formatting process will begin, with its progress indicated at the bottom of the Floppy Disk Formatter window.

4. When the process is complete, another window will appear telling you so. Just click **OK** in that window, and the process will be complete.

Reading Data CDs or DVDs

To read a CD or DVD with data on it (images, files, or programs) rather than music, place the disc in your CD or DVD drive. A Xandros File Manager window should automatically open and display the contents of the disc. You can then copy the files on the data CD or DVD to your hard disk using the copy-and-paste or drag-and-drop methods described in Chapter 5.

NOTE *As I mentioned in Chapter 5, any file that you copy from CD or DVD to your hard disk will be write-protected, so you will have to change its permissions if you want to alter it. To do so, right-click the file, select **Properties** in the pop-up window, and then click the **Permissions** tab in the Properties window and change the permissions.*

When you have finished copying files from the CD or DVD, you can eject it by right-clicking the icon that says **DVD-ROM** or **CD-RW** and selecting **Eject Disk** in the pop-up menu.

Playing Music CDs

To play a music CD, insert it into your drive; the Kscd CD player (shown in Figure 6-2) should open automatically and begin playing it. You should also see a small applet in the Panel that looks like a small CD with a pair of quarter notes on it (also shown in Figure 6-2), which you can use to hide or show the player and control its basic functions. If you are connected to the Internet and playing a commercial audio CD, Kscd will also query an online database (freedb.org) in order to gather album and track titles, which it will then display in the player window.

When you have finished playing your CD, you can eject it by clicking the **Eject** button in the player window or by right-clicking the **Panel** applet and selecting **Eject** in the pop-up menu.

NOTE *Closing the Kscd player window does not also close the Panel applet. To do so, right-click the applet, and then select **Quit** in the pop-up menu. Doing this without first closing the player window will accomplish both tasks in one step.*

Figure 6-2: The Kscd player and Panel applet

Playing DVD and VCD Videos

If you have a DVD drive, Xandros can also play unencrypted DVDs via its bundled video playback software, Xine (Figure 6-3). Xine can also play VCDs (video compact discs), which are movies recorded on specially formatted CDs that can be played in DVD or CD drives. VCDs are inferior to DVDs in terms of image quality, but they are much cheaper. Because they are popular mainly in China (especially Hong Kong) and a few other countries, however, you might not come across many of them unless you happen to love more obscure Chinese movies or Canto-pop karaoke. Still, if you do run across any, you will be pleased to know that you can play them.

Figure 6-3: Viewing DVDs and VCDs with Xine

Because Xine is covered separately in Chapter 14, I won't mention any more about it here. If you just can't wait to watch your copy of *A Red Detachment of Women* though, feel free to jump ahead; otherwise, just hang in there for now.

CD-RW Drives

These days, it seems that almost all computers have built-in CD-RW (CD-rewritable) drives. CD-RW drives work just like CD-ROM drives in that they allow you to read data or play music from CDs. They also allow you to burn data to blank CDs. If you don't have a CD-RW drive in your machine, I would strongly recommend your getting one. Drives for desktop machines are relatively cheap ($40 or less) and are easily installed.

If your data storage needs are greater than what can be handled by a CD, consider installing a DVD burner, which in addition to reading and burning CDs can also read and burn DVDs, which have upwards of seven times the capacity of CDs.

Burning Data CDs and DVDs

Burning data CDs and DVDs is easily handled in the Xandros File Manager's DVD Writer (or CD Writer, depending on what kind of drive you have). In fact, burning these discs in Xandros is probably an easier, or at least more straightforward, process than it is in other operating systems or even many other Linux distributions.

NOTE   *One limitation of the Xandros Open Circulation Edition (the one that comes with this book) is that it limits you to 2X CD burning speed and does not allow DVD burning. The DVD Writer icon in the file tree in the left pane of the XFM window will thus be captioned CD Writer even if you happen to have a DVD burner installed on your machine. You can have full-speed CD and DVD burning by upgrading to any other version of Xandros.*

Setting Up the Files You Want to Burn to a CD or DVD

Your first step is to set up the files you want to burn to disc. The files you gather together for this purpose are referred to as a *project*.

To get started with your project, open XFM and click the **DVD Writer** or **CD Writer** (depending on the hardware you happen to have) icon in the file tree in the left pane of the window. The disc-burning options will appear in the right pane of the XFM window (Figure 6-4).

Click **Create data disc**. The right pane of the window should look like the right side of Figure 6-5. Next, drag or paste the files you want to burn to that pane.

Figure 6-4: CD- and DVD-burning options listed in an XFM window

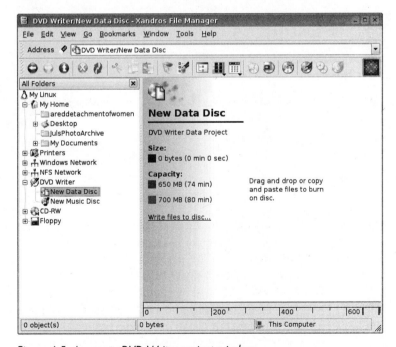

Figure 6-5: An empty DVD Writer project window

As you add your files to your new project, the ruler-like gauge at the bottom of the window (Figure 6-6) will show how much of the target disc's capacity you will be using and how much remains. The maximum capacity for CDs is indicated by a red vertical bar for 650 MB discs and a green bar for 700 MB discs. You do not, of course, want to exceed the maximum capacity of the disc you are going to be using or it won't burn correctly.

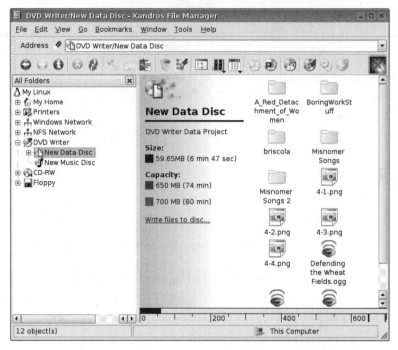

Figure 6-6: Disc-space availability indicator at the bottom of a DVD Writer project window

Burning Your Files to Disc

Once you have gathered all of the relevant files together in the project window, you can move on to actually burning them to disc. To do this, follow these steps:

1. Click the words **Write files to disc** at the left side of the right pane. A small window will appear telling you that Xandros recommends closing all other open programs before writing data to disc. (I've burned many a disc without any problems while other programs have been running, but to play it safe, go ahead and obey.) Click **OK** to close that small window.

2. A Create Disc window (Figure 6-7) appears, showing you the hardware device (your DVD or CD drive, whatever the case may be), the preferred write speed (*Maximum* is the default), the amount of data to be burned to disc, and the amount of time estimated for completion of the process. Because the default settings are probably fine for your purposes, go ahead and click **OK**.

Figure 6-7: Checking your disc-burning settings

3. Two windows will then appear in rapid succession. The first window is explained in the next step. The second window asks you to place a blank disc in your drive. Do what that window says, and then once the blank disc has been swallowed into your machine and the little LED on the drive stops flashing, click **OK**. The burning process will then begin.

4. The remaining window (Figure 6-8) will indicate the progress of the burning process. The process itself consists of three steps, all of which are hands-off for you: preparing the track, recording the track, and fixating the disc. When complete, your disc will be automatically ejected from the drive, and you can click the **Done** button. You are now basically finished.

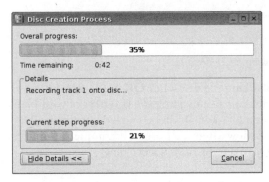

Figure 6-8: The Disc Creation Process window

If you won't be burning any more discs with the same exact group of files, go ahead and do a bit of system housecleaning. Go to the file tree in the XFM window, right-click the project you just burned to disc, and then select **Delete** in the pop-up menu.

Dealing with Rewritable Discs

CD-RW and DVD-RW (rewritable) discs are pretty much like their CD-R and DVD-R counterparts, except that they can be erased and then written to again. They are also quite a bit more expensive. Also, if you are interested in copying or creating a music CD, CD-RW discs cannot be played in the majority of standard audio CD players, such as in your home or car.

Using rewritable discs is much like working with standard write-once CDs and DVDs. If the disc is blank, there is no difference in the process at all, which makes things quite simple. If, however, you want to reuse a rewritable disc that already has data on it, you must first erase, or *blank*, it.

To blank a disc:

1. Insert the disc in the drive, and when the XFM window appears, click **DVD Writer** or **CD Writer** (whichever is appropriate in your case) in the file tree in the left window pane.

2. From the list of choices that then appears in the right pane, click **Blank disc**. A new window, *Blank Disc* (Figure 6-9), should appear.

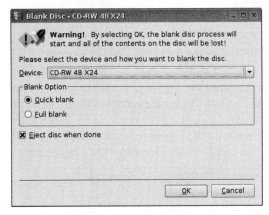

Figure 6-9: Blanking a CD-RW disc

3. To start blanking the disc, click **OK** in the Blank Disc window. Another window will appear indicating the progress of your blanking. When the disc has been blanked, it will be ejected automatically. Click **Done** in the progress window when the process is complete. You can then go on to use the newly blanked disc as if it were new.

Duplicating Audio and Data Discs

Here's how to duplicate audio and data CDs:

1. To get started, open XFM and click the **DVD Writer** or **CD Writer** icon in the left pane.

2. Next, click **Copy disc** in the right pane. When you see a warning window telling you to close all other running applications before burning data to disc, close them if you want to, and then click **OK**.

3. A Copy Disc window should open, followed by another window telling you to insert the source you want to copy. That means that you should insert the disc that you want to copy. Go ahead and insert it. Once your drive light stops flashing, click **OK**.

4. Click **OK** in the next window, and you'll be asked to check the destination media (meaning the blank disc). I don't do it, but click **Check** if you like; otherwise, click **Skip**. The copying process should begin, with the progress indicated in a separate window.

5. When the copy phase of the process is complete, your disc should be ejected automatically, and a small window (bottom of Figure 6-10) will appear that asks you to insert a blank disc.

NOTE   *At this point in the process, the progress bars in the Copy Disc window will not indicate 100 percent progress (also shown in Figure 6-10). This is because they indicate the total progress of both the copy and burning processes, so don't worry.*

6. Insert the blank disc as requested, and then click **OK**. The burning phases of the process will begin. When it finishes, your disc will be ejected automatically, and you can then go ahead and close the Copy Disc window by clicking the **Done** button in that window.

Figure 6-10: DVD Writer asks you to insert a blank disc midway in the disc-copy process

Burning ISO Images to Disc

When you download Xandros or other Linux distributions from the Internet, you usually download them as one or more disc images, commonly referred to as *ISOs*. An ISO is an image of a CD, which means that it is the CD minus the media itself. To put it another way, if CDs had souls, the ISO would be the soul of a CD; take away the CD's metal and plastic, and the remaining data would be an ISO. After downloading an ISO, you burn it onto a blank CD in order to give the image back its body, so to speak, and in the process create a working install disc.

It's simple to burn an ISO to disc using the Xandros File Manager.

1. Double-click the ISO on your hard disk, which you will be able to recognize by its .iso extension. A Create Disc window (like that in Figure 6-7) will appear. After that, the process is exactly the same as for burning other CDs.

2. Click **OK** in the Create Disc window. Two windows will now appear. Place a blank CD in your drive, and then, after the indicator on your drive stops flashing, click **OK** in the second window.

After that, the burning process will begin, with its progress shown in the remaining window. Once the process is complete, your newly burned disc will be ejected from the drive automatically.

USB Storage Devices

Universal Serial Bus (or *USB*) devices, recognizable by their narrow rectangular connector plugs (Figure 6-11), can be plugged and unplugged while your computer is running (called *hot plugging*). These devices include not only the USB printers, scanners, and digital cameras with which you are probably already familiar but also a number of USB storage devices that you can use to back up or transport your data.

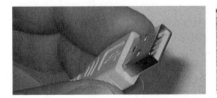 

Figure 6-11: A USB connector plug and USB ports

These USB storage devices include external hard disks, flash memory card readers, and the tiny, finger-sized devices known as flash drives (Figure 6-12). These simple flash drives are quite popular today, and deservedly so, because they are quite inexpensive; extremely handy when you need to transfer fairly large, but not gigantic, amounts of data from computer to computer (from work to home, for example); and pretty safe in terms of Linux compatibility.

Accessing Your USB Storage Devices

To work with your USB storage device, plug it into one of the USB ports on your computer. The XFM window should appear, displaying the contents of that device. An icon for the device, *Removable Disk*, will also appear in the left pane of the window (Figure 6-13). If you see only a single folder with a name like *partition1*, or something to that effect, just double-click that to access your files.

Once you finish with your device, unplug it by clicking the **Removable Disk** icon in the file tree in the left pane and then the words **Eject disc** in the right pane. The contents of the right pane will change, and the light on your device will do a bit of rapid flashing. Once the flashing stops, it's safe to physically unplug the device from your machine.

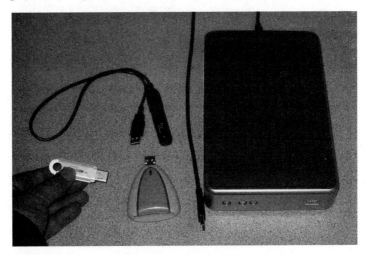

Figure 6-12: USB storage devices

NOTE   *Removing your device before the LED stops flashing can result in your losing data if Linux was saving information to it when you unplugged it. If your device doesn't happen to have an indicator light, just wait for a few seconds (slightly longer if you have copied rather large files to it) before unplugging it.*

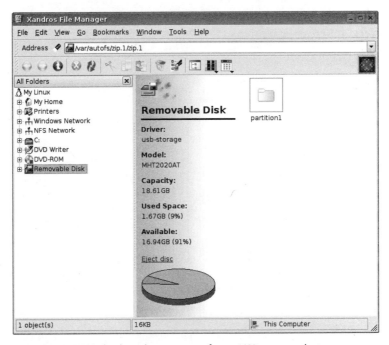

Figure 6-13: XFM displays the contents of your USB storage device

7

CONTROL FREAKS

Getting Things the Way You Want via the Xandros Control Center

The Launch menu and the Xandros File Manager, which were introduced in Chapter 3 and Chapter 5, respectively, are two of the three most important parts of your system. It is now time to meet the third member of what is your system's troika of power: the Xandros Control Center, which you may already have used when you set up your Internet connection in Chapter 4.

You have already worked with several of your system's settings windows in previous chapters, such as when you learned to change your desktop wallpaper. The Control Center provides you with a centralized location from which you can also gain access to such settings windows. You can thus think of the Control Center itself as a kind of settings browser.

While that may rightfully sound quite useful to you, it also probably comes across as rather boring. But the Control Center is much cooler than that, as it also allows you to do things such as add users, install fonts, and even change the look of your application windows and controls.

The capabilities of the Control Center are truly great, but to cover each and every thing it can do would take up a lot of space, be of limited interest to some people, and possibly provide a rather dull read to boot. That being the case, I will instead limit myself to introducing those areas most likely to be of most interest or use to you.

Using the Control Center

To run the Control Center, just go to the **Launch** menu and select **Control Center**. The Control Center window (Figure 7-1) will then appear.

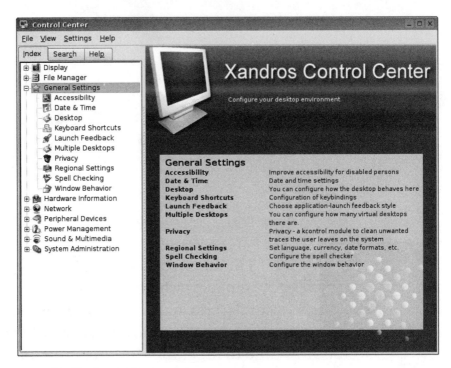

Figure 7-1: The Control Center window

The window is divided into two panes: browsing (on the left) and display (on the right). To use the Control Center, click the + sign next to one of the headings in the left pane; the various subcategories available for that heading will appear directly underneath the heading.

When you then click any of the subcategories, the information or settings options will then appear in the right pane. You can go ahead and have a look through things right now, if you like. You'll be able to get some hands-on experience using some of them in the following projects and sections.

When you installed Xandros, you set up a user account for yourself. However, as mentioned in Chapter 2, you can also add additional user accounts to your system. Doing this allows each user to log in to his or her own account where their files are kept separate from everyone else's. This is where they can change any settings and customize things whatever way they want without affecting anyone else.

If you, for example, want to have a picture of the Green Bay Packers as your desktop wallpaper, and your daughter wants one of the Smashing Pumpkins, there's no problem—you will both have your own desktop environment to work in that can be made as gaudy, simple, or macho as you like. It's almost as if each user has his or her own computer.

7A-1: Creating Additional User Accounts

Even if you are the only person using your computer, you might want to go ahead and follow along with this project so that you will get the hang of how things work. Creating a new account also allows you to follow along with the customizations you will be performing in Projects 7B through 7D without affecting your own user environment—just in case things get a bit too gaudy for your personal tastes.

To add a new user to your system, here's what you need to do:

1. Click **System Administration** in the left pane of the Control Center window, and then in the subcategories that appear directly beneath that heading, click **User Manager**.

   When the User Manager options appear in the right pane of the Control Center window (Figure 7-2), you will notice that almost everything is grayed out, and that there is a red line surrounding the message at the top of the pane telling you that changes to the User Manager module can be performed only by the system administrator—in other words, the person who knows the root password you created during the installation of your system.

2. Assuming you are the possessor of the root password, click the **Administrator** button at the bottom of the window, type the root password when prompted to do so, and then click **OK**.

   The entire right pane will now be surrounded by a red line. This means that you are now in administrator (root) mode—at least in the Control Center.

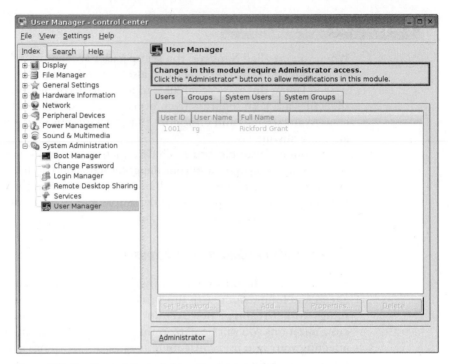

Figure 7-2: The Control Center's User Manager module

3. Now, click the **Add** button at the bottom of the pane, which will bring up the Add User Wizard (Figure 7-3).

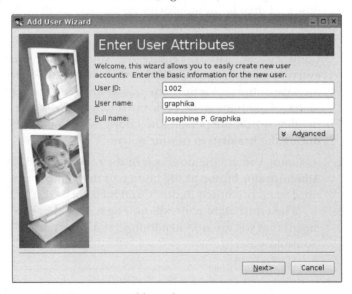

Figure 7-3: Creating an additional user account

4. In the first page of the wizard, type in the username and full name of the user you will be adding. I'm calling the account (User Name) *graphika*

because I'm a graphics lover, and I'm using *Josephine P. Graphika* as the full name, though I could just as well use *A Graphics Lover* in its stead. I'll be referring to this account by name later. Once you have finished typing, click **Next**.

5. In the next page, type and confirm (by retyping) the user password for your new user. If you would like your new user to change passwords after logging in for the first time, so that he or she can pick a new password, check the box next to the words *Force user to change password on first login*. Once you have finished, click **Next**.

6. The next page of the wizard allows you to give your new user access to various system functions. Most of the standard items (dialout, video, audio, and so on) are already set, so you can just click **Next**.

7. If you are using the Xandros Deluxe or Surfside Editions, there will be another page at this point where you can encrypt the new user's Home folder so that the files in that folder will only be visible when that user is logged in. If you want to do this, select **Encrypt user's home folder**, allocate the size of the home directory for that user, and then click **Next**.

8. In the last page of the wizard, just click **Finish**.

After a few seconds, the wizard will close, and the new username will appear beneath your own in the user list in the right pane of the Control Center window (Figure 7-4).

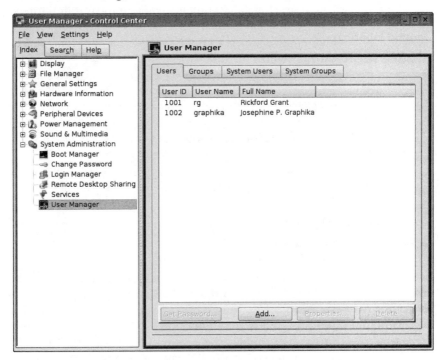

Figure 7-4: A new user listed in the User Manager module

7A-2: Switching Between User Accounts

Now that you have added your new user, it might be good idea to give that new account a spin in order to see how things work. Basically, the process differs only slightly from what you use when shutting down your system. Start off by quitting any open applications you are running (including the Control Center), and then follow these steps:

1. Go the **Launch** menu, and select **Logout**.
2. In the window that appears, click the **Logout** button.
3. When the Login screen appears, click the down arrow at the right side of the box containing your username (next to the words *User name*), and then select your new user account in the drop-down menu.
4. Type the user password for the new account, and then click **OK**.

After a few seconds, you will have arrived at your new user's desktop, and, just like the first time you arrived at your own, the First Run Wizard will appear. You can go through the steps of the wizard now, if you like, or you can do it later by clicking **Cancel** for now. Once the wizard is gone, you will notice that your new user account looks almost exactly like your own, assuming you haven't performed any dramatic changes since installing the system.

If you look a little more carefully, however, you will also notice that the various launchers and applets we added to your desktop in Chapter 3 are not present in the panel of your new account. If you double-click the **Home** folder on the desktop, you will also find that the Home folder is empty, except for the desktop icon and My Documents folder. No need to panic, though, because this is the way things are supposed to be. Remember that I said that *changes made in one user account do not affect those in another*, so you are now face-to-face with the proof of that assertion.

Anyway, as we are soon to embark on a journey into the world of cosmetic customization, you can just stay in your account as you follow along with the next projects. If you would prefer to perform those customizations on your own account environment, go ahead and log out of the new account and back in to your regular one. The choice is yours.

Project 7B: Installing Fonts

Ever since the debut of the first Macintosh way back in 1984, computer users have been obsessed with fonts. That was certainly the case for me the first time I laid hands on a Mac at the UCLA bookstore. Of course, once other operating systems went graphical, font fun was available to all, and so it was with Linux as it began to develop. In the past, however, installing fonts in a Linux system could prove a rather challenging endeavor. This is fortunately no longer the case, and the Xandros Control Center makes even easier work of things.

7B-1: Downloading New Fonts

Before you can install any new fonts, you first have to get some. The Internet is an excellent source of these, with numerous freeware, shareware, and for-sale fonts being available. Remember one thing: you want to use Windows fonts, not those for the Mac. A favorite font-supply source of mine is www.fontfreak.com, which I'll be using as the source of the fonts in this project. The Font Foundry (www.fontfoundry.com) and Font Paradise (www.fontparadise.com) are also excellent sources that you might want to check out.

Get started by going to the FontFreak site and clicking the **ENTER** link on that page. On the next page on that site, there is a message notifying you of the fact that you can purchase all of the 4,700 files it has available.

If you're really into fonts, you might consider doing that later, but for now, just click the **No Thanks** link. Finally, once on the main FontFreak page, click the **PC Fonts** link in the small menu on the left side of the page. Oh, and if you end up on a completely different website, you have clicked the wrong PC Fonts link, so don't be surprised if it happens to you. If you want to follow along with me, and keep things simple, just download the fonts Action Jackson, Airmole, and Airstream from the first page; otherwise, just browse around until you find three fonts that you like. Try to find some that are somewhat gaudy, or at least ornate, so that they will be clearly distinguishable from the ones that come with your system. Once you have downloaded three fonts, close your web browser.

7B-2: Preparing Your New Fonts for Installation

The fonts that you download from FontFreak will come as compressed ZIP archives, so before you can install them, you will have to extract them, as you learned to do in Chapter 5. To make things easier, first create a new folder called My Fonts, and then place the various fonts into that folder once you have extracted them.

7B-3: Installing Your New Fonts

Once your fonts are downloaded and unzipped, you can install them by following these steps:

1. Open the Control Center.

2. In the left pane of the Control Center window, click **Display**.

3. In the list of subcategories that then appears, click **Font Installer**; the Font Installer module will appear in the right pane of the window (Figure 7-5).

    As you will immediately notice, the list of fonts in the module window will be empty, which may come as a surprise given the fact that your system comes bundled with a good number of fonts of its own. The reason for this is that the Font Installer is displaying only the fonts installed exclusively in your user account. Fonts installed in this way will be available for use only in the account in which they were installed. Thus, the fonts you install while in your *graphika* account will not be usable in your regular user account and vice versa.

This might sound like a somewhat odd arrangement, but imagine what would happen if your son, for example, developed a real thing for fonts and installed over a hundred of them. If he were able to install those fonts system-wide, rather than strictly for use in his own account, you would end up having to scroll through your font menu forever when trying to switch fonts while writing a document in OpenOffice.org Write, for example. It really is all for the best, as you will hopefully never have to find out.

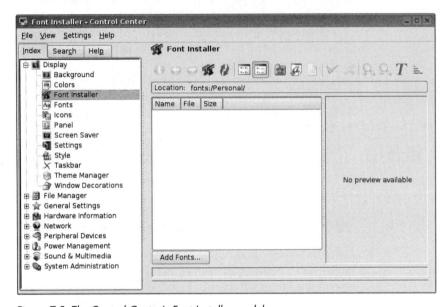

Figure 7-5: The Control Center's Font Installer module

4. Continue the installation process by clicking the **Add** button; the Add Fonts window will appear.

5. Double-click the **My Fonts** folder icon in that window, and while holding down the CTRL key, click each font file in the window.

6. Once you have selected the fonts, release the CTRL key, and click **Open**.

7. A small window will then appear telling you that any running applications will have to be restarted before the font changes will take effect in those programs. Remember what it says (I'll remind you later, in case you forget), and click **OK** to close that window.

You have now successfully installed your fonts, which will appear in the previously empty list in the Font Installer module window. If you now click one those fonts in the list, a preview of that font will then appear in the right pane of the module (Figure 7-6).

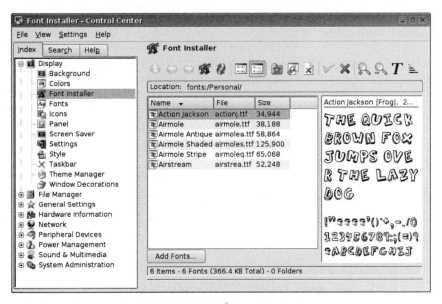

Figure 7-6: Previewing fonts in the Font Installer module

Remember that if you had any applications open when you installed the fonts, you will first have to restart those applications before you can use your new fonts in them. If you have experience using OpenOffice.org in earlier versions of Xandros or other Linux distros, you will also be happy to know that your new fonts will also be immediately available for use in that application as well, which is quite a change from how things used to be even in the recent past.

Windows Fonts for Dual-Booters

If you created a dual-boot setup when installing Xandros, you will be pleased to know that all of your Windows fonts will also be available for use in Xandros, because they are automatically recognized by the system. No special steps are required.

Project 7C: Having Some Fun with Your System's Font Settings

Now that you have some new fonts to play around with, let's move on to gaudying up your system a bit by changing some of the system's font settings. If you are a little worried about creating an aesthetically dreadful mess of your system in the process, don't be—just a few mouse clicks will bring everything back the way it was before we got started. Let's move on and have some fun!

7C-1: Changing Your System's Fonts

In the previous project, I mentioned that the fonts you installed via the Control Center will be immediately available for use once you restart any applications that were open when you installed the new fonts. The only exception to this rule, however, is the Control Center itself. In order to use the fonts you just installed from within the Control Center, you will first need to restart the whole system. So, that said, go ahead and restart your system now, and be sure to log in to the same account in which you installed the fonts.

Waiting . . . . . . Hmmmm . . . . . Duh dum duh dooo . . . Should be ready soon . . . . . Bingo!

Assuming your system has now restarted and you have logged back in, let's get started with our font-customization project. Here's what you need to do:

1. Run the Control Center, and then click **Display** in the left pane of the window once it appears.

2. Now click **Fonts** in the list of subcategories that appears.

    In the right pane, you will see a list of the fonts currently in use for the various components of your system (Figure 7-7). For example, the font used for the text below the various icons on your desktop is Bitstream Vera Sans 12, the font used for the titles that appear at the top of your windows is Bitstream Vera Sans 12 Bold, and so on.

    For our immediate purposes, these fonts are all just too staid and stuffy, so let's get a bit wilder. Let's start off by changing the font for the text displayed on the desktop.

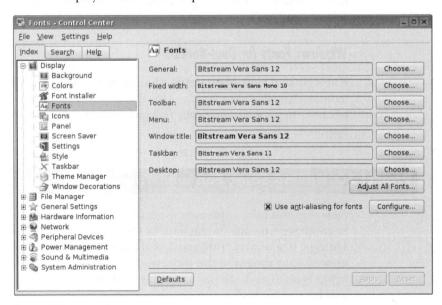

Figure 7-7: System font settings

3. Click the **Choose** button at the far right of the row beginning with the word *desktop* (that would be the bottom row).

4. In the Select Font window that now appears, select **Airmole Stripe** in the Font column and **14** in the Size column by clicking once on each of those items.

5. After making the selections, click the **OK** button to close the Select Font window.

6. The font you chose will now appear next to the word *desktop* in the Control Center window. Assuming it does, click the **Apply** button and you will see the text under the icons on your desktop immediately change to the new font you just selected

NOTE   *Because the new font and font size you selected for your desktop may be somewhat larger than those originally used, the position of the icons on your desktop will probably have changed. To get them all nicely lined up again, right-click anywhere on the desktop and select **Arrange Icons** ▸ **Line Up Vertically** in the pop-up menu.*

Following essentially the same approach as that in steps 3 through 5, select **Action Jackson 24** for Window titles and **Airstream 14** for General.

Once you have made the changes, click **Apply**. Things should now look pretty much similar to what you see in Figure 7-8.

Figure 7-8: Changing system font settings

Well, I didn't say it would be pretty, but at least you know how to do it now. Anyway, to get things back to the way they were, assuming you want them the way they were, just click the **Defaults** button in the Fonts module of the Control Center window (Figure 7-7), click **Apply**, and there you have it: instant *déjà vu*.

You've just seen how you can have a bit of fun with your system by changing the fonts it uses for everyday system-related display tasks. Of course, when it comes to fonts, the choices you make are not just based on your individual sense of aesthetics; you also have to consider readability. Some fonts look really cool, to be sure, but if you can't read anything when you use those fonts, there isn't much point bothering. When it comes to customizing the components that give your system its distinctive look, however, you can really let loose and get wild.

While it is possible to customize the looks of both Windows and Macintosh OS X, in my opinion the options available to you there are actually quite limited. In Xandros, and most other Linux distros, however, you can happily and freely go absolutely berserk. In Xandros, not only can you change the colors of the various components of your system, but you can also even change the window decorations and control themes to such an extent that you practically won't be able to recognize your system by the time you've finished.

7D-1: Changing Window Borders

The most immediately gratifying graphical customization you can make is to the window borders that surround the various system and application windows you use every day. It is also one of the easiest things you can do. Just follow along with these steps:

1. Click **Display** in the left pane of the Control Center window.

2. In the list of subcategories that appears, click **Window Decorations**.

    As you can see in Figure 7-9, the module display consists of a sample of the window decoration currently selected (Plastik is the default), and directly above that, a drop-down menu button that you can use to browse and select from among the various window decorations available.

3. Click that drop-down menu button and select **Keramik**, which, although not one of my personal favorites, is pretty popular in the Linux world in general and (if nothing else other than that) strikingly different.

    Once you've made the selection, a sample of the Keramik window decoration will appear in the right pane of the Control Center window along with the various options available for that decoration below it. If you then click the **Apply** button, the border of the Control Center itself will be . . . well, Keramikized (Figure 7-10).

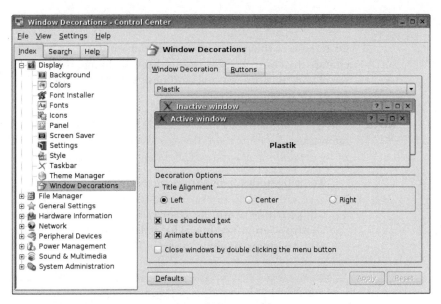

Figure 7-9: Changing window borders via the Control Center

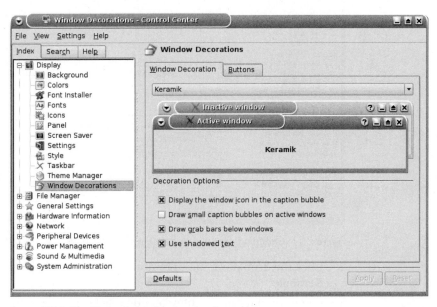

Figure 7-10: The Keramik window-border decoration

7D-2: Changing Control Styles

Okay, so now that you've changed your window borders, the next step is to change the control styles. Doing this will change the looks of the various scroll bars, buttons, menus, and bevels that make up the bulk of an application or system window.

NOTE *Changes to the control-style themes will be fully realized only in KDE-based applications, which fortunately includes your system itself. There will be little or no difference in the appearances of certain applications, such as OpenOffice.org or RealPlayer.*

To bring about the change, here's what you have to do:

1. Click **Style** beneath the Display heading within the left pane of the Control Center window. The Style module will appear in the right pane of the window, as you can see in Figure 7-11.

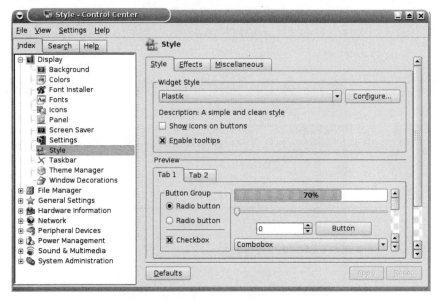

Figure 7-11: Changing control styles via the Control Center

2. Click the drop-down menu button below the words *Widget Style* and select **Keramik**.

3. Once you have made the selection, click **Apply**, and the changes will immediately take effect. The results can be seen in Figure 7-12.

7D-3: Doing a Bit of Coloring

So now that we have some big ol' clunky window borders and rather goopy semi-industrial-looking controls, let's go for a total gaud-out by playing around with the colors of those elements. To get started, click **Colors** beneath the Display heading in the left pane of the Control Center window to bring up the Colors module display in the right pane (Figure 7-12).

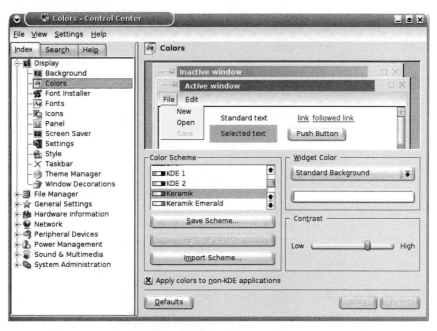

Figure 7-12: Changing the colors of your window borders and controls

As with the module displays for Window Decorations and Styles, the Colors module display includes a previewer, though this time it is at the top of the pane, and a color-scheme selector (to the left just below the previewer). By clicking on the various items within the Color Scheme selector pane, you can see in the previewer the color changes that will take place with the scheme you have just selected. As you will notice, the default this time around is Keramik, which means that we have thus far created an all-Keramik window interface theme. Of course, this is not what we ultimately intend to do, so go ahead and give the other Color Scheme choices a look-through before we move on. Be sure to try out Blue Slate and Solaris, because they are rather striking. Anyway, click **Apply** for at least a couple of these schemes so you can see what things really look like.

Creating an Original Color Scheme

Assuming you have now played around a bit, let's get back to where we were. If you have changed to one of the other color schemes, as I suggested you do, go ahead and change things back to Keramik by clicking the **Defaults** and then **Apply** buttons.

Once everything is back to relative normal, here's what you need to do:

1. In the previewer at the top of the right pane, click the blue area just to the right of, but not directly on, the words *Active Window*.

2. The drop-down menu button in the Widget Color section at the right side of the pane should then say *Active Title Bar*. If it does, click the color button directly below that menu button (Figure 7-13).

Figure 7-13: The color-selector button

3. In the rainbow-colored box of the Select Color window that then appears (labeled *1* in Figure 7-14), click at the very top-left corner of the box in the red area.

4. The small box to the left of the words *Name* and *HTML* (labeled *2* in Figure 7-14), which shows you the color currently selected, should now have changed from blue to red. If it did, click **OK**; the Select Color window will close.

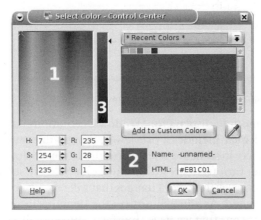

Figure 7-14: The parts of the Select Color window

5. Back in the Control Center window, the left half of the Active window bar in the previewer should now be red. Assuming it is, click the remaining blue area at the right end of the bar.

6. The drop-down menu button in the Widget Color section of the right pane will say Active Title Blend. Go ahead now and click the color bar directly below that button to bring back up the Select Color window.

7. In that window, click the bottom, or black, end of the vertical color bar to the right of the rainbow-colored box (labeled *3* in Figure 7-14).

8. The box showing the currently selected color (labeled *2* in Figure 7-14) will now change from blue to black. Once it has, click **OK**.

9. To round up our color-scheme process, click the colored area surrounding the words *Selected Text* in the previewer; the Widget Color drop-down menu button will then read *Selected Background*.

10. Finally, click the color button directly below, as you did in the last two steps, but this time around, select any color you like in the Select Color window, though preferably something on the light side. Once you have made your selection, click **OK**.

11. To witness the majesty, or lack thereof, of your new creation, click the **Apply** button, after which the changes will immediately take place. Your results should look something like mine in Figure 7-15, but don't be cross if you don't like what you see—this is, after all, just a learning exercise.

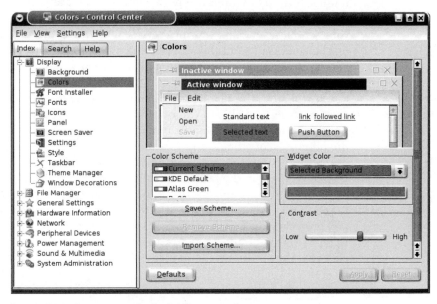

Figure 7-15: Customizing the look of your windows

Even though you most likely are not very pleased with your creation, you can save and name it (or a better one you create in the future) by clicking the **Save Scheme** button. Assuming that you don't want to do this at the present time, however, just go ahead and click the **Defaults** and **Apply** buttons to get things back to the original less nerve-wracking visual state.

7D-4: Cleaning Up

Now that we've finished our haphazard customization process, you most likely want to get things back to normal, which we've already done in regard to our rather disastrous color scheme.

To get the window borders back to normal, here's what you need to do:

1. Click **Window Decorations** under the Display heading in the left pane of the Control Center.

2. In the right pane, select **Plastik** in the drop-down button menu.

3. Finally, click **Apply**.

4. To get the control styles back to what they used to be, simply do this:

   a. Click **Style** in the left pane of the Control Center window.

   b. Select **Plastik** in the drop-down button menu in the right pane of the window.

   c. Click **Apply**.

Screen Savers

You may already have noticed that when you leave your computer running unused and untouched for five minutes or so, the screen will go black, though it will return to life when you move your mouse or tap on your keyboard. This is not some glitch in your system causing your machine to act up—it is your screen saver snapping into service. Of course, usually when you think of a screen saver, you think of pretty pictures or geometric patterns dancing about your screen, so the idea of a blank-screen screen saver might come across as quite the dud.

Fortunately, this blank-screen screen saver is just one of the many screen saver modules available to you on your system. There are actually close to a hundred different screen saver modules for you to choose from, including the perennial favorite, Flying Toasters.

To access and select these modules, click **Screen Saver** beneath the Display heading in the left pane of the Control Center window.

You will now be able to try out the various screen saver modules available to you in the right pane of the window (Figure 7-16) by selecting the module and then clicking **Test**. A sample will then appear in the small monitor at the right side of the window. When you find a module you would like to use, just click the **Apply** button.

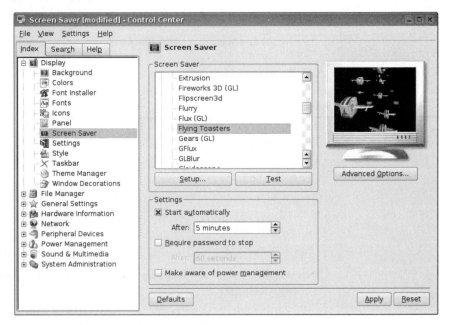

Figure 7-16: Selecting screen saver modules

You can also decide when you want your screen saver to kick in by adjusting the Start Automatically settings, the default setting for which is five minutes of nonuse. Many screen saver modules also allow you to configure them individually, but the nature of the configuration options depends on the module in question. For example, in the case of Flying Toasters, you can choose the animation speed, the number of toasters, the number of slices of flying toast, and even the look of the toasters themselves.

To make changes of this sort, select the module in question, and then click **Setup**. A configuration window (Figure 7-17) will then appear. Once you have set things up the way you like, click the **OK** button in that window and then the **Apply** button in the Control Center window.

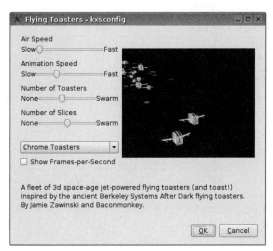

Figure 7-17: Configuring a screen saver module

Enabling Auto-Login

I mentioned earlier in the book that it is possible to set up your system so that you won't have to type your user password when you log in each and every time you start your machine. If you are the only one using your machine, and are in an environment where no one else has access to your machine, this might not be a bad idea.

If you want to set things up this way, here's all you need to do:

1. Click **System Administration** in the left pane of the Control Center window.

2. In the subcategories that appear below System Administration, click **Login Manager**.

3. When the Login Manager module appears in the right pane of the window, click the **Administrator** button at the bottom of the window, type your root password when prompted to do so, and then click **OK** in that password window.

4. Once in root mode, click the **Convenience** tab in the right pane of the Control Center window.

5. In that page, check **Enable auto-login**. Your window should then look something like mine in Figure 7-18.

6. If everything in your window looks hunky-dory, click **Apply**, and the deal will then be sealed. Good-bye, login password!

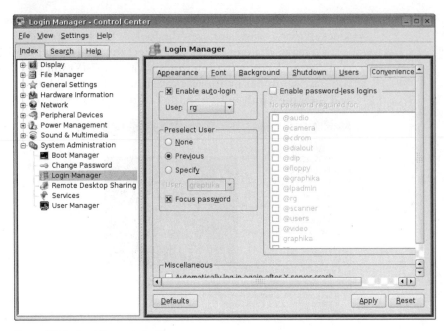

Figure 7-18: Enabling auto-login

Configuring User Accounts

In Project 7A, you learned how to set up additional user accounts, a pretty easy endeavor, all things told. There are, however, a few settings you can apply to those user accounts that might be of interest of you. In order to access these features, you must first open the User Accounts module by clicking **System Administration** in the left pane of the Control Center window, and then clicking **User Manager**. When the User Manager module appears in the right pane of the window, click the **Administrator** button at the bottom of the window, and then supply your root password when prompted to do so. You will then be ready to perform either of the settings changes I will now describe.

Limiting Login Availability

One of these settings that you might find handy is limiting the time and/or days that a user can log in to the system. For example, let's say that you don't want your kids playing around with the computer when you are at work or when they should be doing their homework . . . or playing outside to get some exercise.

To set things up in this way, just follow these steps:

1. Select the username of the user for whom you wish to limit access in the User Manager module (by clicking on that user's name once), and then click **Properties**.

2. In the User Properties window that appears, click the **Account** tab.

3. Once in that tab, click the checkbox next to the words *Only allow user to login between.*

4. Now set the times and days that you want the user in question to have access to your computer. When done, your window should look something like that in Figure 7-19.

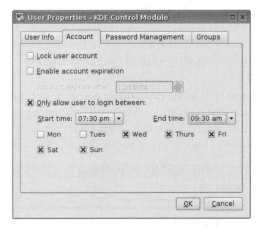

Figure 7-19: Changing user-access privileges

5. Once you have finished, click **OK** to close that window, and then click **Apply** in the Control Center window.

Locking an Account

You can also just lock an account, thus prohibiting a given user from accessing your computer until you wish to allow them to use it again. For example, you might want to make sure that your daughter finishes that essay that is due next week, and so until she does you don't want her to be playing around on the Internet. You can block her account from the same Account tab mentioned in the previous section. Click her username before opening the User Properties window, and then click the checkbox next to the words *Lock User Account.* Of course, when you are ready to provide access again, just uncheck the box, and all will be back to normal.

Dual-Booters: Changing the Default Operating System on Boot-Up

If you have a Xandros/Windows dual-boot setup, you no doubt already know that when you start up your machine, you are given the choice of which operating system to boot up. The default system in such a setup is Xandros, which means that if you make no choice at the time, your machine will automatically boot up into Xandros, but you will have to use your cursor and ENTER keys to select Windows.

If you would prefer to have Windows as the default boot-up system, you can do so in the Control Center window by following these steps:

1. Click **System Administration** in the left pane of the Control Center window.

2. In the subcategories that appear below System Administration, select **Boot Manager**.

3. When the Boot Manager module appears in the right pane of the window, click the **Administrator** button at the bottom of the window, type your root password when prompted to do so, and then click **OK** in that password window.

4. Once in root mode, click the drop-down menu button next to the words *Default operating system* (the button itself will be showing the version of Xandros you are using, such as *Xandros Desktop 3.0.1 OC*), and then select the version of Windows you are using in the drop-down menu (Figure 7-20).

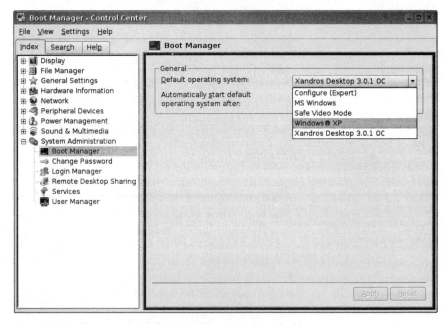

Figure 7-20: Changing the default operating system in dual-boot setups

5. If you would also like to decrease the default auto boot-up time (the time before the system automatically boots up when you do nothing—the default is 30 seconds), adjust the numbers in the box to the right of the words *Automatically start default operating system after*.

6. Once you have finished making the changes, click the **Apply** button, and then quit the Control Center.

The next time you start up your machine, you will, as usual, see the boot-up screen; however, if you do not manually select Xandros at that time, your machine will automatically boot up into Windows.

8

THE KEYS TO THE GATES OF OZ, OR THE GATES OF XANDROS ANYWAY

Expanding and Updating Your System via Xandros Networks

I mentioned in Chapter 1 that the first time I ever heard of Xandros was from a friend who described the system as "cool." Well, when I first gave Xandros a try, I thought it was really good and, more importantly, incredibly easy to use—easier, in fact, than Windows. The word "cool," however, didn't immediately pop into my mind. That is, until I first used Xandros Networks.

What is Xandros Networks? Well, it is sort of a combination of things—a simple-to-use application (Figure 8-1) and a set of online repositories that houses an amazing array of applications and related files. The Xandros Networks (XN) application acts as an interface via which you can access those repositories and then easily download and install whatever you find of interest there. Now, I admit that what I've just described, on its own, might not initially sound all that impressive, but if you have a better understanding of what it is normally like to install an application in Linux, however, you will see why Xandros Networks is nothing short of a godsend.

Figure 8-1: The Xandros Networks application

When you install an application in Linux, that application usually requires that you also install one or more other files that it needs in order to function. These files are called *dependencies*, and some dependencies have dependencies of their own. And, need I say that some of those dependencies have dependencies of their own. Chasing down, installing, and getting all those different parts to work correctly on your own can be a time-consuming and sometimes frustrating experience. This recurring dependency chase is often referred to as *dependency hell*, and rightfully so.

This is where the "cool" comes into play. When you use Xandros Networks to download and install an application, XN also automatically downloads and installs all of the dependencies required in order for the application to run. So you don't have to do any chasing down of this or that file, and you can be pretty sure that whatever you download will, in fact, run—and run as it is supposed to.

Impressed yet?

If you still aren't convinced, think about this: almost 98 percent of the applications available via Xandros Networks are free. Sure, you don't get the pretty boxes and shiny shrink-wrap that you do when you buy a Windows application at the local computer store, but, hey . . . I said *free!* How can you not love that, eh?

And what about that other 2 percent that aren't free, you ask? Well, most of those apps are commercial offerings that you would have to pay for anyway, but when they're downloaded and installed via Xandros Networks, you can be sure that they will work on your system. These include applications such as CrossOver Office, which allows you to run certain Windows applications (such as MS Office) on your Xandros system, or popular games such as Quake III and Return to Castle Wolfenstein.

Xandros Networks First Time Out

Well, let's stop babbling about what Xandros Networks is and instead put it into action. To run XN, just double-click the **Xandros Networks** icon on the desktop, or go to the **Launch** menu and select **Xandros Networks**. (Xandros Networks is an Internet application, so you will have to be connected to the Internet when doing this.) After a few seconds, the Xandros Networks application will appear, and the first time out, it will go through a series of steps that are mostly hands-off for you.

The first thing Xandros has to do, and it will do this every time you start it up, is take inventory of what is already in your system, thus providing it with a database that it can check in the future when you download applications. This allows Xandros Networks to know just what it needs (and doesn't need!) to download in order to make your application work. During this time, you will see a Progress Update window (Figure 8-2), which will automatically disappear when the process is finished.

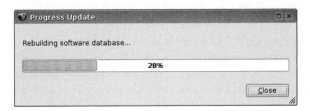

Figure 8-2: Xandros Networks indicates its progress as it takes inventory of your system

In the next phase, Xandros Networks has to check out its online repositories in order to see what is available for you there.

In the small window that appears (Figure 8-3) asking for your permission to do so, click **OK**, and the process will be strictly hands-off from there on in.

Figure 8-3: Xandros Networks asks your permission to do an online search of available packages

Oh, and in case you're worried about mysterious things being downloaded to your hard disk, don't be. XN will be downloading only lists and descriptions of what is available on its repositories, not the applications or files themselves.

Xandros Networks will show you what it's doing in the Progress Update window, which will look like the window shown in Figure 8-4 during the package-list download phase.

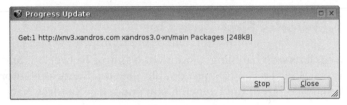

Figure 8-4: Xandros Networks lets you know what it's up to while it downloads package lists from its online repositories

When the package lists are downloaded, you will once again see the mercurial slide of the progress bar in the same window (see Figure 8-2) while Xandros Networks rebuilds its package database. When the process is complete, the Progress Update window will disappear, and the various blank parts of the Xandros Networks window will fill in, finally looking like what you saw in Figure 8-1.

Project 8A: Taking Xandros Networks Out for a Spin

Now that Xandros Networks is up and ready to go, let's take it out for a spin so that you can get a feel for how it works. In this project, we will do this by using it to download and install a simple-but-fun strategy game called Lines (also known as Klines) in which you try to remove the marbles that appear by lining them up in groups of five, as shown in Figure 8-5.

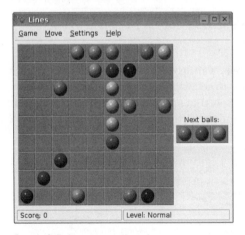

Figure 8-5: Lines

Here are the steps for downloading the game; it's a good example of how to download any application in XN:

1. Click the + symbol next to New Applications in the left pane of the XN window.

2. When the list of subcategories appears under New Applications, click the + symbol next to Games.

3. When the list of subcategories appears under Games, click **Strategy**.

4. A list of the various strategy games available via Xandros Networks will then appear in the top half of the right pane of the XN window. Click **Lines**.

5. A description of Lines will now appear in the bottom half of the right pane (Figure 8-6). Click **Install Lines**.

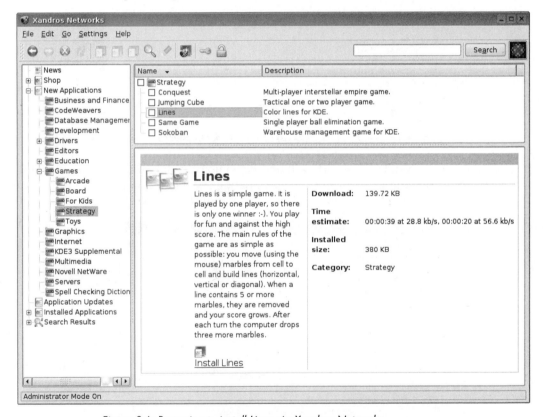

Figure 8-6: Preparing to install Lines via Xandros Networks

A new window, Install Software (Figure 8-7), will now appear, showing you what you are about to install, how big the download will be, and how much hard disk space will be used once the installation is complete.

6. Click **OK**.

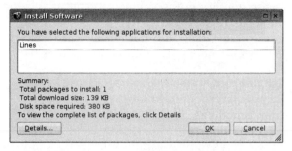

Figure 8-7: Xandros Networks tells you what you are about to install

7. You will now be asked to provide your Administrator's (root) password in another window (Figure 8-8). Type your root password, not your user password, and click **OK**.

Figure 8-8: Xandros Networks asks for your root password

Xandros Networks will now begin downloading the necessary files and will indicate its progress in an Updating System window (Figure 8-9). You can just sit tight for now, because there is nothing for you to do.

Figure 8-9: Xandros Networks shows the progress of the download process

Once the download is complete, XN will begin installing the application and required dependencies. When it has finished, the word *Done* will appear in the Updating System window (Figure 8-10), and you can click the **Close** button, thus ending the process.

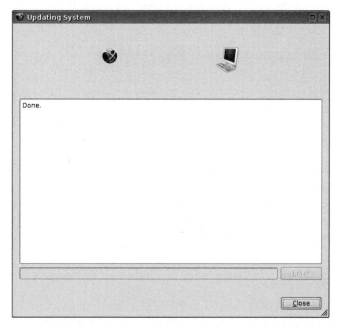

Figure 8-10: Xandros Networks tells you when it has completed the installation process

Now that the download and installation are complete, you can run Lines by going to the **Launch** menu and selecting **Applications ▶ Games ▶ Strategy ▶ Lines**. If you've finished with your downloading for now, you can also go ahead and quit the Xandros Networks application.

Installing More Than a Single Application in One Shot

Now you know how to install an application via Xandros Networks, but what if you want to install more than one application at the same time? Well, if you click one of the categories in the left pane of the XN window while browsing through the available applications, a small box will appear next to each application in the list within the upper half of the top pane, as shown in Figure 8-11.

Figure 8-11: Installing multiple applications simultaneously in Xandros Networks

If you check that box (by clicking in it), you can then browse for other applications to install. When you find another one, click the checkbox for that one too, and then repeat the process for each additional application you would like to install. Finally, when you have finished checking boxes, click the **Install Selected Applications** button (Figure 8-12) just below the **Settings** menu or select the same item from the **File** menu itself.

Figure 8-12: The Install Selected Applications button in Xandros Networks

After you click the Install Selected Applications button, the installation process will be essentially the same as the process you just performed in Project 8A. The only difference will be that the window that shows you what you are about to download and install (like that in Figure 8-7) will now show all of the applications you are about to install, rather than just one.

Uninstalling Applications via Xandros Networks

Xandros Networks not only allows you to install files and applications, but also allows you to remove them. For example, let's say that you just installed Lines in the previous project, but don't really think you'll ever be using it. Well, no sweat, because you can remove it as easily as you installed it in the first place. Here's how you go about it:

1. In the text box next to the Search button, type the name of the application you want to remove. If you want to remove Lines, for example, you would type **lines**.

2. Once you have typed the name of the application you want to remove, click **Search**. A list of packages matching, to some degree, the item you have entered will then appear in the top part of the right pane of the Xandros Networks window (Figure 8-13).

3. Locate the item you want to remove, and then click **Remove**.

After that, it is all pretty much the same process that you followed when installing the application, so I won't go through the steps again here. When the process is done, however, you can go back to the **Launch** menu to look for the application. Unless you did something terribly odd, the application will be gone.

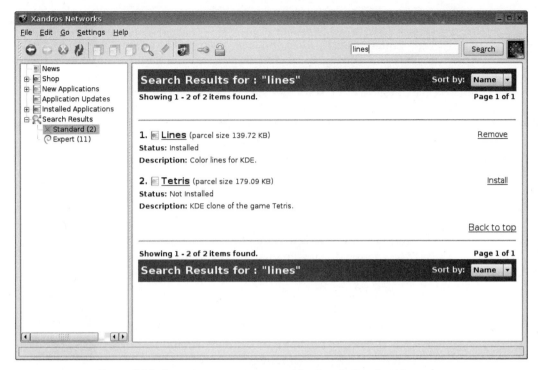

Figure 8-13: Preparing to remove an application via Xandros Networks

Project 8B: Browsing and Installing Applications via Expert View

If you actually did try to remove Lines in the previous section, you may have noticed that in the Search Results section at the bottom of the left pane in the XN window, there were two sets of results: Standard and Expert (Figure 8-14).

Figure 8-14: Xandros Networks search results divided by Standard and Expert Views

By enabling Expert View, you will be able to access yet another bundle of applications available to you via Xandros Networks, some of which can be rather interesting. In addition, once you've worked your way down to the next project, you will discover that Expert View is your key to an absolute gold mine of yet other applications available to you.

In this project, you'll get the chance to work with XN in Expert View by installing an utterly useless, but nevertheless amusing, little application called *kodo*, which is an odometer for your mouse. C'mon, haven't you ever wondered how many miles of desktop travel you've covered? Anyway, here are the steps:

1. Enable Expert View by going to the **Settings** menu and selecting **Expert View**.

2. After a few seconds, a string of new categories will appear under the New Applications heading. If that heading happens to be closed, meaning you can see the heading but not the item categories beneath it, first click the + symbol to the left of that heading. Once the categories are visible, click **Games**.

3. In the top half of the right pane in the XN window, scroll down until you find kodo. When you do, click it, and a description will appear below.

4. Scroll down to the bottom of the explanation at the bottom of the right pane and click **Install Kodo**.

Once you have completed these steps, the rest of the process is the same as the process you performed in Project 8A, so if you've forgotten, you can have a look back at the instructions in that section. After kodo is installed, you can give it a whirl, quite literally, by going to the **Launch** menu and selecting **Applications ▶ Games ▶ Toys ▶ Mouse Odometer**.

Soon thereafter, kodo will appear at one of the corners of your desktop (Figure 8-15). If and when you want to quit kodo, just click it, with either mouse button, and select **Quit** from the pop-up menu.

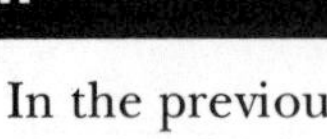

Figure 8-15: A desktop mouse odometer—kodo

Project 8C: Accessing Even More Applications and Having a Bit of Fun

In the previous project, I let you in on an often-overlooked little secret— Xandros Networks not only allows you to install the applications that appeared in the various categories listed in the left pane of its window (both in Standard and Expert Views), but it also gives you access to a whole slew of other applications—applications not directly supported or guaranteed by Xandros, but applications that should work fine on your system. These are the applications from what Xandros refers to as the *Debian Unsupported Site*. It is this cornucopia of easily accessible applications, and the ease with which you can find and install them, that makes the cool side of XN get downright groovy, to resurrect a term I was loathe to use in its day. Ah, but I was so much older then. . . .

8C-1: Enabling the Debian Unsupported Site Repository

To get started, you must first enable the Debian Unsupported Site repository, which you can do by following these two simple steps:

1. Go to the **Edit** menu and select **Set Application Sources**.
2. When the Set Application Sources window appears, check **Debian Unsupported Site**, and then click **OK**.

The Xandros Networks application will then have to access the new repository site to see what is there. Because of the great size of that repository, this may take some time. Be a bit patient, because when it's done, you'll be ready for some real exploratory excitement.

8C-2: Browsing Through the New Offerings

Once Xandros Networks has finished its reading of the online repository files, it might be fun to have a look at what is offered. Just click the **New Applications** button in the main Xandros Networks window and have a look around. I am sure you will be overwhelmed at all there is to see.

NOTE   *Expert View must be enabled in order for you to do this.*

8C-3: Giving the Debian Repositories a Try and Having Some Fun with SuperKaramba

Now that you see that you are much more greatly empowered than you were just moments ago, let's give the new repository a try by downloading, installing, and working with a fun application called SuperKaramba, which is, in the words of its creators, "a tool that allows you to easily create interactive eye-candy on your KDE desktop."

Well, we won't be using SuperKaramba to create any eye candy, which is probably a bit beyond the realm of the average user, but we will be using it to display and use eye candy created by others. Called *themes*, some examples can be seen in Figure 8-16.

Phase One: Downloading and Installing SuperKaramba

1. Type **superkaramba** in the text box at the top of the XN window.
2. Click the **Search** button.
3. In the list of results that appears below, click **Install** next to *superkaramba*.
4. After that, just proceed in the manner you learned earlier in this chapter.

Figure 8-16: SuperKaramba themes

Phase Two: Downloading Some Themes

In order to use SuperKaramba, you first need to have some themes. There are hundreds of these available, and most are available from the KDE-Look website. For the purposes of this project, we are going to try out three of the six themes shown in Figure 8-16: "New" TuxBar, Chrome Clock, and Karamtop. The others, in case you would like to try them out on your own, are KWeather-Karamba, Liquid XMMS, and Flat Calendar.

To get the themes, just follow these steps:

1. Open your web browser, and go to www.kde-look.org.

2. Once the KDE-Look page has loaded, scroll down about halfway or so, and then click **Search Content**.

3. In the search page, select **Karamba** from the drop-down menu next to *type*; type the name of the first theme, **tuxbar**, in the second box (Name Contains); and then click **Search**.

4. In the list of results that appears below, click **"New" TuxBar**.

5. When the page for that theme appears, scroll down just a bit, and click the **[download]** link.

6. Once the New TuxBar theme is downloaded, repeat the process for each of the remaining two themes, using *kweather* and *karamtop* as your search items.

Phase Three: Extracting the Theme Tarballs

The themes you've just downloaded are all in the form of compressed tarballs, so before you can use them, you will have to extract each one using the methods you learned in Chapter 5. Once you extract them, it would be a good idea to create a special folder in which to place them and all other themes you download in the future; KarambaThemes would be a fitting name for that folder. After creating the folder, move the folders for the three themes into it.

Phase Four: Running SuperKaramba

Okay, so now that you have all of what you need in place, it is time to give SuperKaramba a try. As is the case with a good many of the applications you install from the Debian Unsupported Site repository, there will be no launcher for SuperKaramba in the Launch menu. This being so, you will have to run it via the Run Command window (**Launch ▸ Run Command**). In that window, type **superkaramba**, and then click **Run**.

Once SuperKaramba's Welcome window appears (Figure 8-17), open one of the themes you've downloaded by doing the following (I'll be starting with karamtop, so it's probably best you do that one first):

1. Click **Open**, which will bring up the Open Themes window.
2. In that window, navigate to and double-click your new **KarambaThemes** folder. You should now be able to see the Karamtop, ChromeClock, and NewTuxBar folders.
3. Double-click the **Karamtop** folder, and then click once on the **karamtop.theme** file therein. Karamtop will appear on your desktop.

In case you're wondering what Karamtop is, it is a system monitor that shows you how much memory each of the active processes at work in your system is using up. Look at it for a while, enjoy its intrinsic beauty, and then once you get bored with it, move on and open Chrome Clock.

You can open Chrome Clock in this way:

1. Right-click the **Karamtop** applet, and in the pop-up menu, select **Open new theme**. The Open Themes window will then open up to the Karamtop folder.
2. Navigate back to the **KarambaThemes** folder and then to the **ChromeClock** folder within it. Once there, double-click that folder.
3. Inside that folder, click **ChromeClock.theme** once, and then click **Open**.

Once you've finished oohing and ahhing over how beautiful time can be, move on to opening the New TuxBar theme. Before doing that, however, it is probably best to move Karamtop and Chrome Clock so that they are away from the bottom of the screen. To do this, right-click each of them, and then select **Toggle locked position** in the pop-up menu.

Figure 8-17: SuperKaramba's Welcome screen

The icon next to *Toggle locked position* will then change from a blue square emblazoned with a white padlock to black crosshairs, examples of which are shown in Figure 8-18. Once the crosshairs icon is visible, you can move each applet by dragging it.

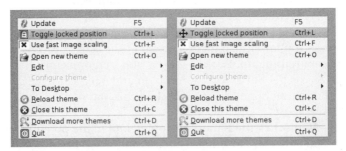

Figure 8-18: Examples of position locked and unlocked icons in a SuperKaramba theme's pop-up menu

Now that Karamtop and Chrome Clock are out of the way, go on and open New TuxBar, which will appear at the very bottom of your screen. Because your usual desktop panel will just be in the way, minimize it for now by clicking the arrow button at the far right side. Once you have done that, open New TuxBar by following these steps:

1. Right-click either **Karamtop** or **Chrome Clock**, and in the pop-up menu, select **Open new theme**.

2. Navigate to the **NewTuxBar** folder and double-click it.

3. Inside that folder, you will find two themes. Click **tuxbar.theme** once, and then click **Open** (the other theme in the folder is automatically opened when you do this). The New TuxBar will then appear at the bottom of your screen as promised.

Phase Five: Configuring New TuxBar

Well, some of you may be using a screen size and resolution different from what New TuxBar is set up for. As a result, you may be able to see only the top half of New TuxBar when it appears. If so, you will have to configure the theme. Configuring SuperKaramba themes is a bit different than what you might be used to, but it is relatively easy. They are all nothing more than text files.

To configure the New TuxBar theme so that you can see all of it (remember, you don't have to do this if you can see it all already), just follow these steps:

1. Right-click anywhere on what you can see of the New TuxBar. Then select **Edit ▸ Edit Theme** in the pop-up menu. The Text Editor will then appear, opened to the TuxBar theme file.

2. In the fifth line of that file, change *H=100* to **H=150**.

3. Now save the file (**File ▸ Save**), but leave Text Editor open for now because you will be using it again in a moment.

4. Now, right-click on the New TuxBar again, but this time select **Reload theme** in the pop-up menu. Within a second or two, you will be able to see all of New TuxBar.

Phase Six: A Bit More Configuring

Now that all of the New TuxBar is visible, you can probably figure out that is supposed to look and behave somewhat like the Dock in Mac OS X, assuming you know how the Dock in Mac OS X is supposed to work. If not, take my word for it. Of course, it isn't quite as versatile as the real Dock, as it really only acts as a set of application launchers. But it does look cool. One problem with New TuxBar, however, is that the programs it is configured to launch are not exactly what you as a Xandros user are most likely to be dealing with. No problem, however, because you can set it up to run whatever applications you want.

To configure New TuxBar so that it will launch Xandros-relevant applications, you will have to go back to the still-open Text Editor window and make some more changes in the file that you edited just a short while ago. The changes will all be to those lines listed together below the line *<GROUP> X=0 Y=0*, as you can see in Figure 8-19.

```
<GROUP> X=0 Y=0
CLICKAREA        X=110     Y=38  W=50 H=90 SENSOR=PROGRAM ONCLICK="konsole"
CLICKAREA        X=174     Y=38  W=50 H=90 SENSOR=PROGRAM ONCLICK="firefox"
CLICKAREA        X=240     Y=38  W=50 H=90 SENSOR=PROGRAM ONCLICK="sylpheed"
CLICKAREA        X=304     Y=38  W=50 H=90 SENSOR=PROGRAM ONCLICK="konqueror"
CLICKAREA        X=368     Y=38  W=50 H=90 SENSOR=PROGRAM ONCLICK="ajunta"
CLICKAREA        X=438     Y=38  W=50 H=90 SENSOR=PROGRAM ONCLICK="gimp"
CLICKAREA        X=502     Y=38  W=50 H=90 SENSOR=PROGRAM ONCLICK="kcontrol"
CLICKAREA        X=565     Y=38  W=50 H=90 SENSOR=PROGRAM ONCLICK="kfind"
</GROUP>
```

Figure 8-19: Launcher commands in the New TuxBar theme file

These lines basically tell TuxBar what applications to launch when a certain region within the bar is clicked. The changes you will make are all to the word that is surrounded by quotation marks at the very end of each line; these are the application commands. Just follow these steps:

1. In the top line, replace *konsole* (the command console) with **oowriter** (OpenOffice.org Writer).

2. If you are using Mozilla instead of Firefox as your web browser, replace *firefox* in the second line with **mozilla**; otherwise, leave this line as is.

3. In the third line, change *sylpheed* to **thunderbird**, or if you're a Standard or Deluxe Edition user, **mozilla -mail** (the second option for Standard and Deluxe Edition users who don't plan on installing Thunderbird).

4. In the fourth line, replace *konqueror* with **XandrosFileManager $HOME**.

5. In line five, change *ajunta* to **kopete**.

NOTE *Leave the command in the sixth line,* gimp, *as is, because you will be installing and using this application later on in the book.*

6. In the next line, replace *kcontrol* with **XandrosNetworks**.

7. Finally, change *kfind* in the last line to **xmms**.

Once you have made the changes, things should look like the lines in Figure 8-20. If they do, save the file (**File ▸ Save**), and then quit Text Editor. If they don't, go back and make the necessary changes before saving the file.

```
<GROUP> X=0 Y=0
CLICKAREA        X=110     Y=38  W=50 H=90 SENSOR=PROGRAM ONCLICK="konsole"
CLICKAREA        X=174     Y=38  W=50 H=90 SENSOR=PROGRAM ONCLICK="firefox"
CLICKAREA        X=240     Y=38  W=50 H=90 SENSOR=PROGRAM ONCLICK="thunderbird"
CLICKAREA        X=304     Y=38  W=50 H=90 SENSOR=PROGRAM ONCLICK="XandrosFileManager $HOME"
CLICKAREA        X=368     Y=38  W=50 H=90 SENSOR=PROGRAM ONCLICK="kopete"
CLICKAREA        X=438     Y=38  W=50 H=90 SENSOR=PROGRAM ONCLICK="gimp"
CLICKAREA        X=502     Y=38  W=50 H=90 SENSOR=PROGRAM ONCLICK="XandrosNetworks"
CLICKAREA        X=565     Y=38  W=50 H=90 SENSOR=PROGRAM ONCLICK="xmms"
</GROUP>
```

Figure 8-20: Changes made to the New TuxBar theme file

Next, click on **New TuxBar** at the bottom of your screen, and select **Reload Theme** to allow your changes to take effect. After that, give it all a try by clicking the various icons with the TuxBar (except for those you haven't installed, of course).

If by any chance, New TuxBar suddenly appears in a new position on your desktop after you reload it, which it might do (and who knows why?), just drag it back to its original position. Unlike the other themes you've worked with thus far, the menu option for toggling the theme's locked position in New TuxBar is inactive, so in order to drag it, you will have to hold down the ALT key while dragging.

Oh, and one more thing . . . when using New TuxBar, you will probably notice that when the icons pop up in their enlarged state, they look rather fuzzy, which allows the icons to pop up more rapidly. Because your hardware may be fast enough to negate the need for that speed enhancement, you may be able to avoid the fuzziness without any problems in terms of pop-up speed. You can quite easily do this by right-clicking the TuxBar and deselecting **Use fast image scaling** in the pop-up menu. If, after doing this, you find the pop-up animation speed to be too slow, go back and select **Use fast image scaling** again.

If you like New TuxBar, but would prefer that it had icons reflective of your needs as a Xandros user, you are in luck.

I have a modified version (shown in Figure 8-21) available free for download via the website for this book (www.edgy-penguins.org/LME). Just click the link for the file on that page.

Figure 8-21: A more Xandros-friendly TuxBar with a definite OS X–ish flair

The file comes in the form of a tarball, which includes not only the theme file itself but also a document explaining how I modified the file, in case you want to play around with things yourself. There is also a link on that page for a KDE theme, Acqua, which, used in conjunction with my modified version of New TuxBar, will give your desktop a very OS X–ish flair, albeit heavily nuanced in the flavor of Linux.

Using Xandros Networks to Install Applications from CD (Deluxe and Business Edition Users Only)

If you happen to have purchased the Xandros Deluxe or Business Editions, a good number of the applications available via the sources we've mentioned thus far are included with your Xandros system on the Application Disc that came along with your system installation disc. To view the contents of this CD and install the applications on it, slip the disc into your drive, and then go to the **Edit** menu in the XN application and select **Set Application Sources**. When the Set Application Sources window appears, check either **CD-ROM drive 1** or **CD-ROM drive 2**, depending on how many drives you have and which one you've placed the CD in, and then uncheck all other items in that window. When done, click **OK**, and you'll be ready to start browsing.

In later releases of the Deluxe and Business Editions, a separate window (Figure 8-22) will automatically appear after you insert the disc labeled Application Disc in your drive. In that window you can check off the applications you wish to install, and then click **Install**. The Xandros Networks application will then start up, prompt you for your root password, and go on to install the items you chose.

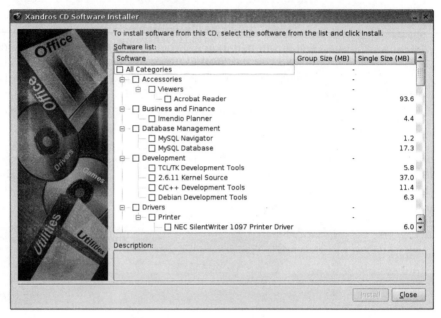

Figure 8-22: Installing applications on the Application Disc in later releases of the Deluxe Edition

Updating Your System and Applications via Xandros Networks

Xandros Networks not only allows you to download and install software, but also allows you to download and install updates when they are available. There are a couple of ways that you can check for updates. The easiest way is to simply look at the Xandros Update applet, right next to the volume controller on your desktop Panel.

If everything is up-to-date, the icon will have a little green arrow on it. If you aren't convinced, or just want to double-check, click the applet, and a Xandros Update Status window (Figure 8-23) will appear. In that window, click the **Check Now** button, and the results will be shown to you.

Another way to go about checking is via the XN application window. In that window, click on **Application Updates** in the left pane. If any updates are available, they will be displayed in the right pane of that window, and they can be installed in the same way as the other applications you've installed so far in this chapter.

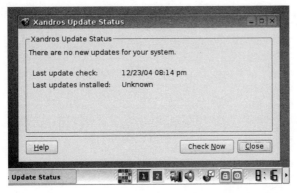

Figure 8-23: Checking for updates via the Xandros Update Status Panel applet and window

Registering with Xandros Networks, and Why It Won't Hurt You to Do So

If you want to get even more out of Xandros Networks, it is worth your while to register. Now, I know registering seems like a big bother, but it's not. Really. Registering with Xandros Networks is easy and doesn't require any credit card information, if you're concerned about that.

What do you get for your efforts if you do register? Well, at the least you will have access to a few other choice applications that you can download and install for free. Nothing wrong with that, right? Of course, once you do register with Xandros Networks, you can also later purchase an XN Premium membership, which allows you to download a host of other cool stuff; purchase other commercial applications, such as CrossOver Office; or upgrade to the Deluxe Edition of Xandros, with which you can get the full shebang. Of course, these purchase options are strictly up to you—nobody is going to be knocking at your door (or inbox) demanding that you do so.

Anyway, once you ready to register, here is how to go about it:

1. Click the + symbol next to Shop in the left pane of the Xandros Networks window.

2. When the list of categories appears below Shop, click **My Account**.

3. A Sign In page will then appear in the right pane of the window. Click **Continue** in the New Customer section to the right.

   A KWallet wizard will now appear (Figure 8-24).

   KWallet has no relation to Xandros Networks; it is a part of your system that allows you to store passwords and other information safely in an encrypted file. I am sort of paranoid about saving passwords on my computer, except for those accounts that really house little information about me, such as forums. If you want to skip on KWallet, click **Cancel**. If you want to go ahead with it, click **Next** in this window and finish the very simple two-page wizard before moving on.

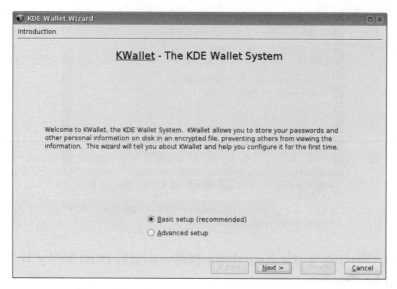

Figure 8-24: The KWallet wizard

4. Once you've bypassed or completed the KWallet formalities, fill out the form in the next registration page that appears in the right pane of the XN window (Figure 8-25).

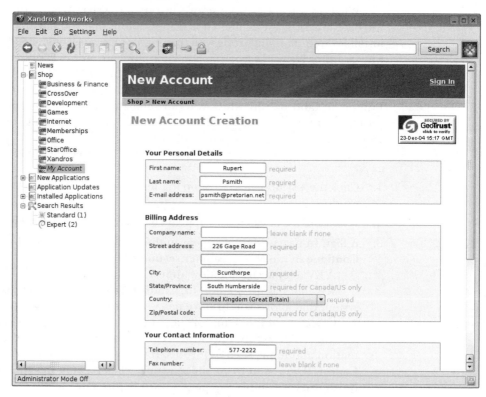

Figure 8-25: Filling out the Xandros Networks registration form

5. When you've finished, click **Continue** at the bottom of the page.

6. Assuming you filled in all the required information, the next page that appears in the right pane will tell you that your registration was successful. Click **Continue**.

7. Finally, you will be presented with a summary of your account (Figure 8-26), basically showing you all the details you entered in step 4.

Figure 8-26: Filling out the Xandros Networks registration form

You are now finished with the registration process. If you like, you can continue browsing though the Xandros Networks Shop and download a few of the cost-free applications that are available there to registered members. Of course, if you are already thinking of upgrading or buying one of the commercial apps available from the XN Shop, you can do that too. Otherwise, sign out by clicking the **Sign Out** link at the top of the right pane in any Shop page.

PART III

GADGETRY

9

MAKING LASTING IMPRESSIONS
Setting Up and Using Your Printer

When personal computers first appeared, people began talking about the dawn of the age of the paperless office, but what actually came to pass is quite different. Because of the PC's desktop-publishing capabilities and the continual decline in the prices of increasingly capable and sophisticated printer hardware, more printing (and paper use) is going on now than ever before. Whether it be for preparing school or business reports, printing out high-resolution copies of images from one's digital camera, creating uniquely personalized business cards, or even producing colorful CD or DVD labels and jewel-case inserts, people are printing more than ever. Unless the only thing you use your computer for is playing games, listening to MP3s, or stopping doors on hot, windy days, you will no doubt want to hook up your machine to a printer.

Is My Printer Supported?

Setting up a printer to work with your new system is actually a very easy task, but you do have to make sure that your printer is supported. Fortunately, printer support in the Linux world is much, much better than it once was. In general, support for Epson and Hewlett-Packard inkjet printers is pretty good, while support for other makers and other printer types is a bit spottier, though improving.

If you really want to make sure that your printer is ready for Linux, probably the best thing to do is go to www.linuxprinting.org. On that site, you can check out the online database to see if your printer is currently supported, and if it is, to what degree. Listings for supported printers also include information on what *drivers*, the little utility applications that basically tell your printer what to do, are best for your purposes. If you're thinking of buying a printer, there is also a page of suggested makes and models.

Project 9A: Setting Up Your Printer

Before you can rush off and start printing, you will first need to set up your printer. To do this, you will have to connect your printer to the computer and then power on the printer. If you connect your printer to your computer's parallel port rather than its USB port, you will first have to turn off the computer before connecting the cable. Once you have made the connection, turn on your printer, and then restart your computer. Of course, if your printer was already connected and powered up when you booted into your system, you can skip this step.

After your printer is hooked up, powered up, and ready to go, setting it up system-wise is merely a matter of following these steps:

1. Open a Xandros File Manager window, and then click **Printers** in the left pane of that window.

2. The right pane of the window should be empty, except for the window title, *Printers*, and a link, *Add printer*, as you can see in Figure 9-1. Click the **Add printer** link.

3. The *Add Printer Wizard* (Figure 9-2) will now appear. In the first page of the wizard, select **Local printer** (the usual setup in home environments) or **Network printer** (if you are using a printer connected to your network but not directly to your computer, as is often the case in office environments), and then click **Next**.

NOTE   *You can also bring up the Add Printer Wizard via the Control Center, if you prefer, by clicking **Peripheral Devices** in the left pane of the Control Center window and then clicking **Printers** in the list of subcategories that appears below. When the Printers module appears in the right pane of the window, click the **Add** button, which will bring up the wizard.*

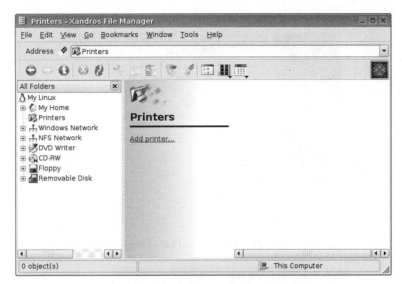

Figure 9-1: The empty Printers window in Xandros File Manager

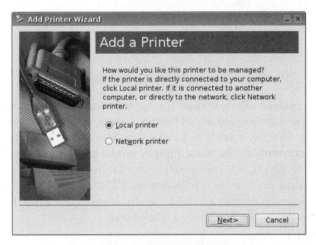

Figure 9-2: The Add Printer Wizard

4. In the next page of the wizard (Figure 9-3), you will see your printer
    listed. Don't get too excited yet; this shows that your system knows what
    kind of hardware you have—it doesn't necessarily mean that it will work.
    Click **Next**.

NOTE   *HP printer users: If you are using a Hewlett-Packard printer, you may be presented
    with a small window at this point telling you that your printer may work better with the
    HPOJ driver (Figure 9-4). This message depends on the model you are using and how
    it is connected to your computer (the parallel port or the USB port). Because my printer
    is connected via the computer's parallel port, I don't get this message, but if you do, skip
    ahead to the "Hewlett-Packard Printers" section of this chapter.*

Figure 9-3: The Add Printer Wizard recognizes your printer

Figure 9-4: Warning to some Hewlett-Packard printer users

5. The wizard will now show the manufacturer, model, and suggested driver for your printer in the next window. These entries should be correct, but this is not true in all cases. Sometimes, when it comes to the printer model, the wizard might not be completely correct. As you can see in Figure 9-5, the model is listed in the wizard as a PhotoSmart 140. Actually my printer is a PhotoSmart 1315, not a 140. In such cases, just choose the correct model from the appropriate drop-down menu button. When you've finished, click **Next**.

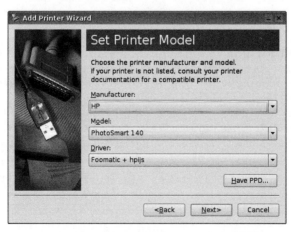

Figure 9-5: Selecting the manufacturer and model of your printer

6. Finally, in the last page of the wizard (Figure 9-6), you will be asked if you would like to print a test page, which isn't a bad idea in order to immediately test that everything has gone according to plan. To do so, just select **Yes**, and then click **Finish**. The wizard will disappear, and your printer will begin to print out a test page almost immediately. If you take a look at the Xandros File Manager window, you will now find a new icon for your printer in that previously empty window. The icon will have a big red check mark on it, indicating that it is the default printer for your system.

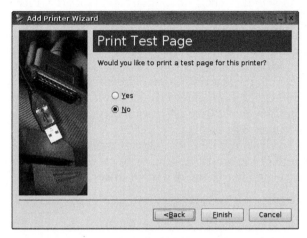

Figure 9-6: The Add Printer Wizard asks you if you want to print a test page before wrapping up

While your printer is at work, you will see two new items appear on your desktop: a Print Jobs window, and on the Panel, a Print Jobs toggle that looks like a small printer, both of which you can see in Figure 9-7. The Print Jobs window shows you what document is currently being printed and what other documents are queued up to print after that. When nothing is printing or queued up for that purpose, the white area of the window will be blank. Clicking the toggle in the Panel acts to either hide or show the Print Jobs window.

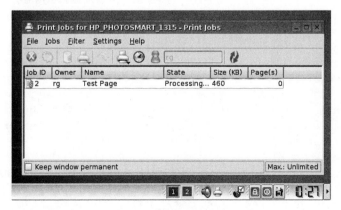

Figure 9-7: The Print Jobs window and Panel toggle

These two items do not appear when printing OpenOffice.org documents.

Hewlett-Packard Printers

As I already mentioned, if you are trying to set up a Hewlett-Packard printer, especially multifunction models or those connected to your computer via its USB port, you will see a small window after clicking the **Next** button in the second page of the wizard. The window will tell you that your printer may work better with the HPOJ (the initials stand for HP Office Jet) driver, as was shown in Figure 9-4.

Because your system probably knows best, click **OK** in that window, and then click the **Cancel** button in the wizard window. After doing that, go ahead and install the driver using Xandros Networks. Just type **hpoj** in the text box next to the Search button in the XN window. Then install the driver, listed as the HP Multifunction Printer Driver, using the procedure you learned in Chapter 8. Once the driver is installed, go back to step 1 of this project and start over again.

This time around, however, when you click the **Next** button in the second page of the wizard, another window will appear asking you whether or not you would like to use the HPOJ driver (Figure 9-8).

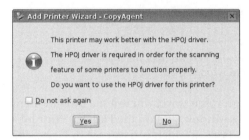

Figure 9-8: Telling the wizard to use the HPOJ driver (HP printer users only)

Unless you went through the trouble of installing it just for kicks, click **Yes**. The window will disappear, and you can then go on to step 3 of the printer setup procedures I just described in Project 9A.

By the way, don't be surprised by the fact that you do not see the HPOJ driver listed in the driver choices in the third page of the wizard; the HPOJ driver is what is called a *low-level driver*, one whose purpose is to provide added functionality to your printer, such as the ability to read memory cards from your digital camera or to scan images. It works in conjunction with other drivers for the actual business of printing.

If you have a show-me sort of personality and want proof that the HPOJ driver is in fact installed, you can easily do so via the Xandros Networks application that you learned to use in Chapter 8. Just type **hpoj** in the text box at the top of the XN window, click **Search**, and then search for the driver in the list of results provided in the pane below. If the word *Remove* appears to the right of the driver in the list, you know it has been installed correctly. If the word *Install* appears instead, you will know that the driver was not correctly installed. In that case, just click the **Install** link to perform the installation.

If Things Don't Go According to Plan

If things do not work out for you (for example, if the wizard doesn't recognize your printer), keep your cool and try doing the following:

1. Right-click the Printer icon that just recently appeared in the Xandros File Manager window, and select **Delete** in the pop-up menu.

2. The printer icon should now be gone. If it is, restart your computer, keeping the printer connected and powered on.

3. Once your system is back up and running, try adding the printer again.

If that doesn't work out, try checking Xandros Networks (with the **Debian Unsupported Site** option selected) to see if there is a special driver available for your printer, or check the Xandros FAQs (http://support.xandros.com) or User Forums (http://forums.xandros.com) for help or advice. You might want to double-check with www.linuxprinting.org, if you haven't already done so, to see if there is anything special they have to say about your particular printer.

If everything seemed to go fine except for the printout quality of the test page you made at the end of the last step of the setup wizard, try using a different driver. To do this, follow these steps:

1. Right-click the icon for your printer in the Xandros File Manager window, and select **Properties** in the pop-up menu.

2. When the Properties window appears, click the **Change Model** button.

3. In the Change Printer Model window that then appears (Figure 9-9), select one of the other driver options listed in the **Driver** drop-down menu, and then click **OK** in that window and **OK** in the Properties window.

4. Try printing out another document.

Figure 9-9: Changing drivers for your printer

Using Your Printer

Now that your printer is set up, you will no doubt want to start printing. This is an easy task and not much different from how it works in the Windows and Mac worlds.

You should be aware, however, that there are two different print dialog windows that might appear when you set out to print. Which of these will appear depends on the application you happen to be using. Most applications will utilize the KDE-based print dialog window *(kprint)*, while OpenOffice.org uses its own. The look and options of the KDE-based dialog window will vary somewhat, depending on the application you are using at the time.

Changing Printer Settings

As you print out various things, it is inevitable that, for one reason or another, you will want to change your printer settings. For example, let's say that you are running low on colored ink and want to keep everything in black or shades of gray for a while. Or maybe you want to print a particular photo at a higher resolution than the default resolution setting of your current printer driver. Or maybe you want to print a page horizontally rather than vertically.

Doing all this is pretty straightforward.

Changing the Print Range and Number of Copies to Print for Your Document

If you are working with a multipage document, your system will automatically print out the whole shebang when you go about printing. This is all fine and dandy, but what if you want to print out only the first three pages of the document? Or what if you want to print out only the page you are currently looking at? Well, none of these possibilities poses any problem, because you can easily print out only what you want via the Print dialog window.

To get started, just select **Print** from the **File** menu in the application you are using. The Print window (Figure 9-10) will appear.

To print a specific range of pages, check the radio button for *Range*, and then type the range of pages you want to print. For example, if you want to print out pages 7 through 13 of your document, you would type **7-13**. If you want to print out just pages 7, 12, 13, and 20, you would type **7,12,13,20**. If you want to print out just page 3, you would type **3** or **3-3**. If you want to print out just the page you are currently viewing, click anywhere in that page before opening the Print window, and then check **Current**.

NOTE *This option is available only in applications that actually separate your document into pages. In the case of a web page, for example, where the document itself is actually a long single page, the option will not be available, even though it will print out on several pages.*

Figure 9-10: A kprint Print dialog window

Other Options

There are also a few other options available to you from the print dialog window. If, for example, you want to print out only odd or even pages, you can select the appropriate option from the *Page set* option button near the bottom-left corner of the window. If you want to print out more than one copy of the document, or parts thereof, select the desired number of copies in the box next to the word *Copies.*

When selecting this option, you also have the option of having the copies collated, meaning that they are printed in ordered sets. For instance, if you set the number of copies at 3, the pages would print out 1,2,3 and 1,2,3 and 1,2,3. This is the default arrangement, so there is nothing you need to do if you like this setup. If you would prefer that the copies print out in 1,1,1 and 2,2,2 and 3,3,3 order, you can do so by unchecking the box next to the word *Collated.* You can also have the pages print out in reverse order, regardless of the number of copies you've selected, by checking *Reverse.*

If you are printing an OpenOffice.org document, most of these options will also be available to you, and there will be an additional option available: *Selection* (Figure 9-11).

The *Selection* option allows you to print out only the text you may have highlighted in the document before bringing up the Print dialog window.

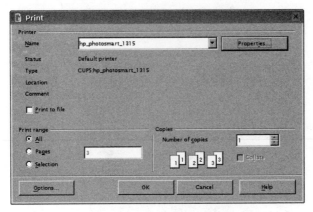

Figure 9-11: An OpenOffice.org Print dialog window

Changing Paper Orientation and Size Settings

To change the size or orientation of the page you are printing, select **Print** from the **File** menu in the application you are using, and then click the **Properties** button in the Print dialog window that appears. You will then see a Configuration window (Figure 9-12).

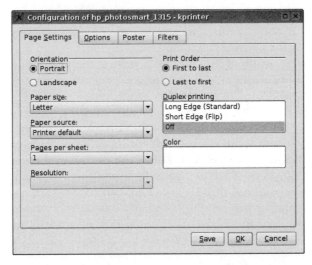

Figure 9-12: Changing paper orientation and size settings

Once in the new window, you can change the orientation of your page from *Portrait* (vertical) to *Landscape* (horizontal) by clicking the appropriate button beneath the word *Orientation*. To change paper sizes, make the appropriate choice from the menu button beneath the phrase *Paper size*. If you would also like to reverse the printing order of your document, that is, printing from the last page to the first rather than the other way around, click the **Last to first** button under the *Print Order* heading. Once you have made your choices, click **OK**. If you would like to use these settings for all your future documents, click **Save** before clicking **OK**.

These same options are available to you when printing an OpenOffice.org document by clicking the **Properties** button in the OpenOffice.org Print dialog window.

When the Properties window appears (Figure 9-13), you will notice that you can also choose to print out the document at a smaller size by adjusting the percentage numbers in the *Scale* box.

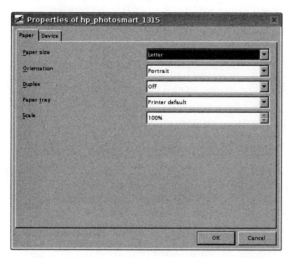

Figure 9-13: Changing paper size, orientation, and scale settings in OpenOffice.org

Okay, so now let's say that you want to print out a copy of one of the photos you downloaded to your hard disk from a digital camera. You may want your photo to come out at as high a resolution as possible. Or maybe you just want to print out a cheap and quick copy of the document you are working on without spending too much time or ink. Well, you can do either one of these things quite easily by changing your printer's color and resolution settings.

To do this, open the Configuration window, as you just learned to do in the previous section, and click the **Options** tab.

Once in the Options tab, click the + symbol next to *General*, and then click **Printout Mode** when it appears beneath it. After doing this, the various printout-mode options available for your printer will appear in the right pane of the tab window (Figure 9-14). These options mainly consist of color, print quality, and paper settings, and they are usually grouped in sets. In case you are not too familiar with such printer settings, I will provide you with a very brief introduction now.

Color settings should be fairly easy to figure out, as the name indicates what it does. Black + Color, for example, allows you to print in both color and black-and-white. Grayscale, on the other hand, allows you to print in black-and-white, such as a typical text document, and every shade of gray in between, as would be the case when printing a black-and-white photo. To vary the printout quality of your document, you adjust the dpi, or dots per inch, settings—the higher the dpi, the better the print quality. The Draft mode option also has an impact on print quality, because if you choose it, the document is printed more quickly. What you gain in terms of speed, however, will probably cost you a bit in terms of print quality. If you are using an old or lower-quality inkjet printer, however, you may actually find your printed output crisper and clearer than in regular printing mode, but a bit of trial and error should show you what works best on your printer. To actually select the color and resolution mode you would like to use, click the appropriate item in the list; it will then be highlighted in blue. If you want to print out a copy of one of your digital images, you will want to select the highest dpi setting for a Black + Color Cartridge. In the case of my printer, the option reads "1200 dpi, Photo, Black + Color Cartr., Photo Paper." If you just want to print out a quick grayscale copy of a document, even one that contains color images, select the lowest dpi Draft Grayscale option available for your printer. In my case, for example, it is "300 dpi, Draft, Grayscale, Black + Color Cartr." Once you have finally made your selections, click **OK**.

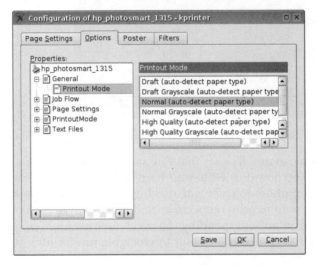

Figure 9-14: Changing your printer's color and resolution settings

To adjust these settings when printing an OpenOffice.org document, click the **Properties** button in the OpenOffice.org Print dialog window. When the Properties window appears, click the **Device** tab, and then click **Printout Mode** in the left pane of that tab.

You can then select from the various options available for your printer in the right pane (Figure 9-15).

Previewing Pages Before Printing

It is often a good idea to see exactly what is going to be printed before actually doing the deed itself. This is very easy to do by going to the **File** menu of the document you want to print and selecting **Print Preview** (**Page Preview** in OpenOffice.org documents). The page will then appear in a separate window, in pretty much the state in which it will be printed. This is very handy when printing web pages (Figure 9-16), as it allows you to see how a lengthy single web page will be divided for printing.

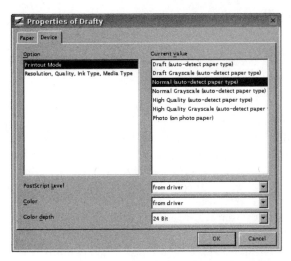

Figure 9-15: Changing color and resolution settings for an OpenOffice.org document

If, for example, the information you want to print appears on page 2 in the Print Preview window, you can choose to print just that page. Once you have had a look through the page in the Print Preview window, you can move on to printing it out by clicking the **Close** button (**Close Preview** in OpenOffice.org). After that, just go ahead and start the printing process by selecting **Print** in the **File** menu.

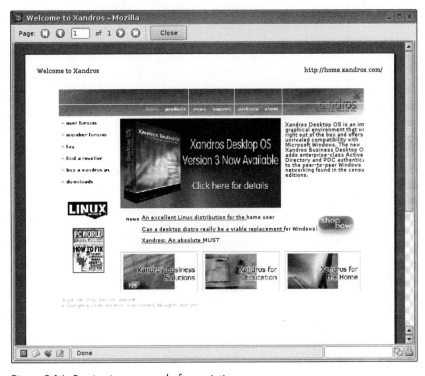

Figure 9-16: Previewing a page before printing

Printing to PDF

A very handy feature in Xandros is the ability to print or save documents to PDF. *PDF (Portable Document Format)* is a file format developed by Adobe that allows you to create documents that cannot be altered by others and yet can easily be read regardless of what word processor program or operating system another person is using. All the recipient of a PDF file needs in order to view that document is a copy of Adobe Acrobat Reader or any other similar PDF reader. PDF files are also usually smaller and can thus be more easily and quickly sent as email attachments. A 5.5 MB OpenOffice.org document of mine shrank down to only 770 KB when I printed it to PDF. It's also a great way to save web pages, as the whole page, graphics and all, becomes one single, easily transportable file. All in all, this ability to create PDF files is a very cool feature that you would have to pay a pretty penny for in the Windows world.

Printing a file to PDF is really simple. Just open the file you want to PDF-ize, and select **Print** in the **File** menu of the application for that document.

In the Print dialog window that then appears, click the drop-down menu button where your printer is listed and select **Print to File (PDF)**, as shown in Figure 9-17. The default name of the file will be print.pdf, so if you want to change that to something more meaningful, you can do so in the text box next to the words *Output file*. Just change the text immediately before the .pdf extension, not the path before that. For example, you might change /home/your_username/print.pdf to /home/your_username/ saturnvuehp.pdf, and so on.

You can do the same thing with OpenOffice.org documents, though the process is slightly different; there, the Print to File (PDF) option becomes Export.

Figure 9-17: Printing a file to PDF

For an OpenOffice.org document, open the document you want to save to PDF, and then click the small button in the OpenOffice.org window that looks like a red and white Adobe Acrobat logo (see Figure 9-18 if you're not sure what one looks like). After that, an Export window will appear in which you can name the file. Once you've done that, click **Export**.

Figure 9-18: Exporting an OpenOffice.org document as a PDF file

Project 9B: Adding Another Printer (Even If You Don't Really Have One)

Because most computers have one parallel port (also often called a *printer port*) and at least two or more USB ports, there is no reason that you can't have more than one printer attached to your machine. You might want to do this, for example, if you have a black-and-white laser printer that you use for your more serious or official documents and an inkjet printer that you use for printing out photos and other fun stuff. Adding the extra printer would be no different from adding the first. Just go back to Project 9A and repeat the steps.

After the second computer has been set up, you can tell your system which computer to use when printing a given document by clicking the drop-down menu button that shows your default printer's name, just as you did when printing to PDF. Then select the printer you want to use from the list, because both printers will show up there.

If you find that you would prefer using the new printer most of the time, while using the original only when needed, you can make the newbie the default printer for your system. You can do this by opening the Xandros File Manager window and clicking **Printers** in the left pane. In the right pane, right-click the printer you would like to set as the default printer for your system, and select **Set as Default** in the pop-up menu. If you want to have the original printer as the default again, just repeat the process for that printer.

9B-1: Adding Your Virtual Printers

Now, you don't actually have to have another printer in order to add another printer. This might sound a bit screwy on my part, but it is true. Let me explain why you might want to do this. The default printout setting for most inkjet printers is Normal mode, which is usually a medium resolution using both black-and-white and color cartridges. This is fine for most people most of the time, and thus is the reason it is called Normal. Well, what if you aren't normal? What if you mostly like to print things out quickly in draft-quality black-and-white, and when you're not doing that, you are printing out high-resolution photos? Normal mode is pretty useless to you in this case.

The perfect solution for your state of affairs, in this imaginary world I am painting, is to add your printer two more times, with each printer set up to print at the resolutions you prefer. You would thus have three printers in the eyes of your system, but only one actually sitting there on your desk. Pretty cool idea, if you ask me.

How do you do this? Well, exactly as you did the first time around. Just go through the printer setup process as you did before, making all the same choices. The only difference this time around is in the second page of the wizard. In that page, you have the option of giving your printer a name. The first time you did this, you just accepted the actual hardware name of the printer, but this time you will have to give each of your two new virtual printers a new and meaningful name. (Be aware that printer names cannot have any spaces in Linux; if you just have to have a space, use an underscore (_) instead.) For example, you might want to call your quick black-and-white draft-mode printer "Drafty," while you could call your photo-printing printer "HiRes." Also, you might as well skip printing out a test copy in the last page of the wizard, because you won't have set things up exactly the way you want at that point. Anyway, once you have finished setting up your two new virtual printers, you can go ahead and do the fine-tuning.

9B-2: Fine-Tuning Your Virtual Printers

Now that you have added your new trusty workhorses, Drafty and HiRes, it is time to set each of them up so that their output matches their names. To do this, open the Control Center, and select **Peripheral Devices ▶ Printers**. When the Printers module appears in the right pane of the window, it should look something like mine in Figure 9-19.

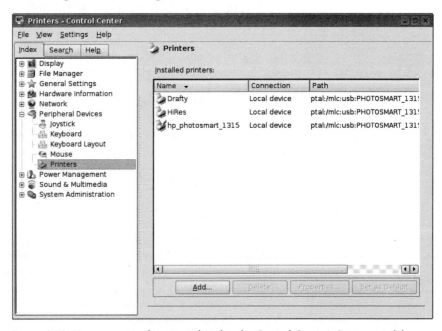

Figure 9-19: Your new virtual printer is listed in the Control Center's Printers module

To get down to business, here's what you need to do:

1. Start off by clicking **HiRes** in the list and then clicking the **Properties** button.

2. When the Properties window appears, click the **Advanced** tab, and then select **General ▶ Printout Mode**.

3. In the right pane of the window, click **Photo (on photo paper)**, which should leave your window looking much like mine in Figure 9-20, assuming, of course, that your printer has a similar setting available.

4. If everything looks just about right, click **OK**.

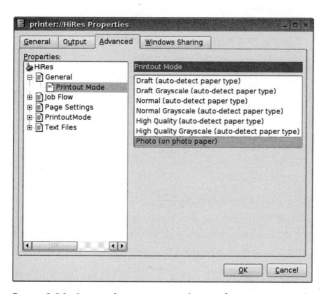

Figure 9-20: Setting the printing resolution of your new virtual printer

You will now be back at the Control Center window, so go ahead and repeat the same process for Drafty. This time around, however, let's pick **Draft Grayscale** in the list at the right of the Advanced tab. Once you have clicked the **OK** button and are back at the Control Center, you can quit the Control Center and move on to trying out your new printers.

9B-3: Selecting and Trying Out Your New Virtual Printers

Now that you have two new printers (and without spending a dime, I might remind you), it is only natural to try them out. Start out with Drafty by printing out a web page. The No Starch Press home page will do fine for this purpose, so here's what you need to do:

1. Punch up **http://www.nostarch.com** in your web browser.

2. When the page has completed loading, go to the **File** menu and select **Print**.

3. When the Print dialog window appears, choose **Drafty** in the drop-down menu button next to the word *Name* in the Printer section of the window (Figure 9-21), and then click **Print**.

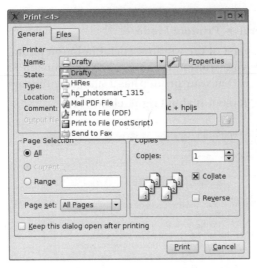

Figure 9-21: Selecting your new virtual printer in the Print dialog window

Within a few seconds, you will have a grayscale printout of that page in your hands. Pretty cool, no? You can go ahead and try out HiRes now, if you like, but I would suggest trying it out at its full potential by printing out one of your digital-camera images on photo-quality paper.

NOTE *If you want to use your new virtual (or even real) printers with OpenOffice.org, you will first have to close all OpenOffice.org modules that happened to be open when you installed the printers and then restart the ones you want. Also, if you would like to set up one of your two new virtual printers as the default printer for your system (Drafty being a more logical choice than HiRes), you can easily do so using the method I described at the very beginning of this project: open a Xandros File Manager window, click **Printer** in the left pane of the window, right-click the printer you want to set as the default, and then select **Set as Default** in the pop-up menu.*

Canceling a Print Job

To wrap up this chapter on printing, let's cover a problem that at one time or another happens to all of us. You wanted to print just one page of a 57-page document, but by accident you started printing the whole thing. What can you do to save your ink and 56 sheets of paper?

Fortunately, the solution is outrageously simple. Just open a Xandros File Manager window, if one isn't already open, and click **Printers** in the left pane of that window.

In the right pane, right-click the printer currently handling your print job, and select **Purge** in the pop-up menu (Figure 9-22). The page currently printing will probably print out to completion, but the printing will stop after that.

Figure 9-22: Canceling a print job

10

FLATBED MEMORIES

Working with Your Scanner

Scanners are both extremely useful and about as cheap a peripheral device as you can get. They allow you to take either images or pages of text and input them in digital form into your computer in much the same way as you duplicate a document on a copy machine. However, even as digital cameras are rapidly overtaking traditional film cameras as the photographic device of choice for the masses, the number of people using scanners to transfer their non-digital images into digital form is slowly decreasing. Despite this trend, scanners are not in immediate danger of extinction because there are more images around than those you take yourself.

Even though scanners have been around for a relatively long time, support for them in Linux is still a bit spotty. Fortunately, this is changing for the better with every new Linux release. The *backend*, the essentially hidden part of your system that handles scanner recognition and support in Linux, is called *Sane*. If you are wondering whether Linux will be able to recognize your scanner, or if you are trying to figure out what type of scanner to buy, you will probably want to go to the Sane website, www.sane-project.org/sane-mfgs.html.

There you will be able to see if your scanner is supported or to get tips as to what scanner to buy. As I have mentioned before, you can also try out the Xandros User Forums (http://forums.xandros.com) and ask for Xandros-specific recommendations there.

Project 10A: Scanning

For those of you who have a scanner, now is the time to get a feel for how to use it with Xandros by following along with this project. To get started, make sure your scanner is plugged into your computer and turned on.

After that, here's what you have to do:

1. Go to the **Launch** menu and select **Applications ▸ Graphics ▸ Scanner**. This will launch the scanning application known as *Kooka*.

2. The Kooka Welcome window (Figure 10-1) tells you which scanning devices you have connected to your machine and asks you to pick one. Assuming you have only one, just click **OK**.

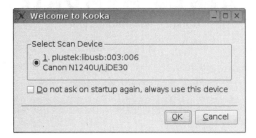

Figure 10-1: The Kooka Welcome window

NOTE   *If the scanner you are using is the only one you are likely to connect to your machine in the near future, then go ahead and check the box next to the words* Do not ask on startup again, always use this device, *which will allow you to bypass this phase of the startup in the future. If you do happen to add, or switch, scanners in the future, you will be able to make the appropriate changes in the Kooka Preferences window at that time. Once you click OK, the main Kooka window will appear.*

Now that Kooka is up and running, you can get down to some scanning. The first thing we'll do is perform a preview scan. This is a quick, low-resolution scan, which allows you to see a thumbnail, a small version of the image you will be working with.

3. Choose a photo you would like to scan, place it on the scanner bed, and then close the cover.

4. Click the **Preview Scan** button in the main Kooka window, after which a small window (Figure 10-2) will appear showing you the progress of the scan.

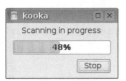

Figure 10-2: Kooka shows your scanner's progress

Once your scanner has finished doing its thing, the progress window will disappear, and you will see a thumbnail of your image in the right pane of the main Kooka window, which at that point should look like Figure 10-3, though your preview image will (unless we move in surprisingly similar circles) be different.

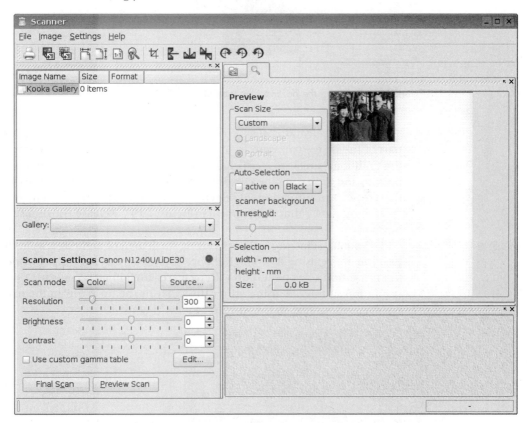

Figure 10-3: The main Kooka window after performing a preview scan

After the thumbnail preview of your image appears, you must select the part of it you want to scan. This can be a very handy feature, as it allows you to perform some after-the-fact digital magic. Imagine, for example, that you have a killer photo of yourself that you want to include in a digital photo album. The only problem is that standing at your side in that photo is your ex, Chris, who, given the course of things in your life, you would rather place squarely into the trash bin of your memory. Of course, rather than stave off a bout of heartbreak by removing your ex, you might, as is the case with my happily married friend in Figure 10-4, just want to isolate a portion of a photo for use as a headshot in a web page or on a letterhead.

Even if you have no need to erase or isolate someone in your image, and you instead want to scan the whole image, you still have to make a selection, in this case from image border to image border. If you don't do this, your scanner, not knowing any better, will scan the entire area of its scanning bed, thus producing an image with an enormous amount of empty white space. In all likelihood, this is something you want to end up with about as much as eggshells in your omelet.

Figure 10-4: Selecting the portion of the image you want to scan

5. To make the selection, place your cursor at one corner of the image or part of the image you want to scan (the cursor's shape will change from the traditional arrow to a crosshair), press and hold down your left mouse button, and then drag the cursor until you have surrounded the area you want to scan with the dashed selection box (sometimes referred to as "marching ants") that then appears (Figure 10-4). Release the mouse button.

    If you are selecting only a relatively small area of an image, as in the example we're using, it would behoove you to increase, perhaps by twice, the resolution so as to end up with a clearer final image. You can adjust resolution settings by using either the slider or the up arrow in the main Kooka window next to the word *Resolution* (Figure 10-5).

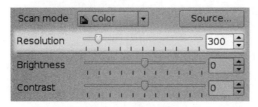

Figure 10-5: Changing the resolution for the final scanned image

6. Now that you have selected the area you want to scan, click the **Final Scan** button to seal the deal.

    A progress window like the one you saw during the preview-scan phase of things will appear again, and, after your scanner spurts out a few tugging sounds, you will hear the long, steady hum of your scanner doing its job. During this time the progress bar will begin its mercurial journey to completion. When the scan is indeed complete, the progress window will disappear, and a Kooka Save Assistant window (Figure 10-6) will open in its place.

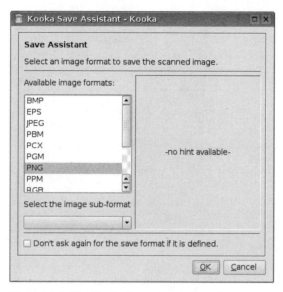

Figure 10-6: The Kooka Save Assistant window

7. Choose a format in which to save your image (I use *JPEG* for images I will use on a web page and *PNG* for everything else), and click **OK**.

Viewing the Results

To see the results of your final scan, you will need to move your mouse over to the right pane of the main Kooka window (Figure 10-3), and then click the tab showing an icon of a folder and file. Since this might be a bit hard to make out, I've highlighted it for you in Figure 10-7.

Figure 10-7: Finding your final scan results

Once you click that tab, the results of your final scan will appear in the right pane of the main Kooka window, as you can see in Figure 10-8.

You will also notice that a thumbnail of the image will appear at the bottom of the pane and that the default filename for that file will be listed in the left pane (in this case, *kscan_0001.png*).

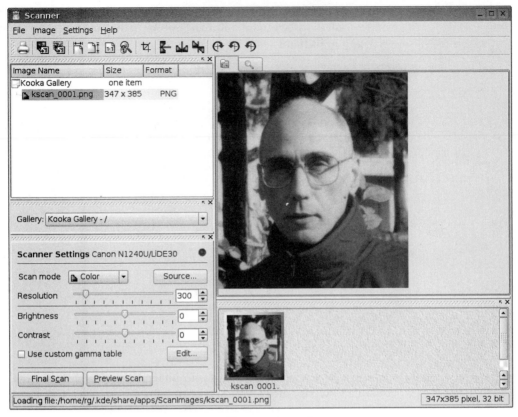

Figure 10-8: The final result of your scanning efforts

Getting a Fuller View

Of course, especially when dealing with larger images or images scanned at much higher resolutions, most often only a part of your final image will be visible in the right pane, as you can see in the left part of Figure 10-9. This is simply because the final image is too big to fit in the relatively small area provided in the Kooka window.

Figure 10-9: Viewing a scanned image before and after scaling

In order to see the entire image, go to the **Image** menu of the main Kooka window, select **Scale to Height** or **Scale to Width**, depending on what is appropriate in your case, and presto! You will then be able to see the whole image that you've just scanned (as in the right side of Figure 10-9).

Where Can I Find My Images?

Once you've finished scanning, you will no doubt want to use your images for purposes all your own. The only problem is that you might not be able to find them. So where are they?

Your images are actually located within your Home folder; however, the folder in which you can find them is hidden from your view and buried in */.kde/share/apps/ScanImages*. You can dig your way to that folder after first going to the **View** menu in a Xandros File Manager window and then selecting **Show Hidden Files**. But there is a simpler way of doing things by which you can save your images to your My Pictures folder (or anywhere else you like), and give each of the files a more meaningful name in the process. After all, an image file with the name Christmas2005.png is certainly more meaningful to you than one called kscan_0076.png, right?

If this all sounds of interest to you, here's what you need to do:

1. Right-click the image you wish to move and rename in the left pane of the Kooka window.

2. In the pop-up menu that appears, select **Save Image** (Figure 10-10).

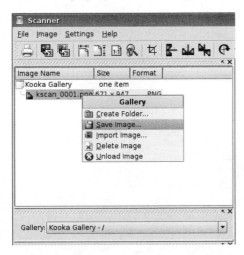

Figure 10-10: Saving your image in a new location (and with a new name)

3. In the Save As window that appears, navigate to the folder in which you wish to save your image.

4. In the File name box, give your image file a meaningful (to you) name.

5. Click **Save**, and you're finished.

Your scanned image will now actually be residing in two locations: the location to which you just saved it and the original Kooka Gallery location buried in the hidden-from-view .kde folder (/.kde/share/apps/ScanImages).

Since you don't really need to have that copy in the Kooka Gallery anymore, you can save some disk space, and keep the left pane of your Kooka window a bit tidier, by deleting that original copy of the image.

Accomplishing this is very similar to what you just did when you saved the image—just right-click the image you want to delete, select **Delete Image** in the pop-up menu (you can see the choice in Figure 10-10), and then in the window that appears asking you if you really want to delete it, click **OK**.

Why Are My Scanned Images So Big?

This is a point that seems to confuse a lot of people, so I'll talk about it a bit. One of the first areas of confusion is that there is a general blurring of how the terms *ppi* (pixels per inch) and *dpi* (dots per inch) are used. Most applications use these terms interchangeably, and yet they aren't really the same thing. To make things simple, when you are talking about images on your screen, you are talking about *pixels* (the little dots that make up your screen image) per inch, and when you are talking about printer resolution, you are talking about *dots* (of printer ink) per inch.

Your computer screen in general has a resolution of 76 ppi, while most modern inkjet and laser printers have a resolution range of 300 to 1200 dpi, sometimes even more. This means that a photo scanned at 76 ppi that looks just fine on your screen ends up looking pretty lame when you print it out. On the other hand, when you scan a picture at 300 ppi, the image will look much better in your printout but will seem gigantic on your screen. This makes sense, as the resolution of your image is more than three times that of your computer's screen resolution. The result is that your computer can accommodate the higher resolution of the image only by displaying that image at three times its original size.

Figure 10-11: Same image scanned at three different resolutions

As an example, have a look at Figure 10-11, where you can see the identical image scanned at three different resolutions: 76 ppi, 150 ppi, and 300 ppi. As you can see, the 76 ppi image at the far left (measuring 132 × 156 mm—about the size of the hardcopy itself) is the smallest, while the other two images are proportionally bigger (265 × 313 mm for the 150 ppi image and 550 × 627 mm for the 300 ppi image).

So What Resolution Should I Use When Scanning?

What resolution you use when scanning really depends on a variety of factors, the most important of which is what you plan to do with the image when you're finished. When I look at Figure 10-12 on my computer screen, the smallest image looks best, the middle image looks okay, and the largest looks a bit odd, not as sharp as the other two. Basically, when scanning images for display on a computer, on web pages for instance, it is probably best to stick with a ppi similar to typical screen resolutions or slightly larger (76 to 150 ppi).

When it comes to printing, a whole new set of considerations comes into play. First of all, there are the limitations of your scanner, different models having different maximum resolutions. The resolution limits of your printer itself are also, naturally enough, a major consideration. These include the type of printer you have, since laser printers and inkjets have different characteristics; laser printers will produce better-quality images than inkjet printers, while inkjet output will be more greatly affected by the type of paper used than will a laser printer. In either case, there is always the question of the printing resolution you ultimately select. Of course, your printed output is not going to suffer if you scan your images at higher resolutions than those at which you plan to print them out, but you will end up with a lot of files taking up too much disk space. Remember: *the higher the resolution of a scanned image, the greater the file size in terms of disk space.* If this is of concern to you, and you would prefer not being so cavalier with your use of disk space, you can follow these very general guidelines:

- If you are using a laser printer, scan at the same resolution at which you are going to print.

- If you are using an inkjet printer with regular paper, scan at about 65 percent of your target printout resolution, about 195 ppi for a 300 dpi print.

- If you are going to use an inkjet printer with photo-quality paper, scan at about 80 percent of your target printout resolution, about 240 ppi for 300 dpi.

Needless to say, these are just suggestions to get you started. What works best for you and your particular scanner/printer setup may be slightly different. That said, it's worth driving home the fact that nothing works better than a bit of experimentation and trial and error. In this case, you can't really go wrong. Just give yourself some time, don't get frustrated, and, most important, don't wait until you desperately need to scan something before trying things out—stay ahead of the game.

Project 10B: Getting a Grip on Resolutions

If all this talk about scanning versus printing resolutions has left you feeling as if you are locked inside a Dali painting, then you might want to join in on this little hands-on experiment. Once you have completed it, you should have a better idea of how resolutions translate into reality and what resolutions work best with your printer. As a bonus, you'll also get a little experience working with the OpenOffice.org application, Draw. To follow along, you will need one clear snapshot (preferably with at least one large object, such as a portrait) and, naturally enough, a scanner and printer.

1. Scan your image at four different resolutions: 76, 150, 300, and 600 ppi. If your scanner cannot handle resolutions as high as 600 ppi, you can skip that one. Save the files that result as **ex76.png**, **ex150.png**, **ex300.png**, and **ex600.png**. Of course, you can name the files anything you want, but using my suggestions will make it easier for you to follow along.

2. Open a Xandros File Manager window, and navigate to the folder in which you saved the images.

3. Select the four files you've just scanned by holding down your CTRL key and then clicking each file individually. When you are finished, the four files will be highlighted.

4. Now right-click any of the four files, and in the pop-up menu that appears, select **Cut**. The files will not immediately disappear at this point, so don't worry.

5. Navigate to your **Home** folder, and right-click any open space. In the pop-up menu that appears, select **Paste**. The four files will then appear (and, incidentally, disappear from the source folder).

6. Run OpenOffice.org Draw by going to the **Launch** menu and selecting **Applications** ▸ **OfficeOffice.org Drawing Editor**.

7. Now go to the **Insert** menu in OpenOffice.org Draw, and select **Graphics**. An Insert Graphics window will then appear.

8. In that window, navigate to your **Home** folder by clicking the **Home** button (as shown in Figure 10-12).

Figure 10-12: Navigating to your Home folder in the OpenOffice.org Insert Graphics window

9. In the list within that window, locate and select the first file you scanned, **ex76.png**, by clicking once on its name. The filename should then be highlighted like that in Figure 10-13. If so, click the **Open** button, after which the image will appear at its full size in OpenOffice.org Draw.

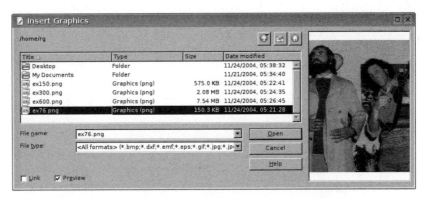

Figure 10-13: Select the file you wish to insert into your OpenOffice.org file

10. Repeat the procedure you just performed in step 9, but this time select the file **ex150.png**.

11. When the image appears, it will be noticeably larger than the first, as you can see in Figure 10-14. Resize the image so that it is the same size as the first by holding down the SHIFT key and then placing your cursor at one of the corners of the image. The cursor will then change into a double-sided arrow. When it does, press your mouse button, and drag one of the raised green squares at the corners of the image until the image is the appropriate size. If you don't see any raised squares, click the image once, after which they will appear. In case you are wondering, holding down the SHIFT key as you do this keeps the proportions of the image intact.

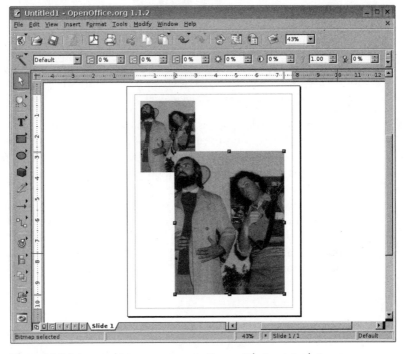

Figure 10-14: Inserted images appear in Draw at their original size

12. Insert and resize each of the remaining two files, **ex300.png** and **ex600.png**, using the methods you used in steps 9 and 11. Once you have completed the insertion process, your OpenOffice.org Draw window should look like that in Figure 10-15. Be sure that your images are placed in the same order as mine so that you will be able to compare your printed results later on.

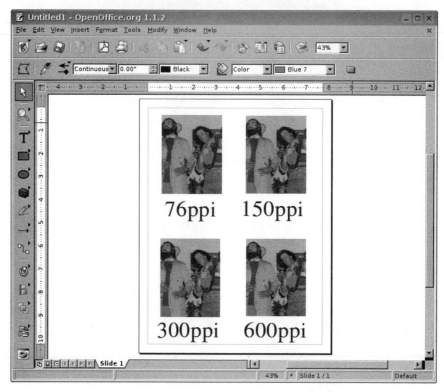

Figure 10-15: Your images set up to print

13. Now that your page is set up, it's time to print it out. Be sure to set your printer's settings to print at 600 dpi, and use a good-quality paper, preferably photo quality. Of course, if you are using a laser printer, your paper choice will matter much less. Once ready, print.

While the four images will probably look more or less the same on your screen, there should be a noticeable difference in your printed output. On the basis of that output, you will be able to see what a difference a few hundred ppi can make and thus have a better idea what scanner settings provide the best results on your printer.

11

BECAUSE MEMORY SOMETIMES FAILS TO SERVE

Digital Cameras

Digital cameras have been around for far less time than scanners, and yet the number of people owning them, as well as the cross section of people using them, is far greater. Seems that just about everyone these days, from Grandma to the kid next door, is snapping up memories of his or her world with a digital camera.

Fortunately, support for digital cameras in the world of Linux is significantly better than that for scanners. In fact, it is probably safe to say that if you have a digital camera, it will most likely work with Linux. Even if your particular model is so old or so new or so obscure a make that it doesn't, you can still get those photos into your computer by removing the storage medium in that camera, popping it into a media reader connected to your computer, and then loading the image files that way into your computer (as covered in Chapter 6). As you can see, one way or another, you will be able to use your camera with Linux.

The *backend*, the essentially hidden part of your system that provides digital camera support in Linux, is the *gPhoto2* digital camera library. The gPhoto2 digital camera library is included in your Xandros system, and, at present, it supports hundreds of cameras. If you are curious to see whether or not your camera is supported, go to the gPhoto2 project page at www.gphoto.org.

Scroll down the page, and click the link that announces some specific number of cameras. As this chapter was being written, the number went from 400 cameras to 500. There's no telling how many will be shown when you read this.

On that page, you will find a complete list of all the cameras supported by gPhoto2. If your camera isn't on the list, it most likely means (as that page points out) that your camera is so old that there is little demand for support for it or that it is so new that there hasn't been enough time to develop specific support for it. Remember, however, that just because your camera isn't on the list doesn't mean it won't work. As I've already pointed out, chances are good that it will.

gPhoto2 is constantly being updated, so if your camera isn't on the list now, it could very well be there in the future. Using Xandros Networks now and then to check for updates should keep you as up-to-date as possible.

Project 11A: Working with Your Digital Camera

All things told, working with images from your digital camera will prove a much easier, and arguably more enjoyable, task than dealing with your scanner. All you have to do to get started is plug the smaller end of the USB connector that came with your camera (which most likely looks like that in Figure 11-1) into the camera, and then plug the other end, which has a standard USB connector, into one of your computer's USB ports. Once you've done that, you're ready to follow along. Oh, and leave your camera's power off for now.

Figure 11-1: Connecting the USB connector to your camera

11A-1: Telling Digikam Where to Store Your Images

Now that your camera and computer are tethered to each other, let's get on to the main task at hand: downloading the images from your camera to your computer's hard disk. The first thing you need to do is run the application that handles basic digital camera tasks in Xandros—*Digikam*. To run Digikam, go to the **Launch** menu and select **Applications ▸ Graphics ▸ Digital Camera**. The first time you run Digikam, a window will appear asking you where you want Digikam to create the My Albums folder it will use to store your downloaded images (Figure 11-2).

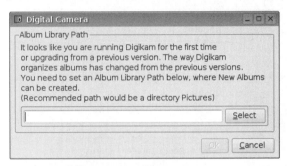

Figure 11-2: Digikam asks you where you want to store your images

A good place to store your digital images would be in the My Pictures folder that Xandros automatically sets up for you within your My Documents folder. To tell Digikam to use that folder, here's what you need to do:

1. Click the **Select** button, and a Select Folder window will appear.
2. In that window, locate the My Pictures folder in the file tree in the right pane of the window by clicking the + symbol next to the **My Documents** folder, and then click once directly on the **My Pictures** folder.
3. The folder will then be highlighted in blue, thus looking like the folder shown in Figure 11-3. When the folder is highlighted, click **OK**.
4. You will be back at the original window, which will now indicate the path to the folder you selected. Click **OK**, and the main Digikam window will appear.

11A-2: Getting Digikam to Recognize Your Camera

Now that Digikam knows where to store your images, let's move on to the even more important job of setting it up so that it knows what kind of camera you have.

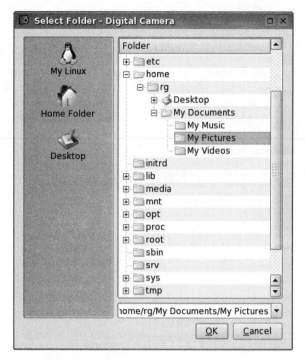

Figure 11-3: Selecting the folder in which to store your images

1. Go to the **Camera** menu and select **Add Camera**. The Configure window will appear (Figure 11-4).

2. At this point, power-on your camera, put it into Play mode (or whatever mode or setting your camera's manufacturer suggests for uploading images to your computer), and then click the **Auto-Detect** button in the Configure window. Digikam will then perform a hardware search in order to see what you have to offer it.

3. Upon finding your camera, Digikam will pop up a message like the one in Figure 11-5, specifying either the make and model or class of camera you have connected. When the window appears, click the **OK** button, and your camera will be listed in the Configure window. Once you see it there, click the **OK** button in that window as well, thus completing the setup process.

Figure 11-4: Getting Digikam to recognize your camera

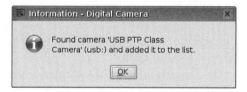

Figure 11-5: Digikam tells you when it has found your camera

11A-3: Downloading Images from Your Camera to Hard Disk

After everything is set up, the next logical step is to put Digikam to use by downloading (also referred to as *importing*) images from your camera to your hard disk.

Here's what you need to do:

1. Go to the **Camera** menu and select your camera, which will now be listed in the drop-down menu (mine says "USB PTP Class Camera"). Once Digikam finishes searching your camera's memory card, it will display the results in a new window (Figure 11-6).

Figure 11-6: Digikam displays the contents of your camera's memory card

At this point, however, the images are not yet on your hard disk, so don't pat yourself on the back just quite yet. You can now choose to download all of the images to your hard disk or to select and then download just the ones you want to keep.

2. To download all of the images to your hard disk, click the **Download** button at the bottom of the window, and then select **Download All** in the drop-down menu that appears. To download only the images you want, hold down the CTRL key, and then click once on each image you want to download. Once you have made your selections, release CTRL, click the **Download** button, and then select **Download Selected** in the drop-down menu.

Digikam will now offer up another window, Select Album (Figure 11-7), in which you are asked where you want to store your images.

The default location is the My Albums folder that Digikam automatically created for you earlier in this project (11A-1) when you specified where you wanted to save your images. The default location is just fine;

however, because eventually you will be adding many more photos, it is probably better to start organizing things from the get-go by creating a separate album for each collection you add.

Figure 11-7: Digikam checks where you want to save your images

3. To create a new album, click the **New Album** button, and a new window, New Album Name (Figure 11-8), will appear.

Figure 11-8: Creating a new album in which to save your images

4. In that window, type a name for your new album (a date or theme would be appropriate), and then click **OK**.

5. The new album will then appear in the original Select Album window as a subfolder of My Albums. Click **OK** in that window to get on with the download process.

6. Digikam will now begin downloading the images from your camera to your hard disk. During this time, it will show the progress of the download at the bottom of the results window (Figure 11-9). When the process is complete, the progress bar will disappear, and you can click the **Close** button and turn off your camera.

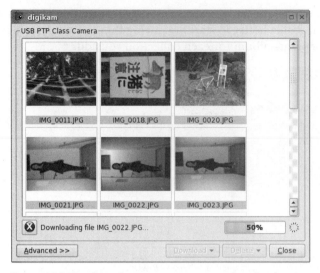

Figure 11-9: Digikam shows its progress as it downloads your images

11A-4: Viewing Your Downloaded Images

You will now be left with the main Digikam window, where you will *not* immediately see your images the first time around. To remedy this, click the drop-down button just below the menu bar that says *By Collection*, and in the drop-down menu that appears, select **By Folder**. Your new album will then appear in the left pane of the window under the *My Albums* heading. Click your new album once, and its contents will appear in the right pane of the window, as you can see in Figure 11-10.

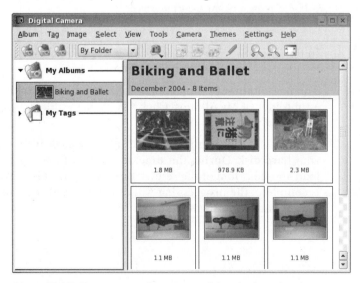

Figure 11-10: The contents of your new album displayed in the main Digikam window

Viewing Options

To view an image at a larger size, double-click it, and the image you chose will appear, slightly enlarged, in a separate window (Figure 11-11).

Figure 11-11: Viewing your images at an enlarged size

To see the image at a yet greater size, either click the maximize button in the three-button cluster located at the top-right corner of the window—it's the one in the middle—or just tug at one of the corners of the window with your mouse until it is the size you want. The image will then automatically enlarge. You can also easily see the other pictures in your album via this window by clicking the left or right arrow buttons just beneath the menu bar.

Project 11B: Fine-Tuning Your Images

Digikam is fairly versatile little program that not only lets you download and display your images but also allows you to fine-tune them. With Digikam you can rotate, resize, crop, and sharpen your images; adjust their brightness and contrast; and reduce red-eye, although the flash units in most digital cameras today pretty much eliminate the need for this feature. Digikam also allows you to transform your color photos into black-and-white or, for a taste of faux nostalgia, sepia tones. All very cool, assuming you go in for that kind of stuff. If you do, most of these manipulation features can be found in the Fix, Transform, and Filter menus of Digikam's enlarged-view windows that we discussed in Project 11A-4.

If you're curious about how to perform some of these basic digital darkroom transformations but don't know where to start, here is a project that can give you some hands-on experience. I'll be covering the most common of these: rotation, cropping, and brightness and contrast adjustments.

11B-1: Rotating Your Images

The most basic transformation you can perform, and at some point it is one that almost everyone needs, is rotation. After all, viewing an upright image sideways is a pretty annoying thing to do, all things considered. Fortunately, however, rotating an image is very easy. Here are the steps:

1. In the main Digikam window, double-click an image that you want to rotate.

2. After the image appears in its own window, go to the **Transform** menu and select **Rotate**.

3. In the menu that then pops out, select the number of degrees you want to rotate the image (90° if the image is lying on its left side, 180° if the image is upside down, or 270° if the image is lying on its right side). Once you release the mouse button, the image will have been rotated to the correct orientation, as you can see in the before-and-after images in Figure 11-12.

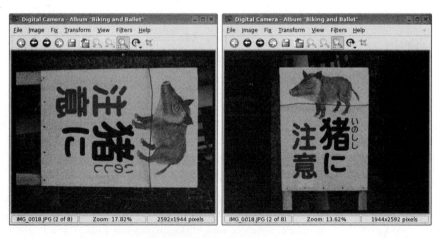

Figure 11-12: Sample image before and after rotation

4. Once you have finished, go to the **File** menu and select **Save**. If you prefer to keep a copy of the original in its unrotated state, select **Save As** instead, and then give the file a new name—but be sure to keep the original file extension.

11B-2: Free Rotation

In some cases, the problem with your image is not that it is sideways rather than upright (or vice versa), but rather that it looks somewhat cockeyed—a common problem with photos I take. Figure 11-13 is a good example: an off-kilter horizon, which really ruins what is an otherwise okay picture.

Figure 11-13: An otherwise fine image spoiled by an off-kilter photographer

To salvage this shot from the uninvited-criticism bin, we can use Digikam's free-rotation feature. If you have a similarly affected image, follow these steps to get things on an even keel:

1. As with all editing procedures, first double-click the target image in order to open it in its own window.

2. Once the window appears, go to the **Transform** menu and select **Free rotation** in the drop-down menu. A small window, Rotate Image (Figure 11-14), will then appear.

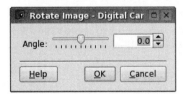

Figure 11-14: Free rotation settings

3. In that window, use the slider or the tiny up and down arrow buttons to adjust the number of degrees you want to rotate the image (negative numbers rotate the image to the left, and positive numbers rotate to the right).

4. Once you have selected your settings, click **OK** and the image will, after a second or so, rotate.

5. If the results are not to your satisfaction, go to the **File** menu, select **Revert** to get things back to the way they were originally, and then try rotating the picture again. As you can see, a little trial and error will most likely be necessary.

6. Once the image is the way you want it, go to the **File** menu and select **Save** or **Save As**, depending on whether or not you want to keep a copy of the original. Your image, allowing for differences in subject matter, should then look something like mine in Figure 11-15.

Figure 11-15: An off-kilter image rescued through free rotation

11B-3: Cropping

After looking at the image you've just rotated, or the example in Figure 11-15, you will realize that your image will have a lot of weird, unsightly, and decidedly off-balance black space at its edges. Needless to say, unless you like having it there because of a rather unique sense of aesthetics, that black space will have to go. For this chore you will need to do some cropping.

To crop an image in Digikam, follow these steps:

1. Place your mouse cursor in one of the corners within the picture area of your image (avoiding the black space), press the left mouse button, and then drag the cursor until it reaches the diagonally opposite corner and you have created a rectangle within the picture portion of the image.

2. When you have finished, release the mouse button, and then everything outside of the rectangle will darken, as you can see in Figure 11-16.

The bright area within the rectangle is what will be left of your image when you have finished the cropping process, while the darkened area outside the rectangle is what will be cropped. That being the case, if you have any black space remaining that still needs to be removed, try selecting the cropping area again. Just click anywhere in the image to deselect the area you've already selected, and then select the rectangular area you want again. This is also a good chance to do some after-the-fact adjustments in terms of composition.

Figure 11-16: Selecting the area to crop

Once the area you have selected is the way you want it to be, you are ready to take your digital scissors to your image and crop it.

3. Go back to the **Transform** menu and select **Crop**. The image will almost immediately be reduced to the area you selected. My own results can be seen in Figure 11-17. Yours should be somewhat similar.

Figure 11-17: The improved final product after rotation and cropping

4. If you are satisfied with the results, go to the **File** menu and select **Save** or **Save As**. If you still aren't satisfied with what you've done, select **Revert** in the **File** menu and start over again.

11B-4: Brightness and Contrast

Let's wrap up our experiment by playing around with the brightness and contrast settings. You surely have taken many a picture that was either overexposed (too bright) or even more likely, underexposed (too dark). In the film-camera world, a trip to your local photo processor (with fingers crossed and a bit of luck) is the only way to deal with this problem after the fact. Fortunately, it is much easier to correct the problem with your digital images. To follow along with this part of the experiment, select an overexposed or an underexposed image that you'd like to improve. For my part, I'll be working with the image shown in Figure 11-18.

Figure 11-18: Dealing with an underexposed image

To correct the brightness of your digital image, here's all you have to do:

1. Double-click the image that you want to fix.

2. Once the image opens up in its own window, go to the **Fix** menu and select **Color ▸ Brightness/Contrast/Gamma**.

3. In the new window that appears, adjust the brightness and contrast of your picture by moving the appropriate slider (Figure 11-19).

4. Once things are to your liking, click the **OK** button, and the changes will be visible in the original image window.

5. If you are satisfied, save your changes by going to the **File** menu, and . . . well, you know the drill by now.

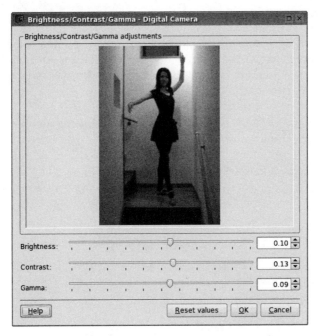

Figure 11-19: Adjusting the brightness and contrast of your image

Tags

Now that we've covered the basics of using Digikam with your camera and images, let's wrap things up with an introduction to one more of Digikam's interesting features: *tags*. In Project 11A, you set up Digikam to organize your images into albums, which are essentially folders in which your images are physically stored. Digikam, however, offers another way to further organize things, in the form of tags, which are essentially category indicators that allow you to view certain groups of pictures together without having to move them physically on your hard disk.

As an example, let's say that you have a daughter (let's call her "Colleen") whose pictures you have scattered throughout your various albums. By creating a "Colleen" tag and assigning that tag to each picture you have of her, you would then be able forever after, with just one or two clicks of the mouse, to see all of her pictures at the same time, though the location of those images on your hard disk would not have changed.

You can also assign more than one tag to any picture, thus allowing a picture to appear in different category groupings. For example, you might want to include your pictures of Colleen with pictures of other members of the family by further assigning those pictures of her an additional "Family" tag.

Creating a Tag

When you create a tag, you are actually creating a new category that you can assign to your photos. The default tags in Digikam are Events, People, and Places, which might be a bit too generic for your tastes or needs.

To create your own tag, follow these steps:

1. From the Digikam main window, go to the **Tag** menu and select **New Tag**. A new window will appear (Figure 11-20).

Figure 11-20: Creating your own tags

2. In that window, name your tag by typing the appropriate text in the *Title* box.

3. To give your tag an icon, click the blank square button next to the words *Set icon.*

4. In the icon browser window that appears, select an icon of your choice, and then click **OK**.

5. The icon you chose will now appear in the Create Tag window. Assuming it does, click the **OK** button in that window to complete the process.

Assigning Tags to Your Photos

Once you've created a tag or two of your own, you will have to assign them to your photos before you can reap any results or benefits. Here's how to do it:

1. Right-click a photo to which you want to assign a tag, and in the pop-up menu that appears select **Assign Tag**. Another submenu will then appear displaying the three default tags that come with Digikam and whatever tags you've created on your own, as you can see in Figure 11-21.

2. To complete the task, select the tag you want to assign to the photo, and you are finished. Now repeat the process for any other photos you want to add to the same tag group.

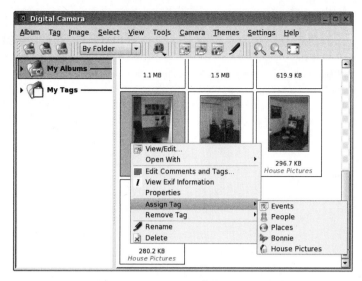

Figure 11-21: Assigning a tag to your photo

Viewing Your Images by Tagged Groupings

Okay, so you have finished assigning tags to your photos and want to see the results. To do this, go to the left pane of the main Digikam window and click on the small black arrow next to the word *Tags*.

A list of all existing tags will appear. When you click any of these tags, the images to which that tag has been assigned will appear in the right pane of the window (Figure 11-22). Of course, no images will appear if you haven't assigned the tag you clicked to any of your photos.

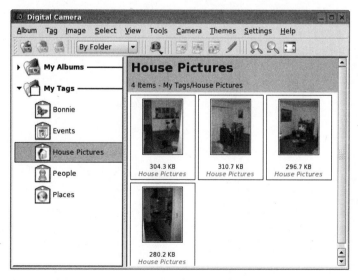

Figure 11-22: Viewing your images by tagged groupings

Moving Beyond

Now that you know how to work with your digital camera and scanner, you will be happy to know that in Chapter 16 you will learn how you can extend even greater control over your images by means of yet other applications that come with your Xandros distribution or are available via Xandros Networks. These include the simple, but highly capable, application *Paint* and the very popular image-editing and manipulation application *the GIMP*.

12

KEEPING TABS ON YOURSELF

Working with Your PDA

When Apple Computer released the first personal digital assistant (PDA), the Newton MessagePad, back in 1993, then-CEO John Scully saw it as the wave of the future. As things turned out, Scully was right; PDAs (often called *hand-helds*) eventually became as popular as chocolates on Valentine's Day. Only problem was that it wasn't the Newton that put PDAs on the map in terms of popularity. Although decidedly cool, the ahead-of-its-time, overpriced, oversized, initially underpowered, and definitely not-yet-ready-for-prime-time Newtons were soon outshone by the smaller, cheaper, and arguably easier-to-use PalmPilots from 3Com (see comparison in Figure 12-1). Yes, eventually it was a-chicken-in-every-pot-and-a-PalmPilot-in-every-pocket sort of world, with the Newton, despite having improved significantly through time, ultimately going the way of the pet rock and the Betamax (yup, I had one of those too).

Other makers would soon join in on the PDA boom by producing their own units, many of which are still being marketed today. These included series such as the Zaurus from Sharp, the CLIÉ from Sony, and the Visor from Handspring. The PalmPilot, however, remains the king of the hill in the world of PDAs.

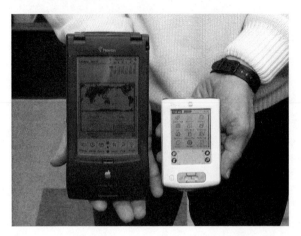

Figure 12-1: An Apple Newton MessagePad and a PalmPilot

But Can I Use My PDA with Xandros?

A friend of mine, who was thinking of switching over to Linux, recently said that one of the things holding him back was the fact that he wouldn't be able to use his PalmPilot if he were to make the switch. His reasoning was logical enough, as each PDA sold today comes with software that you can install on your computer to allow you to synchronize the data on your PDA with that on your computer. Such software disks contain Windows and usually Macintosh versions of the software, but nothing for Linux.

So, no software, no go, right?

Well, no. As I pointed out to my friend, that's just the way it always is with Linux. No matter what hardware device you buy, there is almost never a Linux version of the software for that device included. Instead, and quite fortunately, everything you need to run the device is usually contained within the Linux distribution itself. Such is the case with Xandros when it comes to PDAs. Xandros allows you to work right out of the box, so to speak, with many Palm OS–based PDA models and series including

- Handspring Visor and Treo
- Sony CLIÉ
- Samsung SCH 1300
- Garmin iQue 3600
- Palm M Series
- Palm 1705
- Palm Tungsten
- Palm Zire

The key to setting up your system to work with your PDA is an application called *Palm Pilot Tool*. It doesn't matter if your device is not a PalmPilot; as long as it is one of the models listed in the previous section (and that list could be larger by the time you read this), it will work. To get started, run the Palm Pilot Tool by heading over to the **Launch** menu and selecting **Applications ▸ Utilities ▸ Palm Pilot Tool**.

The first time you do this, a window will appear telling you that the application (also known as *KPilot*) is not yet configured for use (Figure 12-2). Click the **Use Wizard** button to move on to configuring it.

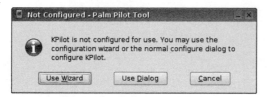

Figure 12-2: The Palm Pilot Tool tells you that it needs to be configured before use

At this point, the first page of the rather plain-looking configuration wizard will appear. Setting up your system to work with your PDA is actually a very simple procedure. Just follow these steps:

1. Before you do anything else, connect your PDA to your computer and power up the device.

2. Once your PDA is attached and powered up, you'll have to teach your system to find the device. You can most easily do this by clicking the **Automatically Detect Handheld & User Name** button in the first page of the wizard (Figure 12-3).

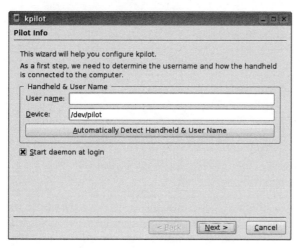

Figure 12-3: Helping your system find your PDA

3. A small window will appear telling you to place your PDA in its cradle and press the HotSync button. Your PDA is already attached to the computer, either by cradle or direct USB connection, so you have already fulfilled the first of these directives.

4. To fulfill the second directive in the message window, press the **HotSync** button on your PDA's cradle, or if you prefer, or just don't have a cradle, use your stylus to tap on the **HotSync** icon in your PDA's home page (left side of Figure 12-4), and then tap the **HotSync** icon again in the following screen (right side of Figure 12-4). Once you have done that, click the **Continue** button in the wizard's message window.

Figure 12-4: Starting HotSync on your PDA

5. The configuration wizard will then search your machine for a connected device, showing the progress of its search in a new window until it finds one. Once it does, click **OK** in that window (Figure 12-5).

Figure 12-5: The setup wizard displays the progress of its hardware search

6. You will now find yourself back at the window where you started, but this time around, the information in the two text boxes will have been completed, reflecting the results of the wizard's search (Figure 12-6). Click **Next** to proceed.

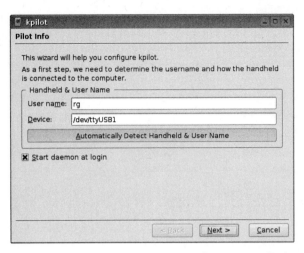

Figure 12-6: Hardware and user settings for your PDA displayed in the configuration wizard window

7. In the final page of the wizard (Figure 12-7), you are asked to choose the application you want to use for syncing purposes. Accept the default by clicking **Finish**.

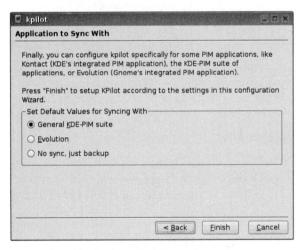

Figure 12-7: The final page of the configuration wizard

8. A small window will appear telling you that the process is complete. Click **OK** to close the window.

The Palm Pilot Tool application window will then appear, and it will try to sync with your PDA. At this point, however, your PDA will probably already have given up trying to sync, so go back to your PDA and tap the **HotSync** button again with your stylus. The synchronization process will begin again, during which time the Palm Pilot Tool will show, in the right pane of the window, a log of what's going on (Figure 12-8).

When the process is complete, you will see the words *HotSync Completed* near the end of the log file. There will also probably be another short string of messages after that saying that the Pilot device does not exist. You can ignore this last set of lines, as it is just the log of the Palm Pilot Tool giving another go at synching while your PDA itself is already done doing any more synching for now. You can also go ahead and disconnect it.

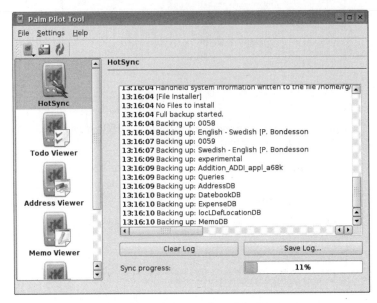

Figure 12-8: The Palm Pilot Tool shows a log of the HotSync process

Synching Forever After

Once you have set up your PDA to work with Xandros, you can perform a HotSync at any time, using the steps you have just learned. To make these steps easier to follow for future reference, I'll rehash and streamline them a bit here:

1. Connect your PDA to your computer.
2. Power up the PDA.
3. Run the Palm Pilot Tool by going to the **Launch** menu and selecting **Applications ▸ Utilities ▸ Palm Pilot Tool**.
4. Press the **HotSync** button on your PDA's cradle or tap the **HotSync** icon on your PDA's home screen and then again in the following screen.

If for any reason your PDA and computer don't sync, quit the Palm Pilot Tool (and its Panel applet), power down the PDA itself, and start over.

Personal Information Manager—Kontact

The Palm Pilot Tool is a handy application, but its real purpose is syncing. To add, edit, or delete data to later sync with your PDA, you should use the various KDE applications that are *conduits* to the categories of information on your PDA. This application group consists of Address Book, Organizer, KNotes, and (if your PDA does email) KMail.

Of course, using this application and that application to check one thing or another can get to be quite the proverbial pain. Rather than bother with all those bits and pieces, you can use the *Personal Information Manager* application, also known as *Kontact*, instead.

Kontact (Figure 12-9) acts as a centralized viewing and editing interface for the other four modules and also to one of the email applications on your system, *KMail* (which I won't be covering because Thunderbird is so much better). It's pretty good-looking to boot.

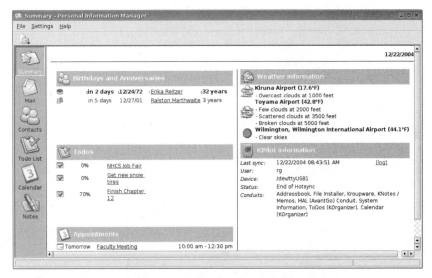

Figure 12-9: Personal Information Manager (Kontact) in Xandros

As you will see, Kontact provides you with a Summary view of all the important information you have stored on your PDA or computer (yes, you can use Kontact without having a PDA). It also warns you when birthdays and anniversaries are fast approaching, and it even tells you the weather conditions in as many cities as you set it up to show, though weather information is supplied by your Xandros system, not your PDA.

You can also easily navigate to the various application modules to input and examine data by clicking the icons in the left pane of the window.

Setting Up the Kontact Summary View Page

Kontact lets you customize the contents of its Summary View page. To add or remove categories from that page, go to the **Settings** menu and select **Configure Summary View**.

The Configure window for the Summary View page (Figure 12-10) consists of two panes: a right pane, which shows the items that can actually appear in the Summary View page, and a left pane, which, when clicked, allows you to configure some of the displayed items. To add an item to the Summary View page, check the box next to the item you want to add. Conversely, you can delete an item from the Summary View page by unchecking the appropriate box.

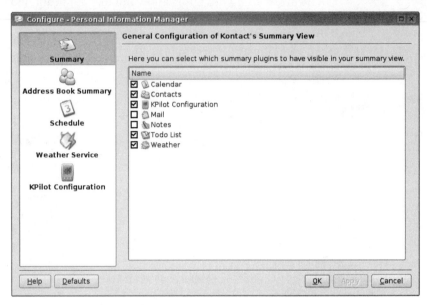

Figure 12-10: Configuring the Kontact Summary View page

I should mention at this point that one of the checked items in Figure 12-10, *Contacts*, may seem a bit bewildering, as it doesn't seem to appear in the actual Summary View page.

This was certainly the case for me. As I later discovered, however, Contact information is in fact displayed in that page in the form of Birthdays and Anniversaries, as this information is stored in the Address Book module, from which Contact information is gathered. This is the only information from the Address Book module that is displayed in the Summary View page.

Adjusting the Address Book Summary Display Settings

If you click the second icon in the left pane of the Summary View Configure window (**Address Book Summary**), you can adjust some of the basic settings for the Contacts, or Address Book, display module. Basically, you have very few options here: whether or not to show birthdays and/or anniversaries and how many days in advance those events should be displayed.

Adjusting the Schedule Summary Display Settings

To adjust the settings for the Schedule module of the Summary View page, click the **Schedule** icon in the left pane of the Configure window. From the settings that appear in the right pane of the window, you can decide how many days of schedule information should be displayed on the Summary View page, and which Todos, all or just those for today, should be displayed in the Todos section of that page.

Setting Up the Weather Summary Display

If you click the **Weather Service** icon in the left pane of the Configure window, you can set up the cities you want displayed in the Weather section of your Summary View page. You can do this via the right pane of the window by clicking the various + symbols in the subpane on the left until you reach the location you would like to add. Once you have found that location, click it once to select it, and then click the **Add** button.

The location will then appear in the subpane on the right (Figure 12-11). For example, if you wanted to add Karachi to your list of weather stations, you would click **+ Asia** ▶ **+ Pakistan** ▶ **Karachi**. You can, of course, add as many locations as you want to show up on the Summary View page.

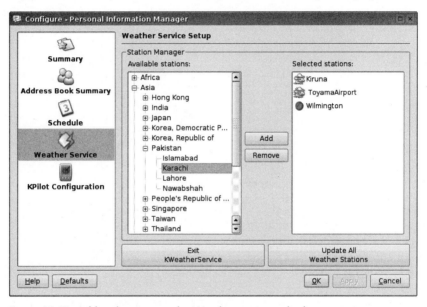

Figure 12-11: Adding locations to the Weather summary display

Using the Various Application Modules That Appear in Kontact

As I mentioned in the previous section, Kontact is really just a centralized environment from which you can view and edit data in a number of otherwise stand-alone applications, each of which can be started on its own via the **Launch** menu. The Address Book, for example, can be opened by selecting **Applications** ▶ **Accessories** ▶ **Address Book**. Because Kontact allows you to conveniently use all of these applications in one place, however, I will focus on using these applications via that framework.

The data in the various application modules in Kontact are all synced with that which you have on your PDA. When you input data into your PDA and then perform a HotSync, the data on your PDA will be copied to the respective application modules in Kontact. Conversely, when you input or edit data in one of Kontact's application modules and then perform a HotSync, the data or changes will be copied to your PDA. All very handy.

This does not mean, however, that you have to have a PDA in order to use Kontact or these modules. You will be happy to know that you can use all of them quite handily without ever joining the handheld fray.

To view, edit, or add data to your address book, click the **Contacts** icon in the left pane of the Personal Information Manager (Kontact) window.

When the Contacts module appears in the right pane of the window, you will see a list of your contacts; and if you click one of the entries in that list, a summary of the data you have saved for that entry will appear at the right side of the window (Figure 12-12).

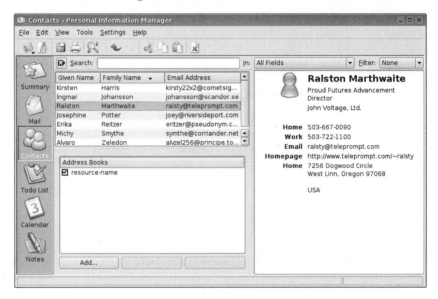

Figure 12-12: Using the Kontact Contacts module

To add a new entry to the address book, click the first icon in the horizontal icon bar below the menu bar, or select **New Contact** from the **File** menu.

An Edit Contact window (Figure 12-13) will appear in which you can input all the data you have. If you would like to input birthday or anniversary information so that it will appear in the Summary View page, click the **Details** tab, and then, once in that tab, enter the information in the appropriate boxes. When inputting birthday information, be sure to input the birth date (9-28-1958, for example), rather than the birthday (9-28).

If you would like to edit the information for a contact already in your address book, just double-click that contact's name from the list in the main page of the module, and the Edit Contact window for that entry will appear. Whether creating a new contact or editing the information for an existing contact, once you are finished, click the **OK** button.

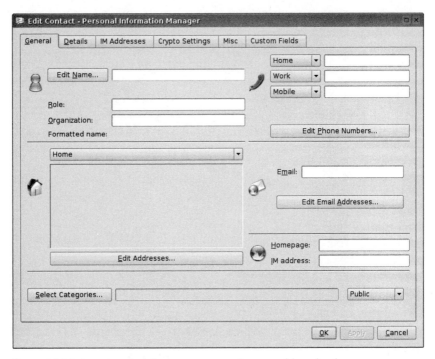

Figure 12-13: Inputting data for a new contact in your address book

Todo List

The Todo List (Figure 12-14), as its name implies, is a simple list of reminders for things that you need to do. You can open the Todo List module by clicking the **Todo List** icon in the left pane of the Kontact window.

When the module appears in the right pane of the window, you can add a new Todo item by clicking directly in the box that says **Click to add a new Todo** in light gray letters. After that, just type your new Todo in that same box, and press ENTER when you are finished. The new item will then appear in the list of Todos below.

If you look at the top of your actual Todo List, you will notice that it is divided into categories, such as Summary, Recursive, and Categories. You can do a bit of fine-tuning to your entry by right-clicking that entry below one of these categories and then choosing from the various options in the pop-up menu that appears (Figure 12-15).

The options listed in the menu will vary according to the category you clicked. To access all of the entries in one go, double-click the entry, and an Edit window for that entry will appear. If you would like to delete an entry from your Todo List, just right-click that entry within the Summary column, and then select **Delete** in the pop-up menu. You can also add new Todos or even sub-Todos from the same menu.

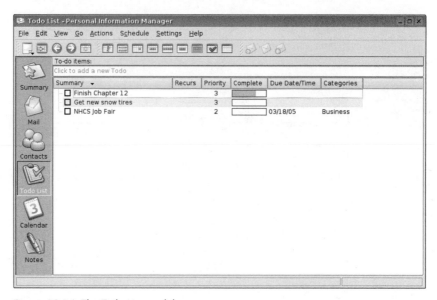

Figure 12-14: The Todo List module

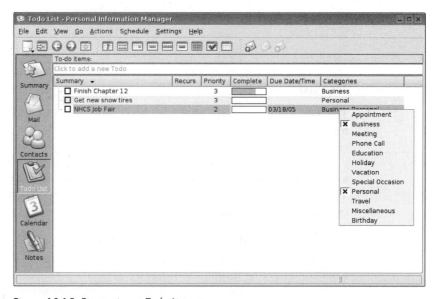

Figure 12-15: Fine-tuning a Todo List entry

Calendar

Tied in with the Todo List to some extent, and sharing the same set of icon buttons in its interface, is the Calendar module (Figure 12-16), which you can open by clicking the **Calendar** icon in the left pane of the Kontact window.

You can view your calendar in one of many views by clicking the various view buttons below the menu bar (Figure 12-17).

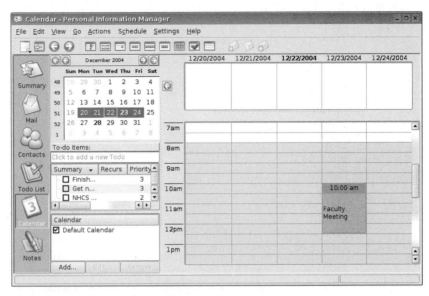

Figure 12-16: The Calendar module

Figure 12-17: The Calendar view buttons in the Calendar module

The views provided by these buttons, moving from left to right, are: *What's Next*, which actually shows the next dated items in your Todo list; *List*, which shows the times on your schedule in list form; *Day*, which shows a calendar view for that day; *Work Week*, which shows your schedule for the entire work week; *Week*, which shows the view for one calendar week; *Next 3 Days*, which provides a three-day view of your schedule starting with the current day; *Month*, which provides a somewhat-traditional one-month view of your calendar, starting with the current week; *Todo List*, which is the same list you dealt with in the previous section; and *Journal*, in which you can keep a daily journal or just jot down and read notes for any given day.

Adding or Editing an Event or Appointment to Your Calendar

Adding an event or appointment to your calendar is quite simple, and there are many ways to go about it. The easiest of these, in my opinion, is to switch to one of the multiday views (Month view is always good), and double-click the day for which you want to make an entry.

Upon doing this, a blank Edit Event window (Figure 12-18) will appear, in which you can provide the relevant details for the event. If you want to edit the details (such as the time or date) of an event you've already entered, you can do so by double-clicking that event in the calendar and then making the changes in the Edit Event window for that entry.

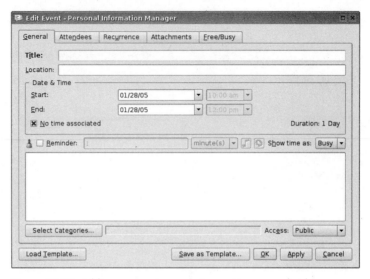

Figure 12-18: Adding an event or appointment to your calendar

Making or Reading a Journal Entry

If you would like to record your reflections or comments for a particular day, you can do so by creating a journal entry. You can do this by clicking the **Journal** view button and then clicking the date for which you want to create an entry in the calendar at the left part of the Calendar module.

A blank area will then appear to the right, in which you can type away. If you would like to make entries for multiple, successive days, just highlight the days in question in the calendar on the left, and a corresponding number of blank boxes will appear to the right. You can then make entries into all or some of those boxes (Figure 12-19).

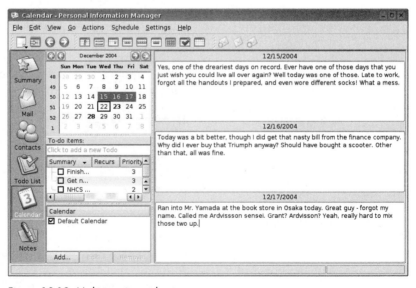

Figure 12-19: Making a journal entry

Notes

Clicking the last item, **Notes**, in the left pane of the Kontact window will bring up the Notes module (Figure 12-20).

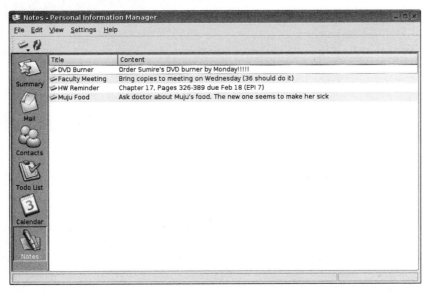

Figure 12-20: The Notes module in Kontact

To add a new note to the list, just click the icon below the **File** menu that looks like a pad of yellow Post-its (it's the one at the bottom). In fact, if you run this module as a stand-alone application (**Launch ▸ Accessories ▸ Popup Notes**), these notes will actually appear scattered about your desktop in that Post-it–like form. You can also add a new note directly from the **File** menu by selecting **New Note**.

Once you have chosen one of the two ways to create a new note, a small window will appear, in which you can give your note a title. Once you have done that, click **OK**, and another small window will appear in which you can write the note. Once you click **OK** in that window, the note will appear in the list within the main Kontact window. To delete a note from the list, just right-click the note you want to remove, and select **Delete** from the pop-up menu.

Installing Applications and Documents on Your PDA

One of the cool things about PDAs is that they are not static, closed systems, as they allow you to install and use third-party applications. There is a vast number of such applications available, especially for Palm OS (Palm Operating System)–based devices, ranging from games and puzzles to spreadsheets, learning tools, and databases (see examples in Figure 12-21). You can even install text documents converted to PalmDOC format (more on how to do that later) that you can then read on your PDA.

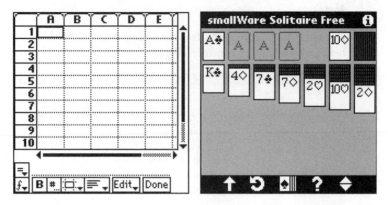

Figure 12-21: A third-party PDA spreadsheet application and solitaire game

To install an application for use with a Palm OS–based device, you must first download it from the Internet to your computer. There are many sites with freeware, shareware, and for-sale applications for Palm OS–based devices, such as www.freewarepalm.com. Files from such sites are usually prepared as ZIP archives, so once you download them, you must first upzip, or *extract*, them using one of the methods you learned in Chapter 5. After that, you can easily install the applications, or other files, on your PDA using the Palm Pilot Tool.

To do this, just follow these steps:

1. Run the Palm Pilot Tool (**Launch ▶ Applications ▶ Utilities ▶ Palm Pilot Tool**).

2. Click the last item in the left pane of the Palm Pilot Tool window, **File Installer**.

3. Next, click the **Add File** button in the right pane of the window, and in the Open window that then appears, locate and select your file.

4. Once you've done that, click the **Open** button, after which the Open window will close. The file you selected will then appear in the right pane of the Palm Pilot Tool window (Figure 12-22). You can also add additional files before syncing with your PDA.

Once all the files you want to install are visible in the Palm Pilot Tool window, you can install them by performing a HotSync with your PDA, as you learned to do earlier in the chapter. When the process is complete, the files will no longer be visible in the Palm Pilot Tool window.

You should note that application files for Palm OS–based devices end with a .prc extension, while the database files required by some applications end in .pdb, which is the same extension used for text documents prepared in the PalmDOC format. Before installing, it is always a good idea to check the contents of the ZIP file for the application you are planning to install in order to see if there is a README file included. The README file should tell you what files to install on your PDA in order to ensure that the application runs as it should.

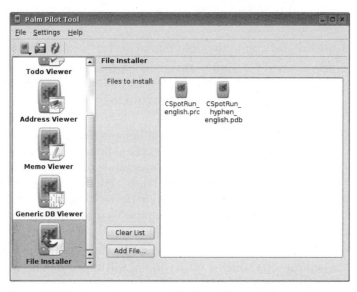

Figure 12-22: An application and database file ready for installation via the Palm Pilot Tool

Converting Text Documents to PalmDOC Format

As I mentioned in the previous section, you can also install text documents (ending in .txt), such as letters, reports, and even whole books, on your PDA. If you want to install a document that is not in text format, you must first save it as text. For example, if you wanted to install a really important email message you received from a colleague, you would first right-click the email message in your email application, select **Save As** in the pop-up menu, and then save it as *yourfilename*.**txt**.

Once you have the text file you want to install, you are just about ready to install it. First, however, you must convert the document to PalmDOC format in order to use it on your PDA. Your Xandros system comes with a special utility to do just that: *Palm Document Converter* (Figure 12-23). To run Palm Document Converter, go to the **Launch** menu and select **Applications ▸ Utilities ▸ Palm Document Converter**.

Figure 12-23: Palm Document Converter

To use the Palm Document Converter, here's what you need to do:

1. Click the icon to the right side of the text box next to the words *Text file*.

2. In the add file window that then appears, navigate to and select the text file you want to convert. Once you've done that, click **OK**, after which the window will close, and the path to the text file will appear in the previously empty upper text box.

3. Next, type in the path to and a filename for the converted file you are about to save in the bottom text box. Be sure to add the extension .pdb to the end of the filename. For example, if you would like to convert a text file called RalstyMessage.txt to a PalmDOC format file by the same name and have it appear in your Home folder, you would type /**home/** *your_username*/**RalstyMessage.pdb**. Your window should then look something like mine in Figure 12-24.

4. Once everything looks right, click the **Convert Text to PalmDOC** button, shortly after which a small window will appear telling you that the conversion was successful.

Figure 12-24: Text file ready for conversion to PalmDOC format

5. Finally, close that message window by clicking **OK**, and then close the Palm Document Converter window by clicking **Close**. Now you can install the new .pdb file on your PDA using the installation method you learned in the previous section of this chapter.

PART IV

APPLICATIONS

13

SURF'S UP

Internet Applications

Now that you've gotten your computer hooked up and online (we did it in Chapter 4), let's take a look at the various software tools you can use to take advantage of the situation. Xandros comes with a wide variety of Internet-oriented applications, with which you will be able to browse the Web, send and receive email, pass instant messages back and forth among your friends, and even make long-distance phone calls cost-free.

Surfing the Web with Firefox

The web browser that comes bundled with Version 3 of Xandros Open Circulation (OC), Surfside, and later releases of all other editions is the new and highly popular offering from Mozilla.org called *Firefox*. Firefox is making great inroads not only in the Linux world but the Windows and Mac worlds as well. In addition to being faster than the other popular browsers out there today, Firefox includes such features as tabbed browsing, pop-up window blocking, spyware prevention, and Live Bookmarks. Together, all of these help to make Firefox a really pleasurable browser to use. As *Forbes Magazine* put it, Firefox is "better than Internet Explorer by leaps and bounds." Can't beat that, eh?

NOTE *Firefox was not bundled with earlier releases of Xandros Standard, Deluxe, or Business Editions V3. If you are using either of those earlier releases but would like to join the fray, take advantage of Firefox's new features, and follow along with the rest of this book, then download and install Firefox now via Xandros Networks.*

Tabbed Browsing in Firefox

One of Firefox's nicest features is what is known as *tabbed browsing*. Tabbed browsing is not unique to Firefox, I admit, as it is a legacy carryover from its stablemate and immediate predecessor, the Mozilla browser—not to be confused with Mozilla.org, which is the creator of the two.

Tabbed browsing is also available, albeit in somewhat hidden form, in Apple's Safari browser and is now even available for Microsoft Internet Explorer as an add-on, even though the MS people for years insisted it was a feature in which their users were not particularly interested.

So what is tabbed browsing? Well, usually when you click a link in a web page, the new page opens in the same window as the one you were in. On some pages, links are coded so that the new page opens in a new, separate window, or maybe you occasionally opt for opening a link in a new window by right-clicking the link and then selecting the **Open Link in New Window** option. This can be very useful; once you have more than a few browser windows open at once, it gets sort of hard to find what you're looking for in them. It can also slow things down a bit on more challenged hardware systems as well.

This is where the tabbed browsing feature comes in handy. To see how it works, and to give Firefox's built-in search function a try at the same time, let's try it out right here and now.

Open Firefox by clicking the **Firefox** launcher on the Panel (or from the **Launch** menu, by selecting **Applications ▶ Internet ▶ Mozilla Firefox**), and then type **nyckelharpa** next to the Google logo in the text box at the top-right corner of the window (Figure 13-1).

Figure 13-1: Firefox's built-in Google search box

Once you've typed that in, press ENTER, after which the results of your search will appear in a familiar Google search results page.

In that page, right-click the top link (**ANA: The American Nyckelharpa Association**), and then in the pop-up menu, select **Open Link in New Tab** (see Figure 13-2). If it's not the first link, just read down the search results until you come to it. You won't have to look far.

Figure 13-2: Opening a link in a new tab in Firefox

After you have done this, the new page will appear in a new tab, and your original page of Google's search results will still be there, ready and waiting in the other tab (see Figure 13-3).

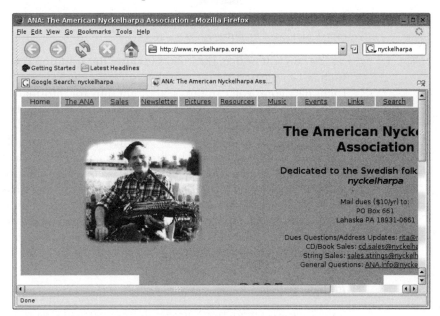

Figure 13-3: A link opened in a new tab in Firefox

I am pretty confident in saying that, once you get used to this feature, you will never miss your old browser.

By the way, if you aren't all that keen on right-clicking and fiddling around with drop-down menus every time you want to take advantage of Firefox's tabbed browsing function by opening a link in a new tab, you can achieve the same thing by clicking the link in question with *both* mouse buttons in unison.

More on Firefox's Built-in Search Feature

In the previous section, you performed a Google search using Firefox's built-in Internet search feature. Well, Google is not the only search engine you can use by means of this feature. In fact, if you click the tiny arrow next to the Google logo in that search box, you will see a whole list of other sites from which you can perform searches (Figure 13-4).

Figure 13-4: Firefox allows you to search for more than just websites

As you will notice, these sites include the traditional search engines, such as Google and Yahoo, as well as such sites as Amazon.com, eBay, and Dictionary.com. You can thus search not only for information or other websites via this handy feature, but also for books, goods, and even the meaning of words.

You will also notice an *Add Engines* item at the bottom of this menu. If you select that item, you will be directed to a page from which you can easily add still other engines. These include the ever-so-useful Wikipedia, Ask Jeeves, and IMDB (Internet Movie DataBase). You can add any or all of these (or the many others available from that site) to your search box list by clicking the link for the search plug-in that interests you. A small window will then appear. In that window, just click **OK**, and the plug-in for that search engine will be immediately added to your list.

In-page Searches

Sometimes you might want to search for a particular word within a certain page. To do this in Firefox, go to the **Edit** menu and select **Find in This Page**, or press the CTRL and **F** keys in unison.

What I have described so far is pretty much standard operating procedure in any browser, and you would probably expect a pop-up window to now appear in which to type the word you want to find. In Firefox, however, things are a tad different, and arguably more convenient, because instead of a search window, you will find a search bar at the bottom of the browser window (Figure 13-5).

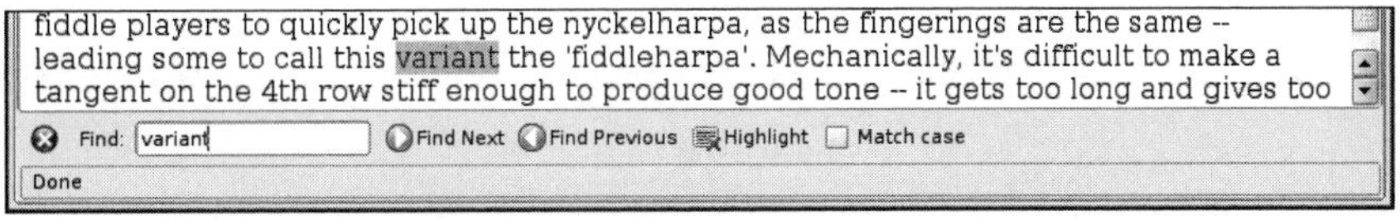

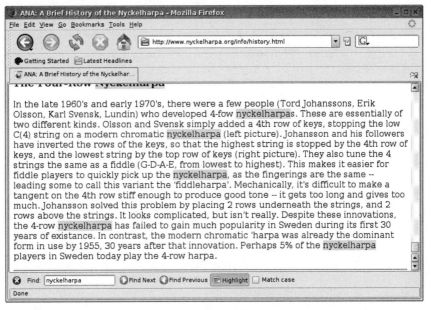

Figure 13-5: Performing in-page searches in Firefox

In that bar you can type whatever word you want to find, and as you are typing, and without pressing another key or clicking another button, Firefox will identify and highlight (in green) the first instance of that word within the document.

Another cool feature within the search bar is its highlight function. If you click the **Highlight** button in the lower search bar after typing in the word you're searching for, all instances of that word within the entire page will be highlighted in yellow (Figure 13-6).

Figure 13-6: Firefox can highlight every instance of the word you're searching for with a single click of your mouse.

When you want to de-highlight the words, simply click the **Highlight** button again, and voilà!

Firefox Popup Manager

Firefox also has a handy feature called the *Popup Manager*, which blocks those annoying pop-up windows that appear when opening certain sites. When you come to a web page that shoots out one of those windows, Firefox will display a banner across the top of the page, telling you that it has prevented a pop-up window from opening (Figure 13-7).

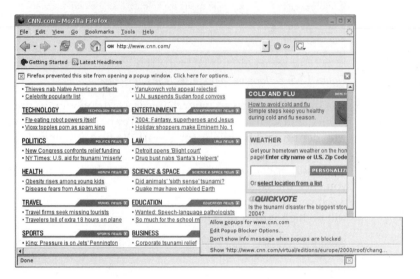

Figure 13-7: Firefox lets you know when it has blocked a pop-up window

It will also display a small icon with a red X in it at the bottom-right corner of the window (also shown in Figure 13-7). If you click either of these items, a pop-up menu will appear, from which you can tell Firefox to allow pop-ups from that site or tell it to let you view just the particular pop-up window in question. Of course, if you are happy with things the way they are and just want to leave the pop-up blocked, you can simply proceed as normal. You can close the top message *(Firefox prevented this site...)* by clicking the red square with a white X in it. Needless to say, this is an extremely useful, effective, and welcome feature.

Live Bookmarks in Firefox

Another cool feature in Firefox is *Live Bookmarks*. Live Bookmarks are essentially bookmarked collections of frequently updated items, such as for news headlines or blogs. Firefox already comes with one such Live Bookmark *(Latest Headlines)*, configured for BBC news, in its Bookmarks Toolbar, which is the bottom-most toolbar of the three located at the top of the window. Every time you click that bookmark button, a list of the most recent news headlines from BBC will appear in a drop-down menu, and clicking one of the links in that menu will bring you to the page for that particular story (Figure 13-8).

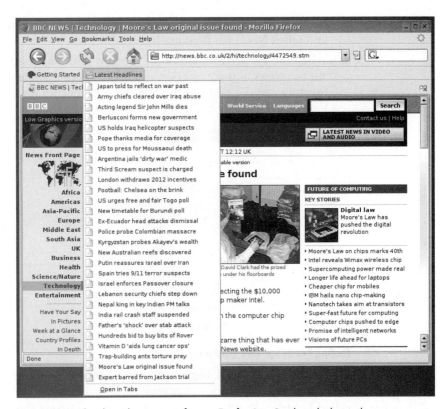

Figure 13-8: The drop-down menu from a Firefox Live Bookmark shows the most recent news headlines

Adding Your Own Live Bookmarks

You can, of course, add your own Live Bookmarks to Firefox for your favorite news feeds or blogs. Most of the URLs for such updated feeds usually contain rss somewhere in the address and end in .xml or .rdf, though you might not always be able to see this ending. For example, the URL for Yahoo News is http://news.yahoo.com/rss/topstories, while the URL for a Live Bookmark is http://rss.news.yahoo.com/rss/topstories. To provide another example, to view Television Without Pity (a site that keeps you up-to-date with your favorite TV shows) in your web browser, you would type **www.televisionwithoutpity.com**, while you would you use **www.televisionwithoutpity.com/rss.xml** in order to set up a Live Bookmark for the site.

NOTE   *If you punch either of the Live Bookmark URLs into your web browser, you will get a page of code that will most likely be of little meaning to you. These URLs are instead used only when setting up Live Bookmarks and are not intended for typical browsing.*

If you want to add a Live Bookmark for one of these feeds, here's what you should do, and I'll use Yahoo News as my example:

1. Go to the **Bookmarks** menu, and select **Manage Bookmarks**.

2. In the Bookmarks Manager window that appears, go to the **File** menu and select **New Live Bookmark**.

3. When the Properties window for the new Live Bookmark appears, type **Yahoo! News** in the *Name* box and **http://rss.news.yahoo.com/rss/ topstories** in the *Feed Location* box. Your Properties window should then look much like that in Figure 13-9. If so, click **OK**.

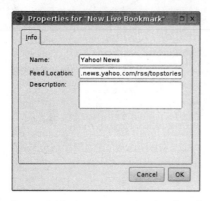

Figure 13-9: Setting up a Live Bookmark of your own

Finding Feeds for Live Bookmarks

Well this is all very cool, but you are probably wondering where you can find feeds that match your personal interests. A good place to start is a site called Feedster. By going to Feedster's Feedfinder page (http://feedfinder .feedster.com), you can type a keyword for the area you are interested in, and you will be presented with a list of results showing all of the available feeds that are relevant to your topic area.

To show you what to do then, let's use Chinese pop star Faye Wong as an example. If you want to search for someone or something else, feel free to make appropriate substitutions if you are going to follow along.

Anyway, here's what to do:

1. Go to http://feedfinder.feedster.com.

2. Type **Faye Wong** in the *Feedfinder* search box, and then click the **Find Feeds** button.

3. In the page of results that appears, click one of the links that sounds the most appropriate to you. When that page appears, there will be a small orange icon in the bottom-right corner of the window (Figure 13-10). The icon's appearance will vary according to the theme you are using.

Figure 13-10: Firefox lets you know when you can create a Live Bookmark for a site

4. If the page seems to be what you are looking for, click that orange icon, and select **Subscribe to...** in the pop-up menu.

5. In the Add Bookmark window, select the location where you would like the bookmark to appear. If you want it to appear in the Bookmarks menu, accept the default location (**Bookmarks**), but if you want it to appear in the Bookmarks Toolbar, change the location in the *Create in* box to **Bookmarks Toolbar Folder** (Figure 13-11).

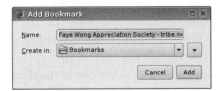

Figure 13-11: Telling Firefox where to create your new Live Bookmark

6. Once you've made your decision, click **Add** to finish the job.

Managing Bookmarks

Anyone who does a lot of web surfing ends up with numerous bookmarks for their favorite sites. Over time, however, you end up with so many that they become somewhat hard to manage. Perhaps you would find it helpful to group some of them together, or maybe you want to rename some so that they are easier to recognize, or maybe you would just like to delete some altogether. Well, you can do all of this via the *Bookmarks Manager* (Figure 13-12). To get started, open the Bookmarks Manager by going to the **Bookmarks** menu and selecting **Manage Bookmarks**.

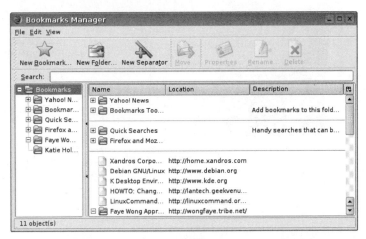

Figure 13-12: Organizing you bookmarks via the Firefox Bookmarks Manager

Grouping Bookmarks Together

You can group bookmarks of a common theme together by creating a new folder and then placing all of the relevant bookmarks within it. For example, let's say that you do a lot of online shopping and thus have numerous bookmarks for the sites with which you do business. In that case, you could create a new folder called Shopping and then drag all of your shopping sites into it.

Here's how to do it:

1. Click the **New Folder** button.
2. When the Properties window for the new folder appears, type **Shopping** in the *Name* box, and then click **OK**.
3. Press the CTRL key, and then click each of the bookmarks related to online shopping in the right pane of the Bookmarks Manager window.
4. Release the CTRL key, and then click—but don't release—any one of the highlighted bookmarks in the right pane. Once you have done that, drag the bookmarks to the new **Shopping** folder in the left pane. Now you can release the mouse button.
5. If you now go to the **Bookmarks** menu in the main Firefox window and select the **Shopping** folder in the left pane, you will see all of your shopping sites nicely arranged together in a pop-out submenu (Figure 13-13).

Figure 13-13: Grouping related bookmarks together in their own folder

Moving a Bookmark or Group of Bookmarks to the Bookmarks Toolbar

Sometimes, when you use a particular bookmark quite frequently, it is more convenient to have it located in the Bookmarks Toolbar than in the Bookmarks menu. In this way, your bookmark is always visible to you and thus only one mouse click away whenever you need it—no scrolling and searching through long menus.

To add a bookmark to the Bookmarks Toolbar, find the bookmark you want to relocate in the right pane of the Bookmarks Manager window, and drag it to the **Bookmarks Toolbar** folder in the left pane. A perhaps even easier way of going about things is to click the icon at the very left end of the URL for the page you're viewing, drag it to the **Bookmarks Toolbar**, and then release the mouse button. The bookmark will immediately appear in the toolbar.

Renaming a Bookmark or Bookmarks Folder

Occasionally one of your bookmarks might be so named that it is impossible to find when you are looking for it. For example, my bookmark for Town and Country Real Estate appears merely as *Home Page*, which is pretty useless as is. To change this state of affairs, or any like it, find and click the file you want to rename in the right pane of the Bookmarks Manager window, or a folder in either pane, and then click the **Rename** button. You can then type the new name for the bookmark or folder in the *Name* box of the Properties window.

Deleting a Bookmark

When a bookmark is no longer of use to you, and just sits there wasting space, you easily can delete it by clicking it once to select it, and then clicking the **Delete** button.

Saving and Transferring a Copy of Your Bookmarks

Friends often ask me how they can save and transfer their bookmarks from one computer to another. Fortunately, this is easy to do once you know how. First, save the bookmarks on the original machine by going to Firefox's **File** menu, selecting **Export**, and then in the Export bookmark file window, giving your collection of bookmarks a meaningful name in the *File name* box, such as **homebookmarks.html**. Just be sure to keep the .html extension when you do your renaming. Once you have done that, your bookmarks will saved as an HTML file, the same format as a web page.

After you have saved your bookmarks, transfer the HTML file to the other machine by floppy, CD, flash drive, or whatever you prefer. Once it is in place in the other machine's Home folder, open Firefox on that machine and then its Bookmarks Manager. Select **Import** from the Manager's **File** menu. In the window that appears, select **From File** and click **Next**. You will then see an Import bookmark file window, and in that window, find your bookmark file. Click on it once to select it, and then click **Open**. Your old bookmarks will then be nicely in place on your other computer.

Firefox Themes

An arguably less useful, albeit more fun, feature of Firefox is that it lets you change its appearance, to varying degrees, through the use of themes. As you can see in the samples shown in Figure 13-14 these themes may merely consist of a different set of buttons in the Navigation Toolbar or a more total and dramatic change in appearance incorporating changes in the buttons, sliders, and background color.

Figure 13-14: Firefox themes

There is only one theme, called *Plastikfox Crystal SVG*, included with the copy of Firefox in your Xandros distro. If you would like to add a few more themes, however, here's what you need to do:

1. Go to the Firefox **Tools** menu and select **Themes**.
2. In the bottom-right corner of the Themes window that appears, click the **Get more themes** link. Mozilla's Firefox Themes site will then appear in your browser.

3. On that page, click any of the themes listed, and a new page with a sample of that theme will open (Figure 13-15).

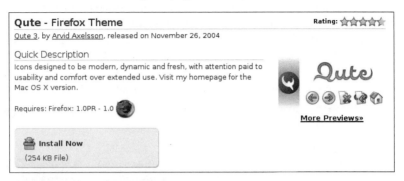

Figure 13-15: Viewing samples of Firefox themes on the Web

4. Once you find a theme you like, click the **Install Now** link on the sample page for that theme.

5. A confirmation window will appear. Just click **OK** in that window, and the download and the installation of the theme will begin.

The progress of the download and installation process will be shown in the left side of the Themes window, which will suddenly reappear. Once the installation is complete, the name of the theme and an icon for it will replace the progress bar (Figure 13-16).

Figure 13-16: Selecting themes from the Firefox Themes window

To use one of the themes you've installed, click the name of the theme in the left pane of the Themes window, click the **Use Theme** button, and then restart Firefox.

The Xandros File Manager as an Internet Application?

You may be surprised to discover that you actually have yet another web browser bundled with your system, and you will probably be even more surprised by what it is. Yes, the Xandros File Manager (XFM) that you learned to use in Chapters 5 and 6 can also act as a web browser. If you find this hard to believe, go ahead and try it out yourself. Just type a URL in the *Address* box at the top of the XFM window, press ENTER, and there you have it (Figure 13-17).

Figure 13-17: The Xandros File Manager doubles as a web browser

Now, I should say that XFM's role as a web browser does have its limitations, especially in regard to the availability of plug-ins, but it can come in handy for quick views of a certain page or for performing quick online searches, and so on. Play around with it, and see what you think. It should be pretty intuitive in terms of usage, so I won't bog you down with redundant details.

Project 13A: Email with Thunderbird

There are two email clients that come bundled with your Xandros system, but the one that is all the rage these days is Mozilla.org's *Thunderbird*.

Thunderbird, in terms of look and feel, is essentially very similar to Windows' Outlook Express, as you can see in Figure 13-18, but it's actually much better. One of the reasons for this claim is that Thunderbird isn't susceptible to the myriad of viruses that perpetuate themselves in the Windows world via the Outlook and Outlook Express address books. It also has a built-in junk-mail filter that helps you cope with that most unwelcome variety of mail—spam. Like Firefox, Thunderbird also allows you to expand its versatility through the installation of various extensions. And if you want to dress it all up a bit, you can even change its appearance though the use of skins. All very cool!

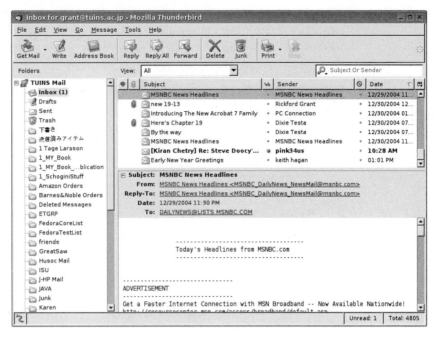

Figure 13-18: Thunderbird

NOTE   *Thunderbird was not bundled with earlier releases of Xandros Standard or Deluxe Editions V3, so if you are a Thunderbird-less user of those releases and would like to download and install Thunderbird, you can easily do so via Xandros Networks.*

13A-1: Setting Up an Email Account in Thunderbird

When you first run Thunderbird, you will be presented with an *Account Wizard* (Figure 13-19), with which you can easily set up your email account.
Here are the steps to do just that:

1. In the first page of the wizard, select **Email account**, and click **Next**.

2. In the second page of the wizard, type the name you would like to appear in the From field of your email messages (in the *Your Name* box) and your email address (in the *Email Address* box). Once you've finished, click **Next**.

3. In the third page of the wizard, select the type of account you are creating, **POP** or **IMAP** (most home accounts are POP, but if you want to be sure, ask your Internet provider). Then type the name of the incoming server and outgoing server in the appropriate boxes. This information should also have been supplied by your Internet provider; if you don't have it, give them a call. When you have finished, click **Next**.

NOTE   *In case you were wondering, a* POP *account is a traditional email account in which new email is downloaded from your provider's mail server and onto your computer. The mail is automatically removed from the server when you download it and thus exists only on your computer, from which you can read it at any time. In* IMAP *accounts,* *the mail resides on the server, and your computer thus acts only as a viewer of sorts. The advantage of this is that you can access and see all of your mail from any computer that connects to the mail server. On the negative side, if your provider's mail server is down for any reason, you cannot read any of your mail.*

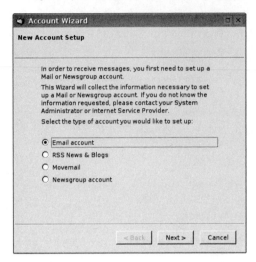

Figure 13-19: The Thunderbird Account Wizard

4. In the next page, type the username for your mail account as instructed by your Internet provider. This is generally not the same as the username you use when logging in to your system. It could be something as simple as your last name or something more complex in appearance, such as **MyCleverEmailName@MyInternetProvider.com**. Click **Next** when finshed.

5. In the next page of the wizard, name your account. This name can be whatever you want it to be, but it should be a meaningful way of differentiating this account from any others you might use now or in the future. A good choice is to your use your name and that of your provider. Thus, for example, if your name is Jack, and your provider is telepathy.com, you might type **Jack's Telepathy Mail**. Once you've named your account, click **Next**.

6. In the final page of the wizard, you will be shown a rundown of everything you have typed thus far. If everything looks right, click **Finish**.

7. If you have set up an IMAP account, you will then be immediately queried for your mail password. If you have set up a POP account, this won't happen until you click the **Get Mail** button in the main Thunderbird window. Whatever your particular case might be, once queried, type your mail password (per your provider's instruction), and then click **OK**.

13A-2: Sending and Receiving Attachments in Thunderbird

One question I am often asked by compu-novices and casual compu-users is how to deal with email attachments. *Attachments*, in case you don't know, are files, such as photos, word processor or spreadsheet documents, compressed archives (such as ZIP files), and even music files, that are sent attached to an email message (hence the name).

Attachments are a very convenient way of sending such files to others, but, unfortunately, they are also a common way of spreading viruses. Although, as a Linux user, you are pretty safe from the viruses that are out there in the world today, a bit of caution is always a good thing. That said, before moving on to the subject of dealing with attachments, let me first lay down some basic ground rules you should follow when dealing with them, regardless of the system you happen to be using.

Here they are:

- Don't open or save attachments if you don't know the sender.

- Don't open or save any attachment that ends in .pif, .scr, or .exe, as these are the most common forms in which viruses are masked and sent. There should be little reason for anyone to be sending you these kinds of files anyway.

- If you do receive attachments of this sort (.pif, .scr, or .exe) from senders you know, don't assume that person is deliberately sending you viruses. As I mentioned earlier, many viruses spread themselves by searching through Windows users' Outlook address books and then mailing copies of themselves to all of the contacts listed therein. A person's computer might thus be sending out hundreds of virus-infected emails without the person knowing it is doing so. If you receive email with such attachments from someone you know, let them know so; their system might be infected. Of course, since such files are created to infect Windows systems, they shouldn't do yours any harm, but still it is best to avoid them.

- Don't open or save any attachment of which you do not recognize the file extension. Most files you receive should end in familiar extensions, such as .jpg, .png, .gif, .sxw, .swc, .doc, .xls, .mp3, and .ogg. Again, even if you recognize the extension, don't open or save the attachment if you don't recognize the sender because virus authors are always finding new ways to worm their creations into your system, even via .jpg files.

- If you receive an email attachment from someone you know, but it, or the email itself, seems suspicious, check with the sender before opening or saving the attachment so as to make sure that the sender did indeed intend to send it.

- Always be suspicious of files attached to mail forwarded to you. Check with the sender first before opening or saving the attachment, and even then be wary. After all, even though you know who forwarded the attachment to you, you can't be too sure where it came from in the first place.

- If the title of an email contains the word "virus," even if it is from someone you know, then it is probably best to be suspicious of it also. After all, even if a message titled "Help, I think I've got a virus!" is legit, it would indicate that the sender's system is infected, right?

Okay, so now that I've hopefully instilled a useful level of paranoia in you, let's get on to dealing with legitimate, nonviral attachments, starting with opening and saving those that you receive.

Opening and Saving Received Attachments

When you receive an attachment, you'll know because the title of the mail will have a small paper-clip icon next to it (Figure 13-20).

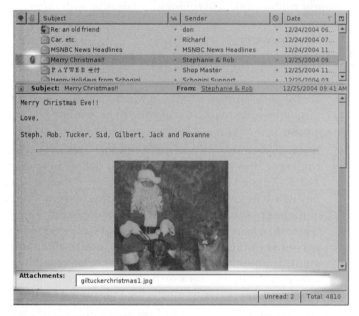

Figure 13-20: Thunderbird lets you know when you have received an attachment

In addition, a small box will appear at the bottom of the email message in an *Attachments* box, displaying the name of that attachment, as you can also see in Figure 13-21. If the attachment is a graphics file, such as a digital photo, the image will also appear within the email message area.

You have two ways to deal with the attachment, both of which involve right-clicking the filename in the Attachments box at the bottom of the window. When you do this, a pop-up menu will appear, and from that menu you can select either **Open**, after which a window will appear asking you which application to use in order to open the attachment, or **Save As**, which is the preferred method. When you select **Save As** in the pop-up menu, the attachment will be saved to your hard disk, from which you can do with it as you see fit. Of course, if the attachment is just a picture, you can just view it in the message area and leave it at that if you have no interest in saving it for future viewing or use.

Sending Attachments

If you want to send your own attachment, simply click the **Attach** button in the Compose window for the email message you are writing, and then navigate to and select the file you want to attach in the Attach File window that appears. If you would like to attach more than one file, you can do so by holding down the CTRL key and then selecting each of the files you want to attach (Figure 13-21).

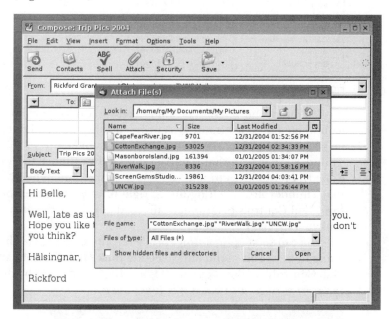

Figure 13-21: Sending email attachments in Thunderbird

When you have finished making your selections, release the CTRL key (if you were selecting more than one file), click the **Open** button, and the files will then be attached to your email message. Once you send that mail, the job will be done.

13A-3: Dealing with Spam in Thunderbird

Well, if you are anything like the millions of other email users in the world today, you are probably deluged every week with hundreds of unwanted and uninvited email messages announcing that you qualify for a mortgage, offering you low-cost prescription drugs, telling you how you can get an online degree, or advising you where you can meet singles in your area. Yes, such are the wonders of the greatest nuisance foisted upon society since the heyday of telemarketers: *spam*.

Fortunately, Thunderbird helps reduce the annoying effects of spam by means of its *Junk Mail Controls* feature. Thunderbird's Junk Mail Controls feature is essentially an adaptive filter that tries to determine which of your email messages are spam. At first, it is none too clever and marks many a good message as junk, while leaving some junk messages as is. You will know when Thunderbird has marked a message as junk by the trash can icon in place next to the sender's name in the list of email messages within the main window (Figure 13-22).

Rena Gill	01/01/2005 09:47 PM
Latisha Gunter	01/01/2005 09:50 PM
Everett Naquin	01/01/2005 09:53 PM
Daniel	01/01/2005 10:22 PM
Secret Admirer	01/01/2005 10:24 PM
Harry	01/01/2005 10:47 PM
Rickie .	01/01/2005 11:04 PM
Cancun Vacation	01/01/2005 11:30 PM
Bonnie	01/01/2005 11:44 PM
Reyes Rubin	01/02/2005 12:16 AM

Figure 13-22: Marking or unmarking messages as junk

If Thunderbird has made a mistake, you can correct it by clicking the icon when a message is not junk or by clicking the small dot icon if the message should be marked as junk (also seen in Figure 13-23). Through time, Thunderbird learns what is junk and what isn't (hence the *adaptive* bit I mentioned), eventually getting it right most of the time. When you are satisfied that Thunderbird is getting things right most of the time, you can set up the Junk Mail Controls to automatically load any incoming email deemed to be junk in a special Junk folder.

You can set it up to automatically reroute such mail to the Junk folder by going to the **Tools** menu and selecting **Junk Mail Controls**. When the Junk Mail Controls window appears (Figure 13-24), click the box next to *Move incoming messages determined to be junk mail to:*.

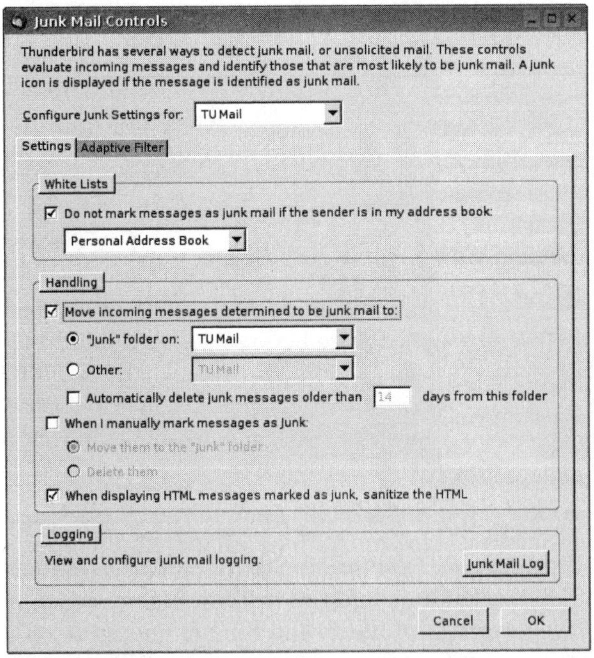

Figure 13-23: Setting up Thunderbird to automate the junk-mail-handling process

The other settings should already be correct, so just click the **OK** button, and your world, at least the world of your inbox, will become a much happier and less-cluttered place.

Of course, spam from new sources will arrive from time to time, so you might still have to mark certain items manually as junk. When you do that, from this point on however, those messages will be automatically moved to the Junk folder. It is also a good idea to check through the Junk folder before trashing its contents—just to make sure that no good messages are inadvertently being placed there.

13A-4: Using Folders in Thunderbird

When you receive a lot of mail from a particular sender, it can be useful for you to set up a folder for that sender. This is especially handy if you happen to subscribe to one or more mailing lists, whose string of messages can quickly fill up your inbox. Just go to the **File** menu and select **New ▸ New Folder**. After that, a small window will appear in which you type in a name for the folder and then click **OK**. The folder will then appear in the left pane of the Thunderbird window. Once the folder is in place, you can simply drag all the email that falls under the category you've just created into the folder.

A still easier way to do this is by typing the name of the sender or group in question in the search box near the top-right corner of the window. Once you do that, only the messages matching that entry will appear in the list of email messages below (Figure 13-24).

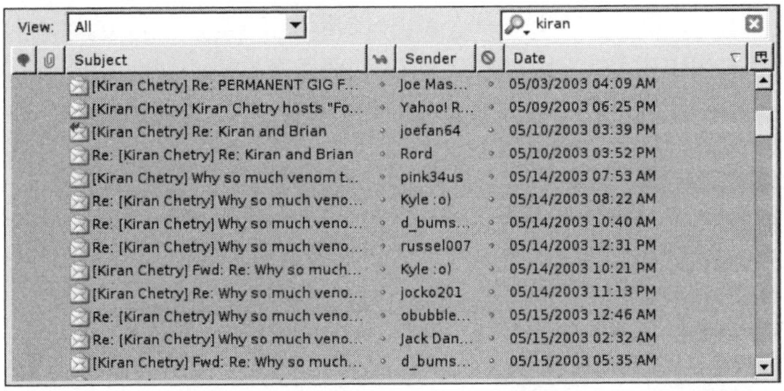

Figure 13-24: Finding and moving mail of a certain type in Thunderbird

If you then click one of the messages in the list, and choose **Select ▸ All** in the **Edit** menu, you can easily select all of these messages in one go. Dragging them to the new folder thus becomes a much easier chore, as all you have to do is click any one of the now-highlighted messages and drag the whole lot into your new folder.

13A-5: Creating a Message Filter in Thunderbird

If you would like to automate things a tad so that certain messages are automatically loaded to your new, or some another, folder in the future, you can create a message filter. To do this, start out by going to the **Tools** menu and selecting **Message Filters**. Once the Message Filters window appears, click the **New** button, which will bring up the Filter Rules window, shown in Figure 13-25.

In that window, here's what you have to do:

1. In the uppermost text box, give your new filter a name.

2. In the same window, choose a surefire way to distinguish the messages that you would like to be automatically loaded into the folder upon arrival. For example, let's say that you created a folder for one of the mailing lists to which you belong. The subject lines of most mailing-list messages are preceded by the name of the list in brackets, such as [Music Lovers] or [Faye Wong List]. Since this is consistent for all mail from the list and is not likely to appear in any of your other email messages, it would be a good candidate for this purpose. That being the case, in the top pane of the Filter Rules window you would select **Subject** in the first drop-down menu, select **contains** in the second, and then in the adjacent box type the bracketed name of the list.

3. In the bottom pane of the window, select **Move to folder**, and then, via the drop-down menu in the middle of the pane, select the folder to which you want the mail moved. In the case of this example, you would be selecting the folder you just created in Project 13A-4.

4. Your Filter Rules window would then look something like that in Figure 13-25. If so, click **OK**. The Filter Rules window will then close, and your new filter will appear in the list of filters within the Message Filters window, which you can then close. Now all of the mail you receive in the future from the person or group specified in your new message filter rule will be automatically rerouted to that folder.

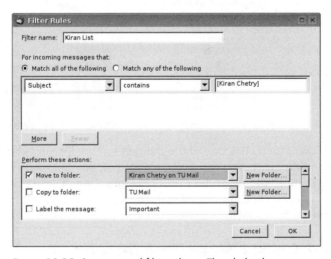

Figure 13-25: Setting email filter rules in Thunderbird

More on Security

Since I've just discussed protecting yourself from email-borne viruses in the previous section, it is worth mentioning at this point that there are some other security features available in various editions of Xandros to help protect you from other network/Internet–related dangers. In addition to the ability to encrypt Home folders, which I mentioned in Chapter 7, the Xandros Surfside Linux and Business Editions have built-in antivirus software (though viruses are not yet much of a problem in Linux world), while the Deluxe, Surfside Linux, and Business Editions have a handy firewall configuration wizard (**Launch ▸ Applications ▸ Internet ▸ Firewall Wizard**), which helps you set up a personal firewall to ward off online intruders. This is especially useful for those with an always-on network or Internet connection.

Project 13B: Instant Messaging (Kopete)

If you are fond of instant messaging, you'll be glad to know that Xandros is ready to serve your needs with its *Instant Messaging* application, also known as *Kopete*. It doesn't matter whether you usually use MSN/Windows Instant Messenger, Yahoo Messenger, AOL Instant Messenger (AIM), or ICQ; Kopete can handle them all. In fact, it can handle all of them at the same time, a really big plus.

Now some of you might not know what instant messaging is, so I'll fill you in before moving on. Basically, *instant messaging* is a service provided by a number of companies (such as those I've just mentioned) that allows you to communicate with your friends or acquaintances online via instant text messages. Once you create an account, you add contacts of people you know who also have accounts of their own. Then, you're ready to go. When any of your contacts are online, Kopete will let alert you, while their instant messaging software will also let your contacts know that you are online. Now you can all contact one another via real-time text messages. The typed conversation that you and your contacts have is displayed in a separate window.

As you can see in Figure 13-26, the conversation looks something like a script. In short, it's sort of like talking on the phone, but instead of talking you're typing. All very fun and handy.

13B-1: Setting Up Kopete

You can run Kopete by going to the **Launch** menu and selecting **Applications ▸ Internet ▸ Instant Messaging**. The first time out, Kopete will bring up its Configure window, in which you can set up an account for each of the services with which you are registered. If you aren't already registered with a messaging service, you will also be able to create one. Get started by clicking the **New** button, and Kopete's Add Account Wizard will appear (Figure 13-27).

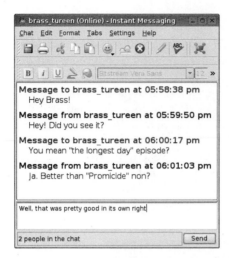

Figure 13-26: Kopete displays a running transcript of your real-time text conversation

Figure 13-27: Kopete's Add Account Wizard

1. In the first page of the wizard, just click **Next**, as there is nothing else for you to do.

2. In the second page (Figure 13-28), select the messaging service for which you want to set up an account by clicking it once and then clicking **Next**. You can add other accounts later, if you wish. If you haven't already registered with the messaging service you've selected, you can do so at this point by clicking the **Register New Account** button.

3. In the third page, enter your account information. For example, if you have an MSN account, you would type in your MSN mail address. If you select *Remember password* (a good idea, in my opinion), you must then also type your password for that messaging service (Figure 13-29). When finished, click **Next**.

Figure 13-28: Selecting the type of account
you wish to set up in Kopete

Figure 13-29: Inputting account information
in the Kopete Add Account Wizard

4. In the final page of the wizard . . . well, there is nothing you really have to
    do, so just click **Finish**.

At this point, Kopete will try to log you onto the service for which you've
just set up an account. If you didn't select the *Remember password* option in the
wizard, A KDE Wallet window will most likely now appear. If so, click **Next** in
that window, type a password for KDE Wallet, and then click **Finish**. You will
then be prompted for the password of the account you've just set up, so type
that in when prompted, and you will be logged in and ready to go.

If you want to set up accounts for other messaging services with which
you are registered, you can do so now, or later, by going to the **Settings**
menu, selecting **Configure Kopete**, and then clicking the **New** button in the
Configure window that appears.

13B-2: Adding Contacts to Kopete

Although you are now set up and logged in, you really can't do anything until you add some contacts to Kopete. If you want to be able to communicate with these contacts via Kopete, they must have accounts with one of the same messaging services as you. To add such contacts, go to the **File** menu and select **Add Contact**, after which an Add Contact Wizard will appear (Figure 13-30).

To help you in following along with the wizard, I'll spell out the steps here:

1. In the first page of the wizard, just click **Next**.

2. In the top box of the next page of the wizard (Figure 13-31), type the name of the contact as you would like it to appear in the Kopete window.

Figure 13-30: Adding messaging contacts in Kopete

3. Next, you must decide to which group you want to add your contact. The default group is *Top Level* (also shown in Figure 13-31), so click the box next to that group, and then click **Next**.

4. In the next page of the wizard, check the box next to the messaging service to which your contact belongs. If, for example, the contact uses Yahoo, check the box next to that service, and then click **Next**. Note that only those services for which you have set up your own accounts will appear in this list, so if your contact is registered with a different messaging service, you will have to register for the same service yourself and then set up a Kopete account for it.

5. In the next page, type the username or email address under which the contact is registered with his or her messaging service. Of course, you will have to get this information from the person in question. Once finished, click **Next**.

6. In the final page of the wizard, just click **Finish**.

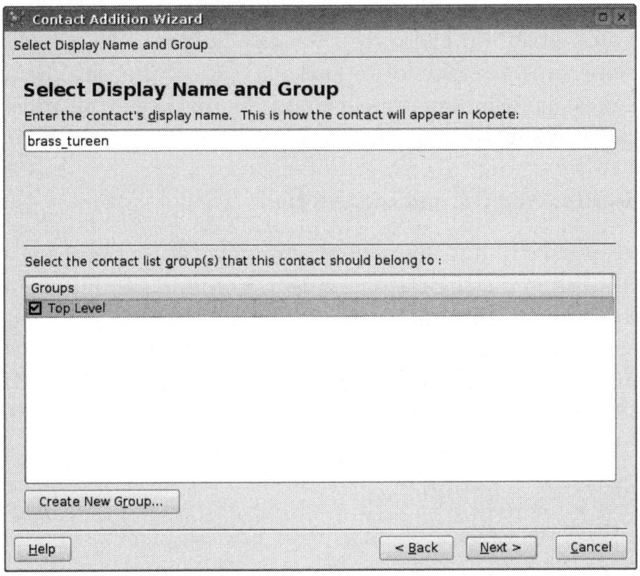

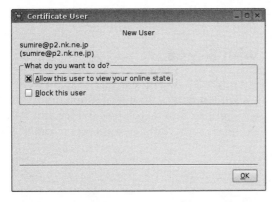

Figure 13-31: Naming your contact in the Kopete Add Contact Wizard

Your new contact will then appear in the main Kopete window, though you will not be able to see that contact's online status until you receive his or her online approval. This is usually requested, and hopefully given, the first time you try to send a message to the contact. The same is true when someone tries to do the same with you for the first time. When that person first tries to contact you, a window will appear notifying you of the fact and asking you whether to allow that person to view your online state or to block the user (Figure 13-32).

Figure 13-32: Certifying a contact request in Kopete

13B-3: Instant Messaging with Kopete

Once you are all set up and have added some contacts, you can move on to doing some text-based communicating. To get started, double-click one of your online contacts in the main Kopete window (Figure 13-33).

An instant messaging window for that contact will appear looking like that already shown in Figure 13-26, albeit blank. To start communicating, just type your message in the bottom pane of the window, and press ENTER. The message will then appear in the top pane, and your contact's response will appear shortly below that.

13B-4: Logging Off and Logging On

When you have had your fill of communication for the day, you can log off of all of your messaging accounts by going to the **File** menu and selecting **Connection ▶ Disconnect All**. When you want to log back on, you can do so in much the same way, by going to the **File** menu again and selecting **Connection ▶ Connect All**. Doing this will log you on to all of the services for which you have set up accounts. The icons for those accounts will then appear at the bottom-right corner of the main Kopete window.

Figure 13-33: The main Kopete window

Internet Telephony with Skype

So your significant other is living in Madrid, and there you are in Grand Rapids spending so much money on international phone bills that you can't afford to hop on a flight and do the ol' face-to-face, eh? Well, you might just be the perfect candidate for a cool new application called *Skype*, shown in Figure 13-34.

What Is Skype?

Skype is an application that allows you to talk to your friends, family, and whomever else you want via the Internet, just as if you were using a telephone. Of course, in order to use Skype, the party you want to speak with must also be using Skype and be online, which may seem like a big drawback. However, when you give Skype a try and hear how good it sounds, get a feel for how well it works, and realize how little it costs (it costs nothing), you won't be worrying about such minor matters any longer.

If you do want to call regular phone lines via Skype, it is also possible via Skype's *SkypeOut* service, which, although not a free service, provides "global calling at local rates." In case, you're wondering, Skype is available not only for Linux but also for Windows and Mac OS X, meaning that just about anyone you know with a computer can use it.

NOTE   *Skype was not bundled with earlier releases of Xandros Standard or Deluxe Editions V3. So, if you are a user of either one of those and would like to get down to some serious long-distance jaw wagging without paying for it all at the end of the month, download and install Skype now via Xandros Networks.*

Figure 13-34: Internet telephony made easy with Skype

Headsets

When using Skype, it is practically a must to use a microphone and a headphone. In fact, to make it all easier, it is a real plus to invest in a headset, which provides a combination of the two. (The Surfside Linux Edition includes a headset in the box!) While you might worry that this is a needlessly geeky thing to buy, you will appreciate it in the long run, since it makes using Skype seem all the more natural and thus fun. In addition, if you and the person with whom you are speaking do not at least use headphones, you will be driven stark raving mad because your voice will bounce back to you as a delayed echo through your contact's mike and vice versa. Trust me, the number-one problem beginning Skype users have is echo, and the reason for the problem is the same: one or both of the two parties are not using headphones.

Running and Using Skype

To get started with Skype, here's what you need to do:

1. Go to the **Launch** menu and select **Applications** ▶ **Internet** ▶ **Skype Internet Calling**.

2. When Skype first appears, you will see the Create Account window (Figure 13-35). In that window, just type a username (no spaces) and password for your new account, and then type your email address.

Figure 13-35: Creating a new Skype account

3. Next, click the box next to *Yes, I have read and I accept the Skype End User Licence Agreement*. Of course, you should give the agreement a read-through first. Once you have done all that, click **Next**.

Skype will then contact its HQ to register you, which might take a bit of time, so be patient. When it is finished, you will be automatically logged in, and the main Skype window will appear (Figure 13-34).

Adding Contacts in Skype

Just as was the case with instant messaging services, you must add contacts before you can communicate with anyone via Skype. A good way to get started, and to test out your setup at the same time, is to call Skype's Echo Test Service.

To do this, just follow these steps:

1. Click the **Contacts** tab, and then click the + icon directly above it.

2. In the Add a Contact window that appears, type the name of the contact you want to communicate with. In this case, type **echo123**, and then click **Next**.

3. The next window that appears tells you that you are about to request authorization to view that contact's online status. Just click **OK**. Skype will then check to see if the user you specified exists, and if so, it will then pop up a window telling you that the user has been added to your Contacts list.

4. Now, click **Finish** in the window I just mentioned, and Skype will go on to send a message to the user you just added to your contacts list, asking that user for authorization (Figure 13-36). Once the user gives that authorization, you will be able to see his or her online status.

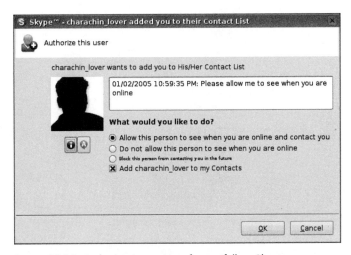

Figure 13-36: Authorization request from a fellow Skype user

Making Calls with Skype

Now that the Echo Test Service is listed in your Skype Contacts list, let's call it up by following these steps:

1. Click the contact name once to select it.

2. Now, click the green telephone icon at the bottom of the page. A picture of the Echo Test Service woman will appear (Figure 13-37). After a second or two more, you will hear her voice telling you to leave a message between the beeps.

3. Do as the Echo Test Service woman says, and leave your message. Then after the second beep, you should be able to hear the message you just recorded played back to you. When the test is all done, the Echo Test Service woman will politely hang up, thus terminating the call.

Once you have set up your real-life contacts, you can call them up in the same way you did the Echo Test Service. When you do, your contacts will hear a ringing on their end, just like a real telephone. Of course, if one of your contact calls you, you will hear the same ringing on your end. If so, just click the green telephone icon at the bottom of the window and start talking. To hang up at any time, just click the red phone icon near the bottom of the page. It's all really simple, intuitive, and lots of fun.

Figure 13-37: The look of a Skype call in progress

Instant Messaging with Skype

If you feel like communicating but don't feel much like talking, Skype (just like Kopete) also allows you to send instant messages to your contacts, though you can send such messages only to fellow Skype users. To do this, click the contact you want to instant message, and then click the **A** icon above the Start tab.

An instant message window will open in which you can send messages back and forth to that contact (Figure 13-38). An identical window will automatically appear on the contact's screen.

Online Dictionary

Let's wrap up this chapter on Internet applications with just about the simplest application of that genre you have: the *Online Dictionary*. Running and using the Online Dictionary is a simple affair. Just go to the **Launch** menu, select **Applications ▶ Utilities ▶ Online Dictionary**, and there it will be on your screen. To put it to use, type in a word you'd like to define, and then press ENTER.

The Online Dictionary will then search its collection of online databases and display the results in the main pane of the window, as you can see in Figure 13-39.

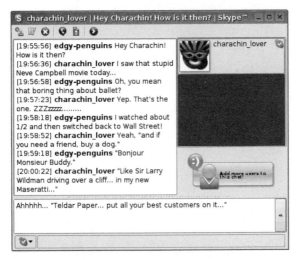

Figure 13-38: Instant messaging with Skype

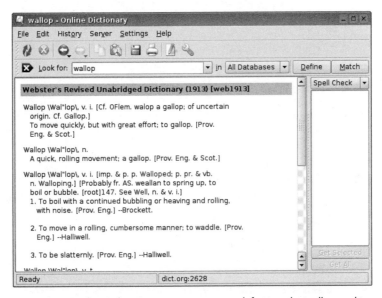

Figure 13-39: The Online Dictionary gives you definition, lexically speaking

If you happen to misspell a word, the Online Dictionary will show you possible substitutions (Figure 13-40).

If you aren't quite sure what the word is you are looking for but know what it sort of sounds like, type that word in the *Look for* box, and then click the **Match** button. The Online Dictionary will offer a list of possibilities in its right pane (Figure 13-41).

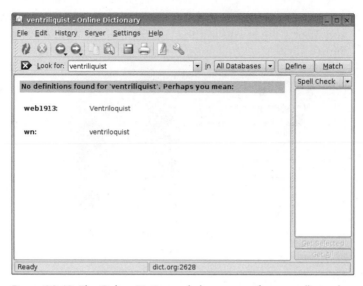

Figure 13-40: The Online Dictionary helps you out if your spelling takes a holiday

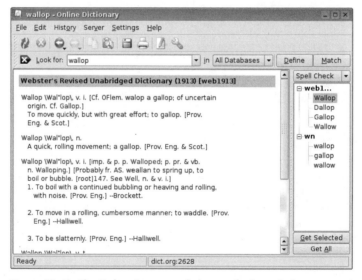

Figure 13-41: The Online Dictionary helps you find words that you can't quite remember

There's Still More in Store from Xandros Networks

If the Internet applications that come bundled with your Xandros distro are not enough to satisfy you, there are still many more available via Xandros Networks. In addition to the popular alternatives Firebox and Thunderbird, Mozilla and Ximian Evolution, you might also want to consider *gftp* for your FTP downloading and uploading needs, or if you're interested in creating your own web pages, the WYSIWYG web page application, *Nvu*. There are, of course, still more, so have a look around and see what else XN has to offer.

14

EAR CANDY

Xandros Does Audio

It's now time to move on to the audio side of things in our Xandros workout. In Chapter 6, you learned about Kscd, your system's default CD player, but in this chapter you will find out even more about your system's other musical talents. You will learn how to rip CDs and create MP3 and Ogg files (which have the .mp3 and .ogg filename extensions, respectively), how to change the tags of such files, and how to play them. You'll also learn how to play the different varieties of Internet broadcast streams.

Audio Formats

Before we start off on our discussion of how to work with audio files in Xandros, it is probably best to first discuss the various formats in which audio data can be stored on your computer, as this is essential information. The de facto audio file standards in the computer world for the longest time have been WAV (created by Microsoft/IBM and using the .wav extension), AU (from Sun/Unix and using the .au extension), and AIFF (from Apple). All of these are uncompressed formats, so files saved in these formats are therefore exceedingly large, with an average WAV file of CD-quality music weighing in at about 10 MB per minute of music. To put that in perspective, back in 1988 my first Macintosh had a 40 MB hard disk—more space than I would ever need, I thought at the time, but not enough to store a WAV file of Nirvana's "Come as You Are."

As computers evolved into the multimedia machines they are today, it became clear that something was going to have to be done about those disk-space-devouring audio files. Audio-compression formats were thus developed. To oversimplify things a bit, these compression formats work by cutting out the portions of the audio signal that the human is less likely to notice if gone—sort of a dog-whistle approach. The most widely known and embraced of these audio-compression formats is MP3 (.mp3). Audio files encoded in MP3 format can end up being as little as one-twelfth the size of the original CD audio (.cda) file without any noticeable loss in quality.

Another audio-compression format that was developed is Ogg Vorbis (.ogg). Ogg Vorbis is a product of the open-source community, and so, unlike MP3, which has always been used under the shadow of yet-to-be-exercised patent rights, it has been free of patent and licensing worries from the get-go. Because of that, and the fact that it was equal to or, as many contend, better than MP3 in terms of quality and performance, Ogg Vorbis has become the darling of the Linux community and its de facto audio-compression format.

The Xandros File Manager as an Audio App?

In Chapters 5, 6, and 13 you learned about many things you can do with the Xandros File Manager. With XFM, you can work with your files, burn CDs, browse through your digital images, and even view web pages. But XFM can also function to some degree as an audio application. Xandros File Manager won't play your audio files for you, but it will allow you to *rip* (copy) files from audio CDs and save those files as is (uncompressed). It can also *encode* them as (convert them to) compressed Ogg files for your own personal use. After you complete Project 14A, you will also be able to encode the tracks as MP3s if you prefer.

Xandros File Manager's DVD-Writer will also allow you to take those files you've ripped and then *burn* (record) them onto recordable CDs or audio CDs that can be played on any standard audio CD player. This allows you to create compilations of your favorite songs and then play them on your living room or car stereo without worry as to whether or not those players are .mp3- or .ogg-compatible.

Using Xandros File Manager to Rip and Encode Audio Files

You will find that ripping the tracks from a CD and then encoding them in the Ogg or MP3 file format is quite simple. Since XFM will first search the CDDB online database for album, artist, and song title information for the

CD you are ripping, it is best to be connected to the Internet when doing so if you want that information encoded in the final MP3 or OGG files. Other than that, all you have to do is follow these steps:

1. Insert an audio CD in your disk drive. Kscd will appear and begin playing the songs on it.

2. Because you have inserted the CD for the purpose of ripping it, not listening to it, quit Kscd and its Panel applet.

3. Next, open a Xandros File Manager window and click the **CD-RW** or **DVD-ROM** icon in the file tree in the left pane of the window. The contents of the CD will appear in the right pane of the window (Figure 14-1), though this might take a bit more time than it does for data CDs. Just be patient and stare at the little paper airplane that will float back and forth in the right pane as Xandros File Manager reads the disc.

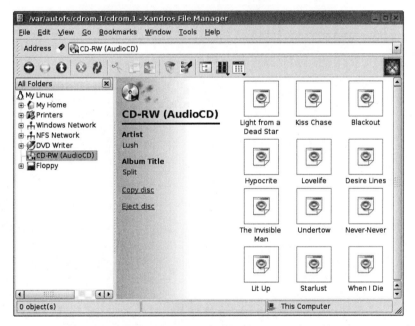

Figure 14-1: The tracks of an audio CD displayed in a Xandros File Manager window

Once the tracks on the CD appear, you are ready to roll. What you do at this point, however, depends on how many of the tracks you want to rip and encode.

4. If you want to convert only a single track, drag that track to a folder of your choice in the file tree in the left panel—your My Music folder would be an appropriate location. If you want to convert more than one track, hold down the CTRL key, and select the target files by clicking once on each of them.

5. Once you've finished selecting the files, release the CTRL key, click, but don't release, any one of the files you've selected, and then drag them all in unison to the destination folder.

When you have done this, Xandros File Manager will begin copying the files from the CD to your hard drive. Again, this will take longer than you may have gotten used to when copying files from a data disc, but they are larger files, after all. Also, do not be too concerned about the progress window; it sometimes seems to give rather odd readings during this process. At some time during the process, another window will appear, asking how you'd like to save the files.

As you can see in Figure 14-2, the choices listed are WAV, CDA, OGG, and MP3, although the MP3 option will not be selectable until after you've installed MP3 encoding support in Project 14A. Unless you choose OGG or MP3, you pretty much will be defeating the purpose of ripping and encoding your audio tracks, so stick with one of those two compressed formats. If you also want to use the files on your Windows side or on your Mac, it is probably best to go with MP3.

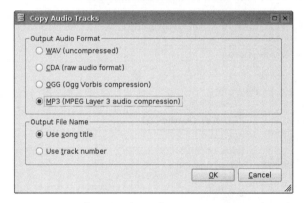

Figure 14-2: Telling Xandros File Manager what to do with your audio files

6. Once you have made your selection, click **OK**. Xandros File Manager will then move on to the encoding process, and when it is done, the progress window will close automatically. The compressed files now reside on your computer.

Get Started Organizing Your Now-Compressed Audio Files

Once the rip-and-encode process is complete, you should organize your files so that in the future you'll know what is what. The standard way of doing this is to create a new folder in your My Music folder named after the artist who performed the tracks you just ripped. Inside that folder, create another folder with the title of the album from which you just ripped the tracks. For example, if you ripped songs from Molly Bancroft's *Get Closer* album, you would create a *Molly Bancroft* folder and a *Get Closer* folder within that. Of course, in the future, if you were to rip and encode songs from a different album by the same artist, you would create a new folder for *that* album within the original folder you've already created for the artist and move all of the newly ripped files into it.

If your encoded tracks are not named with the actual song titles, because you weren't connected to the Internet when you ripped the tracks or because the album you ripped wasn't listed in the CDDB online database, it is probably also a good idea, though not a necessity, to go on and rename the tracks themselves with their appropriate titles. For example, in the case of Molly Bancroft's *Get Closer* album, the filename Track 6.mp3 would be renamed Funky Little Mouth.mp3, and so on.

In this case, if you would like the artist and track names to appear when playing the files in an audio player, you will also need to input each track's tag information. This is a bit tedious when dealing with many files in one go, but it is easy. You will learn how to do it in the XMMS section of this chapter.

Settings

If you would like to adjust Xandros File Manager's encoding settings for Ogg files, you can do so by going to the **Launch** menu and selecting **Control Panel**.

When the Control Panel window appears, click the + symbol next to *Sound & Multimedia*, and then click **Audio CDs**. You can then get to the encoding settings by clicking the **Ogg Vorbis Encoder** tab in the right pane of that window (Figure 14-3).

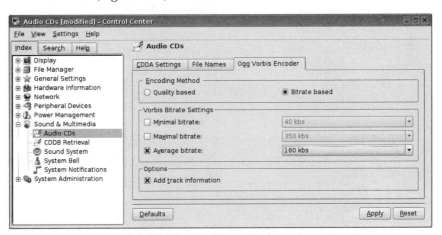

Figure 14-3: Changing the encoding settings for Xandros File Manager

In this tab you can select the encoding bit rate, which allows you to control the sound quality of the final encoded file The basic rule to remember is that the higher the bit rate, the better the sound quality. If you are short on disk space, you should also be aware that higher bit rates take up more disk space, so you'll need to define your priorities in terms of sound and space. The most common choices are 128 kbps, 160 kbps, and 192 kbps though the default, 128 kbps, should provide more than acceptable sound quality if disk space is of great concern.

Creating an Audio CD with Xandros File Manager

As I already mentioned, another cool feature of the Xandros File Manager's DVD/CD-Writer is that it allows you to use your Ogg and MP3 files to create (for your personal use) standard audio CDs that can be played on any standard audio CD player.

The process for doing this is essentially the same as that for creating data CDs, albeit with just one minor exception. Here are the steps:

1. Open a Xandros File Manager window, and then click the **DVD-Writer** or **CD-Writer** icon (depending on the hardware you happen to have) in the file tree at the left side of the window.

2. Next, click **Create music CD** in the right pane of the window (Figure 14-4).

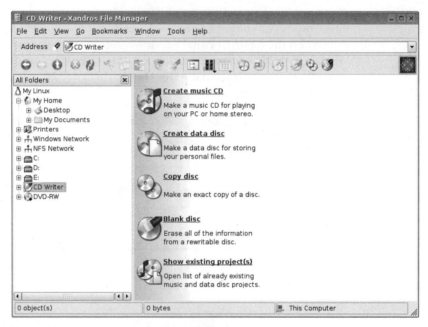

Figure 14-4: Creating an audio CD in XFM

3. Copy the MP3 and Ogg music files you want to include on your CD (and yes, you can mix both file types) to the right pane of the window until you have about 14 songs.

4. Once you've done that, click the words **Write files to disc**, after which the usual window warning you about running programs while burning discs will appear.

5. Click **OK** to follow that bit of sound advice.

6. After the Create Disc window appears, click **OK**. The DVD-Writer will then check to see if you have a blank disc in your drive, and if you don't, it will request that you insert one.

7. Insert a blank disc (my experience is that 650 MB discs seem to work best), and once the light on your drive stops flashing, click **OK**. The process will then begin.

As with all other disc-burning scenarios I have mentioned thus far, the progress of the burning process will be indicated in the Create Disc window, and once the process is complete, the disc will be ejected automatically.

You can now test out your new audio disc by reinserting it into the drive. After doing that this time around, however, Kscd should start up automatically and begin playing the CD.

Be aware that since the disc you've just created is not a standard commercial album, it won't be listed in the freedb.org database. Kscd therefore cannot gather and display track information for the songs on your disc. A small price to pay, as they say.

Project 14A: Adding MP3 Encoding Support to Xandros

As you have learned, you can rip audio files from CD and encode them in Ogg Vorbis format using either the Xandros File Manager DVD-Writer or other applications that I will discuss shortly. You also already know that Xandros does not come with MP3 encoding support; however, as a personal user, you can install such support yourself in the form of an application called *LAME*. Of course, since LAME is not included in the Xandros distribution itself due to licensing concerns over MP3, it is only logical that it is likewise not available via the Xandros Networks repositories. You will thus have to download LAME from outside sources and then install it via the Xandros Networks application. Here are the very simple steps:

1. Open your web browser, and go to http://users.rsise.anu.edu.au/~conrad/not_lame.

2. When that page appears, look for and download the file **lame_3.91-2_i386.deb**. Don't use the newer 3.92 version, as it might not work with your system. There may be still newer versions available by the time you read this, but the file I've listed here works; I can't guarantee any others.

3. Once the download is complete, run Xandros Networks, and then in the **File** menu select **Install DEB File**.

4. In the Browse for Package window that appears, locate the LAME file you've just downloaded, select it (by clicking on it once), and then click the **Open** button.

5. Click the **Install** button in that window.

6. You will then be prompted for your root password, so type it, and then click **OK**. Xandros Networks will then install the file while showing its progress in a separate window.

7. When the installation process is complete, the word *Done* will appear in the progress window. You can then click the **Close** button and drag the LAME file you downloaded to the Trash.

Once the installation is complete, you can encode the audio files you rip from a CD into the MP3 format from the Xandros File Manager.

An Alternative Ripping and Encoding Application—RipperX

Although Xandros File Manager's ripping and encoding capability is very handy, it is not without some minor drawbacks. The fact that it does not create artist and album folders or provide track names can, in the end, mean more work for you, especially if you are doing a lot of ripping. There are, however, a couple of other applications available from Xandros Networks that can do all of these chores for you in one fell swoop, thus making the process much easier and quicker. My favorite of these is called *ripperX*.

RipperX is an alternative ripping-and-encoding application that gathers from the Internet artist, album, and track information for the album you are ripping. It rips and encodes the tracks of that album in either Ogg or MP3 format and then places the encoded files in the artist and album folders it creates on your hard disk. It is extremely easy to use and configure. Best of all, it's pretty quick.

Installing RipperX

To install ripperX, just run Xandros Networks, and make sure that the *Debian unsupported site repository* is enabled in the Set Application Sources window (**Edit ▸ Set Application Sources**). After doing that, type **ripperx** in the text box next to the *Search* button, and then click **Search** or press ENTER. RipperX will then appear in the list of results below (it will probably be the only item listed). Now click **Install**, and then follow the remaining simple installation steps you learned in Chapter 8.

Using RipperX

To use ripperX, just follow these steps:

1. Insert an audio CD in your disk drive, and then quit Kscd and its Panel applet once they appear.
2. Go to the **Launch** menu, and select **Run Command**.
3. In the Run Command window, type **ripperx**, and then click **Run**.
4. When the *ripperX* window appears the first time, a small window, "Wanna create . . . ," will appear asking you if you want to create a config file (Figure 14-5). You do, so click **Yes**.

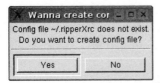

Figure 14-5: RipperX asks if you want to create a configuration file the first time you run it

5. The main ripperX window will appear, and in that window click the **Scan** button in order to read the track information from your CD if it doesn't do it automatically right off the bat.

6. Next, click the **CDDB** button, while connected to the Internet, to gather the artist, album, and track information for that CD. If the album doesn't happen to be listed in the online database, you will have to type in this information yourself in the ripperX window.

7. Select the songs you wish to rip and encode by clicking on the minus symbols to the left of the appropriate tracks. If you wish to rip and encode all of the songs on the album, click the **Select All Tracks** button instead. When you are finished, the ripperX window should look something like that in Figure 14-6.

Figure 14-6: Ripping and encoding audio files with ripperX

8. Once everything looks as it should, click the **Go!!!** button to start the ripping and encoding processes, the progress of which will be indicated in the same, albeit somewhat different-looking, window (Figure 14-7).

9. The first time you rip and encode files with ripperX, you will need to decide where you want it to save your files. To make your choice, click the **Config** button, and the Configuration window will appear (Figure 14-8).

In that window, indicate where you would like ripperX to save your files by clicking the **Target Directory** button to browse to and then select the destination folder you want to specify.

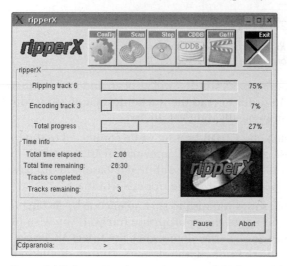

Figure 14-7: RipperX indicates the progress of the ripping and encoding processes

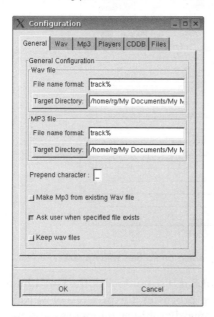

Figure 14-8: Telling ripperX where to save your files

Other Encoding Options with RipperX

In addition to telling ripperX where to save your files, you can tell it in what format to save those files. To do this, click the **Mp3** tab, and then, once on that page, select either **OggVorbis encoder** or **Lame MP3 encoder** from the

drop-down menu button under the words *Encoder plugin* (Figure 14-9).
Remember also that you will be able to create MP3 files only if you have
installed LAME in Project 14A.

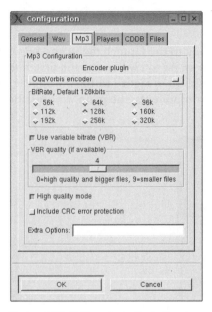

Figure 14-9: Telling ripperX whether to encode
your files in Ogg or MP3 format

After you have made your encoding selection, you can also, if you like,
select the encoding bit rate. As I mentioned before, 128k and 160k are the
most common choices, and either should provide you with very good sound,
though, if you have the disk space, it wouldn't hurt to go with the higher
bit rate.

Playing Audio Files with MP3 Player (XMMS)

Now that you know how to create MP3 and Ogg audio files, you no doubt
want to know how to play them. For this task, you can use the *MP3 Player*
(Figure 14-10) included with your Xandros system.

Figure 14-10: XMMS—The Linux world's #1 audio player

MP3 Player, better known as *XMMS* (X MultiMedia System), is the Linux
world's best-known and most widely used audio player. It is pretty much a
clone of the Windows world's Winamp Classic in terms of what it can do, but
it was written from scratch, and it is very cool and capable. With XMMS, you

can play just about any kind of audio file and even listen to Internet broadcast streams in either MP3 or Ogg format, as you will learn later on in this chapter.

Running XMMS

You can run XMMS by going to the **Launch** menu and selecting **Applications ▶ Multimedia ▶ MP3 Player**. As you will notice the first time you run XMMS, only the main window (as shown in Figure 14-10) will appear; however, XMMS actually consists of three components: the main window, the Equalizer, and the Playlist (Figure 14-11).

Figure 14-11: The three components of XMMS

To open the other components, click the tiny **EQ** button in the main window for the Equalizer, or click the **PL** button for the Playlist. You can also move the various components around, just like a real component stereo, so that they are stacked one on top of the other, side by side, or in whatever configuration you want; just drag them around until they all look the way you want them to. And don't worry about having to fuss with such things again—the next time you run XMMS, the components will reappear just the way you left them when you last exited the program.

Playing Audio Files in XMMS

Of course, the main purpose of XMMS is to play audio files, so to get down to business, click the **Add** button at the bottom-left corner of the Playlist window, and a Load files window will appear. You then have three different ways in which to proceed:

- If you want to play just one song, navigate to the song you want to play, select it (by clicking it once), and then click the **Add** button, which will also close the window.

- If you would like to play more than one song, click each of the songs you want to play while holding down the CTRL key (Figure 14-12). The songs you select will then be highlighted in blue. When you have finished making your selections, release the CTRL key, click the **Add selected files** button, and then click **Close**.

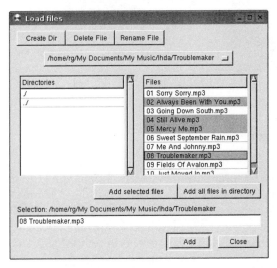

Figure 14-12: Adding multiple tunes from a single folder to an XMMS playlist

- If you would like to play all of the songs in a directory, click the **Add all files in directory** button, and then click **Close**.

If you would like to add still other songs located in still other folders, hold off on closing the Load files window, and navigate to those folders to select the songs you want to add. When you have finally added all the songs you want to add from the various relevant folders, you can then click the **Close** button to close the window. Whatever approach you take, the song or songs you added will then appear listed in the Playlist window (Figure 14-13).

Figure 14-13: Selected songs listed in the XMMS Playlist window

You can then click the **Play** button in the main window to hear your selections.

If you would like to play the songs you've selected in random order and/or over and over in an endless loop, you can tell XMMS to do so by clicking either or both of the **Random** and **Loop** buttons in the main player window (Figure 14-14).

Figure 14-14: The Random and Loop buttons in the main XMMS window

Creating an XMMS Playlist File

If in the future you would like to be able to play the same group of songs you've selected without having to go through all the fuss of selecting them each and every time out, you can do so by creating a playlist file. As you might well imagine, this is a very handy feature. Say, for example, that you want to create a playlist of your favorite songs by various artists, but these songs are located, quite naturally, in a variety of different folders. In this case, coming up with such a list of songs every time you wanted to play them would end up being quite a pain in the posterior, to put it somewhat politely. Creating a playlist file for those songs, however, would make the somewhat tedious playlist assembly process a one-time effort.

To create a playlist file from the songs you've added to the XMMS Playlist window, here's what you need to do:

1. Click, but don't release, the **List** button at the bottom-right corner of the Playlist window (Figure 14-13).
2. Select **Save** from the pop-up menu, and release the mouse button.
3. In the Save Playlist window, which then appears, type in /**home**/*username*/**My Documents**/**My Music**/*playlisttitle*.**m3u** (substitute your own username and playlist title for *username* and *playlisttitle*). In my case, for example, I typed /home/rg/My Documents/My Music/MyFaves.m3u.
4. Once you've finished, click **OK**, and XMMS will save your new playlist.
5. After that, all you have to do to play the list is double-click the M3U file (.m3u is the file extension for the playlists) for that list, and XMMS will start right up playing the songs listed therein.

You can also load a playlist file while already running XMMS. If you already have some tunes queued up in the XMMS Playlist window and would like to remove them, click the **Sub** button (Figure 14-13), but don't release the mouse button. In the pop-up menu, select **All**, and release the mouse button. The songs in the Playlist window will be gone. You can then add your already configured playlist by clicking the **List** button, after which a Load playlist window will appear. In that window, locate your playlist, select it (by clicking it once), and then click the **OK** button. Your saved list will then appear in the XMMS Playlist window.

Project 14B: Using XMMS Skins

One of the most fun things about XMMS, if you're into that sort of thing, is that it allows you to directly change its appearance by using customized interface themes, called *skins*. The default skin for XMMS in Xandros is called *7947-plastik*, and it more or less follows the default theme of the rest of the system. There are, however, several other XMMS skins bundled with your system, examples of which are shown in Figure 14-15.

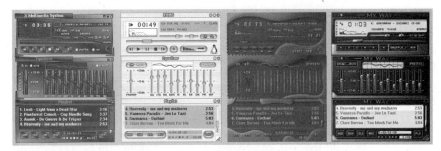

Figure 14-15: Changing the looks of XMMS with skins

14B-1: Changing Skins

What you are going to do in this part of the project is change the default 7947-plastik skin (shown in Figure 14-11) to the *UltrafinaSEM* skin (Figure 14-16), which for my money looks a lot better. You may beg to differ, but just humor me for now.

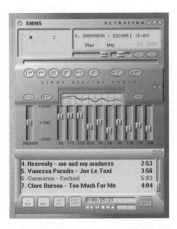

Figure 14-16: XMMS in the UltrafinaSEM skin

To bring about this remarkable transformation, right-click anywhere on the main XMMS program window, and from the pop-up menu select **Options ▶ Skin Browser**.

This will open the *Skin selector* window (see Figure 14-17); scroll down until you find UltrafinaSEM. Once you see it, click it. Like magic, the transformation will be complete.

Figure 14-17: The XMMS Skin selector window

As you no doubt will have noticed as you try out the various skins in the Skin browser, there is a lot of variation in the world of skins. Some can be so wild that you can barely use them, while others may be quite dull and very easy on the eye.

There is also the configuration of your XMMS components to consider. You may agree that the UltrafinaSEM skin looks much more handsome than the default 7947-plastik skin when the components are stacked on top of one another, as in Figure 14-16. However, place the components side by side while using UltrafinaSEM, and it all looks pretty weird, whereas a more traditional stereo-system skin, such as the one shown in Figure 14-18, seems much more the ticket.

Figure 14-18: XMMS components stacked in classic stereo configuration

14B-2: Downloading Additional Skins

If you've gone through the whole lot of skin choices and found nothing to get your heart a-pumping, you can download still other skins from the Web. The XMMS site (www.xmms.org) has quite a few, but even more can be found on the Winamp site (http://classic.winamp.com/skins). Yes, you've guessed right—Winamp skins and XMMS skins are interchangeable. Just be sure *not* to use those skins designed for Winamp 3, which will not work. You can tell which are which by the file extensions: Winamp 3 skins end in .wal, Winamp 2 skins (the XMMS compatibles) end in .zip, and native XMMS skins end in .wsz.

There is an amazing variety of skins available from the Winamp site, so there should be something there to please you. When you find some skins that you like, download them in the usual manner.

14B-3: Installing Your New Skins

Once you have downloaded some new skins, you will have to make them available to XMMS by putting them in the right place on your system. You needn't unzip them, though; you can use them as is, which saves you some minor grief. Anyway, at this stage of the game, this is most easily done by putting them in the *.xmms* folder within your Home folder.

Directories preceded by a dot are normally hidden from view, so to locate the .xmms folder, you will need to go to the **View** menu in a Xandros File Manager window and select **Show Hidden Files**. If you are going to be accessing the XMMS Skins folder often, this would be a good time to use XFM's bookmark function, so as to make navigating back to the folder easier in the future.

From there on in, it's a simple drag-and-drop procedure. Just drag the downloaded skin files directly into the Skins folder inside .xmms, and that's that. The next time you open the XMMS Skin selector, your new skins will be there waiting in the list.

Project 14C: XMMS Plug-Ins

XMMS not only allows you to change its looks through the use of skins, but it also allows you to add various functions to the player through the use of *plug-ins*. Many of these plug-ins are already bundled with your system, while still others are available from Xandros Networks. There is a variety of such plug-ins, and they range in function from visualization modules (which provide you with animated graphical representations of the song you happen to be playing) to timer functions (which allow you to have XMMS start up and shut down, like an alarm clock, when you want).

14C-1: Using What You've Got

Many of the plug-ins you already have on your system are enabled by default in order to allow XMMS to do what it needs to do. To use the other, less-necessary plug-ins, however, you will need to enable them yourself. Let's start out by taking a look at one of the simplest, called *On Screen Display*, which displays the details of the song you are playing on your screen outside the XMMS player itself (Figure 14-19).

Figure 14-19: Song details displayed on-screen with the XMMS
On Screen Display plug-in

To enable the plug-in, follow these steps:

1. Right-click any of the XMMS components, and select **Options ▶ Preferences** in the pop-up menu that appears.

2. When the XMMS Preferences window appears, click the **General Plugins** tab.

3. In the General Plugins tab, select the **On Screen Display** plug-in by clicking it once.

4. Next, check the *Enable plugin* box at the bottom-right corner of the window (Figure 14-20), and then click the **Apply** button. If you then play a song in XMMS, the artist, track number (within the playlist), and song title will appear in green at the bottom-left corner of your screen for three seconds.

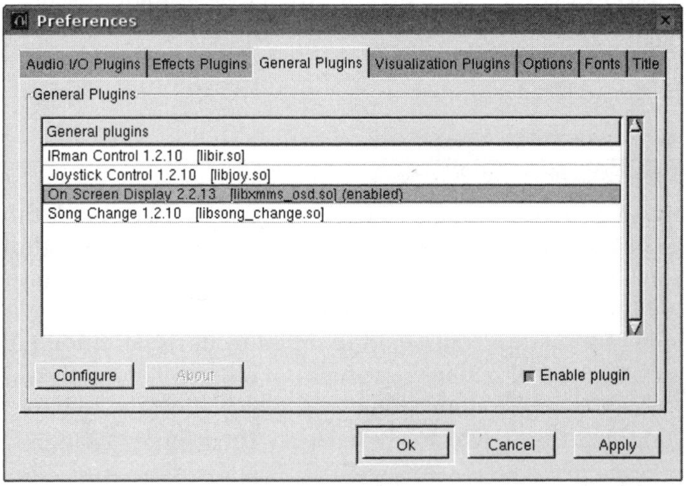

Figure 14-20: Enabling XMMS plug-ins

All very cool . . . but green? And so small! And only three seconds? Fortunately, it is possible to configure most plug-ins to suit your own needs and desires. When you select a plug-in, the Configure button below the list of plug-ins list will become active (clickable) if that plug-in is configurable, as is the case with the On Screen Display plug-in.

14C-2: Changing the Display-Duration and Color Settings

To get a feel for how this works, let's change the behavior of this particular plug-in by doing the following:

1. Select **On Screen Display** in the plug-in list (if you haven't already done so) by clicking it once.

2. Next, click the **Configure** button, which will bring up the Configuration window for the On Screen Display plug-in (Figure 14-21); the options within the Configuration window for other plug-ins will, of course, be different.

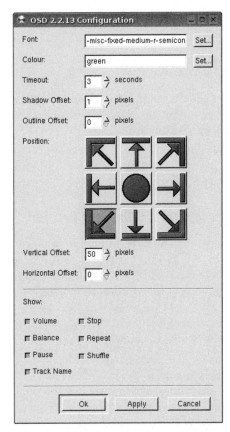

Figure 14-21: Setting the display time of the On Screen Display plug-in

3. In that window, increase the amount of time the song information will appear on-screen by clicking the up arrow to the right of the word *Timeout* until the appropriate number of seconds is displayed in the box to the left of the arrows (I have mine at 20).

4. Once you have set the display time, click **Apply**.

5. To change the color of the onscreen display, click the **Set** button to the far right of the word *Colour*, and a color-selection window (Figure 14-22) will appear.

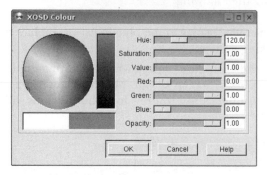

Figure 14-22: Changing the color of the onscreen text displayed by the On Screen Display plug-in

6. In the color wheel, click the color in which you would like your onscreen text to appear. You can then fine-tune your selection by clicking within the color bar to the right of the wheel.

7. Once you have made your selection, click the **OK** button, and that window will disappear. You can then go ahead and click the **Apply** button in the Configuration window to complete this part of the process.

14C-3: Changing the Display Font and Onscreen Position

Now that you've gotten the display time and color taken care of, wrap things up by changing both the font and font size of the display, so as to make it all easier to see. Then change the onscreen location where it will be displayed.

While still in the Configuration window, follow these steps:

1. Click the **Set** button at the far right of the *Font* row, to bring up the XOSD (X On Screen Display) Font window.

2. In the list of fonts in the left pane of the window, scroll down and select **helvetica** by clicking it once.

   You will now notice that just below the preview pane at the bottom of the window the following message will appear: *This is a 2-byte font and may not be displayed correctly*. Well, we certainly don't want anything that may not be displayed correctly, so it's best to change your selection a bit.

3. Scroll down a bit in the middle pane, and select **bold** just below the *iso8859-15* heading.

4. Once you've done that, click the small diamond-shaped **Points** button next to the word *Metric*.

5. Now select **24*** in the *Size* pane on the right side of the window.

6. Your font-selection window should now look like that in Figure 14-23. Assuming it does, click the **OK** button.

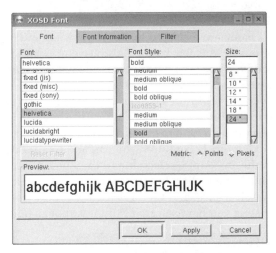

Figure 14-23: Choosing a display font for the On Screen Display plug-in

7. This will bring you back to the Configuration window, where you should then click **Apply**.

8. To wrap things up, change the position of where the song information is displayed on-screen by using the set of arrow buttons that looks something like the navigation controls of the remote control unit for a DVD player (Figure 4-21). Just choose the position you prefer by clicking the appropriate arrow button.

9. Once you have made your selection, click **Apply**.

14C-4: Viewing Your Results

After you have finished the configuration process, go ahead and close the Preferences window by clicking **OK**. In order to see the results of your efforts, play a tune or two in XMMS (or stop whatever tune you have playing, and then click the **Play** button again). The song information for the tune you are currently playing will then appear in its new color and font configuration at a new location on your screen.

Playing Around with Other Plug-Ins

If you are excited by this plug-in business, you might want to try out some of the other plug-ins listed in various tabs of the Preferences window. The visualization plug-ins are always pleasant enough, as are the echo plug-ins, so you might want to try those. If you would like to download and install some other plug-ins via Xandros Networks, try *xmms-alarm* and *xmms-goodnight*, which allow you to start up and shut down XMMS automatically at the times you specify.

Adding or Modifying Tags to Your MP3 and Ogg Files

As you have probably noticed, when you play a piece of music in XMMS or other audio players (such as in iTunes or on an iPod), the song and album titles and artist's name are displayed in the player window. If you've ever used iTunes in Windows or Mac OS, you will also have noticed that such audio files are grouped by genre. The data in each file that provides this and other information is called an *ID3 tag*, or, to keep things simple, *tag*.

As mentioned earlier in the chapter, if you rip a tune from a CD while not connected to the Internet, or if the album or song you are ripping is not included in the online CD lookup database, this information will not be added to your MP3 or Ogg file. Fortunately, you can add or alter this information yourself. To do this in XMMS, select one of the songs in the Playlist window by clicking it once. Then, click, but do not release, the **Misc** button in the Playlist window, select **Info**, and then release the mouse button. A File Info window for the song you have selected will then appear (Figure 14-24).

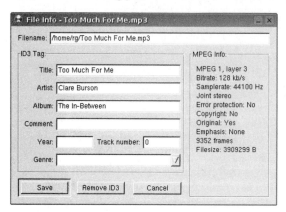

Figure 14-24: Editing the tags of your audio files

To alter or supply any information within the tag, just input the data in the appropriate box or, in the case of genre information, select the appropriate choice from the drop-down menu next to the word *Genre*. When you have finished, click **Save**; the information you added or altered will be added to the tag of the audio file.

EasyTAG

If you have a lot of MP3s and Ogg files that need major tag revisions, a handy program you might want to add to your repertoire is *EasyTAG* (Figure 14-25), essentially a tag editor on steroids. You can easily download and install EasyTAG using Xandros Networks. Just make sure *Debian unsupported site repository* is enabled, type **easytag**, and then press ENTER to locate the file.

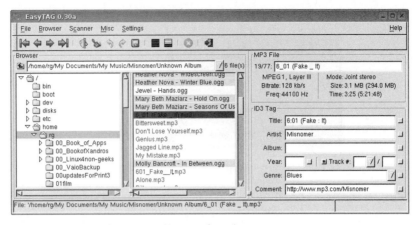

Figure 14-25: Modifying audio-file-tag info with EasyTAG

Listening to Internet Broadcast Streams

One of the coolest features of the Internet is streaming media, which is essentially live or taped, audio or video, Internet broadcasts. Such broadcasts can come in a variety of streaming formats, which are basically compression formats that allow the data to move across the Internet at as small a size as possible. Unfortunately, Linux cannot yet deal with the two most common of these streaming formats, Windows Media Player and Apple's QuickTime, at least not in any simple way, though it can play downloaded files in those formats. Fortunately, there are other media-streaming formats available on the Internet, such as RealMedia. In addition, since streaming-media formats are essentially space-saving compression formats, it is only natural that MP3 and Ogg Vorbis, both audio-compression formats themselves, have also come to be used as streaming-media formats for Internet audio broadcasts.

Project 14D: Real Player 10

RealPlayer (Figure 14-26) is one of the most popular media players in the computer world. Fortunately, it not only comes in Windows and Mac OS versions, but it is also available for Linux. RealMedia streams, specifically geared for use with RealPlayer, are widely available and provided by many mainstream broadcasters, both local and international.

14D-1: Setting Up RealPlayer

To get started, you first need to set up RealPlayer 10. To do this, go to the **Launch** menu and select **Applications ▸ Multimedia ▸ RealPlayer 10**. After you do this, the RealPlayer Setup Assistant will appear (Figure 14-27).

Figure 14-26: RealPlayer

Figure 14-27: The RealPlayer Setup Assistant

There are only four steps in the wizard, and all are simple, requiring you to do little more than click a single button. Here are the steps of the wizard:

1. **Welcome:** Just click **Forward**.
2. **Release Notes:** Just click **Forward**.
3. **License Agreement:** Read the agreement, and then click **Accept**.
4. **About Finished:** Deselect *Check for updates* (it's easier for you, and safer, to check for updates via Xandros Networks), and then click **OK**.

14D-2: Listening to RealMedia Streams with RealPlayer

Once you have completed these steps, the RealPlayer 10 window (see Figure 14-26) will appear, ready for action. For convenience's sake, take it for a test drive by using National Public Radio as the source stream; you can, of course, choose any stream you like. If you don't know any streams offhand, just follow along with me.

Here are the steps:

1. Open your web browser and go to www.npr.org.
2. When the page appears, click the link for the **NPR Program Stream**.
3. The first time you do this, a new window will appear asking you whether you want to use RealPlayer or Windows Media Player to listen to the stream. Click the **NPR** link.
4. Assuming you are using Firefox, a window will appear asking you what to do with the stream. The first item, *Open with*, should already be selected, with RealPlayer listed as the default helper application in the box to the right. That being the case, just click **OK**, and the NPR stream will soon begin playing.

If would prefer not having to see this window every time you click a RealMedia stream, also click the box next to the words *Use this automatically for files like this from now on*, though I would recommend holding off on this step the first time around to make sure that RealPlayer actually does what it is supposed to do—not that it won't, of course.

RealMedia Streams on Your Own

Now that you've got the hang of things, you probably want some more streams to try out right away. There are plenty of sites out there with RealMedia streams, but let me steer you to some of my faves to get you started (you may already know some of these):

Michael Feldman's Whad'Ya Know?   www.notmuch.com/Show

Sounds Eclectic   http://soundseclectic.com

Car Talk   http://cartalk.cars.com/Radio/Show

Radio Netherlands   www.rnw.nl

A Prairie Home Companion   www.prairiehome.org/listings

14D-3: Embedded Versions of RealPlayer

You may find that some RealMedia providers utilize a version of RealPlayer that is actually embedded in the web page itself or another one that the site pops up for that purpose, rather than the usual RealPlayer application window.

If you would like to see an example of an embedded player at work, open your browser and go to Radio Sweden's Svea site at www.sr.se/p3/svea. When the page appears, click the **Lyssna** (which means *Listen*) button, and a small web page will open with RealPlayer embedded therein playing the Svea stream (Figure 14-28).

Svea, by the way, plays pop, rock, and slightly alternative songs by Swedish artists in both English and Swedish, in case you're wondering what you're getting into. It's very cool, so don't worry.

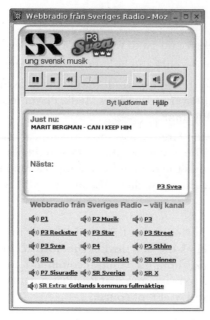

Figure 14-28: An embedded version of RealPlayer

14D-4: Playing Ogg Vorbis Streams with RealPlayer

Not only does RealPlayer allow you to play RealMedia streams, but it also
allows you to play Ogg Vorbis streams. A good example of one of the Ogg
Vorbis broadcasters out there today is Radio France. Radio France has a
number of program streams for Internet listeners in Windows Media Player
format; however, they also have now begun providing Ogg Vorbis streams
for all of their broadcast programs. The stream I recommend you try out is
Fip, which is an exceedingly cool, eclectic collection of music of *all* genres;
you will be constantly surprised by what they play. If you are worried about
language, don't; there is very little talk, and roughly 80 percent of the music
played is in English.

If you want to give streaming media in general, and Radio France in particular, a try, then go to the RealPlayer **File** menu and select **Open Location**.
In the Open Location window that pops up, type **http://ogg.tv-radio.fr:1441
/encoderfip.ogg**. Your window should look like that in Figure 14-29.

Figure 14-29: Entering a play location
in RealPlayer

Once it does, click **OK**. Assuming you are already connected to the Internet, Fip should start playing after a few seconds of pre-buffering. If you would like to be able to play Fip again in the future without having to type in the somewhat lengthy URL each time, you can bookmark the stream by going to the RealPlayer **Favorites** menu and selecting **Add to Favorites**. You can then get your daily dose of eclectia anytime you like by going to that menu and selecting **encoderfip.ogg**.

If you would like to try any of the other Radio France broadcast streams, go to www.radiofrance.fr/services/aide/difflive.php#ogg, and you will find a list of addresses. If, on the other hand, the more traditional variety of pop and rock is your cup of tea, another broadcaster offering Ogg Vorbis streams is Virgin Radio. Virgin Radio has both standard pop/rock and classic rock broadcast streams. To listen to Virgin Radio, go to the Virgin Radio site at www.virginradio.co.uk/thestation/listen/index.html.

14D-5: Playing SHOUTcast (MP3) Streams with RealPlayer

If you happen to be at the Virgin Radio site, you will notice that most streams there are also available in MP3 format. RealPlayer is able to play these streams (referred to as *SHOUTcast* streams) in exactly the same way it does those in Ogg Vorbis format. Click one of the MP3 stream links on that page to give it a go. For a more eclectic variety of streams, you might instead try going to www.shoutcast.com, where you will see an extensive listing of the SHOUTcast MP3 streams. Once you find a stream that seems of interest to you, click the **Tune In** button for that stream. If you are a music lover in need of a tip, **Search** for and try out Radio Paradise, which is exceedingly cool.

Selecting SOUNDcast Streams with Streamtuner

If you've taken a shine to the stations listed on the SHOUTcast site but would like a simpler way of browsing through the many streams available, you might consider installing *Streamtuner* (Figure 14-30). This is a simple application that displays all of the streams available on the SHOUTcast site and allows you to play them via Real Player, XMMS, or any other player of your choice.

Installing Streamtuner

To install Streamtuner, just run Xandros Networks, and make sure that the *Debian unsupported site repository* is enabled. After checking that, type **streamtuner** in the text box next to the Search button, and then click **Search**. Streamtuner will then appear in the list of results below (it should be the only item listed). Click **Install**, and then follow the remaining simple installation steps you learned in Chapter 8.

Running and Using Streamtuner

Now that Streamtuner is installed, you can run it via the **Launch** menu by selecting **Applications ▸ Multimedia ▸ streamtuner**. Then all you have to do is locate a stream you would like to play, double-click it, and then . . . well, that's it. The default audio player for MP3 streams (probably RealPlayer or XMMS) will open up and play the stream.

Figure 14-30: Locating SHOUTcast streams made easy with Streamtuner

To aid you in your search for streams, you can also use the genre entries in the left pane of the Streamtuner window. Click the small arrow to the left of one of the genre headings there, and a list of subheadings will appear below. Click one of those subheadings, and the stations of that type will soon appear in the right pane of the window. Clicking the various tabs in the Streamtuner window will also help you in your search.

To change streams, just double-click another, and the stream currently playing in your audio player will be replaced by your new selection. To stop playing a stream, just use the stop button in either XMMS or RealPlayer. That's it.

If you come upon a stream that you really like and thus want to return to often, you can create a bookmark for that stream by going to the **Stream** menu and selecting **Add Bookmark**, and the bookmark for that stream will be added to the Bookmark tab.

Other Audio Applications

I've covered most of the mainstream audio applications that come with your system and a couple that are available from Xandros Networks. There are, however, many others that you can play around with if you like. For example, *MIDI Player*, which you can run by going to the **Launch** menu and selecting **Applications ▸ Multimedia ▸ MIDI Player**, allows you to play standard MIDI or MIDI karaoke files, as you can see in Figure 14-31.

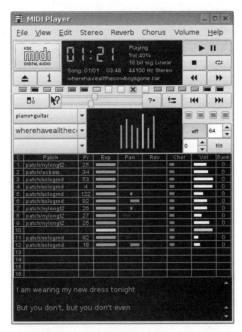

Figure 14-31: Playing a MIDI karaoke file in MIDI Player

If you're interested in that sort of thing, you can find a wide variety of such MIDI or MIDI karaoke files on the Internet by doing a Yahoo or Google search. To get you started, one site you might try out straightaway for MIDI karaoke files is MidiKaraoke.com (http://midikaraoke.com/songdir).

If what you have already isn't enough to satisfy you, there are many other applications available via Xandros Networks. A couple of the applications that you might be interested in are *Rosegarden*, a music-notation editor and MIDI sequencer, and *Audacity*, a multitrack audio editor. There are also numerous XMMS plug-ins available, in addition to those I've already mentioned in this chapter, that will further expand the vast repertoire of things that XMMS can do.

15

COUCH POTATOES

Xandros Does Video

Now that we've covered much of what Xandros can do in terms of audio, let's turn our attention to what is arguably the second most important of its talents in our CNN/MTV-era world: video. Xandros is quite capable in terms of video playback, allowing you to view video files you download from the Internet or from your digital movie camera or watch Internet video streams, video CDs (VCDs), and unencrypted DVDs. If you have a TV tuner card, it even lets you watch television right there on your computer screen.

Media Player (Noatun)

The simplest of players in the Xandros video repertoire is *Media Player* (Figure 15-1), also known as *Noatun*.

Media Player doesn't look like much at first glance, but it is a capable beastie that allows you to play video files in a number of formats, including MPG, AVI (such as those from your digital movie camera), and QuickTime

(.mov). As if that weren't enough, it even allows you to listen to the various types of audio files we've already covered in Chapter 14.

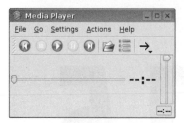

Figure 15-1: Media Player

You may notice when you run Media Player for the first time that there will be no volume controller in the player window that appears on your screen, unlike that in Figure 15-1. If you would like your player to display the controller too, go to the **Settings** menu and select **Show Volume Control**.

Playing a Video File in Media Player

To run Media Player, go to the **Launch** menu and select **Applications ▶ Multimedia ▶ Media Player**. When the player window appears, you can play a file by going to the **File** menu and selecting **Open**. A file selection window will appear, and in that window you can navigate to and then select the file you want to play. Once you've made your selection, click **Open**, and the file will begin playing in a new video playback window.

You can then, if you like, enlarge the viewing size of the Media Player window by simply dragging one of the bottom corners of the player window until it is as big as you want it to be.

The Media Player Playlist

Each time you play a new file in Media Player, whether it be audio or video, it is automatically added to a playlist. Thus, when the file you have just selected has finished playing, the one you viewed or listened to before that, even if it was weeks ago that you did so, will automatically play next. Depending on how you look at the world, this can be considered a rather handy feature . . . or not. If you happen to take a negative view of this default setup, you can configure Media Player so that it will automatically clear the playlist each time you open a new file, thus making it function a bit more like XMMS.

To make this change, just follow these steps:

1. Go to the Media Player **Settings** menu and select **Configure Media Player**.

2. In the Preferences window that appears (Figure 15-2), check the box next to the words *Clear playlist after opening a file*, and then click the **Apply** button to complete the process.

3. Normally, you would now click **OK**, after which the Preferences window would close, but I'll ask you to hold off on doing that for a moment.

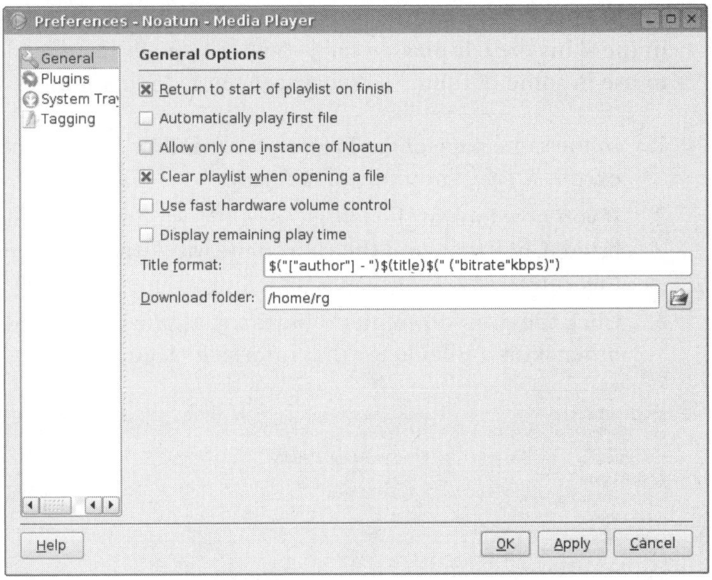

Figure 15-2: Setting Media Player's Preferences

Media Player Plug-Ins

While you have the Preferences window open, it might be fun to play around with the "interface" plug-ins that come with Media Player. These interface plug-ins allow you to change not only the look of the Media Player, as you can with XMMS, but also its size and shape. If you click **Plugins** in the left pane of the window, the various interface choices available to you will appear in the right pane. To see what they all look like in action, deselect the first choice, which is the default interface that you have already seen, and then click all of the others. Click **Apply**, and you will have five very different-looking player windows on your desktop (Figure 15-3). Very cool, you must admit.

Figure 15-3: The many faces of Media Player

Some of these interfaces are configurable both in terms of function and in the skins they display. In fact, you can actually download and install skins to use in some of them. To see what I am talking about, do the following:

1. In the same page of the Preferences window, deselect all of the interfaces except *K-jöfol*, and then click **Apply**.

2. If you now look at the left pane of the window, you will see *K-jöfol Skins* listed. Click that, and the right pane will display the options available for that interface.

3. Click the drop-down menu button that says **kjofol**, and you will see the other skins available for that interface (Figure 15-4).

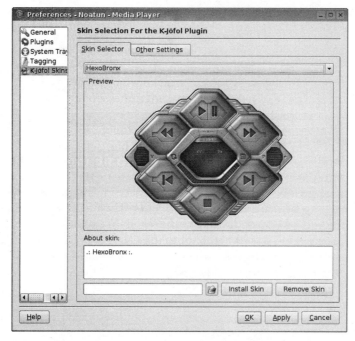

Figure 15-4: Configuring a Media Player interface plug-in

If you would like to install additional skins that you have downloaded, you can do so by clicking the small button that looks like a partially opened folder next to the **Install Skin** button. Navigate to it, select the skin file you downloaded, and click **Install Skin**.

Playing Video Streams with RealPlayer

In Chapter 14, we covered RealPlayer's role as an audio application, allowing you to play Internet audio streams. Audio streams are not the only thing that RealPlayer can handle, however, as you can use it to play video streams as well. If you would like to try out RealPlayer's capabilities for playing video streams, or if you just happen to be a fan of Katie Holmes, point your web browser to http://www.katieholmespictures.com/videos.shtml, scroll down to the section that says *Streaming Katie Videos* (web pages do change through time, so just search a bit through the site if it's not there), and then try out one of the many clips available.

If the Beatles are more your cup of tea, try "The Birth of Beatlemania" at NPR's All Songs Considered site (http://www.npr.org/programs/asc/archives/beatles40). Be sure to click the **Real Media** link on that page. Either way you go, once you have made your selection, RealPlayer will pop up and begin playing the stream in a slightly enlarged window.

If you would like to view the video at an enlarged size, you have two ways of going about it. The first and easiest way, depending on your level of mouse-wielding dexterity, is the same as I mentioned for Media Player in the previous section—just drag one of the bottom corners of the RealPlayer window until it is the size you prefer. The other way is to go to the **View** menu and select **Fullscreen** or **Zoom ▶ Double Size**.

Playing DVDs and VCDs

Your Xandros system also allows you to play DVDs; however, due to licensing concerns, playback is limited to unencrypted discs. Unfortunately, this rules out a vast majority of the DVD movies you buy or rent at your local video shop, thus leaving you with a rather limited choice of movies that you can play on your computer. Of course, DVDs created on personal computers (such as the DVD slideshows that people create these days with applications such as iDVD on the Mac) pose no problem.

DVD Encryption

You may be wondering at this point what encrypted DVDs are, why they are encrypted, and why you can't play them, so I will fill you in. Commercial DVDs are almost always encrypted with CSS (Content Scramble System). The main purpose for encrypting DVDs with CSS is supposedly to prevent piracy. CSS, however, does a bit more than that, as it is also used to enforce regional encodings (more on that in the next section) and to prevent you from skipping through, among other things, those FBI warnings that appear when you first play a DVD.

In order for a device, such as your stand-alone DVD deck beneath your TV or the DVD playback software on your computer, to play an encrypted DVD, it has to have a CSS decryption key. This is available to any company that wants to include it, but in order for that company to do so legally, it has to pay for the right. Most Linux distros, such as Xandros, do not include the key because, among many reasons, they would have to pass on the costs to you if they did. When you buy Mac OS X or most DVD playback software for Windows, on the other hand, you are in fact paying for that key—a hidden cost of sorts.

So I Can't Play My Hollywood Blockbusters in Linux?

Now you may think that this lack of encrypted DVD playback in Linux is a major stumbling block, but that is not actually the case. You can add the CSS key yourself, and it is supposedly legal for you, as an end user, to do so. I'm no lawyer, however, so I won't swear to the fact.

Installing the CSS key (for Xine) is quite easily done, but it is one of the rare cases, in Xandros anyway, when you will have to resort to the command line. If you are interested in adding encrypted DVD playback capability to your Xandros system, I have the steps for you to follow in Chapter 20.

Things to Think About: Television Standards and Regional Encodings

If you do happen to find some movies on DVD that are not encrypted, there are some points you need to consider. If you are strictly a domestic-market sort of buyer, these points may prove to be of little concern to you, but it is still best to be informed so as to avoid any problems down the line. The things that a true DVD aficionado must keep in mind are television broadcast and recording standards and regional encodings.

Television Broadcast and Recording Standards

Whether you are talking TV, video, or DVD, television standards are, whether you know it or not, of concern to you. Have you ever anxiously plopped a videotape you got in the mail from a friend or relative back in Brazil or Poland into your VCR, only to find that you couldn't view it? The reason is different television broadcast and recording standards.

There are three main standards in the world today: *NTSC (National Television System Committee)*, used in North America, parts of South America, Japan, and South Korea; *SECAM (SEquential Couleur Avec Memoire)*, found in France, former French colonies, and former European East-bloc countries; and *PAL (Phase Alternating Line)*, used almost everywhere else. There are also variations of each of these, some of which are incompatible with one another.

The reasons for these differences are rooted in the availability of technology at the time the various standards were adopted and, as with so many other things in life, politics. SECAM, for example, was essentially created to protect French industry, while it was commonly adopted in the former East-bloc countries to discourage citizens of those countries from viewing Western television broadcasts.

DVD Regional Encodings

The other important thing to remember when dealing with DVDs is regional encodings. You may have noticed that on many of the DVDs you buy there is a small logo on the back of the package that looks like a globe with a number in the middle of it. If you are in the United States or Canada, the number will be *1*, usually with the television standard written underneath, which would be NTSC in this case (Figure 15-5).

Figure 15-5: Examples of regional encoding labels on DVD packages

If you were in Japan, that logo would read *2 NTSC*, while if you were in Britain, it would be *2 PAL*. The number within the logo represents the region for which the DVD is encoded. There are six such regions, with the United States, U.S. territories, and Canada forming Region 1. Japan, Europe, the Middle East, South Africa, and Greenland make up Region 2.

This is very important, because DVDs encoded for one region are not playable in machines manufactured for use in another. Thus, if you buy a DVD in the United States and then try to play it on a DVD player in Japan, it won't work, despite both countries using the NTSC standard. If you buy a DVD in Britain (Region 2) and try to play it on a machine in Japan (also Region 2), it also won't work, but this time because of the different television standards (PAL versus NTSC).

When it comes to playing DVDs on your computer, however, things are quite different, in that television standards are mostly irrelevant. Regional encodings are also irrelevant in some ways. When you burn a disc on your DVD burner, or when you play a DVD that someone else burned on theirs, regional encodings are not involved. However, if you buy and then play a DVD movie on that drive, the relevancy of regional encodings comes back into play.

When you buy a computer with a built-in DVD drive, or when you buy an external DVD drive, that drive is usually set up to play DVDs encoded for the region in which you bought your machine. Unlike the DVD players you hook up to your TV, however, those in or connected to your computer allow you to play DVDs of any regional encoding.

This generous feature is limited, however, and this is where you need to be careful. Depending on the manufacturer of your drive, you will be able to switch back and forth between DVDs of differing regional encodings only four or five times. After that, the drive, usually without warning, will be locked into the regional encoding of the disc you were playing for the final switch . . . *forever*. This is unrelated to your operating system—it is strictly a hardware matter.

There is one exception to this region-lock rule. DVDs labeled as *Region Free* or *ALL* (sometimes somewhat inaccurately labeled as *Region 0*) can be played on any DVD player in any region and thus do not register as a regional encoding switch when you plop one of them in your computer's DVD drive. If you therefore play a Region 1 DVD, followed by a Region Free DVD, and then play another Region 1 DVD after that, there will be no change, in your drive's view, as to the number of times you have switched encodings.

If you are curious as to the whys of this rather odd regional-encoding system, it is all based on marketing. The Hollywood studios came up with this system because theatrical releases of their films abroad often lag behind the home releases (DVDs and videos) in the United States. By locking American and Canadian home releases with regional encodings, they can thus be assured that people in other countries will have to wait for the films to be released in theaters in order to see them. In addition, by limiting sales of American and Canadian discs to their respective domestic markets, the studios can then command higher prices when selling distribution rights to foreign distributors.

Depending on how you look at things, it all makes good business sense or may just be an example of unbridled greed. Either way, it is nothing more than a headache for the end user.

Playing DVDs with Xine

Now that you have been forewarned as to the possible pitfalls you may encounter when dealing with DVDs, let's get on to the business of playing them. The application that Xandros, and most other Linux distributions, uses for DVD playback is called *Xine*, which you've already caught a glimpse of in Chapter 6 (see Figure 6-3).

Running Xine

To run Xine, go to the **Launch** menu and select **Applications ▸ Multimedia ▸ Video Player**.

As you will see, Xine consists of two windows: a playback window and a rather handsome controller. These are actually two different applications, with the application that displays the playback window, Xine, providing the main playback capabilities to your system. This may mean little to you, but it is worth noting, because you can use a different controller interface to take advantage of Xine's capabilities if you like, a point I will discuss later on in the "gxine" section of this chapter.

The first time you run Xine, a third window will also appear. This is the Setup window (Figure 15-6), which you can open at any time by right-clicking anywhere in the Xine playback window and selecting **Settings ▸ Setup** in the pop-up menu that appears. For the time being, however, there is probably nothing you really need to do with this window, so you can go ahead and close it for now by clicking **OK**.

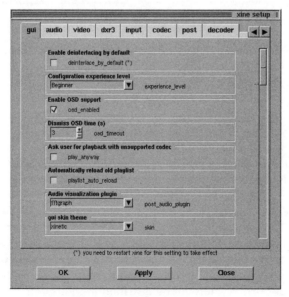

Figure 15-6: The Xine Setup window

Getting to Know the Xine Controller

As you can see by looking at the Xine controller (Figure 15-7), using Xine isn't all that different from using a standard DVD player or VCR, since most of the basic controls (play, back, forward, pause, and eject) are clustered together in a circle, just as they are on the video decks you might have in your home.

Figure 15-7: The Xine controller

There are a few other control buttons that are different, however, so it would be helpful for you to know what they do. The control buttons (they're numbered in Figure 15-7) in the Xine controller consist of the following:

Playlist (1)
Opens a window, in which you can create a playlist of files you'd like to play. This feature is more useful when playing audio tracks (yes, Xine can do that too) or video files on your hard disk than when playing DVDs.

Control (2)
Opens a window, in which you can adjust the color, saturation, brightness, and contrast of the display for the video file you are viewing. As you can see in the right side of the window in Figure 15-8, it also allows you to change the appearance of the Xine controller by applying different skins. You can do this by clicking any of the choices in the list (there are three that come with your system), and the changes will take place immediately.

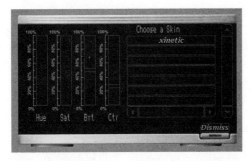

Figure 15-8: The Xine controller and Control window in different skins

Setup Window (3)
Brings up the Setup window (shown in Figure 15-6).

Quit (4)
Quits Xine, thus closing both the playback window and the controller.

Snapshot (5)

Takes a snapshot of the frame currently being viewed in the player window and saves it to your Home folder as a .png file.

Mute (6)

Toggles the audio portion of the file you are viewing or listening to.

Navigator (7)

Brings up the rather primitive-looking Navigator window (Figure 15-9), which allows you to easily navigate through the various menus encoded within the DVD itself.

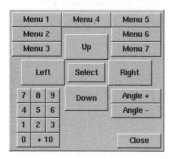

Figure 15-9: The Xine Navigator window

Close Window (8)

Closes only the Xine controller window. You can later reopen the controller window by right-clicking anywhere in the playback window and selecting **GUI visibility**.

Fullscreen (9)

Displays the video you are watching at full-screen width. You can later return to window view by pressing the ESC key.

Playing DVDs in Xine

Actually playing a DVD in Xine is very straightforward. Just place a DVD in your drive and, after the LED on the drive stops blinking, press the **DVD** button in the Xine controller window. The DVD will then start playing in the playback window. That's basically it.

Using Xine to Play VCDs

Xine can also play video CDs, which are better known as VCDs. As I mentioned in Chapter 6, VCDs are videos recorded on CD rather than DVD blanks. Because of the more limited capacity of CD media, an average commercial film comes on two discs. Playing these discs, however, is little different from playing DVDs. Just place the VCD in your drive, wait for the drive's LED to stop blinking, and then click the **VCD** button in the Xine controller window. If that doesn't work, click the **VCDO** button instead.

Oh, and in case you're wondering, VCDs do not have regional encodings.

gxine

As I mentioned in the previous section, the controller that appears when you run Xine is actually a graphical user interface for the normally command-driven Xine. There are, however, other interfaces that you can employ in order to use Xine. My personal favorite is one called *gxine*, which takes a one-window approach to video viewing, as you can see in Figure 15-10.

If you would like to give gxine a go, you can easily do so via Xandros networks. Just type **gxine** in the text box next to the Search button, and press the ENTER key. The installation is a standard one, so there will be no differences from what you learned in Chapter 8.

Figure 15-10: Viewing video files and discs with gxine

Once gxine is installed, you can run it from the **Launch** menu by selecting **Run Command**. When the Run Command window appears, type **gxine** and then click **Run**. When the player opens, you can navigate to and play the file or disc type you want to view via the **File** menu.

TV Time

Many computer users have video capture or TV tuner cards installed in one of the PCI slots within their computers. These cards allow you to take video output from an external source, such as a VCR, and display that output in a separate window on your computer screen—a sort of monitor-within-a-monitor arrangement.

TV tuner cards, an example of which is shown in Figure 15-11, are actually mini–TV tuners connected to an antenna or your cable television source, which allow you to watch live television and change channels in the same monitor-within-a-monitor setup. Some even come with remote controllers. Like video capture cards, they also usually allow you to display output from your VCR or other external video sources on your computer screen. In Xandros, the application that provides the onscreen monitor for displaying the video output from these devices is called *TV Time*.

Installing TV Time

If you are thinking of installing a video capture or TV tuner card in your machine but have yet to do so, hold off on installing TV Time until that card is actually installed. If you already have a card installed, you can install TV Time by running Xandros Networks, typing **tvtime** in the box next to the Search button, and then pressing ENTER. When TV Time appears in the main pane of the XN window, click **Install**, and the installation process will proceed in the usual manner you learned in Chapter 8 . . . except at the very end. Unlike the installation process for most other applications from Xandros Networks, the one for TV Time will include a few configuration steps before the process is complete.

Figure 15-11: A TV tuner card

After the download and installation progress bars reach 100 percent and disappear, you will be asked three simple bits of information in the same Updating System window. Don't worry too much about making a mistake, however, because you can change these settings at any time after the application is installed. The three steps are as follows:

1. Select the default television standard for your location (Figure 15-12). As I explained in the previous section on playing DVDs, different countries use different broadcast standards. Therefore, what you type at this stage depends on where you live. If you live in the United States or Canada, type **1** for NTSC. If you live in France, type **2** for SECAM, and if you live somewhere in the rest of Europe, Australia, or New Zealand, type **3** for PAL. If you happen to live in Japan, as I do at

the present time, type **7** for NTSC-JP. Once you have entered the appropriate choice, click the **Enter** button in the XN window (or just press ENTER on your keyboard).

2. Select the default frequency table. The choices in this step are quite simple. If you receive your television signal via cable, type **1**; if you receive it by antenna, type **2**. Once you have done that, click **Enter** or press ENTER on your keyboard.

3. Do you wish to make '/usr/bin/tvtime' setuid root? Just accept the default (no) here to avoid having to deal with root privileges by clicking **Enter** or pressing the ENTER key.

Once you have completed these three steps, the word *Done* will appear in the main pane of the XN window. You can then click the **Close** button.

Figure 15-12: Following the configuration steps while installing TV Time

Running TV Time

Now that the installation is complete, you can run TV Time by going to the **Launch** menu and selecting **Applications** ▶ **Multimedia** ▶ **TV Time**. TV Time will open as a simple, blackened, menu-less window. The first time you run it, there will also be a configuration menu displayed at the middle of the screen; however, since you will have already performed the basic configuration during the installation process, you can go ahead and close this menu by clicking **Exit**.

NOTE   *If you want to change your settings in the future, you can bring up the settings menu at any time by right-clicking anywhere in the TV Time window.*

After that, what appears in the window is between you and the video output device you have connected to your card or, if you have a TV tuner card, the tuner card itself. TV Time itself is nothing more than a software version of a video monitor.

Getting Your Own Video Capture or TV Tuner Card

If the idea of watching videos or television on your computer screen as you tend to your other business sounds attractive to you, you might consider buying a video capture or TV tuner card for yourself, assuming you don't already have one. These cards are rather inexpensive (some are less than $50 via mail-order outlets), so it is all quite doable. That said, you should also be aware that support for such cards in Linux is rather limited, so it is important to check around before parting with your money. Checking the Xandros User Forums for postings in that regard, or directly asking for advice, is probably a very wise thing to do.

16

DOING THE LEFT BANK

Working with Graphics Applications

Now that you have gotten a taste of Xandros's audio and video capabilities, let's round out this more artistic side of things by focusing on its graphical capabilities. You have already learned to download and view images from your digital camera and how to add yet other images via your scanner, but Xandros doesn't force you to leave things at that. With the graphics applications that come bundled with your Xandros system, and still others available via Xandros Networks, you can go on to enhance and manipulate those images or even create totally different ones of your own. In addition, you will be able to take screenshots of your desktop and other application windows. Basically, if you want to get graphical, your Xandros system comes with the tools that allow you to do so.

Paint

Bundled with your system is perhaps the simplest of graphics applications—*Paint* (also known as *KolourPaint*). When you run Paint (**Launch** ▸ **Applications** ▸ **Graphics** ▸ **Paint**), you will notice that in terms of how you use it and how it functions, it is very similar to the Paint program that comes with Windows systems (Figure 16-1).

Paint is equipped with all of the basic paint tools (brush, pencil, fills, eraser, shapes, and so on) to allow you to create simple images, though not particularly sophisticated or complex ones. This seeming lack of sophistication is one of the reasons that Paint goes largely overlooked by most users. But as the saying goes, you can't judge a book by its cover, and Paint has a lot more to offer beneath the surface than first appearances might seem to indicate.

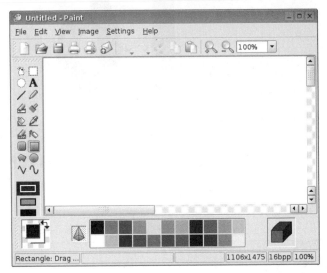

Figure 16-1: Paint—a seemingly simple, but actually surprisingly capable, application

Changing Image File Formats in Paint

Graphics files come in a variety of types. The images from your digital camera, for example, are usually JPEG (.jpg), which along with GIF (.gif) is the most common file type for the images used on web pages. There are, of course, still others. Sometimes you may need to convert an image from one file type to another, for example, when you are preparing an image to use on a web page of your own. Paint is capable of performing many of these conversions, though not all of them. However, since Paint can read images in the most common graphic formats (.gif, .jpg, .bmp, .png, .pcx, .ico, .tif) and can write files in many of the formats most likely to be of interest to you (.bmp, .jpg, .png), it can prove to be quite useful when performing such conversions.

Let's say that you have a .bmp image that you would like to use in a new home page you are working on. In this case, you want to convert the .bmp image into a web-friendly .jpg image. Here's what you would do:

1. Open the .bmp image in Paint by going to the **File** menu and selecting **Open**.

2. Without doing anything else, go to the **File** menu again and select **Save As**.

3. When the Save Image As window appears (Figure 16-2), select **JPEG image** from the drop-down menu button next to *Filter*.

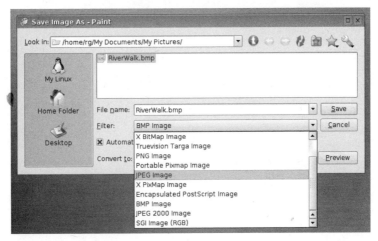

Figure 16-2: Changing the file format of an image in Paint

4. If you want to reduce the time it will take to load the picture on your web page, decrease the quality of the picture by using the sliding bar next to the word *Quality* (this slider will appear in the Save Image As window once you have selected **JPEG image** in the drop-down menu). The trade-off between image quality and load time is something you will have to come to terms with yourself, but a bit of trial and error should provide you with a happy medium.

5. Once finished, click **Save**, and that's all there is to it.

Resizing Your Images in Paint

You have no doubt found yourself with images that are just a tad bigger than you would like them to be, especially if you have one of today's multimillion-megapixel digital cameras. There are many applications that allow you to shrink such images down to size, so to speak, to make them easier and lighter to use in email messages, web pages, and whatever else you have in mind. Using Paint for this purpose is especially handy. To reduce the size of an image, open it in Paint (**File ▶ Open**), and then follow these steps:

1. Select **Resize/Scale** in the **Image** menu.

2. In the Resize/Scale window that appears (Figure 16-3), click the **Scale** button. If you are resizing a line drawing, you might want to try **Smooth Scale** instead in order to reduce the jaggedness of the lines. If you're not sure which to use, try one first, undo your work once you've had a look, and then start over and try the other.

3. In the same window, check the box next to *Keep aspect ratio*. This retains the ratio between the width and height of the image, so that you don't end up with a peculiar-looking stretched-out result.

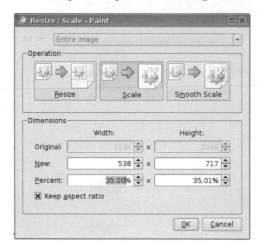

Figure 16-3: Shrinking an image down to size in Paint

4. Finally, in either of the boxes next to the word *Percent*, set the percentage of reduction you would like to perform.

5. When you have finished, click the **OK** button, and the results will be seen immediately in the main window.

6. If the size of the resized image is what you were hoping for, go to the **File** menu, select **Save As**, and save the file with a new name, thereby retaining a full-sized copy of the original, which is always a good idea. If you would instead like to have a second go at things, so as to make the image a bit smaller or larger, go to the **Edit** menu, select **Undo: Scale**, and then start over again from step 1.

Cropping an Image in Paint

Sometimes, the problem you have with an image is not its size (or not only its size) but rather that what you really want to see in the image is too small. For example, let's say that the only things you are really concerned with in the image in Figure 16-4 are the horse and buggy.

That being the case, you could crop the photo to include just that portion of the image. Here's how you go about it:

1. Use the **rectangular selection tool** (the top-right icon in the tool panel at the left of the window in Figure 16-4), and then select the portion of the image you want to crop. Once you have done that, a dashed line will appear surrounding that portion of the image.

2. Next, go to the **Selection** menu, and select **Set as Image (Crop)**.

Figure 16-4: The focus of your image lost in superfluous details

The image will now appear in the main window reduced to the area you selected in step 1 (Figure 16-5).

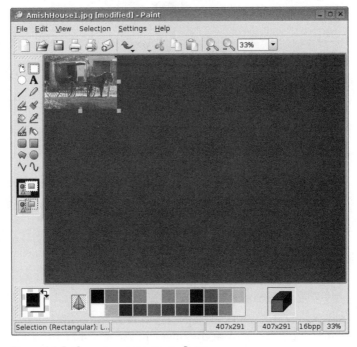

Figure 16-5: Cropping an image in Paint

3. The image may seem uncomfortably small if you were viewing the original at a reduced size. If so, go to the box next to the two magnifying-glass icons and choose **100%** or thereabouts. You will then be able to see the image at its new full size.

4. If you like the results, go to the **File** menu, select **Save As**, and save the file with a new name.

Converting Color Images to Grayscale in Paint

Paint also allows you to easily convert color images into black-and-white grayscale images, should you want to do so for whatever reason. To make the transformation, just go to the **Image** menu and select **Reduce to Grayscale**. You can then go to the **File** menu and select **Save As** to save the newly transformed image with a new name.

Rotating Images in Paint

Paint also allows you to rotate or skew pictures that are incorrectly oriented. To rotate an image, just go to the **Image** menu and select **Rotate**.

When the Rotate Image window appears (Figure 16-6), select **Counterclockwise** or **Clockwise** (depending on the direction in which you want to rotate the image), and then select the number of degrees you want to rotate the image. Once finished, click **OK**.

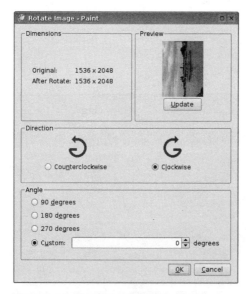

Figure 16-6: Rotating an image in Paint

Skewing Images in Paint

Sometimes the angles of objects in your pictures may be so off as to be almost annoying. If you look at the image in the left of Figure 16-7, you can see that the lighthouse tower is severely skewed.

Figure 16-7: Michigan's Tawas Lighthouse in need of some corrective skewing

If you like, you can correct this in Paint, though the building to the left of the tower will then look a bit off as a result. It all depends on what matters most to you.

Anyway, to skew an image in Paint, first open the image, and then select **Skew** in the **Image** menu.

When the Skew Image window appears (Figure 16-8), you can adjust the number of degrees you would like to skew the image, either horizontally or vertically (or both), using the two boxes below. When finished, click **OK**.

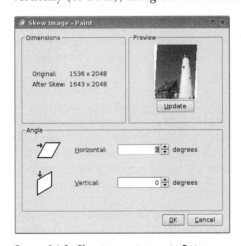

Figure 16-8: Skewing an image in Paint

As you will no doubt notice, in the results (shown in the left side of Figure 16-9), your now properly skewed image will have some unsightly white areas at its top-left and bottom-right sides.

Figure 16-9: An image skewed in Paint, before and after cropping

To get rid of these unwanted white spaces, crop the image so as to eliminate those areas, which will leave you with a more appealing final product, as you can see at the right side of Figure 16-9.

Playing Around with Effects in Paint

Paint allows you to modify your images in still other ways via its More Image Effects window (**Image ▶ More Effects**). When that window first opens, you will see the traditional brightness and contrast settings controls, which are very useful for that purpose. However, there is a bit more lurking behind this window's skin . . . actually within its Effect menu, to be exact. By clicking the drop-down menu button next to the word *Effect*, you can see still other options available to you.

These effect options include *Emboss*, an example of which is shown in Figure 16-10; *Flatten*, which allows you to reduce the image down to two colors of your choosing for some very psychedelic results; *Invert*, which provides you with results that look like a photo negative; *Reduce Colors*, which allows you to lower the number of colors in the image or change it to grayscale; and *Soften and Sharpen*, which allows you to do exactly what its name implies.

You might not be familiar with many of these functions, so go ahead and play around with them. Just remember that, regardless of what you do while experimenting with these various effects, no permanent damage will be done to your image unless you select **Save** from the **File** menu. That said, don't do it.

Figure 16-10: Embossing an image via Paint's More Image Effects window

Project 16A: Getting Arty with the GIMP

Well, if Paint isn't enough to satisfy your budding artistic urges, and you are aching for a bit more excitement, then it's time to go for the *GIMP* (Figure 16-11).

The GIMP, often compared very favorably to Adobe's Photoshop (albeit without that application's exorbitant cost), is a graphics application that allows you to create original images and, more important, retouch or completely doctor image files, such as those from your digital camera. Want to put some color in your cheeks, you say? Or how about getting rid of that red-eye that makes you look like one of the ghoulish characters out of an episode of *Buffy the Vampire Slayer*? The GIMP lets you do not only these things but others, such as airbrush out unwanted shadows (or even facial blemishes), give your image a canvas texture, change a photo into an oil painting, or even add a bell pepper or a pointing hand here and there.

Just in case you're wondering, *GIMP* stands for *GNU Image Manipulation Program* (and *GNU*, the organization that promotes the development of Linux and related free software, is a recursive acronym for *GNU's Not Unix*).

16A-1: Downloading and Installing the GIMP

Although the GIMP does not come bundled with your Xandros system, it is available via Xandros Networks. To get it, run **Xandros Networks**, type **gimp** in the search box near the top of the window, and then click the **Search** button. When the results of your search appear in the pane below, click **Install** next to *GIMP Image Editor* (it should be the only entry in the list), and then follow the usual drill for installing files via Xandros Networks.

Figure 16-11: The Gimp

16A-2: Running the GIMP

Once you have downloaded and installed the GIMP, you can run it by going to the **Launch** menu and selecting **Applications ▸ Graphics ▸ GIMP Image Editor**. The very first time you do this, you will be presented with the *GIMP User Installation Wizard* (Figure 16-12), but working through it is strictly a no-brainer, as all you have to do is click **Continue** in each screen of the wizard until it is finished.

16A-3: Familiarizing Yourself with the GIMP's Interface

As you saw in Figure 16-11, the GIMP is a multi-window application. It first opens as a set of two rather tall palette-like windows and then adds still others as you open images or other tools. While this approach works out quite well, it can be somewhat disconcerting at first. Basically, the left window is the main GIMP window, which is divided into two sections, shown separately in Figure 16-13.

Figure 16-12: The GIMP User Installation Wizard

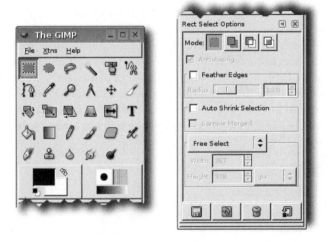

Figure 16-13: The top and bottom halves of the main GIMP window

The top half is a collection of the various drawing and selection tools available. The bottom half, on the other hand, shows the options available for each of those tools. This being the case, when you click a different tool in the top half of the window, the options in the bottom half change to reflect the options for the tool you've just selected.

The right GIMP window, like the left, also consists of two halves, each of which you can see in Figure 16-14.

The top half of the window shows the layers (a topic I'll cover in greater detail later on in this project), channels, and paths for a selected image. The contents of the window thus change when you click different open image windows.

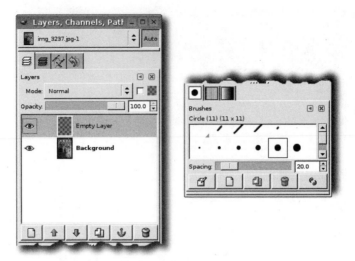

Figure 16-14: The top and bottom halves of the GIMP's Layers, Channels, Paths window

The bottom half, unlike that of the left window, really has no relation to the top; it is merely where you select from the various brush styles, patterns, and gradients available in the GIMP, regardless of whether or not you have selected a tool that can utilize such options.

Finally, we come to the matter of menus. In most applications, the main menu selections are available via the menu bar in the main program window. In the GIMP, however, the menu bar provides only three entries, and the options within those are quite limited. The main options in the GIMP are instead to be found in the menu bar of each image window, as you can see in Figure 16-15. This is where you will be able to, among other things, save, add various effects to, and resize your image.

Figure 16-15: GIMP menu bars in the main and an image window

16A-4: Putting It All Together (and Learning a Bit More) by Creating a Custom Desktop Wallpaper

I could describe and explain all of the GIMP's various tools, filters, and other features, but to cover them all one-by-one would fill up an entire book. Given the many other topics that must be covered within the confines of these covers, however, I just can't do that. What I can do is give you a chance to play around with what the GIMP has in store and in the process create something that might actually be of some use. What I have in mind is a custom-made desktop wallpaper.

So that you will know what sort of images you will need to complete this project, let me first describe what the final creation will look like. Basically, we are going to take a main background image, such as a landscape or cityscape, and add snapshots of people on top of it. For example, let's say that you took a family trip to Walt Disney World last summer. In this case, you would use a landscape shot of Disney World, preferably one with lots of open top space (aka sky), and then add snapshots of each person who went on the trip. Of course, you can add pictures of your favorite film stars if that's what you want to do. It's all up to you. Just make sure that you have a background image that has a lot of top space. For pasting purposes, four snapshots should do nicely. It's also nice if you can choose two vertical and two horizontal shots, for maximum effect.

For my part, I will be using the photo of Wilmington, North Carolina, that I took last summer (shown way back in Figure 11-17) and, to paste on top of that, some photos of friends I visited at that time (Figure 16-16).

Figure 16-16: Examples of photos to be used in a custom desktop wallpaper (excluding the background image)

Once you have selected your pictures, open them all in the GIMP, and then save each one under a new name, such as donnyatdisney_project.jpg, to protect the originals. After you've done that, you'll be ready to follow along. Here goes. . . .

Phase One: Cropping

The first thing you may (or may not) have to do is crop all or some of the images you will be pasting onto the background image. Since these images will be much smaller than the background, you will want the content of those images to be clear . . . and big. That being the case, if the person you are going to be focusing on in a particular image is dwarfed by his or her surroundings, you'll need to crop.

The image on the left side of Figure 16-17 is a good example, where my friend is barely visible, while his house clearly is. Since it is my friend whom I wanted to add to my wallpaper, not his house, I had to do some cropping.

Figure 16-17: An image before and after cropping

To crop the image to about the size I wanted, as seen on the right side of Figure 16-17, I clicked the **cropping tool** (second row, last tool in Figure 16-13) and then, with that tool, outlined the area I wanted to crop, as seen in Figure 16-18. When finished, I clicked the **Crop** button, and the job was done.

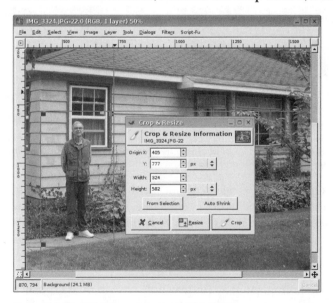

Figure 16-18: Cropping an image in the GIMP

Phase Two: Resizing

Once you've cropped any images in need, the next thing you have to do is resize the photos so that they all pretty much have the same dimensions and so that they will appear at an appropriate size in contrast to the much bigger background image. Here are the steps:

1. Determine the size of the background image by clicking the window for that image and then selecting **Image ▸ Canvas Size**.

2. When the Canvas Size window appears (Figure 16-19), note the larger of the two numbers near the top of the window, whether it be Height or Width. In the case of Figure 16-19, note the dimensions of the image as displayed near the top of the Canvas Size window (1986 × 1452 pixels in this case).

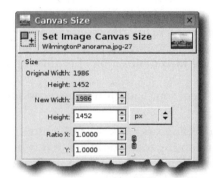

Figure 16-19: Determining the size of an image

3. The size of the vertical images you paste onto the background image should be approximately one-fourth the height of the background, so once you know the height of your background image, do the math. In my case, the ideal size would be around 360 pixels (4 × 360 = 1440); yours will most likely be slightly different.

    It is probably helpful, though not absolutely necessary at this point, to view all of your images at their full size. This helps avoid confusion in terms of perception. You can tell the size at which you are viewing an image by looking at the title bar, where it will say, at the very end of the title, *100%* or *37%* or whatever (see top of Figure 16-18). You want them all to be showing at 100%, so look for any that aren't, click them (one-by-one, of course), and then select **Zoom ▸ 1:1 (100%)** in the **View** menu. When you have done this for each of the photos in question, you are ready to move on and resize the images.

4. Choose one of the vertical paste-on images by clicking it or its window, and select **Scale Image** in the **Image** menu.

5. When the Scale Image window appears, adjust the number for the *Height* box in the top half of the window so that it matches the number you

determined to be appropriate in your case. Don't worry about the width, as the height-to-width ratio will be retained automatically.

6.   When finished, click **OK**, and then repeat the process for the other vertical image.

Next, move on to the horizontal paste-on images. The process for these is the same, but this time, after the Scale Image window appears, adjust the number of the pixels in the *New Width* box so that it is the same number of pixels as that you used for the height of the vertical images. Doing this will make the horizontal images as wide as the vertical images, which will produce a better-looking final product. Anyway, once you have done that, click **OK**, and then move on and do the same for the remaining paste-on image.

Phase Three: Turning Your Background Image into a Work of Art

Okay, now that you've gotten everything ready, it's time to start playing around with filters and effects. The first thing you're going to do is turn your background image into an oil painting. Although this sounds like a rather spectacular thing to do, it is incredibly simple. Just follow these steps:

1.   Go to the **Filters** menu of your background image window and select **Artistic ▸ Oilify**.

2.   Once the Oilify window appears, click the **OK** button, after which a progress bar will start moving to the right at the very bottom of the background image window, signaling the progress of the oilification process. Once it is complete, you will notice the changes.

      If you would like things to look a bit more oilified, go to the **Edit** menu, select **Undo**, and then repeat the Oilify steps. However, this time around, when the Oilify window appears (Figure 16-20), click the box next to *Use Intensity Algorithm*, and increase the number of the *Mask Size* in order to increase the effect. In case you're wondering, the Intensity Algorithm helps retain the colors and detail of your original image, while the Mask Size refers to the brush size of the oilified image—higher numbers produce larger strokes and thus oilier looking results.

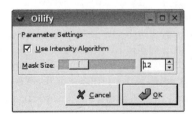

Figure 16-20: Adjusting settings for the Oilify filter in the GIMP

3.   Now that your background image has become a work of art, it seems only fitting that it be on canvas rather than flat paper. To do this, go to the **Filters** menu and select **Artistic ▸ Apply Canvas**.

4. When the Apply Canvas window appears, click **OK**, and within a few seconds your new work of art will look like something that should be hanging in a museum.

NOTE *If you are not viewing your background image at full size, which is quite likely given the fact that it should be a very large image, things will look like a mess at this point. In order to feel a bit more comfortable with what has just happened, go to the **View** menu and select **Zoom 4 1:1 (100%)**. You will then see that things actually look pretty much as I just described them, as you can see in the selection from my own background image shown in Figure 16-21.*

Figure 16-21: A close-up section of an oilified image on canvas

Phase Four: Adding the Paste-on Images

Now that your canvas is ready, it is time to add your paste-on images. Rather than just stick them on in their upright positions, however, we are instead going to rotate each of them a bit so as to achieve a more lively pattern, looking something like that in Figure 16-22.

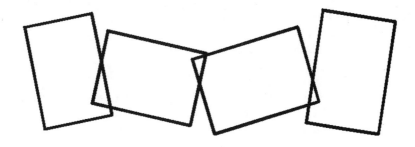

Figure 16-22: The pattern in which the paste-on images will be applied

Whether you want to overlap the images or not depends on the sizes of your images and your own personal tastes.

We'll be adding the images one-by-one, so start with one of your vertical images first by clicking its window and then copying it by going to the **Edit** menu and selecting **Copy**. After that, follow these steps:

1. Click the window of the background image.

2. Now go to the *Layers, Channels, Paths* window (Figure 16-14), and make sure that the title of your background image is listed just below the title bar. If so, click the **New Layer** button, which is the first button on the left in the middle of the window. If you're not sure which one it is, just move your mouse over the buttons without clicking, and a small box will appear telling you what each is (Figure 16-23). Once you do this, a new layer, titled *Empty Layer*, will appear highlighted in the pane above the buttons.

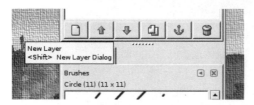

Figure 16-23: The New Layer button

Before moving on, it is probably a good idea at this point to explain briefly how layers work. In the case of our wallpaper project, the easiest way to envision this is to think of your background image as a painting on paper. On top of that, you are adding clear sheets of plastic (the layers) upon which you will draw other elements. If you don't like what you've added on one sheet, you can simply throw the sheet into the trash, and your other sheets will remain as they were before, untouched and intact. You can, of course, add still more sheets to add still other items. Every step is thus protected from any slip-ups you might make in the next step. All very useful and convenient.

If this explanation comes across as somewhat obtuse, perhaps it will help to put it into the context of what we are going to be doing in this project.

If you take a look at Figure 16-24, you will see that you will be adding two layers for each paste-on image you add to your background image, one for the paste-on image itself and one for its shadow. That means that you will actually be adding eight different layers (assuming you are adding four paste-on images) in total. Well, all that said, let's get back to work.

3. Now that you have added an empty layer to your background image, click that image, and then select **Paste** in the **Edit** menu (remember, we copied the image just before we started step 1). Your first paste-on image will then appear within the background image (actually in its own layer), surrounded by a dashed-line selection box.

4. Next, drag the image and place it somewhere in the upper-left portion of the background image. Remember that your desktop has icons on it, so you don't want to place the image too far to the left. Also be careful not to click anywhere except within the area of the selected paste-on image, since you want to keep it selected.

Figure 16-24: The layers required in this project to add a paste-on image to the background

5. Now we are going to the rotate the image a tad so as to match the pattern in Figure 16-23. To do this, click the **rotation tool** (first button, third row) (Figure 16-11), and then click within the selected paste-on image in your new layer.

6. The paste-on image will then be covered by a grid. Click the top-left corner of that grid, and rotate the image until it is at an angle of about -11 or -12 degrees. You can see the angle of rotation in the Rotate window, which will have automatically appeared along with the grid covering your paste-on. Your image window should then look pretty much like mine in Figure 16-25.

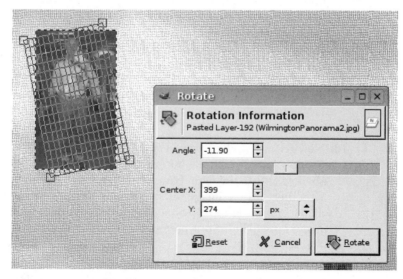

Figure 16-25: Rotating your paste-on image

7. Once everything looks about right, click the **Rotate** button to actualize the rotation of the paste-on image.

8. Now you will add a drop shadow so as to enhance the pasted-on look of the image. To do this, go to the **Script-Fu** menu in the menu bar of your main image window and select **Shadow ▶ Drop Shadow**. When the Drop-Shadow window appears, click the **OK** button.

   When you now look at your image, you will probably be in for a bit of a shock because your newly created shadow will be on top of your paste-on image rather than under it, where it should be (Figure 16-26). This is, odd as it may seem, how it is supposed to be, so don't panic.

Figure 16-26: A seemingly misplaced shadow

9. To correct this peculiar situation, first click the **rectangular selection tool** in the main GIMP window, and then click once anywhere within the background image, but not within the area of the paste-on image therein. Once you do this, the dotted line immediately surrounding your paste-on image will disappear.

   You may be wondering what that seemingly unimportant mouse click is all about and whether it is really necessary. Well, it is necessary, and the reason for it is quite simple. When you paste an image into another, the pasted image actually resides in a floating layer. This is allows you to perform the rotations and drop shadowing we have done so far without affecting the rest of the layer. The click in this last step releases the floating layer, thereby allowing it to finally join with the layer into which it was pasted.

10. Now go back to the Layers, Channels, Paths window, click the **Drop-Shadow layer**, which was automatically created when you created the shadow, within the main pane of that window, but don't click the eye icon there, or the image will become hidden. Then, click the down arrow button. The Drop-Shadow layer should then be listed below the *Empty Layer*, where your paste-on image is located, as you can see in Figure 16-27.

11. If you now take a look at your image, you will see that the shadow is where it belongs, beneath your paste-on image (Figure 16-28).

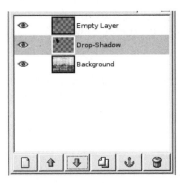

Figure 16-27: Your new layers listed in the Layers, Channels, Paths window

Figure 16-28: A shadow in its proper place

12. You are now pretty much finished with the process of adding your first paste-on image, but to make things less confusing for you as you add additional images, it is a good idea to merge the paste-on image's layer with that for its shadow, thus turning that particular pair of layers into one. To do this, go back to the Layers, Channels, Paths window and click the top layer listed in the main pane of that window, **Empty Layer**.

13. Now go to the **Layer** menu and select **Merge Down**.

     If you now go back to the Layers, Channels, Paths window, you will see that you now have only two layers—*Background* and *Drop-Shadow*. Because each time you add a shadow for your additional paste-on images a new Drop-Shadow layer will be automatically created, it is best to rename this layer now, so as to avoid confusion later on.

     To do this, perform the following step:

     a. Double-click the title area of the **Drop-Shadow layer**. The title area will then become a text-input box, in which you can type the new name for the layer. The name of the person in the paste-on photo would be appropriate. I'm calling mine The Great Saw. When finished, click anywhere else within the window, and the process will be complete.

Now that you have finished adding your first paste-on image, go ahead and repeat the process for each additional image.

Phase Five: Final Adjustments

Once you have added all four images, you should have a total of five layers listed in the Layers, Channels, Paths window, one for each paste-on/shadow combo and one for your background image, as you can see in Figure 16-29.

Figure 16-29: All of your new paste-on images and their shadows listed as separate layers

Everything is now set up, so you can go on to arrange the placement of the various paste-ons. If you want to move one of the paste-on images, just do the following:

1. Click the paste-on's layer in the Layers, Channels, Paths window.

2. Click the **rectangular selection tool** in the main GIMP window.

3. Select the area surrounding the paste-on image (you don't have to get it too exact, as long as the area is greater than the image and its shadow), and then drag the image to the location you want.

4. Once you've completed the move, click anywhere within the background area, but not within the area of the paste-on image itself. You can then move the other images in the same way.

   If you want to overlap your images, you may find when you move them that they are not overlapped in the order you would like, and remember that for maximum effect you want the shadowed right and bottom edges of an image to be on top of the next image. So how do you get things right in terms of overlap? Well, for example, let's say that the image of your cat, Roxanne, appears under the image of your dog, Charlie, but you want it the other way around. In this case, here's what you would do:

   a. Go to the Layers, Channels, Paths window, and click the **Roxanne** layer.

   b. In the same window, click the up arrow button as many times as necessary until the *Roxanne* layer is listed above that of the *Charlie* layer.

c. Take a look at the image itself now to make sure that things are as you want them to be.

d. If so, repeat the process for whatever other layers you need to reorder.

Phase Six: Wrapping Things Up

Once you have everything positioned where you want it, it is time to save the image, and this you should do in two different formats. First, save a copy in the native GIMP format so that you can retain all the layers as is, thus allowing you to add or remove images in the future. To do this, follow these steps:

1. Go to the **File** menu and select **Save As**.

2. When the Save Image window appears, type a title for your image, and then add the extension **.xcf** at the end. For example, I'll be saving mine as WilmingtonWallpaper.xcf.

3. Once you've done that, click the **OK** button to complete the process.
    Next, you will save the image in PNG format for actual use as your desktop wallpaper. Before you can do this, however, you must first merge all of your layers together into one, because PNG cannot handle layers.

4. Go to the **Image** menu and select **Merge Visible Layers**.

5. When the Merge Layers window appears, click **OK**.

6. Now save the image as a .png file by selecting **Save As** in the **File** menu.

7. Next change the extension at the end of the filename from .xcf to **.png** (or giving the image yet another name with the .png extension).

8. When you have finished typing in the filename, click **OK**.

9. When the Save as PNG window appears, just click the **OK** button, and the job will be done.

You can then close all of your still-open GIMP windows and quit the GIMP itself.

Phase Seven: Unveiling Your New Creation

Now that you've created your custom desktop wallpaper, it would certainly be a waste not to use it on your desktop. You learned how to do this in Chapter 7, but to refresh your memory, I'll run through the process again here:

1. Right-click your desktop, and then select **Properties** in the pop-up menu that appears.

2. When the Configure window appears, click the tiny icon that looks like a half-opened folder at the opposite end of the word *Picture*.

3. In the Select Wallpaper window that appears, navigate to and select your new wallpaper (by clicking it once), and then click the **OK** button.

4. After the Select Wallpaper window closes, select **Scaled** in the drop-down menu button next to the word *Position*.

5. After that, click the **OK** button, and voilà! There it will be before you— your new custom desktop wallpaper (Figure 16-30).

Figure 16-30: Your new creation displayed on your desktop

Moving Out on Your Own with the GIMP

Well, you've gotten some hands-on experience with the GIMP, but there is still a lot more under the hood for you to play around with. Go ahead and try things out on your own, which can be a lot of fun if you're into that sort of thing. Just be sure to save a copy of whatever image you are going to work with before getting down to it. After all, "an ounce of prevention . . . ," as the saying goes. If you prefer working through tutorials instead of just finding things out by goofing around, the GIMP Documentation page (www.gimp.org/tutorials) has a number of links to tutorials covering various functions, features, and skill levels.

Project 16B: Screenshots

Call it an obsession or whatever you like, but it does indeed seem to be a fact that Linux users love to take screenshots. Look at just about any Linux-related web page, whether it be the project page for some application or the personal page of a Linux user, and you will invariably find a hefty load of screenshots. Why this should more often be the case in the Linux world than in that for

Windows or Mac OS X isn't clear, since both of those operating systems have the built-in capacity to allow their users to do the same. Still, web pages related to those systems do not seem to be anywhere as well endowed in the screenshot department.

Now that you are a Xandros user, there is no reason that you too cannot join in on this obsession. Fortunately, it is all quite easy to do using the *Screen Capture* application that comes bundled with your Xandros system. To get started, run Screen Capture by going to the **Launch** menu and selecting **Applications ▸ Graphics ▸ Screen Capture**.

16B-1: Taking Full-Screen Screenshots

Taking a full-screen screenshot with Screen Capture is extremely easy. In fact, each time you run Screen Capture, it automatically takes a screenshot of your entire desktop and anything that happens to be open there at the time it starts up. After that, once it is up and running, all you have to do is select **Full Screen** in the drop-down menu button next to the words *Capture mode*, and then click **New Snapshot** (Figure 16-31).

Figure 16-31: Taking a full-screen screenshot with Screen Capture

Screen Capture will then take a shot of everything that is visible on your screen, except your mouse cursor and Screen Capture itself.

16B-2: Taking Screenshots of a Single Window

If all you want is a screenshot of a single window, select **Window Under Cursor** in the *Capture mode* menu, and then click **New Snapshot**, after which Screen Capture will hide itself, as it always does at this point. Now, click anywhere on the window you want to capture, and Screen Capture will immediately take a shot of it.

NOTE *If you would like to take a screenshot of a window without its window borders, uncheck the box next to the words* Include window decorations *directly below the words* Snapshot delay *in the Screen Capture window.*

16B-3: Taking Screenshots of a Single Menu or of an Open Menu Within a Window

So far, so good, but what if you want to take a screenshot of a single menu or of an open menu within a window? Well, this is where the Snapshot delay function comes into play. Until now, we have been using Screen Capture without a delay, as the words *No delay* in the *Snapshot delay* box indicate (Figure 16-31).

To take a screenshot of an open menu, select **Window Under Cursor** in the *Capture mode* menu, change the delay to something like 4 or 5 seconds, and then click the **New Snapshot** button. Once you have done that, rush over to the menu you want a shot of, click it (then release your mouse button), and leave the cursor in place anywhere within that menu. After the 4 or 5 seconds are up, Screen Capture will take a shot of that menu.

If you would like a shot of that menu within its window, the process is almost the same. This time, however, once the menu is open, move the mouse cursor outside the menu area, so that it is instead somewhere in the target window area. Just leave it there until the 4 to 5 seconds are up, and you will have taken a shot like that in Figure 16-32.

Figure 16-32: Taking a shot of an open menu within a window

16B-4: Taking Screenshots of a Region

Screen Capture, like the application *Grab* in Mac OS X, also allows you to take screenshots of a *region*. As you can see in Figure 16-33, a region can include any part of the desktop, a window, a combination of windows, or whatever.

To do this, select **Region** in the *Capture mode* menu, and then click **New Snapshot**. Unlike what happens when you take a full-screen or single-window screenshot, however, Screen Capture will not immediately take the shot this time around. Instead, you must first select the region you'd like to capture.

Figure 16-33: A screenshot of a region

Once you have clicked the **New Snapshot** button, you can select a region by clicking your mouse (but not releasing it) at one of the four corners that will make up the region you are going to define. When you then start dragging the cursor, which will now look like a crosshair, a dashed line will appear surrounding the area you are defining. Continue dragging until you have included everything you want to include, and then release the mouse button. Immediately, the shot will be taken.

16B-5: Taking Screenshots of Screen Capture

Well, now we've covered all there is to cover in regard to using Screen Capture. Still, you might be wondering how you can take a shot of Screen Capture itself if it always hides itself when you click the **New Snapshot** button. It must be possible, after all, since I have screenshots of it in this book. Well, the solution to this seeming paradox is simple: the GIMP.

You see, Screen Capture is not the only application in your system that allows you take screenshots. The GIMP, which we just discussed in the previous project, also allows you to do the same thing and works in pretty much the same way. To take a screenshot via the GIMP, go to the GIMP's **File** menu and select **Acquire ▶ Screen Shot**, after which the GIMP's Screen Shot window (Figure 16-34) will appear.

Figure 16-34: Taking a screenshot with the GIMP

As you can see, the concept is all pretty much the same as that for Screen Capture, albeit with fewer features, so using it should now be easy. Just remember that when you save the screenshot in the GIMP, you will have to type in the file extension yourself, so to keep things consistent with Screen Capture, go ahead and use **.png**.

Image Viewers

In Chapter 4 you learned that the Xandros File Manager can act as an image viewer, providing you with both thumbnail and full-sized views of your various images. But sometimes you want just a bit more. For example, you might want to be able to print out your images via your image viewer, resize or rotate your images, or view full-screen slideshows. Well, Xandros, via Xandros Networks, has at least four different image viewers available that might be just what you've been looking for. These include *GQview, GImageView,* and my two personal favorites, *showimg* (Figure 16-35) and *gThumb* (Figure 16-36).

It is hard for me to say which of these many viewers is best for you, since everyone's tastes are different. If you have a broadband connection, why not download and install all of them, and then, once you've found the one that tickles your fancy, remove the others via Xandros Networks. If you use a dial-up connection to get onto the Internet, then the choice is a bit easier, as showimg will be the quickest download for you, while gThumb will prove to be the longest.

Figure 16-35: showimg

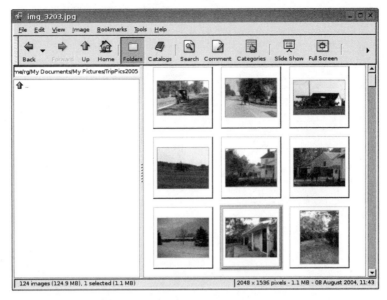

Figure 16-36: gThumb

Other Graphics Apps You Might Want to Consider

If you're looking for still other applications to work with, you might want to consider *Sodipodi*, which is a drawing program. Drawing programs, in case you didn't know already, produce images in which the various shapes are based on a series of mathematical formulae. This is in contrast to painting programs, such as Paint or the GIMP, which save data as a collection of dots, or bits, in which the location and color of every single pixel is recorded. Images created with paint programs are thus often referred to as *bitmaps*.

The advantages of drawing programs over paint programs are that their files are smaller because they don't need to hold as much information and that the actual drawings can be increased to near gigantic sizes without losing their shape. When you do the same thing with an image you create in a paint program, curved edges will become more and more jagged as you increase their size. Of course, on the other hand, paint programs are much more intuitive and thus easier to use.

If you are a real graphics aficionado, you might also want to consider installing *Blender*, which is a widely respected and exceedingly sophisticated 3-D modeling, animation, and rendering application that is widely used in the Linux, Windows, and Macintosh worlds.

Both Sodipodi and Blender are available from Xandros Networks. Just type the name of the one that interests you in the text box at the top of the XN application window, click the **Search** button, and then click **Install** next to the application in the list of results in main pane of that window.

17

STUFFED SHIRTS

Office and Other Productivity Applications

Well, now that we've covered the systemic, mechanical, and aesthetic side of things, let's move on to what is of the highest priority to many, if not most, users—productivity. Of course, in a sense, we've already covered several of these so-called productivity apps in previous chapters, since many Internet applications and the Personal Information Manager suite (covered in Chapter 12) certainly qualify as such. Still, when most users think of productivity, they are thinking office suites, and in this area Xandros is sure to please.

Xandros comes bundled not only with a number of utilities that fit nicely into the productivity category but also with the very popular OpenOffice.org office suite, which is a viable and very capable contender in this last-man (or *person*)-standing arena. To make things all the better, the three main components of OpenOffice.org's office suite (*Writer, Calc,* and *Impress*) are also compatible with their Microsoft Office equivalents (*Word, Excel,* and

PowerPoint), meaning that you won't be missing out on much, if anything, by using OpenOffice.org's offering instead—other than that feeling of emptiness in your wallet, of course. Ouch!

NOTE *Xandros Business Edition comes with Sun Microsystems' OpenOffice-related Star Office, which provides a few more bells and whistles and slightly greater MS Office compatibility than OpenOffice.org's suite.*

If what I've said so far isn't enough to get your frugal stuffed-shirt heart a-pumping, there are still numerous other productivity applications that can be downloaded and installed via Xandros Networks, including a completely different office suite, *KOffice*, so whatever it is you are looking for, you will more than likely be able to find it.

OpenOffice.org Writer

When it comes to office suites, the application that gets used the most by a great many users is the word processor.

In Microsoft's office suite, you are talking *Word*; however, when it comes to OpenOffice.org's suite, we're talking *Writer*, which is one of the three OpenOffice.org applications I will be discussing in this chapter.

As you can see in Figure 17-1, Writer is laid out much like other word processors and is thus pretty straightforward in terms of use. That said, I won't be going into an undue amount of explanation here, since most folks know how to use a word processor these days. Still, there are many features in Writer that even seasoned users tend to overlook, and it is on those features that I will be focusing in this section. Again, since covering all the features in Writer would fill up an entire tome, I will limit my discussion to those features I have personally found to be of great use and those about which I am frequently asked.

Adjusting Line Spacing

The single question I am most frequently asked is fortunately the easiest to answer: "How do I adjust the line spacing in my document?" All you have to do to adjust the line spacing in a paragraph, say from single- to double-spacing, is to right-click in the paragraph in question and then select **Line Spacing ▸ Double** (or whatever other spacing option you prefer) in the pop-up menu that appears. If you do this when you first start writing your document, subsequent paragraphs will follow suit in terms of line spacing.

If want to change the line spacing for an entire multiparagraph document you have already written, go to the **Edit** menu and choose **Select All** before doing your right-clicking. If you would like to change the line spacing for several noncontiguous paragraphs in an already written document, you can change each of them, one-by-one, in the way I first described or go on to the next section to find out how to bring about your changes most easily.

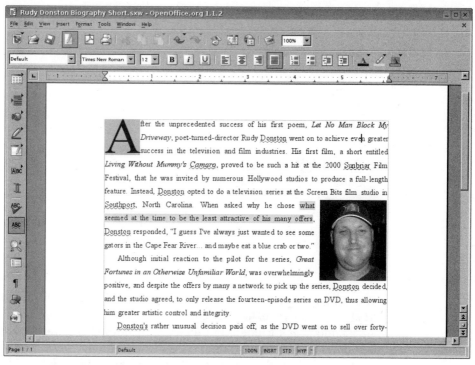

Figure 17-1: OpenOffice.org's word processor: Writer

Multiple Selections

A definitely oft-overlooked feature of OpenOffice.org Writer is its ability to allow multiple selections. You are no doubt already familiar with the fact that you can change the font, font size, or font style of an individual word, sentence, or paragraph by highlighting (or *selecting* or *blocking*, if either of those terms is what you use to describe this action) that particular element within your document and then performing the desired change. But what if you have several such elements scattered throughout your document that you want to change in the same way? Well, this is where multiple selections can come in handy.

Let's say that you are writing a piece on cinema and would like to italicize all of the film titles within your document. To perform the changes in one fell swoop, hold down the CTRL key, and then highlight each of the titles within your document. Your document would then look something like that in Figure 17-2.

Once you have selected all the relevant bits of text, click the **italics** button, and all your highlighted titles will be italicized.

This feature can prove very handy when changing the line spacing of several noncontiguous paragraphs in one go. After selecting the various paragraphs in question, you can simply right-click any one of them, select the appropriate line spacing in the pop-up menu, and be done.

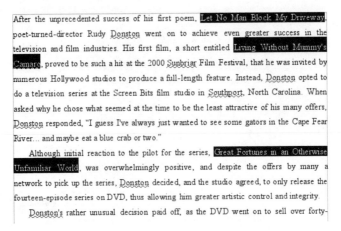

After the unprecedented success of his first poem, Let No Man Block My Driveway, poet-turned-director Rudy Donston went on to achieve even greater success in the television and film industries. His first film, a short entitled Living Without Mummy's Camaro, proved to be such a hit at the 2000 Sunbriar Film Festival, that he was invited by numerous Hollywood studios to produce a full-length feature. Instead, Donston opted to do a television series at the Screen Bits film studio in Southport, North Carolina. When asked why he chose what seemed at the time to be the least attractive of his many offers, Donston responded, "I guess I've always just wanted to see some gators in the Cape Fear River... and maybe eat a blue crab or two."

Although initial reaction to the pilot for the series, Great Fortunes in an Otherwise Unfamiliar World, was overwhelmingly positive, and despite the offers by many a network to pick up the series, Donston decided, and the studio agreed, to only release the fourteen-episode series on DVD, thus allowing him greater artistic control and integrity.

Donston's rather unusual decision paid off, as the DVD went on to sell over forty-

Figure 17-2: Selecting multiple blocks of text in Writer

Find & Replace

A definitely noticed, but too often overlooked, feature in Writer is *Find & Replace*. Perhaps you, like so many others, have had the experience of writing up a multipage document in which a certain word or phrase appears numerous times, only to find that you used the wrong name or date or word. For example, let's say that you were writing a report on the Norman invasion of England, in which you frequently mentioned 1492 as the date for that event. Later, it suddenly dawns on you that 1492 was the year of Columbus's ocean-blue voyage, while William's long-term frolic in England began in 1066. Well, rather than scrolling through the entire 27-page document, changing each of the 47 instances of that mistakenly stated date, and uttering an untold number of obscenities, you could instead use the Find & Replace function to do the job for you, and all in a matter of seconds. Here's how to do it:

1. Go to the **Edit** menu and select **Find & Replace**.
2. When the Find & Replace window (Figure 17-3) appears, type the text you want to correct in the top box next to the words *Search for*. In the case of my historical screw-up example, that would be 1492.
3. In the bottom box *(Replace with)* type what it is you want to replace that text with (1066 in my example). Once finished, your window would look something like mine in Figure 17-3.
4. Finally, click the **Replace All** button, and all instances of the targeted word will be replaced within a second or two by the replacement text.

The Find & Replace function not only allows you to replace text, but it also allows you to change the format of the text you are replacing. Let's say that you want all instances of the word you are replacing to appear in a different font, in a different color, and in boldface type. To do this, you would type the appropriate text entries, and then click the **Format** button within the Find & Replace window.

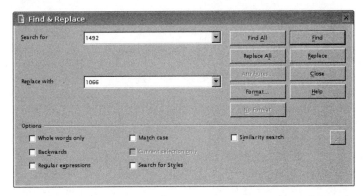

Figure 17-3: Performing multiple corrections in one go via Find & Replace

Once the Text Format (Replace) window appears (Figure 17-4), you could go on to make your various formatting selections and then click **OK** when finished. After that, you would click the **Replace All** button and voilà!

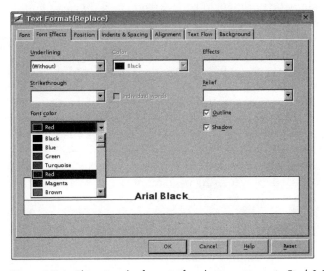

Figure 17-4: Changing the format of replacement text via Find & Replace

Word Count

A common feature that is very easy to use, but not so easy to find, is *Word Count*. To take a tally of the number of words, characters, images, and lines in your document, just go to the **File** menu within your document and select **Properties**. When the Properties window for your document appears, click the **Statistics** tab, after which you will see all of the information clearly laid out before you, as in the example in Figure 17-5.

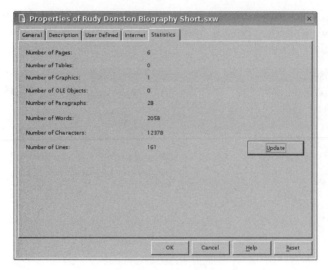

Figure 17-5: Checking the stats for your document

Headers, Footers, and Page Numbering

Adding page numbers to your document is an easy enough thing to do, and yet many people still go about the process manually, by typing in the number at the bottom of each page. There is a much easier and more automatic way of doing this, by means of *headers* and/or *footers*.

Headers and footers, in case you don't already know, are text fields at the top (header) or bottom (footer) of your page that hold a variety of elements that you would like to appear on every one of your pages. These elements could consist of the title, the author's name, the date, and so on. They are handy because you need to input the text only once, after which it will appear automatically on every page in the document.

Within the headers and/or footers, you can also place other fields, such as the one used for displaying page numbers. The page number field is extremely handy in that it is *dynamic*. By that I mean that it will automatically show the correct page number for each page. Thus, it will read *1* on the first page, *2* on the second page, *3* on the third page, and so on.

Here are the steps:

1. From within your document, go to the **Insert** menu, and select **Header ▶ Default** if you would like the page number to appear at the top of your pages or **Footer ▶ Default** if you would like it to appear at the bottom. Once you do this, a small empty field will appear at either the top or bottom of each page in your document.

2. Your cursor should already be in your header or footer, but if it's not, click in whichever of the two you are working on so as to place the cursor there.

3. Next, go to the **Insert** menu again, but this time select **Field ▶ Page Number**, after which all of the pages in your document will be automatically paginated. You can use the justification buttons (left, center, right) in the menu bar to place the page number where you would like it.

4. If you would also like to include a page count, in order to show the total number of pages in the document, in addition to a page number, go to the **Insert** menu yet again, and select **Field ▸ Page Count**. You will then have two numbers side-by-side.

To make it easier to figure out what these two numbers mean, you can add some text. For example, you could simply type a slash between the two numbers so that, for example, the pages of a four-page document would be numbered *1/4, 2/4, 3/4,* and so on. Or, instead of that, you could type the word *of* between the two numbers, and, if you like, also type the word *Page* before the first number, thus producing pages numbered as *Page 1 of 4, Page 2 of 4,* and so on (Figure 17-6).

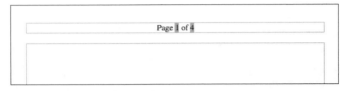

Figure 17-6: Adding Page Number and Page Count fields to a header or footer

NOTE *Although the Page Number and Page Count fields in your header or footer appear as gray boxes on your screen, only the numerals within those boxes will actually appear in your printout.*

Removing Headers and Footers

Well, now that you know how to add headers and footers to a document, you may also be wondering how you can get rid of them. Here are the steps:

1. Go to the **Format** menu and select **Page**.
2. In the Page Style window, click on the **Header** or **Footer** tab (depending on which of the two you want to remove).
3. In that tab, uncheck the box next to *Header on* or *Footer on.*
4. Finally, click **OK**, and it'll be bye-bye header or footer.

Creating a Header-less (or Footer-less) Cover or Title Page

You can see how easy it is to add and remove headers and footers, but sometimes you might merely want to remove a header or footer from just your top (or first) page. Although this seems as if it would be a very easy thing to do, figuring out how to do it can be rather challenging. Fortunately, I've done the figuring for you, so here's all you need to do:

1. Click anywhere in the first page of your document.
2. Next, select **Stylist** in the **Format** menu.

3. When the Stylist window appears, click the **Page Styles** button (fourth button from the left), and then double-click **First Page** in the list of styles below (Figure 17-7). Your first page will then become a header-less cover page.

Figure 17-7: Changing page styles via the Stylist window

If you change your mind and want to switch your page back to the way it was before, just double-click **Default**, or whatever page style you happened to have been using, and all will be as it was.

Taming AutoCorrect/AutoFormat

Arguably, the handiest features of most major word-processing applications are their auto-correction and auto-format functions. *AutoCorrect/AutoFormat* automatically corrects and/or formats various elements within a document as you type. Forgot to type a capital at the beginning of a sentence? Auto-Format will capitalize it for you. Typed *recieved* instead of *received*? AutoCorrect will fix that misspelling for you on the fly.

The only problem with all this is that AutoCorrect/AutoFormat sometimes ends up annoying you with some of its changes. A good example would be that of URLs. Whenever you type in the URL (address) of a website, AutoFormat automatically converts that URL into an actual link, which, if you click it, will bring up that page in your default web browser. This could be handy, but not if you're creating your document just for printing.

Fortunately, you can take control of AutoCorrect/AutoFormat and thus get it do only what you want. To get started, go to the **Tools** menu and select **AutoCorrect/AutoFormat**. In the AutoCorrect window that appears, you can go about getting things the way you want.

For example, for some reason or other, every time I type the word *Internet*, I mistakenly type *Intenret*. Since this is a very common mistake for me, and one that is not covered by the AutoCorrect replacement dictionary, I can add it in myself in the **Replace** tab by typing **Intenret** in the left box *(Replace)* and **Internet** in the right box *(With)*, as you can see in Figure 17-8. After that, I would click the **New** button, and the pair would be added to the dictionary.

To do away with the annoying URL problem I mentioned earlier, click the **Options** tab, and then uncheck the two boxes next to *URL Recognition.* Once you finish configuring things, click **OK**.

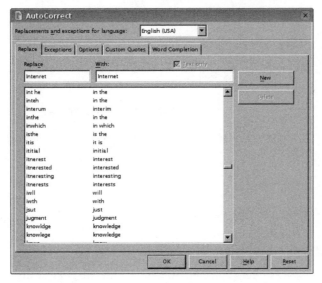

Figure 17-8: Taking control of AutoCorrect

Drop Caps

A pretty cool feature that can add some oomph to your documents is *Drop Caps.* Drop Caps takes the first letter of the first word of a paragraph and blows it up so that its height equals that of the first two or three lines of your document. You can see an example in the document shown in Figure 17-1.

On an aesthetic note, having a drop cap at the beginning of every paragraph within your document really lessens the overall effect and instead makes things look a bit overdone.

That said, it is easiest in the long run to add a drop cap to your first paragraph after you have already typed in your second. If not, every paragraph you write after the first will automatically begin with a drop cap.

Here are the steps required to add a drop cap to your document:

1. Start out by clicking once anywhere within your first paragraph.
2. Next, go to the Format window and select **Paragraph**.
3. When the Paragraph window opens (Figure 17-9), click on the **Drop Caps** tab.
4. In that tab, check the box next to *Display drop caps.* If you like, you can then go on to play around with the other settings, though the defaults should be fine.
5. When finished, click the **OK** button, and the drop cap will be added to your document.

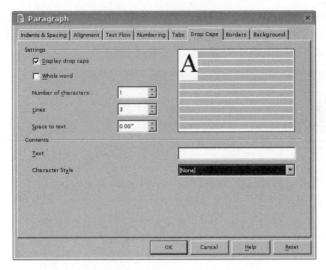

Figure 17-9: Adding a drop cap to your document

Inserting Images into a Document

With all the images available to you via the Internet, your scanner, or your digital camera, it is hard to resist jazzing up your documents a bit by adding an image here and there. To insert an image into your document, just follow these steps:

1. Click once wherever you want the image to appear in the document.
2. Go to the **Insert** menu, and select **Graphics** ▶ **From File**.
3. When the Insert Graphics window appears, check the box next to *Preview* (to make it easier to select images), and then navigate to and select the image you want to insert by clicking it once (Figure 17-10).
4. Once you have selected you image, click **Open**, and the image will appear within your document.

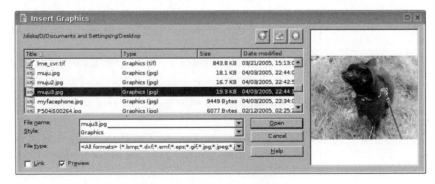

Figure 17-10: Inserting an image in a Writer document

Resizing an Inserted Image and Adjusting Text Wrap Properties

If the image you've inserted is a large one, it may be way too big to deal with within the confines of your letter-size page. Conversely, if the image is a small one, or if you click in the bottom third of a page before inserting the image, it may end up being too small to use. In either case, you will need to resize the image to get things right. Here's what you need to do:

1. Press and hold down the SHIFT key (to retain the image's horizontal to vertical aspect ratio), and then, from within the document, drag one of the image's four corners until the image is the size you would like it to be.

2. Once you have done that, release the SHIFT key.

After you have resized the image, it will be positioned either between, above, or below the lines of text in the document, as you can see in the left half of Figure 17-11.

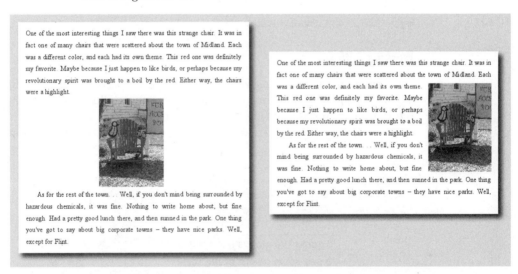

Figure 17-11: An image within a text document, with and without text wrapping

It is possible, however, to have the text wrap around the image, so as to produce more of the newsletter-ish look shown in the right half of Figure 17-11.

1. Double-click the image within the document to bring up the Graphics window (Figure 17-12).

2. In that window, click the **Parallel** button and then **OK**.

When you now look at your document, you will notice that the text comes out flush to one or more sides of the image, which you most likely do not want. That being the case, open the Graphics window once again, and adjust the appropriate numbers in the *Spacing* section. Increasing the numbers will increase the distance between the text and the image. Trial and error will help you to get it just right.

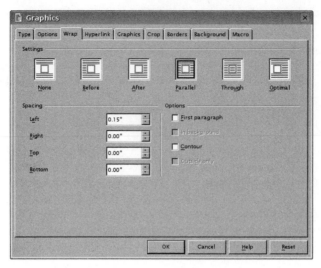

Figure 17-12: Adjusting text-wrap settings

Working with Frames

You have no doubt seen magazine articles with excerpts or quotations embedded within the text in a much larger text size. You can do this within your Writer documents as well (Figure 17-13) by using *Frames*. If it helps you any, you can think of a frame as a kind of movable document within a document.

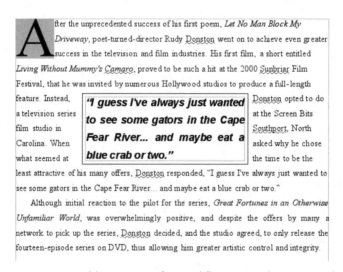

After the unprecedented success of his first poem, *Let No Man Block My Driveway*, poet-turned-director Rudy Donston went on to achieve even greater success in the television and film industries. His first film, a short entitled *Living Without Mummy's Camaro*, proved to be such a hit at the 2000 Sunbriar Film Festival, that he was invited by numerous Hollywood studios to produce a full-length feature. Instead, Donston opted to do a television series at the Screen Bits film studio in Southport, North Carolina. When asked why he chose what seemed at the time to be the

"I guess I've always just wanted to see some gators in the Cape Fear River... and maybe eat a blue crab or two."

least attractive of his many offers, Donston responded, "I guess I've always just wanted to see some gators in the Cape Fear River... and maybe eat a blue crab or two."

Although initial reaction to the pilot for the series, *Great Fortunes in an Otherwise Unfamiliar World*, was overwhelmingly positive, and despite the offers by many a network to pick up the series, Donston decided, and the studio agreed, to only release the fourteen-episode series on DVD, thus allowing him greater artistic control and integrity.

Figure 17-13: Adding some professional flair to your documents with Frames

To add a frame to your document, go to the **Insert** menu and select **Frame**, after which a Frame window will appear (Figure 17-14). In that window, you can adjust the settings for the new frame in terms of size, borders, background, and so on. To start off with, however, just click the **OK** button, and the frame will appear within your document.

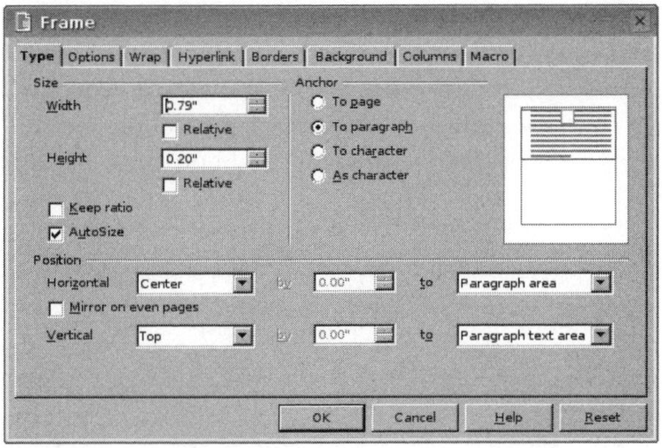

Figure 17-14: Inserting frames in a Writer document

Once the frame appears, you can move it to wherever you would like to place it by clicking anywhere within the frame (but not on its borders) and dragging. Just as with images (discussed earlier in this section), you can adjust a frame's size by tugging on any of the green squares that appear on each of its borders and corners until the frame is the size you want.

To type text in the frame, first deselect it by clicking anywhere on the page outside the frame itself. Once you've done that, the small green squares on the edges of the frame will disappear. You can then click within the frame (but not on its borders) and start typing. As I mentioned before, the frame is kind of a document within a document, so you can format the text (font, font size, font color, text justifications, and so on) within it as you would in any document.

If you would like to go on to further adjust the frame's attributes, such as eliminate or change the thickness of its border, select the frame by clicking its border (the green boxes at its edges will reappear), and then double-click within the frame itself, thus bringing back up the Frame window.

Project 17A: Figuring Out What to Do with and How to Use a Spreadsheet

Next to the word processor, the second most coveted application in an office suite is its spreadsheet, which in OpenOffice.org is called *Calc* (Figure 17-15).

Spreadsheets are extremely useful calculating and graphing tools, and many a person who has built up a certain expertise with such applications has founded a rather profitable career based on his or her abilities in that regard. Still, in all too many cases, spreadsheets go unused and forgotten, taking up valuable disk space and serving as much purpose as a pack of dried cherries tucked away inside one of your running shoes. Hmmm. . . .

The reason for this neglect is very often that such users (or rather non-users, in this case) just can't seem to find any practical reason to use a spreadsheet. This is logical enough, because spreadsheets are in fact nothing more than electronic ledger sheets, and as we all know, ledger sheets are something used only in businesses. Well, what might be true for ledger sheets isn't necessarily true of spreadsheets, because spreadsheets can be used to perform some pretty mundane, albeit important, everyday tasks. And I'm not just talking numbers here. For example, whenever I get a class schedule or class list here at work, that list is created with a spreadsheet. Ditto for the students' grade transcripts.

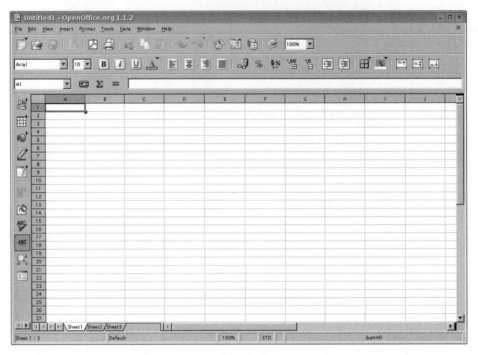

Figure 17-15: OpenOffice.org's spreadsheet: Calc

So what might you want to do with a spreadsheet? Well, a natural thing that comes to mind is budgeting. Suppose that you want to buy a new car and are trying to figure out when you'll have enough money to buy it. Since you're an all-cash type, this could all take some time. Does this situation seem familiar? Plausible? Well, even if a new car is not on your horizon, or even in your present state of consciousness, following along with this project will at least introduce you to some of the basics of using a spreadsheet. That said, here we go.

17A-1: Getting Started and Laying Things Out

Before getting started, it's a good idea to understand how a spreadsheet is set up. A spreadsheet consists of a seemingly endless number of *cells*. It is in these cells that you input the numbers or letters you will be working with. The cells are arranged in *rows* (labeled A, B, C, and so on) and *columns* (labeled 1, 2, 3, and so on). Coordinates are thus given as a combination of these two labels. Thus, if you type something into the third box from the left of the spreadsheet (column C) and the fifth box from the top (row 5), you would be typing in cell C5 (Figure 17-16).

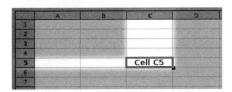

Figure 17-16: Cells, columns, and rows in Calc

Now that you've gotten the basics as to how a spreadsheet is arranged, get started on your budget by running Calc (**Launch ▶ Applications ▶ OpenOffice.org ▶ Spreadsheet**) and then, once it opens, following along with these steps:

1. Type the word **Income** in cell A2, **Total In** in cell A7, **Expenditures** in cell A9, **Total Out** in cell A20, and **Remainder** in cell A22.

2. Now, go back and click cell A1 again, and click the **bold** button (the one that looks like a big black **B**).

3. Click the **fill** button (the fourth-from-the-last button in the second row, with an **A** on it), and hold your mouse button down until a small color-selection palette appears.

4. In that palette, select **yellow**.

5. Repeat steps 2 to 4 for cells A7, A9, A20, and A22.

NOTE   *Steps 2 to 5 are not, strictly speaking, necessary for calculating your budget, but they will make your headings easier to see and at the same time give you some practice with formatting spreadsheets.*

6. Now that you've got your first set of headings done, begin adding in your sources of income (just two for now, and they can be fictitious if you prefer) and then your expenses (six of them) by name, such as *Utilities, Rent,* and so on. Type all of these in the A column, directly beneath their respective headings.

7. After that, fill in the amounts for the various entries in the A column directly next to them in the B column. Remember not to fill in the totals or worry about dollar signs, as that is the spreadsheet's job . . . but more on that in just a moment.

Once you are finished, your spreadsheet thus far should look something like mine in Figure 17-17.

	A	B
1	**Income**	
2	Salary	2890
3	Paper Deliver▸	970
4		
5		
6		
7	**Total In**	
8		
9	**Expenditures**	
10	Rent	725
11	Utilities	120
12	Cell Phone	39
13	Cable	50
14	Car Loan	325
15	Car Insuranc▸	138
16		
17		
18		
19		
20	**Total Out**	
21		
22	**Remainder**	
23		

Figure 17-17: Your new spreadsheet thus far, with income and expenses listed

17A-2: Doing Some Math

Okay, so now it's time to make your numbers look more like money and to do some math. Here's what you need to do:

1. Click the **B** heading at the very top of the B column (*not* the B button that selects bold text). Once you do this, all of the cells in that column will be highlighted in black.

2. Next, go to the **Currency Number Format** button (the one to the left of the percent sign on the toolbar) and click it once, after which the numbers in your B column will be in a more familiar dollars-and-cents format (*$725.00* rather than *725*). Note that this is not strictly necessary, but at least now you know how to do it.

3. Now get on to the math by clicking cell **B7**, typing **=sum**, and then pressing ENTER.

    The equal sign, in case you are wondering, is a signal to your spreadsheet that you are entering a formula, such as =2+2, or =3*4 (three times four), or =3/4 (three divided by four), and so on. Typing **sum** after the equal sign tells the spreadsheet that you will be entering a string of numbers, or cells, that you would like to add.

    As you most likely noticed after pressing ENTER, a pair of dark parentheses appeared next to *=sum* with a flashing cursor between them. It is between these parentheses that you will list the items you want to add together.

4. Now click, but do not release, your mouse button in cell B2, drag the cursor to cell B6, and then release your mouse button. Those cells will now be surrounded by a red line, indicating the same *range* of cells now listed between the parentheses in your formula.

5. The formula in cell B7 should now read *=SUM(B2:B6)*. If so, press ENTER, and you will know your total monthly income without so much as a single gear turning in your head.

Now that you know how easy math can be when you don't use your mind, repeat the process for your total expenses by first clicking cell **B20**, typing =**sum**, and pressing ENTER. This time, when the dark parentheses appear, click your mouse in cell **B10** and drag it to **B19**. The formula in cell *B20* should then read *=SUM(B10:B19)*. If so, press ENTER, and you will immediately know how much money you spend each month. I like to show my Total Out figure in red boldface, so do the same if you're so inclined.

To do this, assuming cell B20 is still selected (and if it isn't, click it first to do so), click the **bold** button in the button bar, and then click the **font color** button (two buttons to the right of the bold button—the one with a big **A** on it). In the font color palette that appears (Figure 17-18), click the color you want for your text, which in this case would be red, and the text within the cell will automatically change to that color.

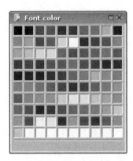

Figure 17-18: Changing the format of text within a cell

Finally, let's see how well off you'll be once your bills have been paid by determining your monthly remainder. To do this, click cell **B22**, type =, and then without typing or pressing anything other than your mouse button, go on to click cell **B7**, press the minus key (-), and then click cell **B22**. Your formula should now read *=B7-B20*. If it does, press ENTER, and you'll instantly know what you'll be worth at the end of the month. Your spreadsheet should now look like that in Figure 17-19.

	A	B
1	**Income**	
2	Salary	$2,890.00
3	Paper Deliver▸	$970.00
4		
5		
6		
7	**Total In**	$3,860.00
8		
9	**Expenditures**	
10	Rent	$725.00
11	Utilities	$120.00
12	Cell Phone	$39.00
13	Cable	$50.00
14	Car Loan	$325.00
15	Car Insuranc▸	$138.00
16		
17		
18		
19		
20	**Total Out**	$1,397.00
21		
22	**Remainder**	**$2,463.00**
23		

Figure 17-19: Your spreadsheet shows you your monthly worth

17A-3: Performing Some After-the-Fact Adjustments

You may have wondered why I asked you to set up more cells than seemed necessary, considering the data I asked you to input. Well, unexpected things do occasionally happen and memories do sometimes fail, so it's always good to be able to make allowances for such unforeseen occurrences. For example, let's say that after setting up your spreadsheet you suddenly remember that you also get a bit of money each month from your once-a-week tutoring sessions at the local junior college and, very important, that you forgot to include your food and entertainment expenses in your list of expenditures. Now, because you have space for these items and have set up your formulae to automatically include them, making an adjustment is hardly a problem.

Give it a try yourself and see what I mean, by adding one new source of income under the *Income* heading and two more expenditures under the *Expenditures* heading. After you type in the amounts for these new items, the totals in your various formula fields will automatically change to account for the new entries. Pretty cool, don't you think?

17A-4: Doing a Little More Math

Now that you know your monthly worth, let's get back to the business of that car of yours. To figure out how many months it will take you before you've saved up enough for your new $40,000 SAAB 9-7X, click in a cell away from everything you've just typed, such as cell **F4**, and type in a new formula. What you want to include in this formula is the total price of your new car, minus the $9,000 estimated trade-in for your present one, divided by 70 percent of your monthly leftover cash, which is the amount you want to put toward the purchase of your new wheels. You would thus start by typing =**(40000-9000)**/. What you have typed so far is the cost of the car, minus the trade-in amount, divided by . . . well, that comes next.

Now click cell **B22**, press the asterisk key (*), which is the symbol used to represent multiplication. Type **.70** (for 70 percent) and a close, or right, parenthesis. Your formula should now be something like *=(40000-9000)/ (B22*.70)*, or (car cost, minus trade-in) divided by (monthly savings times 70 percent). Now press ENTER to see how many months you have to wait.

Since cell B22, which is included in your formula, is in currency format, your result in cell F4 will also be in that format. After all, your spreadsheet doesn't know what you are driving at (or, in our case, would that be *driving in?*). If this bothers you, right-click in that cell, and then select **Format Cells** in the pop-up menu.

When the Format Cells window (Figure 17-20) appears, click the **Numbers** tab, and then click **Number** in the *Category* box and **-1234.12** in the *Format* box. If you prefer a rounded-off number to one ending in a fractional amount, click **-1234** in the *Format* box instead. Once you are finished, click **OK**, and your cell will no longer be in currency format.

17A-5: Printing Your Spreadsheet

The area of a spreadsheet is quite large, so if you want to print out just the area that you have actually used, you need to first define the print region, or *Print Range*. In the case of your spreadsheet, you would highlight just the area you actually used (we'll leave out the calculation bit you did in section 17A-4) by clicking your mouse button in cell **A1** and then, while holding down your mouse button, drag it to cell **B22**. The entire area will then be highlighted in black. Now go to the **Format** menu and select **Print Ranges ▸ Define**, and that area will be bordered by a solid black line. If you want to see what your document will look like when printed, go to the **File** menu and select **Page Preview**.

It might be pretty hard to see things clearly in the preview window. If so, go to the small drop-down menu button with a percentage in it at the far right of the first row of buttons, and select **100%**. Your window, and the document within it, should then look something like that in Figure 17-21. If things look right, you can go ahead and print it.

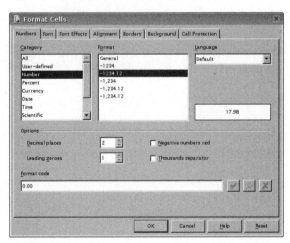

Figure 17-20: Changing font properties within a cell

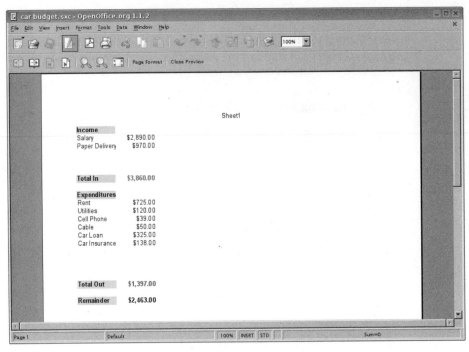

Figure 17-21: Previewing your spreadsheet before printing

An overlooked, but actually quite useful, application within OpenOffice.org's suite is *Draw* (Figure 17-22). Draw, as its name implies, can be used to create vector-based drawings, images in which the various shapes are based on a series of mathematical formulae, as I mentioned in Chapter 16. More important for many users is the fact that it can be used as a simple page-layout program. To get a feel for what you can do with Draw in this department, I will lead you through a little project from which you will learn how to create a simple newsletter.

17B-1: Getting Started

To get started, first run Draw by going to the **Launch** menu and selecting **Applications** ▸ **OpenOffice.org** ▸ **Tools** ▸ **Drawing Editor**. Once Draw appears, change the margins of your new document by going to the **Format** menu and selecting **Page**.

When the Page Setup window appears, reduce the margins for all sides to **0.50** in the *Margins* section in the bottom-left quadrant of that window in order to give yourself more room in which to work. When complete, your window should look like that in Figure 17-23.

In case you're wondering, yes, you can change your margins within OpenOffice.org Writer in the same way.

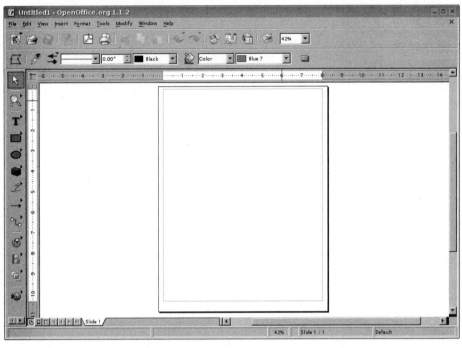

Figure 17-22: OpenOffice.org Draw

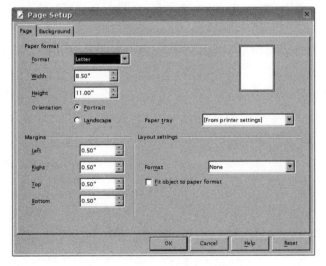

Figure 17-23: Changing page margins in Draw

17B-2: Creating a Title Banner

Now let's start adding elements to the page by working first on a title banner. To get started, just follow these steps:

1. Click the **text tool** button on the left side of the main window, the button with a big T in it. Click your mouse in the top-left corner of the page; then drag your mouse until you get to the right margin, but, of course, a bit farther down so as to create a fairly large rectangle.

2. In that rectangle, type a title for your newsletter, press ENTER, and then give it a subtitle.

3. Once you've done that, highlight the title text, and then choose a rather dynamic-looking font from the drop-down font menu box in the button bar, and increase its font size so that it is in the 50 to 72 range, depending, of course, on how long the title is and on the font you've selected. Then set the title in boldface by clicking the **bold** button (remember, that's the one that looks like a big B).

4. Now highlight the subtitle and increase its font size, but keep it significantly smaller than the title.

5. When finished, your title banner thus far should look something like that in Figure 17-24. If so, click anywhere else in the page to deselect the text box.

Figure 17-24: Creating a title banner in your newsletter

6. Now add a background to your banner by clicking the slashed border around your text box.

   At this point, the border should disappear, but the little green squares around its periphery should remain. This means you are no longer in text-input mode and can now apply border and fill attributes to the text box itself.

7. In the drop-down menu box next to the paint-can icon in the second row of buttons, select **Gradient**, and then in the drop-down menu box next to that, select **Gradient 1** (Figure 17-25).

8. Your title banner will now have a rather nice background; however, as you will probably notice, the title text will be rather hard to see. To correct this, get back into text-input mode by double-clicking your title banner, and then, once the slashed borders reappear, select the title

text and change the font color to white or any other light color. You can also change font colors via the font color button, which is the one right next to the underline button.

9. Everything now should be pretty much hunky-dory except for the fact that title text may be too close to the top of the banner box.

Figure 17-25: Creating a gradated background in your newsletter banner

10. To remedy this, click the slashed border once, to exit text-input mode. Then, assuming the slashed border is gone but the green squares are still there, right-click the banner area, and select **Text** in the pop-up menu.

11. When the Text window appears, change the figure in the *Top* box within the *Spacing to borders* section to something like **0.24"** or so, and then click **OK**. The text in your title header should now look more appropriately placed.

To finish off the title-banner area, you might want to add another text box in which to show the volume number, location, and date for your newsletter. Place this beneath the one already in place containing your title and subtitle. Type in the appropriate data, and then highlight the text and change the font to boldface and white. The font size should also be smaller than that for your subtitle. You can choose any font you think looks good for this purpose.

After that, exit text-input mode by clicking the border of the text box once. Now, in the drop-down menu next to the paint-can icon, select **Color**, and then select **Black** in the drop-down menu next to that. When you have finished, click anywhere else in the page to deselect your new text box. At this point, your title banner should look something like that in Figure 17-26.

Figure 17-26: Your new title banner with a gradient background

17B-3: Adding Text and Image Fields

Now that you have your title banner set up, it's time to add some content to your newsletter. You will be setting up your page so that it will have two columns, with an image at the top of the right column. To do this, just follow these steps:

1. Create a new text box on the left side of the page but beneath your title banner. Start at the left margin, about an eighth of an inch below your banner area, and then drag your mouse until the box reaches the margin line at the bottom of the page. The column should cover just under 50 percent of the page in terms of width.

2. Now type in whatever you want in this column, differentiating between titles and body by means of font size and style.

3. When you are finished, click anywhere else on the page to deselect this text box.

4. Next, add an image to the right side of the page, much as you did with Writer, by going to the **Insert** menu and selecting **Graphics**.

5. Once you have inserted the graphic, resize it (again, much as you did in Writer) so that it will fit within the area for the right column, again at just under 50 percent of the page in width. Remember to hold down the SHIFT key as you do this in order to retain the height-to-width aspect ratio of the image.

6. When you've finished, click anywhere within the page to deselect the image.

7. Finally, add a text box beneath the image, and type whatever information you want in it.

8. Now click in any open space within the page to deselect that text box, and you will have the makings of a newsletter, something like that in Figure 17-27.

If you would now like to move on and create a second page for your newsletter, you can add a page by going to the **Insert** menu and selecting **Slide**, which is Draw parlance for *page*.

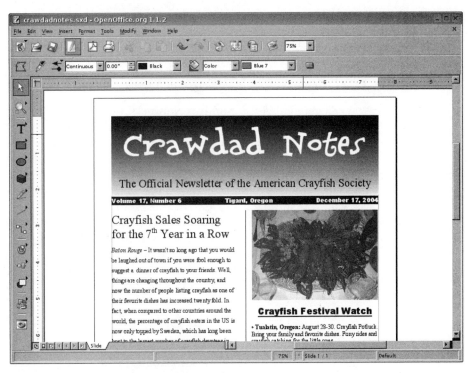

Figure 17-27: Your new newsletter in Draw

Other OpenOffice.org Applications

There are also a few other applications included with the OpenOffice.org suite that I will not be covering for lack of space. These include the Microsoft PowerPoint-compatible presentation program, *Impress*, a mathematical formula editor, and a web page editor, all of which can be run from the **Launch** menu (**OpenOffice.org** ▸ **Presentation**, **OpenOffice.org** ▸ **Tools** ▸ **Formula Editor**, and **OpenOffice.org** ▸ **Tools** ▸ **HTML Document**, respectively).

Project 17C: Creating a Business Card with gLabels

You can create business cards and various kinds of labels in OpenOffice.org Writer, but my favorite application for this particular task is *gLabels*, a very-easy-to-use label and business-card design and printing application. It supports pretty much all of the preformatted card and label stock available from companies such as Avery, which means that it can also be used to design and print CD labels and jewel case inserts.

17C-1: Downloading, Installing, and Running gLabels

You can get gLabels via Xandros Networks, but you must first be sure that you have selected **Debian Unsupported Site** in the Application Sources list (**Edit ▸ Set Application Sources**). Then just type **glabels** in the text box at the top of the window, and click the **Search** button. When the results of your search appear in the pane below, click **Install** next to *glabels*, which should be the only item listed, and then follow the usual procedures for installing files via Xandros Networks.

Once gLabels is installed, you can run it by going to the **Launch** menu and selecting **Applications ▸ Office ▸ gLabels Label Designer**. If it doesn't happen to be there yet (it will be the next time you start up your system), run it via the Run Command window instead (**Launch ▸ Run Command**), by typing **glabels** and then clicking **Run**.

17C-2: Setting Up Your Business Card

To get started with your card project, click the **New** button, and the New Label or Card window will appear (Figure 17-28).

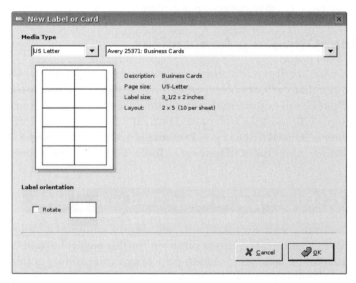

Figure 17-28: Selecting paper size and card or label stock in gLabels

In that window, first select the paper size of the card stock you will be using (the default is *US Letter*), and then select the brand and type of the card stock itself. The choices are listed with description and product number, so you should have no problems. Once you have made your selection, click the **OK** button, and a design grid will appear in the main window.

17C-3: Designing Your Business Cards

For learning purposes, we will be creating a rather elaborate, some might say gaudy, business card that includes a graphic, a shape, a line, and two or three different fonts. Of course, when you create one of your own, you might prefer something a bit tamer, but, as I said, this is for learning purposes.

Phase One: Adding an Image to Your Card

To start out, you will add an image to your card. You can choose anything you like—a photo, a logo, a line drawing, or whatever else you come up with. To insert the image into the design grid, here's what you need to do:

1. Click the **image** button, which is the sixth item in the second row of buttons (the one with a little house on it).

2. Next, click your mouse button at one of the corners where your graphic will actually be situated, and then drag your mouse until the area that you would like to fill with that image is covered in a checkerboard-patterned rectangle, much like the one you see in Figure 17-29.

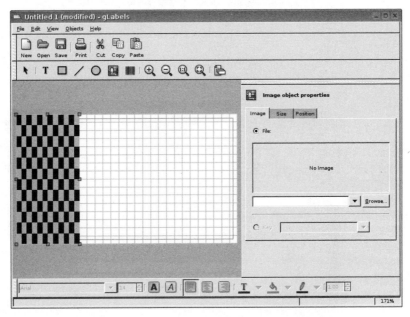

Figure 17-29: Inserting a graphic into your business-card layout

3. Now insert the image by clicking the **Browse** button in the right pane of the window and navigating to and selecting your image (by clicking it once) in the Load image window that appears.

4. Once you have made your selection, click the **OK** button. Your image will then appear within the previously checkered rectangle within the design grid.

NOTE *At this point, you might want to go ahead and save your image so as to take a load off your system's memory (and to avoid any unfortunate mishaps).*

Phase Two: Adding Text to Your Card

Now we'll add some banner text to spread across the top of the card. Here are the steps:

1. Click the **font** button, which is the second button in the second row of icons (the one that looks like a capital T), and then click once in any empty area within the design grid.

2. In the right pane of the window, type whatever you want to place in the banner—for example, your name or a real or fictitious business name.

3. Once you've done that, drag the text box within the design grid to the very top red line, and then stretch it so that the green dots along the borders of the box fill the available space within the red borders of the design grid.

4. Next, choose a substantial-looking font and as large a font size as will fit in the appropriate boxes at the bottom of the window. Also be sure to click the **center** button and, if you like, the **bold** button as well. You might also want to choose a new color for the banner text.

When you are finished, your window should then look something like that in Figure 17-30, making allowances, of course, for your own font, text, and image selections.

Figure 17-30: Adding banner text to your business card

Phase Three: Adding Subtext to Your Banner Text

Now that you have your image and banner text in place, let's add some subtext to that banner. This could be a message or a slogan that would have meaning in relation to the content of the banner text. For example, if your banner text consists of your name, the subtext could be something like *Nice Guy Extraordinaire.*

Anyway, go about this in the same way you added the banner text, but this time around choose a slightly more modest and less-heavy font in a different color and in a smaller font size. Then center the subtext directly beneath the banner text.

Phase Four: Adding a Line Beneath Your Banner

Before moving on to adding your address, phone number, and email address, you might want to differentiate the banner area of the card by adding a horizontal line beneath the two banner elements (the banner text and subtext). Here's what you need to do to bring it about:

1. Click the **line tool** button (that's the fourth button in the second row of icons).

2. Next, click below the left end of your banner area and then drag your mouse straight across the screen until you reach the other end, whereupon you can release the mouse button.

3. Finally, go to the right pane of the window and select a different, preferably bright, color for the line (red is nice). Once you've done all that, your card should look like a variation on that shown in Figure 17-31.

Figure 17-31: Adding a line to your business card

Phase Five: Adding Your Address, Phone Number, and Email Address

Now that most of the main elements are in place, go ahead and add your more vital statistics. You can do this in the same way you added your banner text and subtext, but this time be sure to use a smaller and more conservative font and in a darker color. You will also probably want to increase the line spacing in this text field. You can do this by selecting the address text field, clicking on the **Style** tab in the right pane of the window, and adjusting the numbers in the *Line Spacing* box (Figure 17-32).

Figure 17-32: Adding your address, phone number, and email address

If you want to have a bit more fun, you can also add an additional message or slogan at the bottom of the card in a different and slightly larger font. At this point, for safety purposes, you might also want to save your project one more time. Better safe than sorry, right?

Phase Six: Adding a Geometric Shape to Your Card

You are just about finished, but in order to get just a tad more experience, why not add a big circle to the card as a background graphic? If you're interested, here's what you need to do:

1. Click the **ellipse** tool, which is the sixth button in the second row and looks like a tan circle.

2. Click near the top-center edge of your banner text, and then drag your mouse until you reach the bottom of the lowest element within the design grid.

3. Drag both sides of the circle to form as perfect a circle as you can.

4. Get rid of the circle's black border by clicking the **arrow** button to the right of the color-selection button in the right pane and selecting **No line**.

5. Once you've done that, click the **Fill** tab in the right pane, and then select as light a color for the circle as you can. Yellow, pink, or light blue would be a good choice.

6. Finally, move the circle layer behind those of the other elements by right-clicking the circle itself and then selecting **Order ▶ Send to Back**.

You are now finished, but to get a better view of your card before printing it out, go to the **View** menu, deselect **Grid**, and then go back again and deselect **Markup**. Doing this eliminates the background setup grid and takes you out of the default markup mode (this is the mode for creating a card) and into a viewing mode.

Your card should look something like mine in Figure 17-33. Now go ahead and save your project.

Figure 17-33: The final product of your (or at least my) business card project

Phase Seven: Printing It Out

The only thing left for you to do now, should you want to take that final step, is print out the card. It is a good idea to first print a single copy on regular paper to see how it all looks. After that, insert the card stock in your printer, click the **print** icon (or select **Print** in the **File** menu) in the gLabels window, and then click the **Print** button when the Print window appears. If you would like to see what your final printed page will look like before actually printing, click the **Print Preview** button first, which will show a whole slew of your cards ready to be transferred to card stock (Figure 17-34)—the number of cards that will appear in your preview window will equal the number of cards in the sheet of card stock you chose in section 17C-2.

Figure 17-34: Print Preview shows what your printed page will look like

Other Productivity Applications You Already Have and Others You Might Want to Consider

In addition to the applications I have covered in this chapter and elsewhere in the book, there are a few others that are included with your Xandros system. These include *Flow Chart* (also known as *Kivio*), which is an easy-to-use flowchart- and diagram-creation app (**Launch ▶ Applications ▶ Graphics ▶ Flow Chart**); *Time Tracker* (also known as *KArm*), which helps you to keep track of how much time you spend on your various projects for billing purposes (**Launch ▶ Applications ▶ Utilities ▶ Time Tracker**); and *Reminder Message Scheduler* (also known as *KAlarm*), which can give pop-up reminders for events that you want to keep in mind, or even run certain applications or commands automatically at specified times (**Launch ▶ Applications ▶ Utilities ▶ Reminder Message Scheduler**).

There are also numerous other productivity applications available via Xandros Networks in the Debian Unsupported Site repository, including *AbiWord*, a stand-alone, multiplatform word processor; and the well-known *KOffice* suite (Figure 17-35), which I mentioned earlier in this chapter. KOffice comes with applications similar to those found in OpenOffice, plus a couple more.

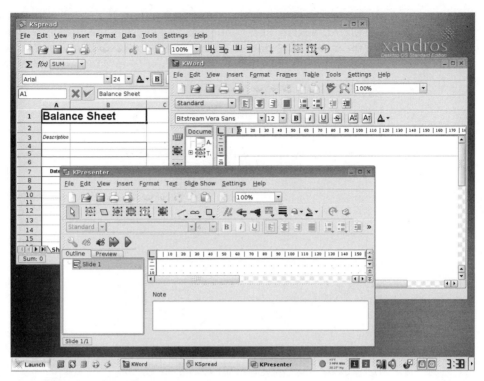

Figure 17-35: KOffice

For Those of You Suffering Separation Anxiety

If you are having trouble weaning yourself away from Windows completely, there is good news for you in the form of CrossOver Office, a 30-day trial version of which comes with the Open Circulation (the one in this book) and Surfside Editions of Xandros V3. If you want the full version, it can be had by upgrading to Xandros V3 Deluxe or Business Editions or can be purchased and downloaded via Xandros Networks.

So what is it? Well, CrossOver Office is an application that allows you to run Microsoft Office and a number of other Windows applications and web browser plug-ins from within Xandros even if you do not have a dual-boot Window/Xandros setup. To see which Windows applications and plug-ins are compatible with CrossOver Office (and to what degree they work), go to the CodeWeavers compatibility page at www.codeweavers.com/site/compatibility /browse and have a look.

Using CrossOver Office

CrossOver Office usually runs invisibly in the background every time you run a Windows application in Xandros. The only times you actually need to deal with it directly are when you run it for the first time and when you actually install Windows apps. To set things up the first time around, go to the **Launch** menu and select **Applications ▸ CrossOver ▸ Office Setup**.

A very simple setup wizard will appear. Just click **Next** in the first screen of the wizard, **Next** in the second page, and **Finish** in the third. After that, you will see the usual setup window (Figure 17-36), from which you can install applications from setup files on your hard disk or from Windows application CDs.

Figure 17-36: The CrossOver Office Setup window

You can also use CrossOver Office to download and install various plugins for your web browser that are normally not available in Linux (see Figure 17-37). To do so, just click the **Install** button, and then in the Install Software window that appears, select the plug-in you want to install (QuickTime, Windows Media Player, and Shockwave are the ones most people want). Click **Next**, and then follow the remaining steps in the installation wizard.

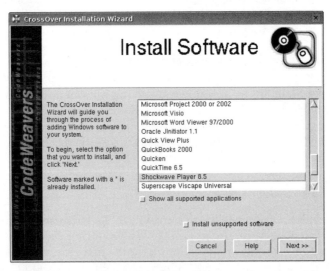

Figure 17-37: Installing web browser plug-ins via CrossOver Office

To show you how you can install a Windows application via CrossOver Office, I will use the example of a freeware text editor called *NoteTab Light* (Figure 17-38). A text editor, in case you are wondering, is something like a word processor after liposuction—it allows you type in your text but doesn't, in its purest form, do any formatting. That means no fonts, no font sizes, no colors, and so on; and all of that means more speed when typing and scrolling.

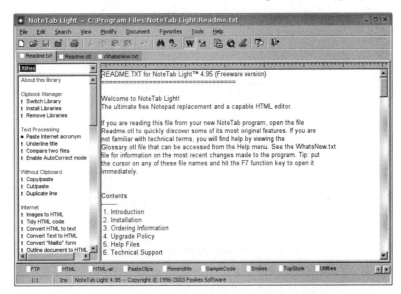

Figure 17-38: A Windows application, NoteTab Light, running in Xandros

Although your Xandros distro already has a text editor of its own (Text Editor), it is worth your while to try out NoteTab Light as it is a bit different in the way it is set up. If nothing else, it is a quick and easy download and will give you the chance to have some hands-on, no-cost experience installing a Windows application via OpenOffice. That said, go ahead and give it a try.

17D-1: Downloading NoteTab Light

To get NoteTab Light, go to www.notetab.com, and click the **EXE Package** button under the *NoteTab Light 4.95* heading (the version number might be higher by the time you read this). Once the download is complete, the file NoteTab_Setup.exe will appear in your Home folder (or wherever else you happened to have saved it) with a CrossOver Office icon (Figure 17-39).

Figure 17-39: Windows .exe files appear with CrossOver Office icons

17D-2: Installing NoteTab Light

To install NoteTab Light, just follow these steps (this is essentially the same procedure as for installing all other Windows applications):

1. Double-click the **NoteTab Light Setup** file in your **Home** folder. If you are using the demo version of CrossOver Office, a warning window will appear telling you how many days you have left on your tryout period. Just click **OK** to continue.

2. A window will then appear asking if you want to install NoteTab Light (Figure 17-40). Click **Yes**.

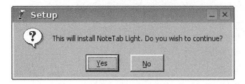

Figure 17-40: CrossOver Office checks with you before installing NoteTab Light

3. Another window will then most likely appear telling you that an access violation has occurred. Just click **OK**.

4. The NoteTab Light Setup Wizard will then appear (Figure 17-41). Click **Next** to continue.

Figure 17-41: The first page of the NoteTab Light Setup Wizard

5. In the next page of the wizard, select **I accept the agreement**, and then click **Next**.

NOTE   *The actual text area in this license agreement window will be blank.*

6. In the next page of the wizard, accept the default installation directory by clicking **Next**. This directory is actually a fake Windows directory in your Linux partition—not the real Windows partition in a dual-boot setup.

7. In the next page, click **Next** for a full installation of NoteTab Light.

8. Click **Next** in the next page to accept the default Start menu shortcut location.

9. In the next window, accept the default shortcut location (your desktop) by clicking **Next**.

10. In the next window, click **Install** to begin the installation process.

11. When the installation is finished, the wizard will tell you so (Figure 17-42). Click **Finish** to complete the process.

Figure 17-42: The Setup Wizard tells you when the installation process is complete

17D-3: Running NoteTab Light

Once installed, you have two ways of running NoteTab Light. The first way is to simply double-click the desktop icon created by the installer. The alternative is to go to the **Launch** menu and select **Windows Applications ▸ Programs ▸ NoteTab Light ▸ NoteTab Light** (Figure 17-43). If you don't happen to remember having seen a menu item called *Windows Applications* before, you would be remembering correctly—the menu item is added by CrossOver Office the first time you successfully install a Windows application.

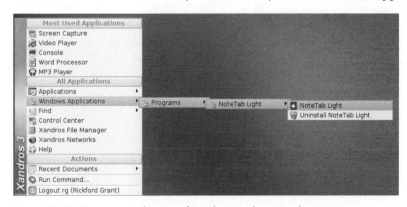

Figure 17-43: Running applications from the Windows Applications menu

18

TIME TO UNWIND

Gaming

Many a person is loath to admit it, but games are a big attraction to almost everyone at the helm of a personal computer. Even those who deny being gamers often find themselves caught in the act of rapping off a quick round of solitaire between work projects. The popularity of games is even suggested by the fact that most Linux distributions come bundled with more games than any other type of application. Xandros, for example, comes with 11 games, and many others are available via Xandros Networks.

Of course, unlike most other applications, games are tied in to the user's personality, and not everyone takes a fancy to the same game or even genre of game. For example, many people, especially in or from the Windows world, continue to love the game *Minesweeper* (Figure 18-1), while it is pure snoresville for me. Thus, although there are already many games included in your system, there are probably only two or three that will actually ever get played more than once or twice.

Figure 18-1: Minesweeper

Things being what they are, gamers and neo-gamers alike seem to be in a perpetual search for new games that will satisfy whatever it is that their game-playing side finds enticing. This no doubt explains why store shelves are so often filled with games for the Windows market. Fortunately for Linux users, while there are many games for sale, there are even more games that can be downloaded from the Internet for free, many of which are available via Xandros Networks.

Taking Stock of What You've Got

As I already mentioned, your Xandros system comes bundled with 11 different games. A quick look through the **Launch** menu (**Applications ▸ Games**) will show that these are broken into four different categories: *Arcade, Board, Cards,* and *Strategy*. If you installed the mouse odometer, *kodo*, in Chapter 8, there will also be another category—*Toys*. Most of these games are variations on other well-known games that you may have played in the past and thus require no explanation. The only two exceptions are *Miniature Golf* (also known as *Kolf*) and *Atomic*.

Miniature Golf

Miniature Golf (Figure 18-2), as its name implies, is a miniature golf–simulation game.

You can play it with any number of additional players, or you can have a run at the course solo, if you prefer. Conceptually, the game is quite easy to play, but setting it up can stump you a bit the first time out.

To start playing Miniature Golf, go to the **Game** menu and select **New**, and a New Game window (Figure 18-3) will appear.

The game is set up by default for two players, but you can add more players by clicking the **New Player** button. Once you have added whatever number of players you'd like, name each of the players by typing their name or initials in the text boxes that say *Player 1, Player 2*, and so on. If you would like to play the game alone, type your name or initials in the box that says *Player 1*, and then click the **Remove** button to the right of *Player 2*.

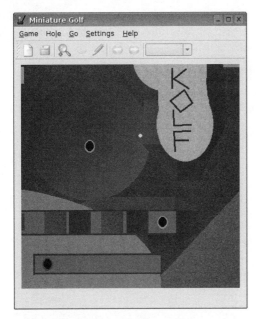

Figure 18-2: Miniature Golf

Figure 18-3: Choosing the number of players for Miniature Golf

Once you have chosen the number of players, you have to go on and pick your course, since the default is an essentially unplayable *Create New*. Here's what you need to do:

1. Click **Course** in the left pane of the New Game window.

2. Select the course you want from the list in the right half of the window (Figure 18-4).

3. Finally, click the **OK** button, and you'll be ready for action.

Once you begin playing, it should all be simple enough to figure out, as it is pretty much the same as a regular game of miniature golf—just stroke your ball through the whole course, dealing with mounds, bumpers, sand traps, and ponds along the way, while trying to do so with as few strokes as possible. Just remember that the power of your stroke is determined by the duration of your mouse click—the longer you hold down the mouse button, the stronger your stroke will be.

Figure 18-4: Selecting the course you want to play in Miniature Golf

Atomic

Atomic (Figure 18-5) is a fun (perhaps even somewhat educational) puzzle-like game that can be quite frustrating, depending on how you look at things.

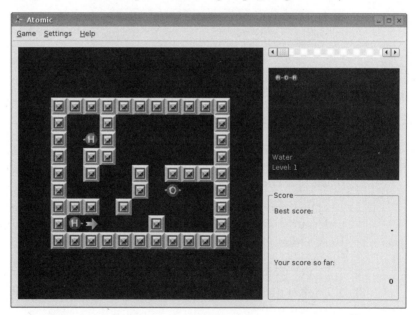

Figure 18-5: Atoms made fun: Atomic

The idea is quite simple: assemble the scattered atoms in the main playing area in the left half of the window so that they match the example of the assembled chemical molecule shown in the right half of the window. Yes, that's right, even if you don't know anything about atoms or chemicals, you can still follow along because you have an example right there in front of you, so knowing how things should go together is the easy part. Actually putting them together, though . . . well, that's the challenge.

If you prefer things a bit more complex, you can spice things ups by building capsaicin or caffeine rather than fiddling around with the likes of mere water or methane. To do this, just use the scroll bar or arrow buttons above the preview window in the right side of the window (Figure 18-6), and select the molecule that suits your tastes.

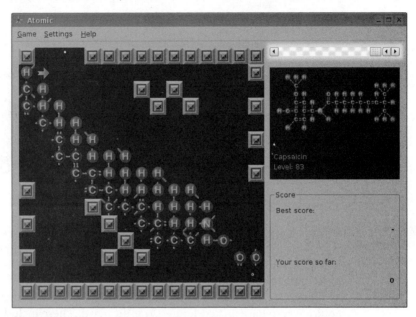

Figure 18-6: Choosing your atoms in Atomic

Expanding Your Game Collection via Xandros Networks

If you are quite the gamer and thus not satiated by what you already have in your Games menu, you can, as I mentioned earlier, expand your gaming repertoire via Xandros Networks. There are a number of games available there via Standard and Expert modes, if you register with Xandros Networks. You can even download the very popular *Tux Racer* (Figure 18-7) from the Shop for free, though you will need to have an accelerated graphics card if you want to run that particular game happily, since it's painfully slow if you don't.

How do you know whether you have an accelerated graphics card? Well, the easiest way to find out is to go through the documentation that came with your computer. If you don't have that, or if you can't find the answer within the docs, just go ahead and install Tux Racer, and see how it goes. If it runs at a seemingly normal game speed, you'll know you have an accelerated graphics card, while if it runs in molasses mode, then you'll know you don't (or at least don't have one that is compatible with the game).

Figure 18-7: Tux Racer

If you do happen to find that things are just too sluggish to deal with, there's no need to worry, as no harm has been done to your system. Just try to get your mouse down to the **Quit** button, and exit the game by clicking it. After that, you can remove the game from your system via the Xandros Networks application.

There are a far greater number of games available from XN that do not require you to have an accelerated graphics card. These include various clones of familiar games, such as *Tetris*; *Same Game*, the freeware classic from Japan; *Battleship*; and the German card game, *Lieutnant Skat*, which comes bundled with most other Linux distros. For my part, however, I will be focusing on two other games that may not be particularly familiar to you, if at all, but are loads of fun and classics in their own right: *Frozen-Bubble* and *Pysol*.

Frozen-Bubble

Frozen-Bubble (Figure 18-8) is a classic, and although it has been ported over for use in the Windows and Mac worlds, its roots and soul are pure Linux.

The objective of Frozen-Bubble is simple: shoot down all the bubbles in a screen in order to move on to the next. While this may sound so simple as to border on being boring, that is not the case. And best of all, you can live eternally in the world of Frozen-Bubble because you just cannot die; every screen you fail to clear the first time around will repeat over and over and over again until you get it right. Pretty cool (the life-eternal bit, at least), you have to admit.

Figure 18-8: Frozen-Bubble—a Linux classic

Installing Frozen-Bubble

To get Frozen-Bubble, just run Xandros Networks, type **frozen-bubble** in the search box, and then click **Search**. After that click **Install** next to *Frozen-Bubble*, and you'll be on your way.

Running and Playing Frozen-Bubble

Once you've installed Frozen-Bubble, you can run it by going to the **Launch** menu and selecting **Applications ▸ Games ▸ Arcade ▸ Frozen-Bubble**. The game will appear in a window, which will be black until it finishes loading, after which you will see the main-menu screen for the game (Figure 18-9). You cannot use your mouse in Frozen-Bubble, so navigate through the choices with your up and down cursor keys, and then press ENTER to make your selection. The default setup is one-player window mode with sound on, so if that sounds fine enough for you, just press ENTER straightaway to get started playing.

Game Play in Frozen-Bubble

As I mentioned, the idea of the game is to shoot down all the bubbles in the screen in order to move on to the next screen. You shoot the bubbles down with more bubbles, and you must hit a group of two or more bubbles of the same color with another of the same color in order to bring them all down. Once the bottom-most bubble makes contact with the bottom of playing area, all the bubbles will freeze over (hence the game's name), and you will have to start the level over again. Remember, you can play any level over and over and over until you get it right, with no penalties for your persistence.

Figure 18-9: The main-menu screen in Frozen-Bubble

Controls

Since you cannot use your mouse in Frozen-Bubble, you need to use your left and right cursor keys to aim the bubble you are going to shoot, and then use the up cursor key to actually shoot it. When you are finished playing the game, usually because you are worn out, just press the ESC key, which will bring you to the *High Scores* screen, where you can record your high scores by entering your initials and then hitting ENTER. Hit the ESC key again, and you'll be back at the options screen; hit ESC one more time, and Frozen-Bubble will close itself down completely.

The King of Solitaire Games: PySol

Well, now that we've installed one classic Linux game, let's jump right over to another, and this one has to be considered the king of solitaire games— PySol. PySol includes just about every solitaire game known on your part of the earth and then some, thus providing you with over 200 different games. These include poker-based solitaire games, such as *Poker Shuffle* and *Poker Square*; solitaire games played with Japanese *Hanafuda* cards (as shown in Figure 18-10), such as *MatsuKiri* and *Oonsoo*; card puzzles, such as *Pegged* and *Hanoy*; and card-based memory games, such as *Concentration* and *Memory 24*. All in all, an exceedingly cool and eclectic collection!

Installing PySol

To install PySol, run the Xandros Networks application, type **pysol** in the search box, and then click the **Search** button. After that, click **Expert View** in the bottom-left corner of the window, beneath the words *Search Results*. The choices available to you will appear in the right pane. In that pane, click **Install** next to *xandros-pysol,* and then follow the usual steps you learned in Chapter 8 to finish the job.

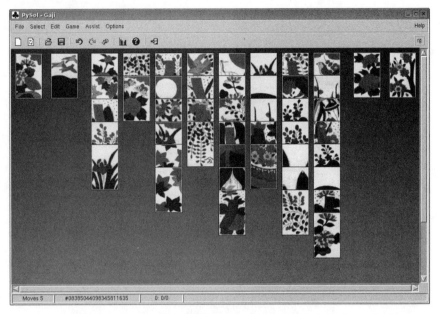

Figure 18-10: Playing the Hanafuda solitaire game Gaji in PySol, the king of solitaire games

Running and Playing PySol

In order to play PySol, go to the **Launch** menu and select **Applications ▶ Games ▶ Cards ▶ PySol**. PySol will then start up and be ready to play. To select the game you want to play, just go to the **Select** menu and choose from the many games listed there. Of course, since there are an awful lot of games in PySol, it would be a bit beyond the scope of this book to explain how to play every one of them. Fortunately, PySol comes with a pretty thorough help system that provides you with instructions for each of the games. To use this system, select the game you want to play, and once it appears, click the question mark button. Once you do this, the rules for the current game will appear in a separate window (Figure 18-11).

In addition to its help system, PySol allows you to see a demo of each game being played so that you can get a better feel for how things are done, a decidedly handy feature. In order to view one of these demos, select the game you want to play, go to the **Assist** menu, and select **Demo**. PySol will then begin playing the game for you. To make things all the clearer and easier to understand, it will display giant arrows to indicate its next move, as you can see in Figure 18-12.

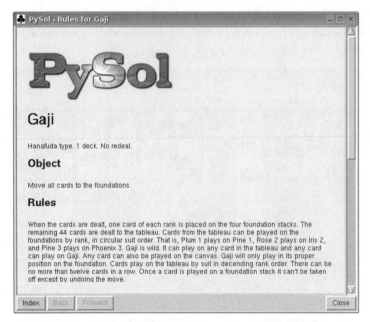

Figure 18-11: Individual game rules shown in a separate window in PySol

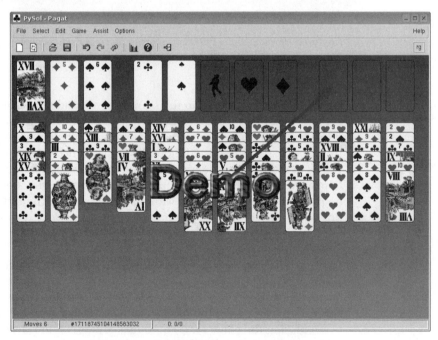

Figure 18-12: PySol's demos show you how each game is played

Project 18A: Getting a Little Adventurous with Njam

Now that you've gotten a taste of the games that come bundled with your system, and of some of those available via Xandros Networks, it's time to move on and have a bit of adventure. There are other games available on the Internet that are not specifically designed for use with Xandros—or even available via Xandros Networks—but will still run on your system. These are not guaranteed or supported by Xandros, so if anything goes wrong, you are on your own. That said, you might feel a bit easier knowing that the game that I will be covering in this project is not actually installed per se, so there is no chance of conflict or breaking your system. I can vouch for this myself, as I have used this game on my system without any problems arising, so you should be fine.

The game you will be installing is called *Njam* (Figure 18-13).

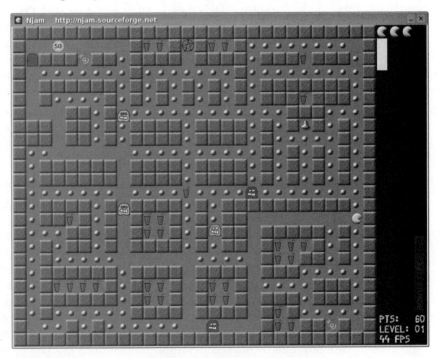

Figure 18-13: A new take on an old theme: Njam

Njam is basically a clone of *Pac-Man*, that most popular of computer and arcade games in days of yore. Of course, with its 3-D-like graphics, cooler music, and new twists and turns, Njam is in many ways more fun to play, or at least different enough to make it all seem a bit fresh to any player who spent his or her fair share of quarters playing the original in the good ol' days of dark and noisy video arcades.

By the way, if you are wondering what *Njam* means, it is Serbian for *yummy*, which seems quite appropriate given that the whole concept of the game is to eat as much as you can. I suppose you might think of it as a non-caloric, no-carb way to pig out. Atkins Diet followers take note.

18A-1: Downloading and Extracting Njam

To get Njam, follow these steps:

1. Go to http://njam.sourceforge.net, and click the **Linux binary** link.

2. On the next page that appears, click any one of the files in the *Download* column. Selecting the file from the location geographically closest to you will probably provide you with the fastest download time, though it doesn't always work out that way.

3. Once you have chosen a site from which to download Njam, another page will appear, but you won't need to click anything there; the download should just automatically begin. You will know when it does, because your web browser will pop up a window asking you what to do with the file.

4. In that window, select **Save to Disk**, and then click **OK**.

    When the download is complete, you must extract the tarball, as you learned to do in Chapter 5. Once you have done that, you will have a new folder with a name something like njam-1.21-i386 (the version number on yours might be higher if the application has been updated in the time after this book was released).

5. Right-click that folder, and select **Rename** in the pop-up menu. Then go ahead and shorten the name to **njam**. This will make it easier to handle in the future.

18A-2: Installing Njam's Dependencies

Now you are ready to play Njam . . . well, just about. As is stated on the Njam site, Njam has certain dependencies that must be met in order for it to be able to run.

These consist of *libsdl-image*, *libsdl-mixer*, and *libsdl-net*. As you already know, when you install an application via Xandros Networks, any dependencies that application requires are automatically downloaded and installed at the same time. This time, however, since you downloaded Njam without using Xandros Networks, you will have to find and install its dependencies yourself.

Luckily for you, all of these files are available via Xandros Networks, as they are required by many other applications. In fact, if you've already installed Frozen-Bubble, libsdl-mixer and libsdl-image will already have been installed on your system, meaning that the only file you'll have to install yourself is libsdl-net.

To install the files upon which Njam depends, run the Xandros Networks application, and then type **sdl** (that's a lowercase *l*, not the numeral 1) in the text box next to the *Search* button. Then click the **Search** button, and a list of files containing *sdl* will appear in the bottom half of the right pane of the XN window (Figure 18-14).

In that list, locate the three files I just mentioned, and install each of them using the method you learned in Chapter 8. If the file has the word *Remove* next to it, then you know that the file is already installed.

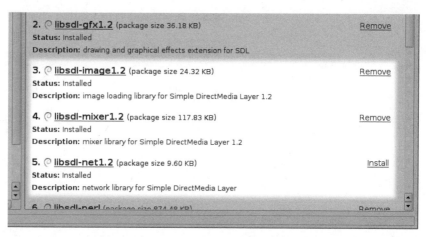

2. libsdl-gfx1.2 (package size 36.18 KB)   Remove
Status: Installed
Description: drawing and graphical effects extension for SDL

3. libsdl-image1.2 (package size 24.32 KB)   Remove
Status: Installed
Description: image loading library for Simple DirectMedia Layer 1.2

4. libsdl-mixer1.2 (package size 117.83 KB)   Remove
Status: Installed
Description: mixer library for Simple DirectMedia Layer 1.2

5. libsdl-net1.2 (package size 9.60 KB)   Install
Status: Installed
Description: network library for Simple DirectMedia Layer

6. libsdl-perl (package size 874.48 KB)   Remove

Figure 18-14: Installing the dependencies for Njam via Xandros Networks

18A-3: Running Njam

Once the three dependency files are installed, the only thing you really have to do is run Njam. Because there is no menu launcher for you, however, you will have to run it via the Run Command window (**Launch ▸ Run Command**). Once the window appears, type **/home/yourusername/njam/njam -w** in the *Command* box in that window (being sure to place *your* username in the appropriate spot within the string). After you've done that, click **Run**, and Njam will start right up.

In case you're wondering, that -w flag (you'll learn a bit more about flags in Chapter 20) causes Njam to open in a window (hence the *w*) rather than in full-screen mode. This is important, since running Njam in full-screen mode (without the -w flag) might cause some machines to freeze and then log out, which isn't something you would normally want to happen. No damage done if it does, of course, because all you have to do in that case is log in again, but why bother, right?

18A-4: Creating a Menu Launcher for Njam

Rather than typing in a command each and every time you want to run Njam, you might like to create a menu launcher for it in order to make things a tad more convenient. You can also use the same process to add menu launchers for any other applications you need, so it is indeed worth having a go.

Here are the steps for creating a menu launcher for Njam:

1. Close the still-open Njam window by pressing the ESC key.

2. Next, go to the **Launch** menu and select **Applications ▸ System ▸ Menu Editor**.

3. When the Menu Editor appears, click the + symbol next to *Games* and then the + symbol next to *Arcade*.

4. After that, click **Arcade** itself, and your window should look like mine in Figure 18-15.

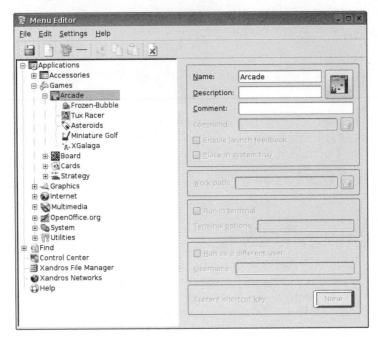

Figure 18-15: Preparing to add a new menu launcher for Njam via the Menu Editor

Assuming everything looks pretty much as it should, you are ready to add a new menu item.

5. Go to the **File** menu and select **New Item**, and a small New Item window will appear.

6. In the text box in that window, type **Njam** (as in Figure 18-16), and then click **OK**. The *Name* box in the right panel of the Menu Editor window should now say *Njam*.

Figure 18-16: Naming a new menu item in the Menu Editor

7. In the *Comment* box, type **A Pacman clone** (or just leave it blank if you prefer).

8. In the *Command* box, type **/home/yourusername/njam/njam -w**.

9. To start rounding things up, give your new launcher an icon by clicking the square box to the right of the *Name* and *Description* boxes.

10. In the Select Icon window that appears, scroll down until you find an icon called *package_toys*, which looks like a happy face sticking out its tongue (Figure 18-17).

Figure 18-17: Selecting an icon for the Njam menu launcher

11. Once you locate the icon, click it once to select it, and then click the **OK** button. The Menu Editor window should then look like that in Figure 18-18.

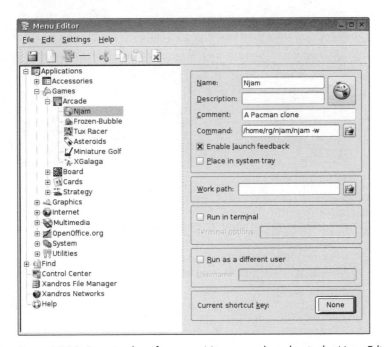

Figure 18-18: Data in place for a new Njam menu launcher in the Menu Editor window

If everything looks as it should, go to the **File** menu and select **Save**. Then you can test out the new launcher by quitting the Menu Editor and selecting **Applications ▸ Games ▸ Arcade ▸ Njam** in the **Launch** menu. Njam should then reappear in its own window, as before. If not, go back to the **Menu Editor,** click **Njam** in the left pane, and then check to see if you have typed in the correct command.

Playing Njam

Now that Njam is up and running, you will be looking at its menu screen (Figure 18-19), from which you can select what game mode you want to play, choose what other options you would like (sound effects, BGM, and skins), or, if you are so inclined, create new levels yourself.

Figure 18-19: The Njam opening menu screen

You won't have any mouse control in Njam, so use your up and down cursor keys to navigate through the menu, and then press ENTER to make your selection. Assuming you have chosen one of the game options, you will next be presented with a list of course choices. Use your cursor keys to select the one you want to play, and press ENTER. Before the game starts, you will see one more screen, in which you must select the course you want to play. Select the course of your choice using your cursor keys and press ENTER; then you will be able to start playing Njam.

Controls

For a single-player game, the Pac-Man-esque *chomper*, as I call it, is controlled by your keyboard cursor keys. When one of your chompers dies, you can get back into the action by pressing the SPACEBAR. When your last chomper dies, the stats page will automatically appear, showing your points for the game. If you then press the SPACEBAR, you can type in your name to include it in the high-scores list (assuming your score is high enough to make it). After that, you will be back at the main menu screen, from which you can decide what to do next.

While you can quit Njam by selecting **Exit** in the menu screen and pressing ENTER, you can also accomplish the same thing by pressing the ESC key as many times as needed, the number of presses necessary depending on the screen you are in at the time, until the game closes.

Game Modes

As you can see in the Njam menu (Figure 18-19), there are essentially four game modes to choose from: single-player, two-player cooperative, two-player duel, and two-player network duel. While you can easily figure out what single-player mode is all about, you may be wondering what the difference is between a two-player cooperative game and a two-player duel. I will fill you in so as not to leave you in the dark.

Both the cooperative games and the duels are played with two players at one keyboard operating two separate chompers. The first player controls his or her yellow chomper with the cursor keys, while the second player operates his or her green chomper with the R, D, F, and G keys. As long as neither player is extremely broad-shouldered, this arrangement should work out well enough, and the close physical proximity of the players could even actually work out to be quite advantageous in some select circumstances, if you catch my drift.

The duels are simple enough to understand: one player tries to beat the other by winning four games. Winning a game is achieved by getting the most points, which, with two players manning the same keyboard, can be quite exciting (watch out for the unethical use of elbows, though). Cooperative games, on the other hand, are quite a different thing, though equally simple to understand. They are essentially the same as single-player games, albeit with two players (and two chompers) working together to get the same job done. Something to be learned in that, I suppose.

Skins

A nice feature of Njam is the fact that it allows you to change the look of the various game elements through the use of *skins*, which are alternative graphic sets (like the themes for your web browser, *Firefox*) that give Njam a new appearance.

These skins, shown in Figure 18-20, can be selected by going to the opening menu. In that screen, just use your cursor keys to move down to **Options**, and then press ENTER. This will bring you to the **Options** menu, where you should again use your cursor keys to move down to **Skin**. Press ENTER, as many times as you like, to browse through the skins available. Once you have found a skin that you like, use the down cursor key to select **Back**, and then press ENTER. That's all there is to it.

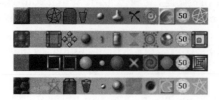

Figure 18-20: Njam skins

Finding Out More About Njam

If you would like to learn a bit more about Njam, check out the pretty complete documentation available from the Njam project page (http://njam .sourceforge.net/doc.html). In addition to the basic overview of the rules that I have provided, you will learn a bit more about the characteristics of the various elements within the game and how to use the level editor to create your own new playing levels.

Project 18B: A Final Bit of Fun with Fish Fillets—the Next Generation

Fish Fillets—the Next Generation, or *Fillets NG* to keep it simple, (Figure 18-21) is a wonderful port of the Windows puzzle game *Fillets.*

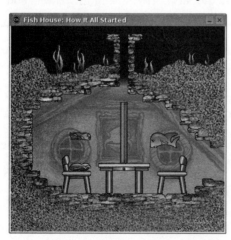

Figure 18-21: Fish Fillets—the Next Generation

Basically, the whole point of the game is to guide two hypersensitive, and sometimes witty, fish through a rather intriguing underwater labyrinth without getting the fish pulverized by the various obstacles that might inadvertently come crashing down on their sweet little heads. Fillets NG is very easy on the eyes with its attractive graphics (boy, do those jars of marmalade look tasty!), and with its great background music, it is equally kind on your ears.

Downloading, Installing, and Running Fillets NG

Fish Fillets—the Next Generation can be easily downloaded and installed via Xandros Networks. Be forewarned, however, that it is a very hefty download (over 60 MB), so if you are using a dial-up connection to the Internet, you might want to hold off on getting it until the middle of the night while you are asleep because the download will take hours. To get it, run Xandros Networks, but first make sure the *Debian Unsupported Site repository* is enabled. Then type **fillets** in the text box at the top of the window. Click **Search**, and then, once the list of results appears in the pane below, click **Install** next to *fillets-ng*.

Again, just as was the case with Njam, you will have to run Fillets NG via the Run Command window. To do that, go to the **Launch** menu and select **Run Command**. In the Run Command window, type **fillets** and click **Run**.

Creating a Menu Launcher for Fillets NG

Since typing a command to run Fillets NG can get to be a bit of a nuisance if you end up playing the game quite often, you will no doubt want to create a menu launcher for it as you did for Njam. Fortunately, the process is essentially identical. First, quit Fillets NG by clicking **Exit** in the game window, and then follow the same procedure you did for Njam. This time, however, name the new menu entry **Fillets NG**, and then type the following additional information:

> *Comment:* **An underwater puzzle maze**
>
> *Command:* **fillets**

For the icon, choose **bluefish** (which looks something like the blue fish in Fillets), and then go to the **File** menu, select **Save**, and then quit the Menu Editor. After that, you can more easily run Fillets NG by going to the **Launch** menu and selecting **Applications ▶ Games ▶ Arcade ▶ Fillets NG**.

Playing Fillets

The first thing you should see upon running Fillets NG is the menu screen, from which you can choose from among the *Credits*, the (as of this writing) still-under-construction *Intro*, the various game *Options*, and the level you want to start wandering through.

The level selections are made by clicking on the shiny balls in the path at the middle of the screen (Figure 18-22), though you will be able to select only the first level the first time out, and after that you will be able to choose from among only those levels you have already completed. In other words, you cannot just bypass levels and jump ahead. To return to the menu screen, just press the ESC key at any time.

Figure 18-22: Selecting playing levels from the menu screen of Fillets NG

Your job when playing Fillets is to get the two fish safely through each room of the labyrinth in order to move on to the next room. There are more than 70 rooms in all. The movement of the fish is handled from the keyboard via the cursor keys. You can switch between fish by pressing the spacebar. You can also control the fish using your mouse. To move a fish, click it with your left mouse button and drag it. To have the fish push objects, click the fish with the right mouse button and then drag it. You can return to the opening screen at any time by pressing ESC.

Moving through the each room is not as simple a task as it might seem because there are a variety of impediments to make things more challenging, a number of which you can see in the second room shown in Figure 18-23. The most important of these is the fragility of the fish themselves, which die whenever anything drops directly on them or on anything they are supporting on their backs. Push a puny snail off a cup and onto a saucer that's on the big fish's back, and say *sayonara* big fish. The likelihood of such cases of piscicide is increased by the fact that there are a number of potentially unstable obstacles that the fish have to move in order to travel from place to place within a given room. In some levels, there might also be some other living creatures that appear, but they do not have anything to do with solving the puzzle and are essentially nontoxic to the fish. They are only there to, as the author of the game puts it, "make the game more lively."

As far as moving objects is concerned, neither fish has a problem with lifting. Lowering such objects is another matter entirely, as trying to do so will turn either fish involved with the task into pickings from an alley cat's trash can. Pushing objects is less of a problem, though only the big fish can budge the heavier or larger items. The small fish does more of a finesse job, pushing the smaller objects around (cups, snails, shells, and the like) in order to clear the way for the bigger fish to put his or her (I'm not sure which) muscle to work. Of course, pushing some objects can cause others to fall, so be careful.

Figure 18-23: Even more impediments await in the second and subsequent rooms of Fillets NG

It is also important to remember that the fish can push only objects that are supported, or will be supported, by other objects, or the other fish, upon completion of the push. This does not include pushing an object directly onto another fish, since this is not possible. It is possible, however, to push an object onto another object that is already supported by the other fish. Support of most objects can also be transferred from one fish to the other fish from beneath that object. Figure 18-24, taken from the Fillets help files, shows some of the various moves that the fish can and cannot perform.

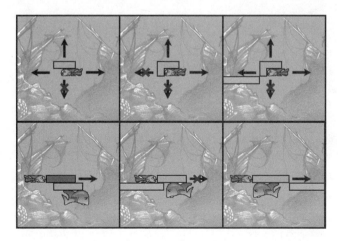

Figure 18-24: Some permitted and prohibited moves in Fillets NG

Finding Out More About Fish Fillets—the Next Generation

If you would like to find out more about Fillets NG and game-playing rules, go to the project site at http://fillets.sourceforge.net, and click the **How to Play** link at the left side of the page for more details. You can also access the same information right there on your computer by digging through the **data** folder you placed within the **fillets** folder. Just double-click the **doc** folder within **data**, the **html** folder within that, and finally **manual.html** within that, after which detailed rules for playing the game will appear in your web browser. You do not have to be online if you take this approach.

Even More Games In Store

In addition to the games I have mentioned thus far in this chapter, there a still many more available via Xandros Networks (Debian Unsupported Site repository). These include clones of old arcade classics such as *Burgerspace* (run around making hamburgers while avoiding the roaming weenies) and *Pingus* (Figure 18-25), in which you must try to save the hundreds of cute little penguins that appear on-screen from falling over cliffs and so on. *Blobwars* and *Tuxpuck* are other games that might be worth checking out if you are a classic arcade game lover.

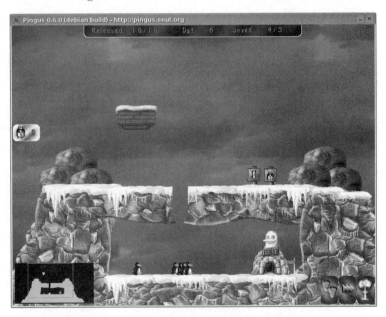

Figure 18-25: Pingus

If arcade games aren't really your cup of tea, you might want to try *Flight Gear,* a very attractive flight simulator (**fgfs** is the command you need to type in order to run it), *GNUChess* or *3D Chess* (run command=**3Dc**) if you're a chess lover, or even the *Xshogi/GNUshogi* combo (yes, you need to install both of them; run command = **xshogi**) or *Cgoban* if you are a fan of the Japanese board games *shogi* and *go.* There are, of course, many, many others. Enjoy the search.

19

KIDS' STUFF

Applications for Children

Given Linux's well-earned, though no-longer-accurate, reputation as an operating system for geeks, you would probably be totally surprised if you were to find any Linux applications out there for children. Well, start spitting out your oohs and wows, because Linux does indeed have offerings for the little ones. After all, even geeks have children.

While there probably aren't as many of these kids' apps out there for Linux as there are for Windows or Mac OS, there are still enough to give your little ones just cause to demand the right to man your keyboard once in a while. Oh, and lest you get the wrong impression, the somewhat-limited number of these applications is no indicator of their quality. Some are so nicely designed and fun to play around with that they have become popular enough to warrant being ported over to the Windows and Mac OS worlds.

Unfortunately, none of these applications comes bundled with your Xandros system, but don't let that discourage you, because almost all of the ones I will be discussing in this chapter are available from Xandros Networks.

And what about those that aren't? Well, you will have to download them yourself, but you will still use the Xandros Networks application to install them, so, either way, things will be quite easy at your end.

Potato Guy

Let's get started with an application that is probably quite familiar to you in its non-digital form—*Potato Guy* (Figure 19-1).

Yes, Potato Guy is the computer equivalent of the old Mr. Potato Head game that you may well have played with as a kid. In case you lived a slightly deprived childhood, and thus do not know Mr. Potato Head (or just don't remember him), the idea is simple: take an otherwise-normal everyday tuber, albeit one with arms and legs; stick a hat, nose, eyes, mouth, ears, or whatever else you want on it; and end up with a spud you can call your bud, like that in Figure 19-1.

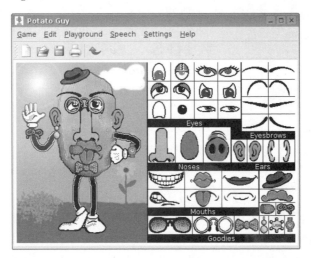

Figure 19-1: Potato Guy

Potato Guy has a few other differences from the Mr. Potato Head you played around with in your day, as this digital version even talks. Stick a nose on your *tuberfreund*, and you will hear "nose." Kind of cool. If potatoes aren't your thing, or at least your kids' thing, you can opt for an aquarium motif or for the Linux penguin, Tux, himself (Figure 19-2).

Installing and Running Potato Guy

To download and install Potato Guy, run Xandros Networks, type **potato guy** in the text box at the top of the window, and click **Search**. After that, just click **Install** next to *Potato Guy* in the results that appear below. You can then run Potato Guy from the **Launch** menu by selecting **Applications ▸ Games ▸ For Kids ▸ Potato Guy**.

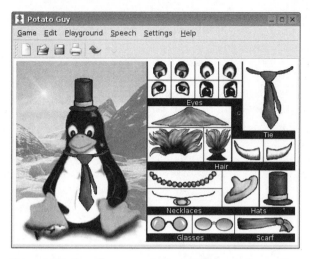

Figure 19-2: Tux offers a respite from potatoes in Potato Guy

Tux Paint

Now let's move on to what is perhaps the most successful and popular Linux application for children—*Tux Paint* (Figure 19-3).

Tux Paint is a cute and colorful paint program that allows your children (or anyone else's, for that matter) to tap into their artistic side by creating their own works of art, simple as they may turn out to be.

Figure 19-3: Tux Paint

The collection of tools in Tux Paint is pretty much like that found in most paint programs (brush, line, shapes, eraser, text, and so on). But there are also special features such as the Magic button, which allows your children to alter whatever they've painted in rather sophisticated ways (blur, fade, drip, mirror), and the Stamp button, which functions like a rubber stamp, allowing the kids to plop down various images (fish, birds, planets, and even Euros, to name but a few) anywhere they like within their creation. There are no menus in Tux Paint, so all the kids have to do to select a tool is click the appropriate button with the mouse, making everything very easy to deal with. To make things all the more appealing, there are even sound effects that ring out every time the brush (or other tool) hits the canvas. In fact, it is all so entertaining that you might end up wanting to play around with Tux Paint for a while yourself.

Installing and Running Tux Paint

As with all of the applications I'll cover in this chapter, Tux Paint can be easily installed via Xandros Networks. Just type **tuxpaint** in the text box next to the *Search* button, and then click **Install** next to *tuxpaint* in the results that appear below. All three items listed in the results will be installed, which is what you want, believe me. After that . . . well, you know the drill by now. Once Tux Paint is installed, you can run it by going to the **Launch** menu and selecting **Applications ▸ Graphics ▸ Tux Paint**.

Using Tux Paint

Using Tux Paint should be quite straightforward, since everything is controlled via large buttons that are easy for kids to manipulate. Just remember that when they click one of the tool buttons on the left side of the window, the option buttons on the right will change, showing the various options available for the tool they've selected.

Your kids can also save what they have created by clicking the **Save** button, and their creations will be automatically saved to a special directory without any potentially baffling file-system navigating.

To open one of their saved creations so that they can proudly show them off to you, all they need to do is click the **Open** button, and all of their saved files will appear as thumbnails within the Tux Paint window (Figure 19-4).

Letter Order Game

Letter Order Game (Figure 19-5), also known as *KMessedWords*, is a simple and very traditional game that is essentially exactly what both of its names imply.

Your child is presented with a group of scrambled letters from which he then tries to figure out the correct word.

Figure 19-4: Saved files are easily accessed from within the Tux Paint window

Figure 19-5: Letter Order Game

Installing and Running Letter Order Game

You can get Letter Order Game via Xandros Networks by typing **letter order game** in the text box at the top of the XN window and clicking **Search**. Click **Install** next to *Letter Order Game* in the results below, and then follow the usual drill for installing applications via Xandros Networks that you learned in Chapter 8. Then you can run Letter Order Game by going to the **Launch** menu and selecting **Applications** ▸ **Education** ▸ **Language** ▸ **Letter Order Game**.

Playing Letter Order Game

When the Letter Order Game window appears, you can start playing by selecting your level (*Easy* is the default) and then clicking the **Randomize** button.

A messed-up word will appear in the main part of the window (as shown in Figure 19-5); then, in the *Your guess* box at the bottom of the window, you type your guess as to what word those letters actually represent.

Click the **Try** button, and if you have typed in the word correctly, a window will pop up congratulating you on spelling the word correctly (left side of Figure 19-6).

Figure 19-6: Letter Order Game tells you whether your guess is correct (left) or incorrect (right)

You can then click the **Play Again** button in that window to go on to the next word. If your guess was incorrect, you will see a different window telling you that you missed (right side of Figure 19-6). Click the **OK** button in that window, and you will get another crack at solving the puzzle. If you finally give up, click the **Randomize** button again, and you will get a new word to work with.

Hangman Game

Hangman Game, as its name implies, is a computerized version of that most traditional of word games, Hangman. On the off chance that you're not familiar with the game, I'll give you a brief description. When you start a game, a series of lines representing the letters in a word appears at the bottom of the game window. You then try to guess what letters go in the blanks. If your guess is right, all the instances of that letter will appear in the appropriate blanks. Each time a letter you guess isn't in the word, construction of the noose and the person hanging from it will proceed, piece-by-piece and limb-by-limb. The object is to guess the word before getting hung.

Despite the essentially innocent nature of the game, as a parent you might not want your child playing a game that uses a gallows and noose as its motif. Well, let's just say that in those cases where your child does lose a game, the hangman figure will at least not be in the noose but rather hanging onto it by its hand (Figure 19-7).

Figure 19-7: Here's what your children will see if they lose a game of Hangman

The message that appears at that point, however, does say, "You are dead," so I don't really know what to tell you. At any rate, have a look at the results of a losing round in Figure 19-7 to see what you think, and then decide for yourself.

Installing and Running Hangman Game

Hangman Game is available from Xandros Networks, so just type **hangman** in the text box, click **Search**, click **Install** next to *hangman game* in the results, and then follow the usual process you learned in Chapter 8. After the installation is complete, you can play Hangman Game by going to the **Launch** menu and selecting **Applications ▸ Education ▸ Language ▸ Hangman Game**.

Playing Hangman Game

Playing Hangman Game is quite simple. Just type the letter you want to offer up as a guess, and then press ENTER. If the letter is a part of the word in question, it will appear at the bottom of the screen. If the letter is not part of the word, it will appear in the *Misses* list at the top-left corner of the playing area, and construction of the gallows will begin.

Tux Typing

While we're still on the topic of word and letter games, let's move on to *Tux Typing* (Figure 19-8), commonly referred to as *Tux Type*, a close relative of Tux Paint.

Figure 19-8: Tux Type

Tux Type is a very attractive and well-featured typing-tutor application, complete with music and sound effects that even you can enjoy. There are two different typing games in Tux Type: one called *Key Cascade*, where you type out the letters you see plastered on the falling fish so that Tux can eat them (the fish), and one called *Word Cascade*, where you do the same thing to falling words. Both of the games in Tux Type have three levels of difficulty, so they could well be used by children of quite different ages—even kids in their mid-forties.

Installing Tux Type

To install Tux Type, run the Xandros Networks application, type **xandros-tuxtype** in the text box, and click **Search**. The list of results will be empty at first, but you will be instructed to click **Expert** under *Search Results*, so do that (at the bottom of the left pane). When *xandros-tuxtype* appears in the right pane, click **Install**, and then follow the usual drill.

Running Tux Type

You can run Tux Type from the **Launch** menu by selecting **Applications** ▸ **Education** ▸ **Tools** ▸ **Tux Typing**, but before you actually run it, be aware of the fact that Tux Type is set up by default to run in full-screen mode. If you would prefer to have the game appear in its own window, or if your computer is just hostile to full-screen applications, as some are, go to the **Launch** menu and select **Run Command**. When the Run Command window appears, type **tuxtype -w**, and press ENTER.

Creating a Menu Launcher for Using Tux Type in Window Mode

If you would always like to use Tux Type in window mode, it would behoove you to create a menu launcher that will allow you to do that more easily. Just follow these steps:

1. Go to the **Launch** menu and select **Applications** ▸ **System** ▸ **Menu Editor**.

2. When the Menu Editor window appears, click the + symbol next to *Education*, and then click the + symbol next to *Tools*.

3. When the subcategories appear under *Tools*, click **Tux Typing** (it should be the only entry there).

    You would think at this point that the only thing you would have to do is add a -w flag to the command for the present Tux Type launcher. Unfortunately, given the parameters I have set for this book, that is not possible because the game was installed in root mode, as are all games installed via Xandros Networks. What you will have to do instead is create a totally new launcher, which, paired with the original launcher, will give you the freedom to play the game in whichever mode you please.

4. With *Tux Typing* now selected in the left pane of the Menu Editor, go to the **File** menu and select **New Item**.

5. When the New Item window appears, type **TuxType (Window Mode)**, and then click **OK**.

6. In the right pane of the Menu Editor window, type **tuxtype -w** in the *Command* box, and then click the icon square to the right of the *Name* and *Description* boxes.

7. When the Select Icon window appears, scroll down and select **tux**.

8. Once you've done that, click **OK** in the Select Icon window to close it.

9. Your Menu Editor window should now look like mine in Figure 19-9. Assuming it does, go to the **File** menu and select **Save**. You can then quit the Menu Editor.

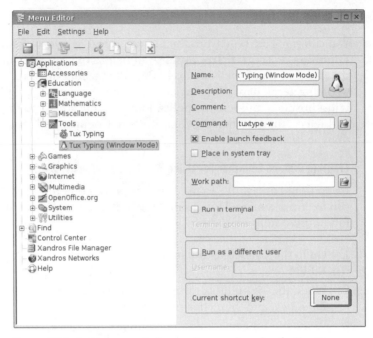

Figure 19-9: Setting up a window-mode menu launcher for Tux Type

Using Tux Type

When the Tux Typing window first appears, it will be opened to its menu screen (Figure 19-10).

Figure 19-10: The opening menu screen in Tux Typing

In that screen, you can use your mouse to select the game you want, and then you will be presented with a choice of skill levels. Once you select one of those, the game begins.

The game is all about typing. See a fish with a *w* on it? Press **w** on your keyboard to guide Tux over so he can gulp it up. When you successfully complete a level, Tux will congratulate you (as in Figure 19-11), and when you don't, you'll be told so as well. That's just about all there is to it.

Figure 19-11: Tux Typing congratulates you when you successfully complete a level

MathWar

Now that we've covered quite a number of graphical and lexical applications, let's move over to the mathematical side of things by introducing *MathWar* (Figure 19-12).

MathWar is a simple mathematics tutor that pops out simple math problems to which you, or preferably your child, input the answers. The time in which you have to answer is set at 10 seconds (though you can adjust this in either direction), and questions are divided among three operators: addition, subtraction, and multiplication (no division). Although you can adjust the percentage of questions for each operator so that, for example, 20 percent of the questions would involve multiplication, 30 percent division, and 50 percent subtraction, you cannot configure the level of difficulty. Sorry.

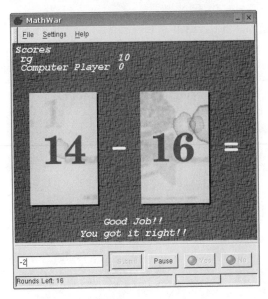

Figure 19-12: MathWar

Installing and Running MathWar

To get MathWar via Xandros Networks, type **mathwar** in the text box at the top of the XN window, click **Search**, click **Install** next to *MathWar* in the results below, and then follow the usual drill for installing applications via Xandros Networks. You can run MathWar by going to the **Launch** menu and selecting **Applications** ▸ **Education** ▸ **Mathematics** ▸ **MathWar**.

Playing MathWar

When the MathWar window appears, go to the **File** menu and select **New Game**. A simple problem will appear, and your job is to type in the correct answer within the time allotted and click **Submit**. A small timer bar at the bottom-right corner of the screen will show you how much time you have left for each question. If you do not answer within the allotted time, either you will be told that time is up and provided with the correct answer (an instant miss) or the computer will offer up its own solution, and you will be then asked whether you think the computer is correct. Make the right choice and you get points; make the wrong choice and the computer gets points. All quite fair and simple.

Changing MathWar's Settings

As I mentioned, you can change many of MathWar's settings. This is done by going to the **Settings** menu and selecting **Preferences**. In MathWar's preferences window (Figure 19-13), you can adjust the number of rounds and the number of seconds per round (in the *General* tab), decide what percentage of the time the computer will offer up an answer of its own when you can't come up with one yourself (in the *Computer Player* tab), and determine the percentage of questions that will be based on each of the three operators available (in the *Operators* tab).

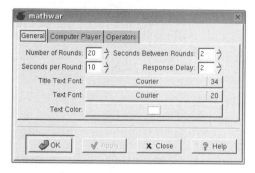

Figure 19-13: Changing MathWar's settings

LPairs

The next application we will be dealing with is a memory matching game by the name of *LPairs* (Figure 19-14).

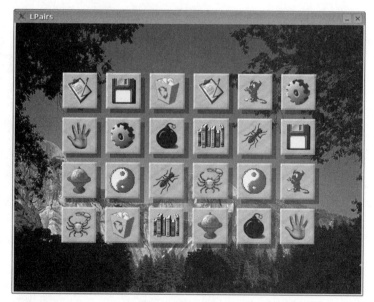

Figure 19-14: LPairs—a pure and simple memory matching game

The images shown in LPairs are not of a particularly childish variety, so the game shouldn't be offensive to older kids or even adults. You might thus end up with a broader audience for this game than is the case with most of the other applications in this chapter. Still, it is really simple in concept, so the little ones should find it fun too.

Downloading, Installing, and Running LPairs

You can download and install LPairs via Xandros Networks by first making sure that the *Debian Unsupported Site repository* is enabled and then typing **lpairs** in the text box at the top of the window. Click the **Search** button, and then click **Install** next to *lpairs* in the pane below. Once the installation is complete, you can run LPairs via the *Run Command* window. Just type **lpairs** and then click **Run**.

Playing and Configuring LPairs

When you run LPairs, it will open right into its main, and only, menu (Figure 19-15).

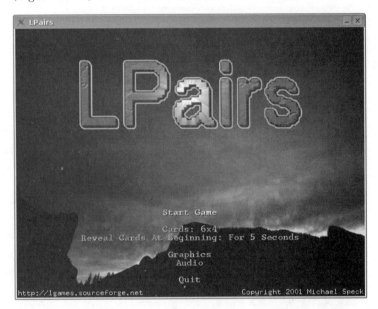

Figure 19-15: The main menu screen in LPairs

The options within the menu are few, and basically all you have to do is to click any item for it to take effect. For example, to choose the number of tiles in the game, click **Cards** as many times as it takes to come up with the number of tiles you would like. Your choices are (in tiles-per-row format) 4×4, 5×4, 6×4, 6×5, and 8×5. Once you have gone through the other items and made your choices and are ready to play the game, just click **Start Game**.

The game will start up with all of the tiles facing down, which means they will all appear blank. To get started, just click a tile and it will flip over, revealing the image on its reverse side. Then click another tile to see if you can match the first. Once you do match a pair of tiles, both will disappear, and you simply keep up that process until all the tiles are gone. If you want to return to the main menu, you can do so at any time by pressing the ESC key.

It just wouldn't be right for me to finish up a chapter on applications for children without including one that concerned geography. After all, geography was my undergraduate major way back when, and no doubt what got me where I am today. Hmm. . . .

Nevertheless, *KGeography* is a pretty cool application that drills your children not only on map identification and U.S. and world capitals but also on the flags of the many nations of our modern world (Figure 19-16).

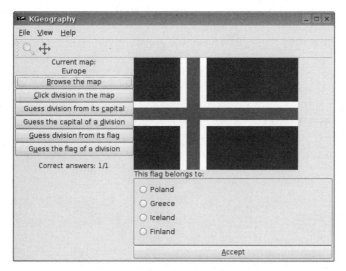

Figure 19-16: Learning the flags of the world with KGeography

Who knows, maybe your child is a budding geographer or vexillologist—a seldom-seen word for someone who studies flags. KGeography will help her find out.

KGeography is not available from any of the Xandros Networks repositories, so you will have to download it on your own. However, because it comes in the form of a Debian package (.deb file), it can be installed easily by means of the Xandros Networks application. Note that Xandros does not support or guarantee applications you install this way, so don't go screaming to them if anything goes wrong. I have used KGeography on my system, however, and found no problems, so you should be all right. Still, if anything does go wrong in your case, don't come screaming to me either. You are strictly on your own in regard to any screaming you wish to do, should it come to that.

19A-1: Downloading KGeography

You can download KGeography by clicking the **Debian – KGeography 0.3** link on the project home page at http://kgeography.berlios.de/download.html. When the list of available downloads appears on the next page, click the **kgeography_0.2-1_i386.deb** link (version 0.3 doesn't actually seem to work), and the download will begin.

19A-2: Installing KGeography

After KGeography is successfully downloaded, you can install it by running the Xandros Networks application and selecting **Install DEB File** in the **File** menu. In the Browse for Packages window that appears, locate and then select the **kgeography deb** package by clicking it once. Then click the **Open** button in that window, and the installation process will begin.

19A-3: Running and Using KGeography

KGeography will create its own menu launcher, so you can easily run it via the **Launch** menu by selecting **Applications ▶ Education ▶ Miscellaneous ▶ KGeography**. Once KGeography appears, you can choose from among various world regions by going to the **File** menu and selecting **Open**. From the window that appears (Figure 19-17) you can select Africa, Europe, France, Germany, North and Central America, Spain, or USA.

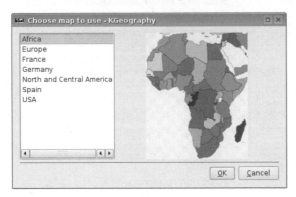

Figure 19-17: Choosing the region to study in KGeography

Once you have made your selection, you have a number of options to choose from. On the left side of the KGeography window is the following list of buttons.

Browse the map

This is not a quiz but rather a way for you to familiarize yourself with the countries or states in the map selected. Clicking on a country or state reveals its name and capital (Figure 19-18).

Click division in the map

In this quiz, you are told in the left pane to click on a specific state or country.

NOTE *In KGeography,* division *stands for a political division.*

Guess division from its capital

In this quiz, you are given a sentence to complete, such as "Hanover is the capital of...," and then given four answers to choose from.

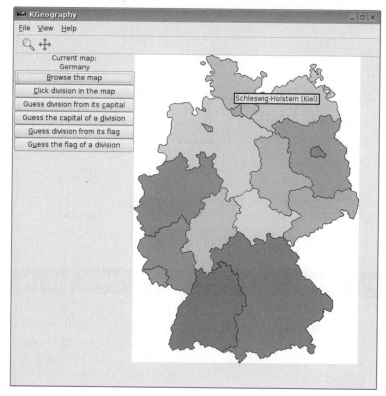

Figure 19-18: Clicking on a state or country reveals its name and capital.

Guess the capital of a division

This is another multiple-choice quiz in which you must name the state or country of the given capital. For example, "Raleigh is the capital of..."

Guess division from its flag

In this quiz, you are shown a flag and then asked to choose from among four possible states or countries to which it might belong. This and the following flag quiz are available only for Europe, Africa, North and Central America, and Germany. Hey, can you recognize the flag of Nordrhein-Westpfalen?

Guess the flag of a division

In this quiz (Figure 19-19), you are asked to select from among four flags in order to complete the sentence given, such as, "The flag of Berlin is..."

At the beginning of any quiz you choose, you will first be asked how many questions you would like (very democratic), the maximum number of which depends on the number of choices available in the real scheme of things; a quiz on the states of the United States, for example, would have a maximum of 50 questions. As you play along, your score is displayed in the left pane of the screen as a fraction, with the number of correct answers on the left and the total number asked thus far on the right.

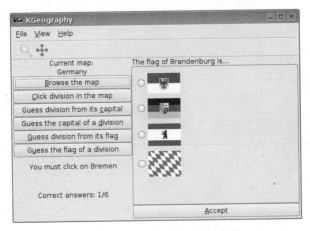

Figure 19-19: Identifying the flag of a specified state or country

Project 19B: Creating a Kid-Friendly (and Kid-Safe) User Account

So now you've installed a heap of applications for your little ones to use, but you still don't feel quite safe leaving them alone at the helm of your computer. What if they screw up something? What if they start viewing web pages that might corrupt their tender young minds? And what if they dump some of your files? The list of possible nightmarish scenarios goes on and on.

Well, the simple answer is to create a special user account just for them and then to customize it so that they can do only what *you* want them to do. Sound interesting? Here's how to do it:

1. Create a new user account for your children via the Control Center, as you learned to do in Chapter 7.

2. Run Xandros Networks, type **eyes** in the text box, and then click **Search**. Once the results are displayed, click to install Eyes. After you've completed the installation, quit Xandros Networks. We'll get back to Eyes in a moment.

3. Log out of your own user account, and then log in to the new account you've just created for your children.

   Now comes the dramatic stuff:

4. Change the desktop wallpaper, as you learned to do in Chapter 3, to something that might make your children feel at home—a picture of Tucker, the family dog, or maybe a scanned image of one of your children's own drawings.

5. Remove all of the desktop icons except for the Trash. Don't worry, the icons are all just links, not the real thing, so no harm done.

6. Now, remove all of the items from the Panel by right-clicking each item and selecting **Remove** from the pop-up menu. To get rid of those nubby little bars, like that for the Taskbar (the section of the Panel that shows you which windows you have open), right-click at the top of the bar itself, and then select the **Remove ItemName** in the pop-up menu (Figure 19-20). Leave only the clock and the Lock/Logout buttons. Yes, remove the Launch menu too.

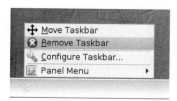

Figure 19-20: Removing the Taskbar from the Panel

7. To make things easier for your children to see and manipulate, increase the size of the Panel by right-clicking it and then selecting **Properties** from the pop-up window.

8. In the Properties window, select **Large** from the drop-down menu button beneath the word *Size* (Figure 19-21). Then click **OK**, and the Panel will bloat up to almost three times its original size.

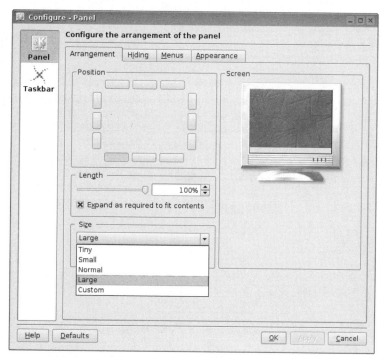

Figure 19-21: Increasing the size of the Panel

9. Now, add to the Panel the pair of eyes you installed just before logging out of your user account. This silly little applet looks like a pair of eyes, twirling around following the movements of your mouse cursor. Do this by right-clicking the Panel and selecting **Add ▶ Applet ▶ Eyes**.

10. Once you have done that, move the eyes by dragging the little nubby bar that appears to the left of the eyes. A good location to place the eyes is just to the left of the Lock/Logout buttons, as it prevents the kids from inadvertently logging themselves out.

11. Now add launchers to the Panel for all of the applications for which you want your children to have access. To add a launcher for Letter Order Game, for example, you would right-click the **Panel** and then select **Add ▶ Application Button ▶ Applications ▶ Education ▶ Language ▶ Letter Order Game**. Go ahead and do this for each application; you might also want to include a calculator, since kids seem to enjoy playing around with them. If you want them to have some sort of word-processing function, consider letting them use the simpler *Text Editor* rather than the more complex *OpenOffice.org Write*.

12. If you want to include a launcher for Tux Type, you will have to create a new launcher for it, since the menu launcher you created previously for that application will appear only in your own user account.

   a. To create a launcher for Tux Type, right-click on the **Panel** and select **Add ▶ Special Button ▶ Non-KDE Application**.

NOTE   *KDE applications usually have a prominent K somewhere in the name—Tux Type doesn't.*

   b. In the configuration window that appears, type **tuxtype -w** in the *Executable* box. Then click the icon button to the right of the *Executable* box, select **tux** in the Select Icon window that appears, and click **OK**. Your configuration window should then look like that in Figure 19-22. Assuming it does, click **OK**.

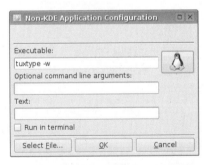

Figure 19-22: Creating a Panel launcher for Tux Type

13. Finally, adjust the spacing between the icons so that they are not too close to one another. You can do this by right-clicking each icon and selecting **Move** in the pop-up window. Then just move the icon in question until it seems to be in a good place.

Basically, that's it for setting up the desktop for the kids. When you've finished, it should all look something like what I've come up with in Figure 19-23, though your dog will no doubt be different.

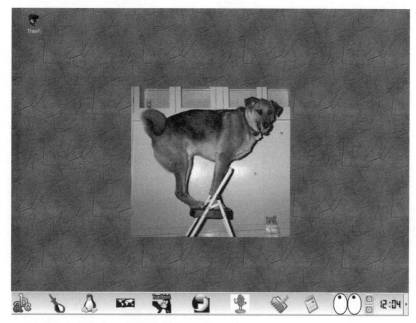

Figure 19-23: Your new, kid-friendly desktop

Now that your new kid zone is ready, the only thing you have left to do is teach your kids how to log in, how to type their password, how to use the various applications, and how to log out. Once your children have the hang of things, you can pretty much rest assured that they can play around on your computer safely without wreaking havoc on your user account or the system itself.

PART V

FOR THE MORE ADVENTUROUS

20

WANT TO GET A LITTLE GEEKY?
Using Linux Commands

Many people shy away from Linux because they envision it as a system for compu-geeks—an environment in which you do everything the hard way by using a command line. In this era of graphical interfaces, the idea of typing in commands to get things done seems a dreadful throwback to the days of DOS, and that puts many people off—especially those who remember what it was like in those "old days." This reaction is fair enough, but it is not really an accurate reflection of the reality of the Linux world. After all, most Linux users today utilize some sort of graphical interface. They can, and often do, achieve all that they hope to achieve through drop-down menus and mouse clicks alone. In fact, with Xandros there is actually no need for the everyday user to resort to typing commands at all.

Be that as it may, many people interested in Linux can't resist having a go at the command line, and many expect any book on Linux to have a chapter covering the subject. There are also, to be quite honest, a few things that cannot be done without the use of the command line, though these are quite limited and not 100 percent necessary to function in the Xandros environment. Still, I have provided some examples of what you can do with the command line in the three projects in this chapter.

Don't Lose Your Nerve

The idea of playing around with commands might sound a bit forbidding to most, but you needn't worry too much. I will limit my introduction to the hardcore basics—essentially just what you need to know in order to follow along with the projects in this chapter and most of the other things you might need to know to get by. And if that isn't enough to soothe your worries, you can feel quite safe skipping over this chapter entirely if you are so inclined. Still, I would encourage you to give it all a try at least once, because using the command line can be as harmless and simple as anything else you do on your system. And, it can actually even provide you with a little fun, if you can believe that.

Meet the Command Console

Open the *Linux Command Console* application in your Xandros system by going to the **Launch** menu and selecting **Applications ▸ System ▸ Console**. When the Console opens, it will, in all its simplicity, look much like Figure 20-1.

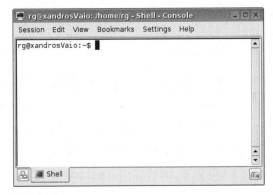

Figure 20-1: The Command Console

As you can see, all it says is **rg@xandrosVaio:~$**. In this case:

The **rg** is my username.

xandrosVaio is the name I gave my computer.

The tilde (~) shows that I am in my Home folder.

And the **$** shows that I am in user, rather than root, mode.

In your case, the username and computer name will be different. If your username is frog and your computer is called officeBeast, for example, the command line will say **frog@officeBeast:~$**.

Typing in the Console is straightforward enough; you just type as you usually do. You can also delete and insert letters or phrases by using the DELETE and BACKSPACE keys and the cursor keys. For practice, try the following:

1. Type **I like strawberries so very much.**

2. Now, change *strawberries* to **cherries** (because cherries are, in fact, so much better). Just use your left cursor key to move the cursor in front of the first *s* in *strawberries.*

3. Next, tap on your DELETE key as many times as necessary to erase the word *strawberries* (uh, that would be 12 times, methinks).

4. Finally, just type **cherries**, and then use your right cursor key to move the cursor back to the end of this meaningful sentence.

Now that you've completed this fascinating bit of typing practice, press the ENTER key. As you will almost immediately see, the Console's response to your efforts thus far is merely a dismissive:

```
bash: I: command not found.
```

Although you've typed a string of text that has meaning to you, it means absolutely nothing to your system. In fact, the system was so short-sighted that it could see nothing other than the first word you typed in the Console: I. Because I is not a valid command, the system had no idea what do to with it.

Shells

You may be wondering at this point what this bash business is all about and why it is talking to you. Well, Bash (Bourne Again Shell) is one of the many shells that are used in Linux systems, and the one that happens to come with your Xandros distro, and most others for that matter. A shell is actually a program that interprets the commands you type into the Console and delivers them to your system so that it can act on them. I like to think of it as a command-handling subsystem. Some scripting languages, as you will find out in the Briscola section in this chapter, also have their own shells, but other than those few exceptions, you generally need not be unduly concerned with shells other than to know what they are.

Nontoxic Commands

As you now know, all of this typing is easy enough, but in order to actually do something useful with your Console, you need to type commands, and there are more of them than you could ever hope or need to know. To get you started, we will begin with some commands that are easy to understand, nontoxic, and completely child-friendly.

$ whoami

There is no command as easy, safe, or even as seemingly useless, as whoami. Rather than help those with multiple-personality disorders discover who they are at any given moment, the whoami command simply tells you which user is currently logged in. Try it out by typing **whoami** after the **$** and then pressing the ENTER key. Remember that commands are case-sensitive; a *W* is not the same a *w*, so type accordingly.

The Console will now tell you the username of the person currently logged in. If you are logged in as frog, you should get **frog** as the answer to your command. My username is rg, so when I run the command, the result, as you can see in Figure 20-2, is **rg**. You might also notice that the screenshot was taken on a different computer, as the prompt is **RGAcer** rather than **xandrosVaio** as it was in Figure 20-1.

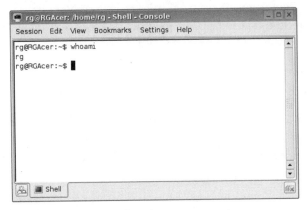

Figure 20-2: Trying out the whoami command

$ pwd

If you essentially know who you are but aren't exactly sure where you are, the pwd command (print working directory) should come in handy. The pwd command tells you exactly where the Console is in your directory tree.

Let's say, for example, that the Console is in my rg Home directory when I use the pwd command; I would, after typing the command and pressing the ENTER key, get **/home/rg** printed to my Console. You should get similar results if you try it out.

NOTE *The word* print, *in this case, has nothing to do with your printer; it merely means that the response will be printed to, or displayed in, the Console.*

$ ls

Another harmless but handy command is ls (list directory contents). The ls command shows you what is in your current directory, whatever that might be at the time. This is the nongraphical equivalent of double-clicking a folder in Nautilus to see what is inside. Try it out by typing **ls** and then pressing the ENTER key.

Your results should list all of the folders in your Home directory (mine are shown in Figure 20-3), which is the default directory when you run the Console.

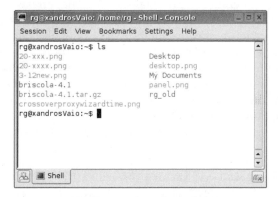

Figure 20-3: The results of the ls command

You can also increase the functionality of the ls command, and almost any other command for that matter, through the use of *flags* (also called *options*). For example, you use the -R (recursive) flag with the ls command to show not only the list of files in the folder but also what is within the subfolders. To use a flag, just type the command, followed by a space, and then the flag, as is the case in $ls -R.

$ su

When you have to change from being a normal user to being the root user via the Console, you can do so by using the su (superuser) command. There are two simple and straightforward steps involved. Open a new Console window, and then type **su** and press ENTER; after which you will be asked for your root password. As you type in your password, the password itself will not appear in the Console window, but that is how things are supposed to be, so don't panic. When you are finished, press the ENTER key, and the prompt you usually see in your Console, **username@computername:~$**, will be replaced by your root prompt: **computername:/home/username#**. Notice that instead of a **$** at the end of the prompt, you now have a **#** instead, which indicates that you are in root mode.

exit

You can get out of root and back to your normal user mode by using the exit command. Just type **exit** and press ENTER, and you will become your old self in user mode again. Very simple and handy. If you use the exit command while in user mode, you will exit the Console altogether—a command-line version of quit.

$ locate

In contrast to the seemingly lightweight commands you have learned so far, the locate command is really quite useful. In fact, you might well find it a much easier, faster, and more effective method of finding files than the graphical search tool in the Launch menu. Using the command is quite easy: you simply type in the command followed by a space and the name of the file you are searching for. You can use this command in either root or user mode.

Give the locate command a try by searching for the icon file for the Instant Messaging application *Kopete*. To do this, type **locate kopete.png**, and press ENTER. The locations of the various kopete.png files will then appear in your Console, as you can see in Figure 20-4.

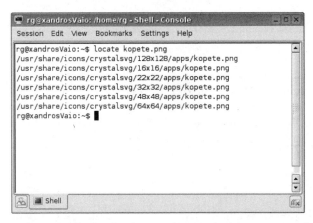

Figure 20-4: The results of a search using the locate command

updatedb

As you have just seen, the locate command can be quite handy; however, as you add files and applications to your system, you will need to update its database of filenames from time to time if you want to keep using it.

To do this, become root using the su command, and then type **updatedb** (update database), followed by a tap on the ENTER key. It will seem that nothing is happening for a while (an even longer while if you have a lot of files), but don't worry—progress is being made. Once your prompt returns, you will have successfully created the database file. After that, you can go on and use the locate command.

Commands with Some Teeth

The simple commands you have tried so far are all of the safe-and-sane, fire-marshal-approved variety; they merely print out information to your Console. Now you are going to try to get some real tangible results from the commands you type in. These commands are also essentially safe and sane if you follow my instructions.

$ mkdir

You have already learned how to create folders by means of menus and your mouse, but you can also do this using the command line by means of the mkdir (make directory) command. To see how this command works, create a folder called *command_exp* (for command experiments) by typing **mkdir command_exp** and then pressing ENTER. The new folder should appear in your Home folder, so go ahead and check to see if it is there by clicking the user's **Home** icon on your desktop.

Okay, good, *bra, bueno!* Now let's create another new folder within that new folder—a *subfolder* if you will. We'll call this one *sub*. So, just type **mkdir command_exp/sub** and then press ENTER. You can now take a peek and see if the subfolder appears within the command_exp folder, if you like.

You have no doubt noticed that in order to create the subfolder, sub, you used a forward slash (/) after command_exp. Basically, when you use the forward slash, you are telling your system to execute a command on the item located to the right of the forward slash, and you are telling the system that the file is located in the folder to the left of the forward slash. You will see still more examples of the forward slash in action in the rest of this chapter.

$ cd

Until now, you have been using the command line from your Home folder. With the cd (change directory) command, you can change from one folder to another via your Console by typing the command followed by the folder you want to enter. To take it out for a spin, let's get inside the command_exp folder by typing **cd command_exp** and pressing ENTER. If you've done this correctly, the prompt in your Console should now read **username@computer-name:~/command_exp$**. If so, you can pat yourself on the back.

$ cp

The cp (copy & paste) command allows you to copy a file and paste it in a new location in one swoop. To do this, the command needs to know where the file you want to copy is, what it is called, and where you want to copy it.

To give it a try, copy any file you happen to have in your Home folder and paste it in your command_exp folder. For example, in my case I want to copy a file called tawas.png in my Home folder to my command_exp folder. I thus type **cp tawas.png command_exp/** and press ENTER, and then I will have a copy of tawas.png in my command_exp folder. The first expression after the cp command is the file you are copying (tawas.png); the second expression is the location where it is to be pasted (command_exp/). After you try it out, have a look within your command_exp folder to make sure the file you copied is there.

So what happens if the file you want to copy isn't in your Home folder? Say, for example, your tawas.png file is in the command_exp folder, and you want to place a copy of it in a happy_pics folder that is also located in the command_exp folder. Well, you actually have a couple of ways of going about it.

One way is to first use the cd command you just learned to move into the command_exp folder. You thus type **cd command_exp**, and then press ENTER, which places you in the command_exp folder. You then use the cp command to copy the tawas.png file and paste it in the happy_pics folder by typing **cp tawas.png happy_pics/** and then pressing ENTER.

The second alternative is to do it all in one fell swoop using only the cp command. To go this route, type **cp command_exp/tawas.png command_exp /happy_pics/** and then press ENTER. This route is equally effective, although it involves a tad more typing.

$ rm

The rm (remove) command, as its name implies, is used to remove files and empty folders—a sort of command-line version of moving things to Trash. The rm command, albeit very useful and easy to use, should be used with caution. Once you remove a file with this command, there is no going back— the file is gone for good.

To play it safe, let's try out the rm command by getting rid of that new copy of the file you moved to your command_exp folder moments ago. The basic rm command structure consists of the command itself, rm, followed by the name of the file that you want to remove. Assuming your Console shows you to be Home, you can remove the file by typing **rm command_exp/** followed by a tap on the ol' ENTER key. The file will then be gone, and gone for good.

If the file is not in the Home folder, just use the cd command to move into the folder in which it is placed, and then use the rm command once there. As with the cp command, you can achieve the same thing in one go by typing **rm foldername/filename** and pressing ENTER.

Now that we are essentially finished with the experimentation process, you might as well get rid of the command_exp folder. However, since that folder has a subfolder (sub) within it, the rm command cannot handle the job. This is because, as I mentioned before, *the command can be used only to remove files and empty folders*. To remove a folder and its contents as well, you need to add the recursive flag, -r. To do this, just type **rm -r command_exp** and then press ENTER. Your command_exp folder and the subfolder within will then be but a memory.

As you learned in Chapter 15, Xandros, for legal reasons, does not come with playback support for encrypted DVDs, which really puts a damper on things, since most commercial DVDs are of the encrypted variety. The good news is that you can install support for encrypted DVD playback. The only way to do this, however, is via the command line, which is a good example of how commands can come in handy once in a while. If you need or want to play DVDs, and get some command-line practice in the process, just follow along with the rest of this short project.

20A-1: Downloading and Installing libdvdread3

To play back encrypted DVDs, you need to install *libdvdcss*, which you can get via the script included in the *libdvdread3* package. That package may already be installed on your system, so it is a good idea to first see if it's there. If not, you can easily install it via Xandros Networks. Here's what you need to do:

1. Open a Console window, type **locate libdvdread3**, and press ENTER.
2. If the locations of the various libdvdread3 files are listed as the result of your search, go on to section 20A-2. If, on the other hand, nothing appears, you need to install the libdvdread3 package, which you can do by running the Xandros Networks application, typing: **libdvdread3** in its search box, clicking **Search**, and then clicking **Install** next to *libdvdread3* in the results that will appear in the pane below.

20A-2: Downloading and Installing libdvdcss

As I mentioned, the libdvdread3 package alone does not allow you to play back encrypted DVDs. It is instead a means by which you can download and install libdvdcss, which is the great enabler in this case. Since libdvdcss must be downloaded (via the Console), you must be connected to the Internet while doing the following:

1. Become root by typing **su**, pressing ENTER, typing in your root password when prompted to do so, and then pressing ENTER again.
2. Type **/usr/share/doc/libdvdread3/examples/install-css.sh** and press ENTER.

This rather long command string tells your system to run the script called *install-css.sh*, which is located in the *examples* folder, located in the *libdvdread3* folder, located in the *doc* folder, located in the *share* folder, which is located in the *usr* folder. Phew! Oh, and that forward slash (/) at the very beginning of the command string tells your system that the usr folder is located at the very root of your file system, not in your Home folder.

NOTE *If you happen to be behind a firewall, and must specify your proxy server in your Internet applications, after step 1, type **export http_proxy=http://yourproxyserveraddress :portnumber/** (example: **export http_proxy=http://proxy.jellyfish.nu:3128/**), and press enter before moving on to step 2.*

The progress of the download and installation will then be shown in the Console window. You will know that the installation is complete when you see your user prompt again. After that, you should be able to run *Xine* via the **Launch** menu (**Applications ▸ Multimedia ▸ Video Player**) and play just about any DVD you want (regional encodings aside), though it would probably be a good idea to restart your machine before doing so.

Project 20B: More Command Practice with Briscola

If you would like to get a bit more practice using the commands we've covered, and to see how the command line can give you access to other programs not available via Xandros Networks, why not give this project a try. The program you will be installing in this project is a simple, yet very traditional, Italian card game called *Briscola* (see Figure 20-5).

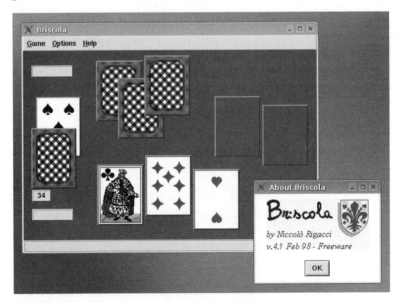

Figure 20-5: Briscola

20B-1: Getting the Briscola Files

Okay, so now you are just about ready to begin installing Briscola, but before you do, you must get the files you need. First of all, you will need Briscola itself, which you can get from the project's home page at www.rigacci.org/comp/ software. If you have trouble getting the file there, you can also get a copy from my website for this book: www.edgy-penguins.org/LME.

Part of the page is written in Italian, but don't let that throw you—just scroll down the page to the section that says *Briscola* and click the **briscola-4.1.tar.gz** link, which will get you the file by the same name.

NOTE   *The .tar.gz ending tells you that this is a tarball.*

Briscola is a script written in a language called *Tcl* and thus requires that you have *Tk* installed, which Tcl utilizes in order to create graphical interfaces. You can easily install Tk from the Xandros Networks Debian Unsupported site by running Xandros Networks, typing **tk8.4** in the *Search* box at the top of the window, clicking **Search**, and then clicking **Install** next to *tk8.4* (not *tk8.4-dev* or *tk8.4-doc*) in the list of results within the pane below (Figure 20-6).

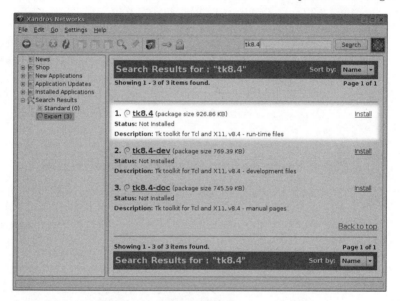

Figure 20-6: Installing Tk via Xandros Networks

20B-2: Extracting the Briscola Tarball

Now that you have installed Tk and have the Briscola tarball on your hard disk, you are ready to get started. First, extract the tarball using the double-click method you learned in Chapter 5. You will then have a new folder, *Briscola-4.1*, within your Home folder. To make things easier as you move along, shorten the name of the folder down to **briscola**.

20B-3: Preparing the Briscola Script

Most applications that come in tarball form include a *README* file, which includes information on what you need to do in order to install and use the application. If you double-click the **README** file in the briscola folder, you will see that the *HOW TO START* section tells you to adjust the first line of the briscola.tk script to point to your Tk shell and to adjust the second line of the script to point to the directory where the various Briscola files are located. To perform the adjustments as instructed in the README file, just follow these steps:

1. Open a Console window and find the Tk shell, called *Wish*, by typing **locate wish**; press ENTER and then note on a piece of paper the location given.

2. Now right-click the **briscola.tk** file itself in the briscola folder, and select **Open With ▸ Text Editor** in the pop-up menu.

3. When the briscola.tk file opens within Text Editor, change the very first line from **#!/usr/local/bin/wish** to **#!/usr/bin/wish**, which should have been the location given as the result to your *locate* search in step 1. The **#!** at the beginning of the line, in case you're wondering, indicates the path to a shell, in this case the Tk shell.

4. Now, in the second line, change **/usr/local/games/briscola/** to **/usr/local/ share/games/briscola/**, which is where you are going to be placing the briscola folder so that all of the users on your computer can play it.

5. Once you have done this, go to the Text Editor **File** menu and select **Save**.

6. Quit Text Editor.

20B-4: Moving the Briscola Folder to a Global Location

If you were to leave the briscola folder where it is now (in your Home folder), only you would be able to play the game. To make it available to others who have user accounts on your machine, you need to copy it to a global location. Since global locations are all in root territory, you will first have to become root before you do any copying. Here's what to do:

1. Open a Console window (if one isn't open already), and become root by typing **su** and pressing ENTER.

2. When prompted for your root password, type it in and press ENTER.

3. Copy the briscola folder to its new global locations by typing **cp -r briscola /usr/local/share/games**. Then press ENTER.

4. Exit root mode by typing **exit** and pressing ENTER.

20B-5: Running Briscola

You can now run Briscola (and double-check your work) by doing the following:

1. In the Console window, move into the new globally located briscola folder by typing **cd /usr/local/share/games/briscola** and pressing ENTER.

2. Now run Briscola by typing **./briscola.tk** and pressing ENTER.

NOTE *In case you were wondering (since there is no briscola.tk command), your system doesn't know what to do with your input. The ./ that you typed in step 2 tells your system to run the script you have signified after the slash (briscola.tk).*

20B-6: Removing the Briscola Folder Within Your Home Folder

Assuming that Briscola ran without problems from its new global location, you can trash the briscola folder that is still in your Home folder. Of course, you can do this by simply dragging it Trash, but to get some more command practice, do it via the command Console.

1. Quit Briscola.
2. In the Console, type **cd** and press ENTER to get the Console back into your Home folder.
3. Remove the briscola folder by typing **rm -r briscola** and pressing ENTER.
4. Quit the Console by typing **exit** and pressing ENTER.

20B-7: Creating a Desktop Shortcut for Briscola

The method of running Briscola that you've just used works well enough, but it can get to be quite a pain in the posterior to open up a Console window and type a couple of commands every time you want to play a few tricks of the game. To make things easier on yourself in the future, it would be a good idea to create a desktop shortcut that you can then simply double-click anytime you want to have a hand at the cards, so to speak.

If you are interested, here's what you need to do:

1. Right-click any open space on the desktop, and select **Create New ▶ Shortcut** in the pop-up menu. A Create Shortcut Wizard will then appear.
2. In the first page of the wizard, select **Program** and then click **Next**.
3. In the text box that appears next to the Browse button in the next page of the wizard, type **/usr/local/share/games/briscola/briscola.tk**, as shown in Figure 20-7. When finished, click **Next**.
4. In the final page of the wizard, change the name of the shortcut to **Briscola**, and then click **Finish**.

   You will now have a new shortcut for Briscola on your desktop; however, as the icon is, graphically speaking, rather dull, you might want to change it to something more colorful.
5. Right-click the **Briscola** shortcut on the desktop, and select **Properties** in the pop-up menu.
6. In the Properties window, click the icon button just below the General tab. This will bring up the Select Icon window.
7. In that window, scroll around until you find an icon to your liking—the icon of two playing cards in the *package...* section would be an appropriate choice.
8. Click once on the icon you've chosen once to select it, and then click **OK**.
9. Finally, click **OK** in the Properties window to wrap things up.

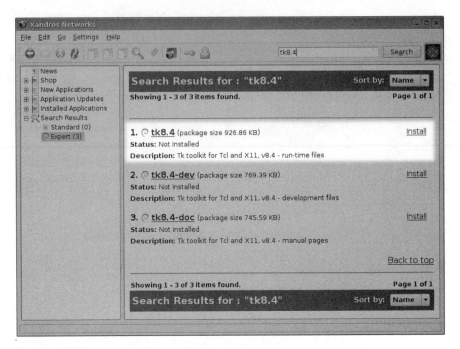

Figure 20-7: Creating a desktop shortcut for Briscola

Playing Briscola

As I already mentioned, Briscola is about as easy a card game as there is. Briscola is a trick-taking game, which means that you put out a card, and then your opponent puts out a card, and the one who puts out the higher point-value card wins the hand, or *trick*, for which points are awarded on the basis of the cards involved in that trick. The winner of the trick then goes on to *lead* the next trick, meaning that the winner puts out his or her card first the next time around. When all the cards are played, the points for each player are then tallied, and the player with the most points wins. It's all much simpler to do than it is to describe.

The Cards and Their Rankings

Like many other Italian and Spanish games, Briscola is played with a 40-card deck, consisting of the following cards: K, Q, J, 7, 6, 5, 4, 3, 2, and the Ace. Traditionally, it is played with either French-suited cards (hearts, diamonds, clubs, and spades) or Italian-suited cards (swords, coins, batons, and chalices), usually dependent upon the region in which it is played. In the software version you have just installed, you will be playing with French-suited cards but with images and patterns in the regional style of Tuscany.

Unlike most card games you are probably familiar with, the ranking and point values of the cards in Briscola are somewhat different, as you can see in the following chart.

Ranking of Cards	Point Value
Ace	11
Three	10
King	4
Queen	3
Jack	2
7	0
4	0
2	0

While this ranking arrangement might seem odd, it is actually fairly commonly used in card games from the southern and Catholic regions of central Europe. With that bit of information in mind, it should all be pretty easy enough to fathom, taking a religious view, that God (Ace) and the Holy Trinity (3) rank higher than the divine-rights-endowed royals (K, Q, J) and their decidedly mortal subjects (7, 4, 2). The rankings are thus quite sensible, albeit slightly ironic.

Game Play in Briscola

Once Briscola starts up, it will deal three cards to each player. It will then take the seventh card and place it face up under the down-facing pile of undealt cards, known as the *stock* or *talon*. That seventh card is called the *Briscola* (from which the game gets its name), and it determines the trump suit for that particular game. This means that any card of the same suit as the Briscola will beat any card of any other suit, even one of a higher ranking. Of course, when you play a trump card against another trump card, the normal rankings of the cards come back into play.

It is important to note at this point that unlike many other trick-taking games, you are neither required to follow the suit of the card led in a trick in Briscola nor to beat it if you can. This means that if your opponent plays a club card, you can play a card of any suit you like, even if you have a card that can beat it, all depending on your own strategy for ultimately winning the game.

It is a good idea to first go to the **Options** menu before getting started and select **Show Score**. This will allow you to know how you're doing as you play. After you've done that, you are ready for action, and since your computer opponent is always kind enough as to allow you to lead, you can begin by clicking the card you want to put into play. The computer will then play its card (Figure 20-8).

Once you've assessed the situation, click one of the blank spaces in your hand, and the points for that trick will be displayed in the *You* box (if you won the trick) or the *Me* box (if the computer won the trick). Of course, if the trick involved only the 7, 4 or 2 cards, no points will appear, as those cards have no point value.

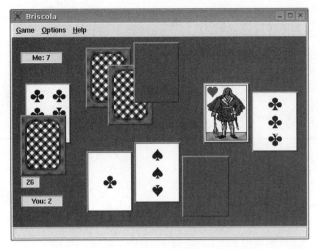

Figure 20-8: Gameplay under way in Briscola (with the author of this
book about to win the trick by playing a trump—the three of clubs)

Want to Know More?

If you would like a more detailed set of rules on playing Briscola (and just
about any other card game in the world), check out www.pagat.com.

Project 20C: Running Java Applications via the Command Line

In addition to the numerous applications covered thus far, there are still more
applications available to you that are written in the Java scripting language.
Your Xandros system comes with the *Java Runtime Environment, J2RE*, installed,
which means that you can run these so-called *Java scripts* on your system without extra effort. You will, however, usually need to resort to the command
line in order to run the applications. Don't worry though, because once
these Java-based applications are up and running, it is all point and click.

20C-1: Downloading a Java-Based Application—Risk

In this project, you will be downloading and running the well-known board
game Risk (Figure 20-9). Risk, as well as many other Java-based applications,
is available from www.sourceforge.net, but to make things easier, just point
directly to the Risk project home page at http://jrisk.sourceforge.net (and
don't forget to type the *j* at the beginning of that URL). Once there, scroll
down to the *Downloads* section, and click the **Risk jar and source** link. You will
then be taken to a page of download locations, so click the one closest to you,
and wait for your download to begin.

Risk comes as ZIP archive, so once the download is complete, you will have to unzip the file using the double-click-then-copy-and-paste method you learned in Chapter 5. Once finished, you will have a new folder, *Risk*, within your Home folder. If you take a look in that folder, you will notice the file Risk.jar. This is the game itself that you will be running via the command line. In the future, should you choose to download other Java-based applications, the file with the .jar extension will be the one you will be trying to run.

20C-2: Running Risk

You can now run Risk without any further work. To get going, open a new Console window and do the following:

1. Move your Console into the Risk folder by typing **cd Risk** and pressing ENTER.

2. Then type **java -jar Risk.jar** (be sure to place a space between java and -jar) and press ENTER. Risk will appear, and you can start playing.

Figure 20-9: Risk

Here's what you just did in that last line: the first part of the command string, java, calls the Java Runtime Environment into action; the -jar flag after that tells Java that you are going to be running a .jar file; and the last part is the actual file you are going to run, Risk.jar. In the future, if you choose to run other Java-based applications, just follow the same pattern: **java -jar application_name.jar**.

Where Do I Go from Here?

Okay, so you sort of enjoyed the slightly geekier side of things and are keen on learning more, eh? Or maybe you're not all that excited about it, but you now see how a bit of command action can be useful. Fortunately for you, the Internet is filled with all sorts of command references and tutorials. Just do a Google search for Linux commands, and see what you get. A sure bet in my book is *LinuxCommand.org*, which has a great step-by-step approach to making the command line understandable to the newbie. It also goes on to teach you how to write shell scripts with which you can do even more interesting things via the command line. Check it out at http://linuxcommand.org.

PROXY SETTINGS

If your Internet provider or network has you behind a firewall, you will not be able to access Internet content, such as web pages and broadcast streams, unless you input the *proxy server settings* given to you by the service provider or network administrator. The method of inputting these settings, however, varies slightly from application to application. Although most KDE apps, such as the Panel Weather applet and Kdict, utilize the proxy settings you input for the system as a whole in the Xandros Control Center, instructions for inputting both system-wide and application-specific settings are provided here.

The information you need in order to input your proxy settings usually consists of a *URL* and a *port number*. The *proxy preferences window* for most applications provides separate input boxes for these two components of the proxy address. In cases where there is only one box for the information, write the two components together, separated by a colon, as in the example proxy.crazyfish.se:3128. Some providers or network administrators may also require you to use your username and password in your proxy settings, so be sure to check the proxy information provided to you before entering your settings.

Control Center—System-wide Proxy Settings

As I noted, many applications gather their proxy information from your system-wide settings in the Control Center. These include Instant Messaging (Kopete), Media Player (Noatun), Online Dictionary (Kdict), Xandros File Manager, and even Xandros Networks. To get to these settings, follow these steps:

1. Go to the **Launch** menu and select **Control Center**.

2. Click the + symbol next to *File Manager*, and then click **Proxy** in the list that appears below.

3. In the Proxy module in the right pane of the window (Figure 1), select the appropriate choice per the instructions of your Internet provider or network administrator.

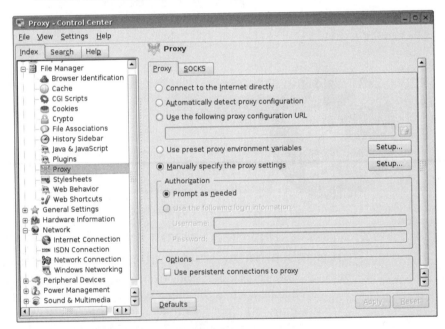

Figure 1: The Proxy module in the Control Center

4. If you are choosing either *Use preset proxy environment variables* or *Manually specify the proxy settings*, click **Setup** for that item. Input the appropriate settings in the window that appears (Figure 2), and then click **OK**, after which that window will close.

5. Once you have finished, click **Apply**, and then quit the Control Center.

Figure 2: Manually inputting system-wide proxy settings in the Control Center

Xandros Networks

As already mentioned, Xandros Networks uses the proxy settings provided in the Control Center. If you are having problems connecting to the Internet via Xandros Networks, make sure that it is using the proxy settings provided in your current user environment by doing the following:

1. Go to the **Edit** menu and select **Proxy Settings**.

2. In the Proxy Settings window that appears (Figure 3), make sure your username is selected in the drop-down menu button next to the words *Use proxy settings specified for this user.*

3. Click **OK** when finished.

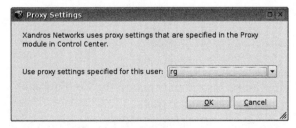

Figure 3: Xandros Networks asks you which proxy settings you want to use

Firefox

1. Go to the **Edit** menu and select **Preferences**.

2. When the Preferences window appears, click the **Connection Settings** button near the bottom of the window.

3. In the Connection Settings window (Figure 4), select the appropriate proxy type, and then input your settings.

4. When you are finished, click **OK**.

Figure 4: Proxy settings for Firefox

Mozilla

1. Go to the **Edit** menu and select **Preferences**.

2. In the left pane of the Preferences window, click the + symbol next to *Advanced*, and then click **Proxies** in the list that appears below.

3. In the right half of the same window, select **Manual proxy configuration**, and then input your settings, as shown in Figure 5.

4. Click **OK** when finished.

RipperX

1. Click the **Config** button to bring up the Configuration window.

2. In that window, click the **CDDB** tab.

3. In that tab (Figure 6), check **Use HTTP**, and then input your proxy information in the boxes below.

4. When finished, click **OK**.

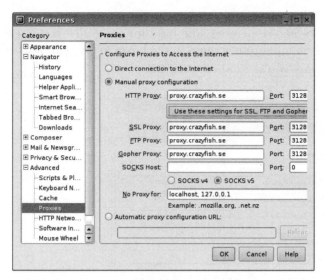

Figure 5: Proxy settings for Mozilla

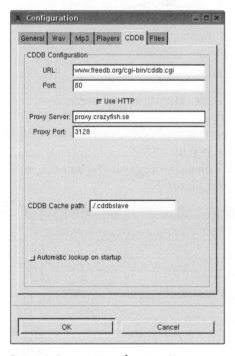

Figure 6: Proxy settings for ripperX

RealPlayer

1. Go to **Tools** ▶ **Preferences**, which will open the Preferences window.
2. Click the **Proxy** tab at the top of the window.

3. Check the box next to appropriate proxy type according to your Internet provider or network administrator (try *HTTP*, if you're not sure), and then input your settings in the boxes to the right (Figure 7).

4. Once you've finished, click **OK**.

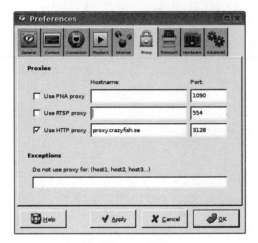

Figure 7: Proxy settings for RealPlayer

MP3 Player/XMMS

For SHOUTcast or Icecast (MP3) Internet streams:

1. Right-click anywhere in the XMMS window and select **Options ▶ Preferences** in the pop-up menu.

2. Scroll through the items in the *Input Plugins* pane, and select **MPEG Layer 1/2/3 Player** (Figure 8).

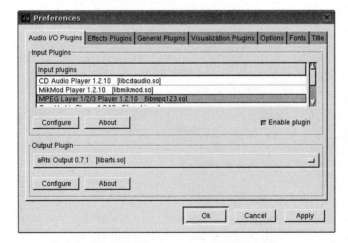

Figure 8: Selecting the MP3 plug-in in the XMMS Preferences window

3. Click the **Configure** button directly below that pane (*not* the *Configure* button near the bottom of the window), which will bring up the MPG123 Configuration window.

4. In that window, click the **Streaming** tab.

5. In the Streaming tab, check *Use proxy*, and type your proxy information in the *Host* box. You should also click the *Enable SHOUT/Icecast title streaming* check box near the bottom of the page to see the titles of songs as they are broadcast.

6. Once you've done all this, and your window looks like that in Figure 9, click **OK** to close the Configuration window, and then **OK** to close the Preferences window.

Figure 9: Inputting proxy settings for SHOUTcast (MP3) streams in XMMS

For Ogg Vorbis Internet streams:

1. Right-click anywhere in the XMMS window and select **Options ▶ Preferences** in the pop-up menu.

2. In the Preferences window that appears, scroll through the items in the *Input Plugins* pane, select **Ogg Vorbis Player**, and then click the **Configure** button directly below that pane (*not* the *Configure* button near the bottom of the window).

3. In the Ogg Vorbis Configuration window, check **Use proxy**, and type your proxy information in the *Host* box (Figure 10).

4. When finished, click **OK** to exit the Ogg Vorbis Configuration window, and then in the Preferences window, click **OK**.

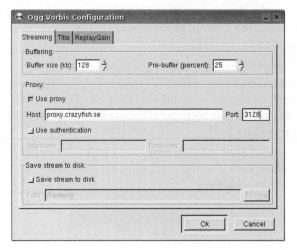

Figure 10: Proxy settings for Ogg Vorbis Streams in XMMS

Streamtuner

1. Go to the **Edit** menu and select **Preferences**.
2. In the Preferences window, click the **Network** tab.
3. Once in the *Network* tab (Figure 11), check *Use a proxy server*, select your proxy type, and then input your proxy settings.
4. When finished, click **Close**.

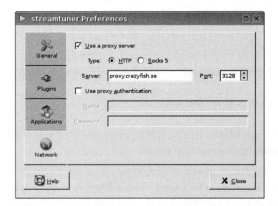

Figure 11: Proxy settings for streamtuner

Video Player/Xine

1. Right-click the playback window (not the controller), and select **Settings ▸ Setup** in the pop-up menu.

2. In the Xine Setup window that appears, change *Configuration experience level* from *Beginner* to **Advanced**, and then click **Apply**.

3. Next, click the **Input** tab.

4. Once in that tab, scroll down to the boxes that say *HTTP proxy host* and *HTTP proxy port*, and fill in the appropriate information (Figure 12). Fill in the two other proxy-related boxes (*HTTP proxy password* and *HTTP proxy username*) if your provider or network administrator requires it.

5. When finished, click **Close**.

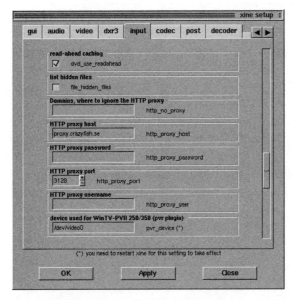

Figure 12: Proxy settings for Video Player/Xine

Gxine

1. Go to the **Edit** menu and select **Preferences**.

2. In the Preferences window, click the **Input** tab.

3. Scroll down to the boxes that say *http_proxy_host* and *http_proxy_port*, and fill in the appropriate information (Figure 13). Fill in the other two proxy-related boxes (*http_proxy_password* and *http_proxy_user*) if your provider or network administrator requires it.

4. Click **Close**.

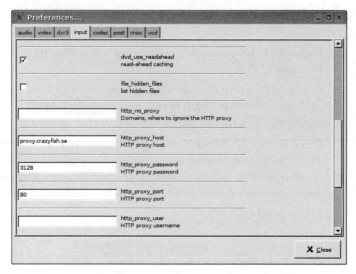

Figure 13: Proxy settings for gxine

CrossOver Office

You can input proxy settings for CrossOver Office in the last screen of the
setup wizard (Figure 14) that appears when you run CrossOver Office for the
first time. Just check *Use HTTP proxy*, type in your proxy information, and
then click **Finish**.

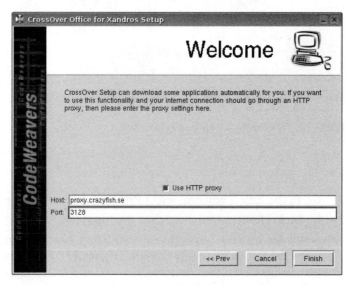

Figure 14: Inputting proxy settings for CrossOver Office in the Setup wizard

You can also input or change your proxy settings at any other time via the Setup window:

1. Go to the **Launch** menu and select **Applications ▸ CrossOver ▸ Office Setup**.
2. In the Setup window, click the **Settings** tab.
3. Once in that tab, click the **Advanced** button.
4. When the Advanced Configuration Settings window appears (Figure 15), check **Use HTTP proxy**, and type in your settings in the two boxes below.
5. Click **OK** to close the Configuration window, and then click **OK** in the Setup window to seal the deal.

Figure 15: Inputting proxy settings for CrossOver Office via the Setup window

GLOSSARY

A

account

Linux allows a number of people to use the same system while appearing that each person is using his or her own system. Each user has his or her own *account*, in which the user's files are kept in separate Home folders, and in which customizations will not affect the files in the accounts of the other users of the machine. See also *root account/mode*.

administrator account/mode

See *root account/mode*.

applet

A mini-application, usually performing a subtask in relation to another application. A good example is the number of applications written in the Java programming language that are run in conjunction with a web browser, such as many online games. See also *application* and *Java*.

application

Often referred to as a *program*, an application is a piece of software designed to allow the user to perform a particular task. Word processors, games, media players, and spreadsheets are all examples of applications.

archive

A file that is compressed in order to save disk space or to reduce the size of a file. Archiving a file makes it easier to transport, either via the Internet or some other form of removable media, such as floppy disks or USB flash drives. See also *tarball* and *ZIP file*.

B

BIOS (Basic Input-Output System)

A chip in a computer that gives your machine the instructions it needs in order to use its basic hardware and to boot up your operating system.

boot

The process, occurring shortly after you power-on your machine, in which your operating system is started up.

boot disk

As described in this book, a floppy disk containing certain system files, which, when inserted into your computer, allows you to boot from a CD-ROM on a computer (usually an older one) whose BIOS does not normally allow you to do so.

burn

The process of writing data to a blank CD or DVD. The term *burn* refers to the fact that the data is written to disc by the laser in your CD or DVD drive.

C

console

The application in which you type commands by which to perform various tasks on your computer.

CPU (central processing unit)

The chip that is the brain of your computer and performs all of the instructions given to it by the software you use.

D

Debian

One of the most popular Linux distributions upon which Xandros is based.

dependency

Any file, application, or library that an application requires in order to run.

desktop

The main workspace on your computer screen. It is what you see when all other windows are closed.

distribution/distro

A Linux distribution consists of the Linux kernel and a variety of other applications and libraries. These usually consist of one or more graphical desktop environments; applications such as word processors, media players, games, and utilities; help files, fonts, and drivers; and some sort of installer with which to simplify the installation of the system. Xandros is an example of a Linux distribution, though there are many others, such as Fedora Core and Mandrake.

download

The process of transferring any file or application from the Internet, network, or other device into your computer.

driver

A small application that allows your operating system to communicate with the hardware devices you have connected to your computer, such as a printer or scanner. Most drivers are built into the Linux kernel, which means that you do not have to install a special driver for the hardware you connect. On the downside, if the current kernel does not contain the driver for your device (often the case for new hardware), you'll probably have to wait for the next Linux release, when it will most likely be included.

dual-boot system

A computer that is set up to run one of two different operating systems, such as Windows and Linux. Both operating systems are installed on the computer's hard disk; when you start up the machine, you are given the choice of which system to use to boot.

E

email client

The software application you use to read and send email.

encode

The process of converting a standard audio file, usually one ripped from an audio CD, and converting it into a smaller MP3 or Ogg Vorbis file. Also see *rip, MP3,* and *Ogg Vorbis.*

Ethernet card/port

An add-on, or built-in, expansion card that allows you to connect your computer to a network via a cable connected to the Ethernet port on that card and, at the other end, the network source.

F

file extension

The three (or sometimes four) letters preceded by a period that come at the end of a filename. The file extension tells the system what kind of file it is and thus with which application to open it. Microsoft Word documents, for example, end in .doc, OpenOffice.org Writer documents end in .sxw, and MP3 audio files end in .mp3.

flash drive

An extremely small, solid-state data storage device that plugs into a computer's USB port. Because of their relatively low price, small size, and lack of moving parts, these drives have become quite popular for transferring files from computer to computer or from home to work, and vice versa.

flash memory card

Any one of several kinds of memory cards that are used in most digital cameras today to store images. Images stored on such cards can be loaded onto the computer by simply connecting the camera itself, with the card installed, to the computer, or by removing the card from the camera and then inserting it into a USB memory card reader already connected to the computer.

Flash Player

A plug-in application that provides a web browser with the ability to display pages created using Macromedia's Flash. See also *plug-in*.

freeware

Software that is available free of charge, though usually with licensing rights retained by its creator. See also *open source* and *shareware*.

G

GNOME (GNU Network Object Model Environment)

One of the two most commonly used graphical desktop environments in Linux. See also *KDE*.

GNU

GNU, a recursive acronym for *GNU's Not Unix*, is a project dedicated to creating a complete operating system consisting entirely of free software.

graphical desktop environment

Essentially the same as *graphical user interface*, though indicating that the interface includes a graphical file manager, trash bin, desktop, and other convenience features.

graphical user interface

A graphical user environment, such as seen in Windows or Mac OS, that allows you to deal with your system and file system by mouse rather than by typed-in commands.

H

HTML (HyperText Markup Language)

The language used for creating web pages. You can see what it looks like by opening a web page in your web browser and selecting **View ▸ Page Source**. A new window will appear showing the HTML source for the page you are viewing.

I

ISO (International Organization for Standardization)

As used in this book, an ISO is an exact CD image—basically the contents, layout, and format of a CD minus the actual disc itself. ISO images can thus be transferred over the Internet and then burned to an actual disc by the user.

J

Java

A programming language developed by Sun Microsystems that can run on any operating system. It is often used to create applets for use over the Internet. Many online games, for example, are Java applets.

JavaScript

A scripting language developed by Netscape and Sun Microsystems that is primarily used by web page authors within their HTML documents to provide greater functionality to the pages they create. Although it was inspired by Java, and has bits of similarity to it in terms of its syntax, it is not at all the same. See also *Java* and *HTML*.

K

KDE

One of the two most commonly used graphical desktop environments used in Linux and the one used in Xandros. See also *GNOME*.

kernel

The core or heart of an operating system.

L

LAN (local area network)

A group of interconnected computers in a limited area, such as an office, a school, or your home.

library

Basically, a helper application that allows another application to function or to provide some other specific functionality to that other application. Libraries are, as a general rule, essentially invisible to the user.

Linux

A UNIX-like computer operating system that is notable for being free software. The term *Linux* actually refers to the Linux kernel itself, but it is most often used to describe the combination of the kernel and all of the other libraries and applications that help make it easier to handle, which should be officially referred to as GNU/Linux. Xandros is an example of a Linux distribution. The name *Linux* is itself a combination of the name of its creator, *Linus Torvalds*, and *UNIX*, after which Linux is to a great degree modeled. See also *distribution/distro, GNU, kernel*.

log out

Exiting your current user session. Once you are logged out, another user can then log in to his or her own account. Logging out, therefore, does not require shutting down your computer.

M

memory

See *RAM*.

modem

A device, either built into your computer or outside it in a separate unit, that allows you to connect to the Internet via a telephone line.

motherboard

The main circuit board in your computer. All of the components in your computer (the CPU, memory, drives, and so on) are connected to this board.

MP3

An audio file compression format that allows you to store audio files, such as songs from CDs, on your hard disk with greatly reduced space. MP3 files are recognizable by the .mp3 file extension.

N

network

Any group of two or more interconnected computers. This could be the various computers in an office, a school, or even in your home (see *LAN*). The Internet itself is a kind of network.

O

Ogg Vorbis

An Open Source audio file compression format that is mostly popular in the Linux world. Like MP3, it allows you to store audio files, such as songs from CDs, on your hard disk at greatly reduced space. Ogg Vorbis files are recognizable by the .ogg file extension.

open source

Software for which the programmer's source code is freely available, viewable, and modifiable to all. Although open-source software is, as a general rule, free of cost, it is not the same as *freeware*. See also *freeware* and *shareware*.

P

package

A single archived file, often an application, containing the application itself and other files it might need to run. Packages for Debian-based systems, such as Xandros, are recognizable by the .deb file extension. This means that when you are installing applications via Xandros Networks, you are installing .deb packages.

partition

A division of, or the act of dividing, a single hard disk into smaller separate parts, each of which appears to the operating system as a separate hard drive.

PC card

See *PCMCIA*.

PCMCIA (Personal Computer Memory Card International Association)

A kind of add-on card (and the slot in which you place such a card) that provides added functionality to your computer, usually laptops. There are various types of PCMCIA cards, with those adding networking capabilities (Ethernet, wireless, modem) to your computer being among the most common.

plug-in

A sort of mini-application that is installed to extend the capabilities or features of another application in some specific way.

pop-under window

Similar in concept and function to a *pop-up window* except for the fact that it appears behind an open web browser window rather than in front of it.

pop-up window

An additional, usually smaller, window, that pops open when you open certain websites. Sometimes these provide an important function to the site itself, but most often they are advertisements.

port

An interface on your computer to which you can attach peripheral devices, such as a printer, scanner, digital camera, and so on.

R

RAM (random access memory)

This is your computer's memory in which information is temporarily stored while you are using various applications. Information held in RAM disappears when the computer is turned off. This is in contrast to your hard disk, which holds information or data somewhat permanently until you erase it.

rip

The process of extracting an audio file from an audio CD.

root account/mode

When you use a Linux system, you normally are using your user account (or, in user mode), in which you have access only to your own data. The owner of the machine, however, also has access to the root account or root (also known as *administrator* or *superuser*) mode. The root user has access to all of the data in whatever user accounts there might be on a given computer. The root user also has the ability to add and remove user accounts, install applications and fonts system-wide, and alter other system-wide settings. The root user must possess the root password in order to access the account or mode.

S

serial port

An increasingly less-used type of connector (and connection port) on most computers. These days, serial ports are mainly used for connecting external modems or, more rarely, your mouse. See also *port*.

shareware

Software that is available initially for free but must be ultimately paid for in order for the user to continue using it. Shareware thus usually has some mechanism by which to encourage or force the user to pay. See also *freeware* and *open source*.

skin

A set of graphical elements that can be installed to change the look of an application or group of applications. Sometimes referred to as a *theme*.

spam

Uninvited and unsolicited junk email.

streaming media

Basically, audio or video broadcasts sent over the Internet and listened to or viewed on your computer by means of some sort of software, such as your web browser or RealPlayer, much as you would with a radio or television set. Such streams are typically not stored on your hard disk.

superuser

See *root account/mode*.

T

tarball

An archived, or *compressed*, file created with a version of the *tar* program, which is commonly used in Linux.

theme

See *skin*.

Torvalds, Linus

A member of the ethnic Swedish population in Finland, who is best known as the creator of the Linux kernel.

V

VCD (video compact disc)

A movie or other video file(s) burned to one or more CDs rather than DVDs. VCDs are cheaper to produce than DVDs, and they work on almost any computer with a CD drive or most other machines that can play DVDs, such as the DVD player you probably have attached to your TV. The video image quality of VCDs, however, is inferior to that of DVDs, and the CD medium has less storage capacity. A typical feature film that fits on one DVD, therefore, takes up two VCDs.

W

wallpaper

Any image used as a decorative background for your desktop.

web browser

The application you use when viewing web pages, such as Firefox, Mozilla, Opera, or, in the Windows world, Internet Explorer.

Wi-Fi (wireless fidelity)

These days used as a general term for wireless computer connectivity between computers, peripherals, and/or the Internet.

wireless access point (WAP)

Devices that permit machines to communicate with one another on wireless networks. The WAP is usually connected by Ethernet cable to an Internet or other network connection and communicates wirelessly with your computer.

wireless card

An add-on card inserted into your computer's PCMCIA slot that allows you to connect to a network or the Internet without a direct wired connection (hence the term *wireless*).

X

Xandros

A Debian-based Linux distribution, noted for its ease of use and installation and its considerable level of Windows compatibility.

Z

ZIP file

An archived, or *compressed*, file created with the WinZip program, commonly used in Windows systems. ZIP files can also be created by other programs, such as PKZIP (Linux) and StuffIt (Linux, Mac OS, Windows).

INDEX

J

J2RE, 418–419
Java language
    command line for, 418–419
    defined, 436
JavaScript language, 437
journal entries in calendar, 204
JPEG images, 290–291
Junk Mail Controls feature, 229–231

K

KAlarm application, 350
Karamtop monitor, 129
KArm application, 350
KDE environment, 437
Keramik styles, 106–109
kernel, 437
Key Cascade game, 386
keyboard settings, 23–24
KGeography application, 393–396
kid's stuff, 379–380
    Hangman Game, 384–385
    KGeography, 393–396
    Letter Order Game, 382–385
    LPairs, 391–392
    MathWar, 389–391
    Potato Guy, 380–381
    Tux Paint, 381–382
    Tux Typing, 386–389
    user accounts, 396–399
killing applications, 42
Kivio application, 350
KLaptop button, 34
Klines game, 120–123
KMail application, 197
KMessedWords Game, 382–385
kodo application, 126
KOffice applications, 320, 350–351
Kolf game, 358–360
KolourPaint application. *See* Paint
        application
Kontact application, 197
    address book, 198
    application modules in, 199–201
        Calendar, 202–204
        Notes, 205
        Todo List, 201–202
    schedules, 198–199
    Summary View page, 197–199
    weather summary display, 199
Kooka application, 162–167
Kopete application, 233
    communicating with, 237–238
    contacts in, 236–237
    logging off and logging on, 238
    setting up, 233–235
KPilot application, 193–196
kprint dialog box, 148–149
Kscd player, 84–85
KWallet wizard, 135–136
KWeather application, 36–39

L

labels. *See* business cards
LAME application, 251–252
Landscape orientation, 150
LANs (local area networks)
    defined, 437
    for Internet connections, 46
Launch button, 33
Launch menu, 39–40
launchers
    for Fish Fillets—The Next
        Generation, 375
    for Njam game, 369–372
    on Panel, 35
    for Tux Typing, 387
LEDs, flashing, 93
Letter Order Game, 382–385
libdvdcss program, 411–412
libdvdread3 package, 411
libraries, 437
license agreement, 18–19
limiting login availability, 114–115
line spacing in Writer, 320–321
Lines game, 120–123
lines on business cards, 347
links
    to files, 67
    in tabbed browsing, 212–214
Linux, 4
    benefits, 4–5
    defined, 437
    distributions, 5
Linux Command Console, 404–405

LICENSE AGREEMENT

Xandros Desktop OS Version 3

Open Circulation Edition

IMPORTANT: CAREFULLY READ THIS END USER LICENSE AGREEMENT ("EULA") BEFORE USING THIS PRODUCT.

CLICKING ON THE "ACCEPT" OR "YES" BUTTON IN RESPONSE TO THE ELECTRONIC LICENSE AGREEMENT ENQUIRY AS TO ACCEPTANCE OF THE TERMS OF THIS LICENSE AGREEMENT, INSTALLING OR DOWNLOADING THE SOFTWARE, INDICATES ACCEPTANCE OF AND AGREEMENT TO, AND LEGALLY BINDS YOU ("YOU" OR THE "END USER") AND XANDROS CORPORATION ("XANDROS") TO THE TERMS AND CONDITIONS OF THIS LICENSE AGREEMENT (INCLUDING ANY TERMS, CONDITIONS AND RESTRICTIONS CONTAINED IN ANY QUOTE ISSUED BY XANDROS RELATING TO THE SOFTWARE). IF THE END USER DOES NOT ACCEPT AND AGREE TO THE TERMS AND CONDITIONS OF THIS LICENSE AGREEMENT THEN EITHER DO NOT DOWNLOAD, INSTALL OR OTHERWISE USE THE SOFTWARE.

1. LICENSE

(a) Xandros Desktop OS Open Circulation Edition (the "Software Product") is a modular operating system made up of individual software components that were created by various individuals and entities ("Software Program").

(b) Subject to the terms and conditions contained herein, Xandros hereby grants to You a non-exclusive license to use the Software Product:

   1. for your personal, non-commercial use; and

   2. for internal business purposes only and only if You are a Developer; where a "Developer" means a person who uses the Software Product in connection with the development of a software application or component.

(c) Many of the Software Programs included in the Software Product are distributed under the terms of the GNU General Public License ("GPL") and other similar license agreements that permit the user to copy, modify and redistribute the Software Programs. Please review the terms and conditions of the license agreement that accompanies each of the Software Programs included in the Software Product.

(d) In addition to the freely distributable Software Programs, some versions of the Software Product may also include certain Software Programs that are not distributed under the terms of the GPL or similar licenses that permit modification and redistribution. Generally, each of these Software Programs is distributed under the terms of a license agreement that grants the licensed user to install each of the Software Programs on a single computer for the user's own individual use. Copying, redistribution (except as permitted under Section 6 hereof), reverse engineering, decompiling and/or modification of these Software Programs is prohibited. Any violation by the user of the applicable license terms shall immediately terminate the license to use the Software Program. In order to view the complete terms and conditions that govern the use of these Software Programs, please consult the license agreement that accompanies each of the Software Programs. If You do not agree to comply with and be bound by the terms of the applicable license agreements, do not install, distribute or otherwise use the relevant Software Program. If You wish to install these Software Programs on more than one computer, please contact the vendor of the program to inquire about purchasing additional licenses.

2. PROPRIETARY RIGHTS

(a) The Software Product is confidential and copyrighted. Title to the Software Product and all associated intellectual property rights is retained by Xandros and/or its licensors. Except as permitted under Section 6 hereof, You may not make copies of the Software Product. No right, title or interest in or to any trademark, service mark, logo or trade name of Xandros or its licensors is granted under this Agreement.

(b) All title and intellectual property rights in and to the content which may be accessed through use of the Software Product is the property of the respective content owner and may be protected by applicable copyright or other intellectual property laws and treaties. This EULA grants the user no rights to use such content.

3. LIMITED WARRANTY

EXCEPT WHERE SPECIFICALLY STATED OTHERWISE IN THIS AGREEMENT AND THE APPLICABLE LICENSE AGREEMENTS WHICH ACCOMPANY EACH SOFTWARE PROGRAM, THE SOFTWARE PRODUCT, INCLUDING WITHOUT LIMITATION EACH SOFTWARE PROGRAM, IS PROVIDED TO THE USER ON AN "AS IS" BASIS, WITHOUT ANY OTHER WARRANTIES OR CONDITIONS, EXPRESS OR IMPLIED, INCLUDING, BUT NOT LIMITED TO, WARRANTIES OF MERCHANTABLE QUALITY, SATISFACTORY QUALITY, MERCHANTABILITY OR FITNESS FOR A PARTICULAR PURPOSE, OR THOSE ARISING BY LAW, STATUTE, USAGE OF TRADE, COURSE OF DEALING OR OTHERWISE. THE ENTIRE RISK AS TO THE RESULTS AND PERFORMANCE OF XANDROS DESKTOP OS IS ASSUMED BY THE USER.

4. LIMITATION OF LIABILITY

NEITHER XANDROS NOR ITS DEALERS, SUPPLIERS OR LICENSORS SHALL HAVE ANY LIABILITY TO THE USER OR ANY OTHER PERSON OR ENTITY FOR ANY DIRECT, INDIRECT, INCIDENTAL, SPECIAL, OR CONSEQUENTIAL DAMAGES WHATSOEVER, INCLUDING, BUT NOT LIMITED TO, LOSS OF REVENUE OR PROFIT, LOST OR DAMAGED DATA OR OTHER COMMERCIAL OR ECONOMIC LOSS, EVEN IF XANDROS HAS BEEN ADVISED OF THE POSSIBILITY OF SUCH DAMAGES, OR THEY ARE FORESEEABLE. XANDROS IS ALSO NOT RESPONSIBLE FOR CLAIMS BY A THIRD PARTY. THE MAXIMUM AGGREGATE LIABILITY TO THE END USER OF XANDROS, ITS LICENSORS, DEALERS AND SUPPLIERS SHALL NOT EXCEED THE AMOUNT PAID BY THE END USER FOR SOFTWARE PRODUCT. THE LIMITATIONS IN THIS SECTION

SHALL APPLY WHETHER OR NOT THE ALLEGED BREACH OR DEFAULT IS A BREACH OF A FUNDAMENTAL CONDITION OR TERM OR A FUNDAMENTAL BREACH. SOME STATES/COUNTRIES DO NOT ALLOW THE EXCLUSION OR LIMITATION OF LIABILITY FOR CONSEQUENTIAL OR INCIDENTAL DAMAGES, SO THE ABOVE LIMITATION MAY NOT APPLY TO YOU.

5. RESTRICTIONS

The End User may permanently transfer all of the rights under this EULA, provided that the End User retains no copies or registration numbers, that the End User transfers all of the Software Product, and that the transferee agrees to be bound by the terms of this EULA. The End User shall: (a) not distribute copies of the Software Product as pre-installed or OEM software; (b) not distribute any Software Program(s) except as permitted under the license agreement relating to such Software Program; (c) not rent or lease the Software Product; (d) maintain all copyright notices on all copies of the Software Product; (e) not reverse-engineer, decipher, decompile, or disassemble the Software Product, except and only to the extent that such activity is expressly permitted by applicable law notwithstanding this limitation; (f) not deploy the Software Product in a commercial, industrial or educational environment except under a separate license agreement with Xandros; and (g) not distribute the Software Product with magazines or books except with the prior written consent of Xandros.

6. DISTRIBUTION

(a) Subject to the restrictions contained in Section 5 hereof, You may distribute copies of the Software Product provided that:

1. a copy of this EULA is included with the Software Program and the user of the Software Program agrees to be bound by the terms and conditions hereof;

2. You do not charge a license fee for the Software Product, provided that you may charge a nominal fee to compensate you for the direct costs associated with Your redistribution of the Software Product;

3. the Software Product has not been altered or modified in any way;

4. the Software Product is the most recent version made available by Xandros;

5. the following copyright notice shall be conspicuously displayed in such distribution: "Xandros Desktop OS Open Circulation Edition, (c) Xandros Corporation 2003-2005. All rights reserved."; and

6. You comply with all export laws, rules and regulations in the jurisdictions where the Software Product, including any Software Programs, are exported or re-exported from time to time.

7. TERMINATION

Without prejudice to any other rights, Xandros may terminate this EULA if the End User fails to comply with the terms and conditions of this EULA. In such event, the user must destroy all copies of the Software Product, and certify in writing to Xandros that this has been done.

8. GENERAL

(a) No waiver by either of the parties hereto of any breach of any condition, covenant or term hereof shall be effective unless it is in writing and it shall not constitute a waiver of such condition, covenant or term except in respect of the particular breach giving rise to such waiver.

(b) This agreement contains the whole of the agreement between the parties hereto concerning the matters provided for herein and there are no collateral or precedent representations, warranties, agreements or conditions not specifically set forth in this agreement and none have been relied on by either party as an inducement to enter into this agreement. This agreement supersedes any prior proposal, representation or understanding between the parties hereto.

(c) This agreement shall be governed by the laws of the state of Delaware. The United Nations Convention on Contracts for the International Sale of Goods shall not apply to this agreement or the transactions contemplated hereunder.

(d) This EULA has been prepared and drawn up in the English language. In the event that this agreement is translated into any other language and in the event of a discrepancy in the interpretation between the English text and the text of the other language, the English text shall govern.

(e) If any provision of this agreement is declared by a court of competent jurisdiction to be invalid, illegal or unenforceable, such provision shall be severed from this agreement and the remaining provisions shall continue in full force and effect.

(f) This agreement shall enure to the benefit of and be binding upon You and Xandros and your respective heir, executors, successors and permitted assigns.

Should there be any questions concerning this EULA, or desire to contact Xandros for any reason, please see our contact information at www.xandros.com/about/contact.html.

COLOPHON

Linux Made Easy was written using OpenOffice.org Writer and laid out in Adobe FrameMaker. The font families used are New Baskerville for body text, TheSansMono Condensed for code text, Futura for headings and tables, and Dogma for titles.

The book was printed and bound at Malloy Incorporated in Ann Arbor, Michigan. The paper is Glatfelter Thor 50# Smooth, which is made from 50 percent recycled materials, including 30 percent postconsumer content. The book uses a RepKover binding, which allows it to lay flat when open.

UPDATES

Visit **http://www.nostarch.com/lme.htm** for updates, errata, and other information.

STEAL THIS COMPUTER BOOK 3
What They Won't Tell You About the Internet

by WALLACE WANG

An offbeat, non-technical book that explores what hackers do, how they do it, and how readers can protect themselves. Thoroughly updated, this edition adds coverage of rootkits, spyware, web bugs, identity theft, hacktivism, wireless hacking (wardriving), biometrics, and firewalls.

MAY 2003, 384 PP., $24.95 ($37.95 CAN)
ISBN 1-59327-000-3

STEAL THIS FILE SHARING BOOK
What They Won't Tell You About File Sharing

by WALLACE WANG

Steal This File Sharing Book peels back the mystery surrounding file sharing networks such as Kazaa, Morpheus, and Usenet, showing how they work and how to use them wisely, and revealing potential dangers lurking on file sharing networks, including viruses, spyware, and lawsuits, and how to avoid them. Includes coverage of the ongoing battle between software, video, and music pirates and the industries trying to stop them.

NOVEMBER 2004, 296 PP., $19.95 ($27.95 CAN)
ISBN 1-59327-050-X

HOW LINUX WORKS
What Every Superuser Should Know

by BRIAN WARD

Shows how the Linux system functions so that system administrators can devise their own solutions to problems. Readers will find coverage of devices, disks, filesystems, and the kernel; how Linux boots; essential system files, servers, and utilities; network configuration and services; shell scripts; development tools; compiling software from source code; maintaining the kernel; configuring and manipulating peripherals; printing; backups; sharing files with Samba; network file transfer; buying hardware for Linux; and user environments.

MAY 2004, 368 PP., $37.95 ($55.95 CAN)
ISBN 1-59327-035-6

THE LINUX COOKBOOK, 2ND EDITION
Tips and Techniques for Everyday Use

by MICHAEL STUTZ

The second edition of our acclaimed *Linux Cookbook* contains step-by-step recipes that show you how to do just about anything with Linux. Organized by general task (such as managing files and manipulating graphics), this edition includes hundreds of new recipes as well as new sections on package management, file conversion, multimedia, working with sound files (including OGG and MP3), Vi text editing, and advanced text manipulation. A perfect introduction to the Linux command line or complete desktop reference for any of the major Linux distributions.

AUGUST 2004, 824 PP., $39.95 ($55.95 CAN)
ISBN 1-59327-031-3

JUST SAY NO TO MICROSOFT

by TONY BOVE

Just Say No to Microsoft begins by tracing Microsoft's rise from tiny software startup to monopolistic juggernaut and explains how the company's practices over the years have discouraged innovation, stunted competition, and helped foster an environment ripe for viruses, bugs, and hackers. Readers learn how they can dump Microsoft products—even the Windows operating system—and continue to be productive. The book also shows how to work successfully and seamlessly with computers and people who are still hooked on Microsoft software. Includes full explanations of alternate operating systems, such as Linux and Mac, and outlines various software applications that can replace the familiar Microsoft products.

SEPTEMBER 2005, 304 PP., $24.95 ($33.95 CAN)
ISBN 1-59327-064-X

PHONE:
800.420.7240 OR
415.863.9900
MONDAY THROUGH FRIDAY,
9 A.M. TO 5 P.M. (PST)

FAX:
415.863.9950
24 HOURS A DAY,
7 DAYS A WEEK

EMAIL:
SALES@NOSTARCH.COM

WEB:
HTTP://WWW.NOSTARCH.COM

MAIL:
NO STARCH PRESS
555 DE HARO ST, SUITE 250
SAN FRANCISCO, CA 94107
USA

Electronic Frontier Foundation
Defending Freedom in the Digital World

Free Speech. Privacy. Innovation. Fair Use. Reverse Engineering. **If you care about these rights in the digital world, then you should join the Electronic Frontier Foundation (EFF). EFF was founded in 1990 to protect the rights of users and developers of technology. EFF is the first to identify threats to basic rights online and to advocate on behalf of free expression in the digital age.**

> ## The Electronic Frontier Foundation Defends Your Rights!
> ## Become a Member Today!
> ## http://www.eff.org/support/

Current EFF projects include:

Protecting your fundamental right to vote. Widely publicized security flaws in computerized voting machines show that, though filled with potential, this technology is far from perfect. EFF is defending the open discussion of e-voting problems and is coordinating a national litigation strategy addressing issues arising from use of poorly developed and tested computerized voting machines.

Ensuring that you are not traceable through your things. Libraries, schools, the government and private sector businesses are adopting radio frequency identification tags, or RFIDs – a technology capable of pinpointing the physical location of whatever item the tags are embedded in. While this may seem like a convenient way to track items, it's also a convenient way to do something less benign: track people and their activities through their belongings. EFF is working to ensure that embrace of this technology does not erode your right to privacy.

Stopping the FBI from creating surveillance backdoors on the Internet. EFF is part of a coalition opposing the FBI's expansion of the Communications Assistance for Law Enforcement Act (CALEA), which would require that the wiretap capabilities built into the phone system be extended to the Internet, forcing ISPs to build backdoors for law enforcement.

Providing you with a means by which you can contact key decision-makers on cyber-liberties issues. EFF maintains an action center that provides alerts on technology, civil liberties issues and pending legislation to more than 50,000 subscribers. EFF also generates a weekly online newsletter, EFFector, and a blog that provides up-to-the minute information and commentary.

Defending your right to listen to and copy digital music and movies. The entertainment industry has been overzealous in trying to protect its copyrights, often decimating fair use rights in the process. EFF is standing up to the movie and music industries on several fronts.

Check out all of the things we're working on at http://www.eff.org and join today or make a donation to support the fight to defend freedom online.

ELECTRONIC FRONTIER FOUNDATION · 454 SHOTWELL STREET · SAN FRANCISCO, CA 94110 · 415.436.9333

Exclusive Special Offers from Xandros for Readers of *Linux Made Easy* by Rickford Grant

20% Discount on Xandros Network Premium Membership

Xandros Networks Premium Membership offers subscribers:

- Free and unlimited access to a vast library of over 3,000 software applications to enhance your Xandros Desktop experience
- Immediate access to system updates, security fixes and management tools
- Advanced access to new Xandros products and third party applications
- Discounts on commercial third-party applications, like StarOffice 8
- Discounts on new Xandros Products
- Voting privileges for new additions to the Xandros Networks application library
- Exclusive, special offers available only to Xandros Networks Premium Members

20% Discount when you upgrade to Xandros Desktop OS Deluxe or Business Edition 3.0

Xandros Desktop OS – Deluxe Edition 3.0

The Xandros Desktop OS - Deluxe Edition 3.0 delivers an unparalleled and easy to use desktop alternative. Its familiar and intuitive graphical environment simplifies the transition from using a Windows computer, and the ability to run popular productivity software, such as Microsoft Office® and Adobe Photoshop® make the transition even easier.

Xandros Desktop OS – Business Edition 3.0

The Xandros Desktop OS - Business Edition 3.0 offers a complete desktop experience including Firefox web browsing, Thunderbird e-mailing, Skype Internet calling, and the Star Office suite. Loaded with security features including Xandros Anti-Virus, the Xandros Firewall Wizard, encrypted home folders, and secure access to virtual private networks – you can finally say goodbye to the frustration related to Windows security.

Xandros Desktop can be installed either standalone or alongside Windows to create a dual-boot "Best of both worlds" machine making using and migrating to Linux from Windows a simple and natural experience.

To take advantage of these exclusive offers please visit Xandros at www.xandros.com/lmeoffers.html

xandros
Making Linux Work For You

Xandros and Skype goodies inside!

This CD packet contains your very own copy of Xandros OCE (Open Circulation Edition) and a FREE 120-minute SkypeOut coupon that will let you call anyone on a regular telephone line using Skype. That's free, as in free. So don't steal this CD because the person who buys this book without the CD will be very, very unhappy :(